Travel in Twentieth-Century French and Francophone Cultures

Travel in Twentieth-Century French and Francophone Cultures

The Persistence of Diversity

CHARLES FORSDICK

OXFORD
UNIVERSITY PRESS

*This book has been printed digitally and produced in a standard specification
in order to ensure its continuing availability*

OXFORD
UNIVERSITY PRESS

Great Clarendon Street, Oxford OX2 6DP
Oxford University Press is a department of the University of Oxford.
It furthers the University's objective of excellence in research, scholarship,
and education by publishing worldwide in
Oxford New York
Auckland Cape Town Dar es Salaam Hong Kong Karachi
Kuala Lumpur Madrid Melbourne Mexico City Nairobi
New Delhi Shanghai Taipei Toronto
With offices in
Argentina Austria Brazil Chile Czech Republic France Greece
Guatemala Hungary Italy Japan South Korea Poland Portugal
Singapore Switzerland Thailand Turkey Ukraine Vietnam

Oxford is a registered trade mark of Oxford University Press
in the UK and in certain other countries
Published in the United States
by Oxford University Press Inc., New York

© Charles Forsdick 2005

The moral rights of the author have been asserted

Database right Oxford University Press (maker)

Reprinted 2009

ISBN 978-0-19-925829-1

Preface

THIS book has emerged directly from the reflections that led to my previous and more precisely focused study of exoticism, *Victor Segalen and the Aesthetics of Diversity*, published with Oxford University Press in 2000. It may be read as an exploration of the historical evolution of the concepts underpinning Segalen's thought, as well as an implicit consideration of the blind spots and potential shortcomings perhaps inevitable given the historical context of his work's production in an early twentieth-century colonial world. If Segalen's work remains a recurrent point of reference in this volume and even seems to haunt some of the present chapters, this is principally because I feel that his complex reflection on the decline of diversity, as well as on its progressive reconfiguration, deserves a wider contextualization in relation to subsequent work in the field (both critical and creative). For, as Chris Bongie, Marie-Paule Ha, Edward Hughes, and others have clearly illustrated, there is still a pressing need to situate Segalen in relation to subsequent twentieth-century attitudes to exoticism, to go beyond the selective quotation and reductive anthologization to which his writings have often hitherto been subject.[1] Such a project, as I explain more fully below in Ch. 1, is part of a wider undertaking to investigate the meanings and fortunes of 'exoticism' and 'diversity', potentially key terms in the exploration of twentieth- and twenty-first century cultures and intercultural contact, yet terms whose importance has often been eclipsed, especially in the anglophone academy, by their postcolonial denigration.

The intention is to consider these two terms in relation to the physical and textual practices of travel in twentieth-century French-language cultures, and to explore, in particular, the ways in which the

---

[1] See Chris Bongie, *Exotic Memories: Literature, Colonialism, and the Fin de Siècle* (Stanford, Calif.: Stanford University Press, 1991), Marie-Paule Ha, *Figuring the East: Segalen, Malraux, Duras, and Barthes* (New York: State University of New York Press, 2001), and Edward J. Hughes, *Writing Marginality in Modern French Literature: From Loti to Genet* (Cambridge: Cambridge University Press, 2001). The recent publication of an English translation of Segalen's important *Essai sur l'exotisme—Essay on Exoticism: An Aesthetics of Diversity*, trans. and ed. Yaël Rachel Schlick (Durham, NC: Duke University Press, 2002)—will, in addition, go some way to encouraging a clearer understanding of the author in relation to postcolonial thought.

literature of travel casts light on the shifts and transformations these terms often conceal. In their recent *Cambridge Companion to Travel Writing*, Peter Hulme and Tim Youngs have underlined the relative underdevelopment of their field of inquiry and its lack of any orthodox critical tradition. Concentrating on the study of travel writing in English, their aim is 'to bring [the] subject into focus in order to accompany it'.[2] This volume has a similar objective in relation to a deliberately eclectic body of material, most of which has been produced in French. As such, it responds to and supplements several recent critical texts that have endeavoured to chart the relatively unstudied field of travel in francophone cultures since the early twentieth century.[3] A substantial body of French-language criticism also exists, but much of this, focused on individual authors, has a generic or narratological emphasis, and so explores textual issues associated with, although often peripheral to, my principal concerns.[4] It is instead with a growing body of English-language criticism, often focused on English-language material and in some cases drawing more obliquely on French-language literature and thought, that I aim to engage.[5] Moving beyond the intention of any

[2] Peter Hulme and Tim Youngs (eds.), *Cambridge Companion to Travel Writing* (Cambridge: Cambridge University Press, 2002), 1.

[3] See e.g. Jan Borm and Jean-Yves Le Disez (eds.), *Seuils et Traverses*, 2 vols. (Versailles: Suds d'Amériques; Brest: CRBC, 2002), Romuald Fonkoua (ed.), *Les Discours de voyages: Afrique–Antilles* (Paris: Karthala, 1998), Jean-Xavier Ridon, *Le Voyage en son miroir: essai sur quelques tentatives de réinvention du voyage au 20e siècle* (Paris: Kimé, 2002), and Jean-Didier Urbain, *Secrets de voyage: menteurs, imposteurs et autres voyageurs invisibles* (Paris: Payot, 1998). Also of note are special issues of journals, such as Roger Célestin, Elaine DalMolin, and Georges van den Abbeele (eds.), 'Travel and Travelers', *Sites*, 5/1 (2001), and Jean-Xavier Ridon (ed.), 'Errances urbaines', *Nottingham French Studies*, 39/1 (2000).

[4] See e.g. Odile Gannier, *La Littérature de voyage* (Paris: Ellipses, 2001), Olivier Hambursin (ed.), *Voyage et littérature: sens et plaisirs de l'écriture pérégrine* (Amay: Maison de la poésie d'Amay, 2001), Sophie Linon-Chipon, Véronique Magri-Mourgues, and Sarga Moussa (eds.), *Miroirs de textes: récits de voyage et intertextualité* (Nice: Publications de la Faculté des Lettres, Arts et Sciences Humaines de Nice; Paris: Centre de Recherches sur la Littérature des Voyages, 1998), Jean Mesnard and Alain Niderst (eds.), *Les Récits de voyage* (Paris: Nizet, 1986), Christine Montalbetti, *Le Voyage, le monde et la bibliothèque* (Paris: PUF, 1997), François Moureau (ed.), *Métamorphoses du récit de voyage* (Paris: Champion; Geneva: Slatkine, 1986), Adrien Pasquali, *Le Tour des horizons: critique et récits de voyages* (Paris: Klincksieck, 1994), and György Tverdota (ed.), *Écrire le voyage* (Paris: Presses de la Sorbonne Nouvelle, 1994).

[5] In addition to Hulme and Youngs' volume, of particular note are: Frances Bartkowski, *Travelers, Immigrants, Inmates: Essays in Estrangement* (Minneapolis: University of Minnesota Press, 1995), Steve Clark (ed.), *Travel Writing and Empire: Postcolonial Theory in Transit* (London: Zed Books, 1999), Michael Cronin, *Across the Lines: Travel, Language, and Translation* (Cork: University of Cork Press, 2000), James Duncan and Derek Gregory (eds.), *Writes of Passage: Reading Travel Writing* (London: Routledge,

general introduction to twentieth-century travel literature in French, the stated objective, as the subtitle implies, is primarily to illuminate a generic feature of travel literature (i.e. its renewed responses to what each generation of travellers seems to perceive as the decline of diversity) that merits sustained attention in its own right. At the same time, the volume addresses a more rarely studied body of French-language texts. Like travel itself, its focus is, however, persistently transcultural or transnational. The understanding of 'travel literature in French' draws on material from a range of regions, countries, and communities in which French is one of a number of principal means of expression; moreover, since travel literature, more perhaps than any other genre, remains a transcultural form, and since any attempt to maintain divisions along national or even linguistic lines is likely to strain credibility, this francophone corpus is inevitably supplemented by material from other traditions.[6] Similarly, this book takes for granted the assumption that any reduction of the study of travel to the perspectives of a single discipline risks restriction of a dynamic and fluid object of inquiry whose successful exploration depends on a genuinely interdisciplinary approach.

This study additionally and logically engages with and endeavours to supplement a growing body of material produced in the field traditionally known as French studies that attempts to open up understandings of what is meant by 'French'. Responding to a series of recent volumes, it employs travel as a changing figure and practice to explore ways in which one might move beyond any exclusive focus on France itself in order to explore the culture and cultural production of a more complex network of French-speaking spaces.[7] In such a rethinking of the object of French studies, the role of travel would seem essential: not only does

1999), Jas Elsner and Joan-Pau Rubiés (eds.), *Voyages and Visions: Towards a Cultural History of Travel* (London: Reaktion, 1999), and Patrick Holland and Graham Huggan, *Tourists with Typewriters: Critical Reflections on Contemporary Travel Writing* (Ann Arbor: University of Michigan Press, 1998).

[6] The excellent journal *Studies in Travel Writing* deliberately addresses material from a range of national traditions, and the series of *Seuils et Traverses* conferences (Derry 1998, Brest 2000, Versailles 2002, Ankara 2003, Birmingham 2004) has endeavoured to provide an international forum in which travel literature scholars from a variety of often contradictory traditions can engage in constructive dialogue.

[7] See Emily Apter, *Continental Drift: From National Characters to Virtual Subjects* (Chicago, Ill.: University of Chicago Press, 1999), Charles Forsdick and David Murphy (eds.), *Francophone Postcolonial Studies: A Critical Introduction* (London: Arnold, 2003), Thomas Spear (ed.), *La Culture française vue d'ici et d'ailleurs* (Paris: Karthala, 2002), and Tyler Stovall and Georges van den Abbeele (eds.), *French Civilization and Its Discontents* (Lanham, Md.: Lexington Books, 2003).

it encapsulate the physical processes of progressive encroachment and uneven exchange on which inter- or transcultural contact depend; but also it describes the often more subtle or imperceptible movements of ideas and influences that allow the construction (and deconstruction) of ideologies and identities at any given moment. Describing the institutional context of these issues, a recent edition of *Yale French Studies* was entitled 'French and Francophone: The Challenge of Expanding Horizons'.[8] The title articulates an uneasiness with any expansion that leads to dichotomies and divisions. A number of contributions to the journal accordingly explore the benefits of a focus on connections rather than disconnections, illustrating the idea that a post-national 'French studies' including all areas where French and its variants are spoken will require what Lawrence D. Kritzman dubs 'hermeneutic strategies that are both comparative and dialogic in nature'.[9] In an article foregrounding the importance of travel, Michael Dash offers a concrete illustration of what such a formulation implies by exploring the subtle intersections of Caribbean and metropolitan travel writing (by André Breton, Pierre Mabille, and Édouard Glissant) around the period of the Second World War.[10]

This book resists, however, any excessive involvement in those turf battles that often tend to monopolize debates over intellectual identity and direction. It distances itself from discussions of whether 'Francophone studies' is potentially a field of 'Francophobic inquiry', or whether 'Hexagonal literature is a branch of Francophone Studies'.[11] The objectives go beyond, I hope, the potentially disabling *impasses* of such disciplinary anxiety. It is intended that this volume's implications will have a more general relevance to ongoing attempts, in a variety of fields, to define and explore its key terms of reference, cognate to if not dependent on each other: diversity, exoticism, and travel. Although these three are explored progressively, one of whose principal aims is a consideration of the evolving semantic fields to which they refer, it seems useful and appropriate to outline at this stage the ways in which

---

[8] See Farid Laroussi and Christopher L. Miller (eds.), 'French and Francophone: The Challenge of Expanding Horizons', *Yale French Studies*, 103 (2003).

[9] Lawrence D. Kritzman, 'A Certain Idea of French: Cultural Studies, Literature and Theory', *Yale French Studies*, 103 (2003), 146–60 (p. 154).

[10] J. Michael Dash, '*Caraïbe Fantôme*: The Play of Difference in the Francophone Caribbean', *Yale French Studies*, 103 (2003), 93–105.

[11] See Sandie Petrey, 'Language Charged with Meaning', *Yale French Studies*, 103 (2003), 133–45 (p. 135), and Mireille Rosello, 'Unhoming Francophone Studies: A House in the Middle of the Current', *Yale French Studies*, 103 (2003), 123–32 (p. 131).

they are understood. The first two terms—diversity and exoticism—are investigated in some detail in the early stages of this study, in the light of (on the one hand) an emphasis in French-language scholarship in fields such as imagology and (on the other) English-language scholarship on colonial discourse and postcolonialism. An awareness of the complex and at times even controversial semantic field of 'diversity' underpins the study, and there is inevitably a consciousness of its range of potential applications (to languages, to ethnography, to biology, etc.). The principal understanding of the term, however, is cultural, relating to the perceived distinctiveness of individual cultures, especially that of the traveller's origin (where recognition of a unified point of departure is possible) and of those through which s/he journeys. Distinctiveness does not, of course, necessarily imply any essentialist understanding, and, as the comments above on Frenchness and the porous frontiers of the Hexagon already make clear, I tend to espouse a view of culture popularized by anthropologists such as James Clifford and Brian Street that eschews essence in favour of process, fixity in favour of dynamism.

The raw material is the actual or imagined experience of travel, often informed by more abstract understandings of cultural identities, but at the same time shaped by the very real contrasts and conflicts that regulate intercultural encounters. Although informed by debates over cultural diversity in the work of scholars such as Michael Carrithers and Tzvetan Todorov, the study does not engage directly in those discussions of biology, culture, and anthropology that have been undertaken elsewhere.[12] The approach adopted inevitably involves considerations of the metamorphic conditions of actually existing diversity at a number of moments in recent history, but the emphasis in what follows is instead on the ways in which diversity is imagined, perceived, and constructed, i.e. the processes of creative variability that permit its persistence. For reasons explored in the introductory chapter, whether travellers are colonial or postcolonial, whether motivated by an ideological belief in their culture's superiority or driven by an apparently more modest desire for genuine dialogue and exchange, their journeys seem to depend on a degree of diversity for their self-justification; with the ubiquity of sameness, travel as a meaningful practice risks becoming redundant. It is the traveller's attitude to the concept of 'diversity' that is

---

[12] See e.g. Michael Carrithers, *Why Humans Have Cultures: Explaining Anthropology and Social Diversity* (Oxford: Oxford University Press, 1992), and Tzvetan Todorov, *Nous et les Autres: la réflexion française sur la diversité humaine* (Paris: Seuil, 1989).

important, for this varies according to the individual, according to cultural origin, and according to chronological context. 'Diversity' undeniably covers, therefore, a range of subject positions and assumptions, and this study makes clear that the imaginary geography undergirding the term can still, in a post-colonial period, remain a hierarchical one of centre and periphery; at the same time, it is important to underline the fact that attempts at a non-hierarchical, post-colonial understanding can themselves be equally hazardous and prematurely celebratory, erasing residual power relationships and ignoring neocolonial contexts. I retain the term, however, fully aware of the pitfalls of its elasticity.

These semantic reservations are equally applicable to the cognate term 'exoticism', used to describe a range of representational and relational practices that allow a member of one culture to observe, interact with, and otherwise process phenomena from a different—and often radically different—culture. As I explain in Ch. 1, there has been a tendency amongst postcolonial scholars to reduce 'exoticism' to an assimilative and ultimately destructive or taxidermic manœuvre, i.e. a cultural or imaginative procedure akin to physical colonization and domestication. Although I accept the validity and necessity of such a critique, I suggest at the same time that to reduce exoticism to a single meaning risks over-simplifying the range of practices to which the term refers. It is accordingly understood more flexibly—as is the French equivalent 'exotisme', to which it is perhaps not wholly synonymous—to refer to a wider range of encounters than postcolonial orthodoxy perhaps permits. The aim is neither to conflate different experiences of other cultures or divergent representational practices relating to them, nor to deny historical context and the impact of colonialism and its legacies. Instead, it is to suggest, on the one hand, that exoticism is not a uniquely French or Western practice, and, on the other, that a specifically French exoticism itself takes a variety of forms that converge with and diverge from ideological orthodoxies predominant at a certain moment—and sometimes converge and diverge, confirm and contest at the same time. To borrow Edward Hughes's terms, in relation to the earlier twentieth century, there exists a more anxious, less categorical exoticism that has the capacity to 'articulate important ambiguities that both define colonialism's culture and hold the capacity to dismantle it'.[13]

---

[13] See Hughes, *Writing Marginality*, 170.

Although 'diversity' and 'exoticism' are general, even abstract terms with theoretical applications, they are intimately related to the concept and activity of travel, a practical mechanism that allows direct, even empirical engagement with the issues that these terms imply. As such, travel is the term through which questions of diversity and exoticism are freighted. The book contributes in part to an ongoing project whose aim is to redefine 'travel', to open up its often narrow meanings, and to allow it to exploit what James Clifford has dubbed the term's 'historical taintedness' in order to describe a more diverse range of spatial practices. Like the pair of terms with which I have associated it, travel lacks semantic stability whether it is considered synchronically or diachronically. Therefore, although this study both acknowledges and explores the exclusions whereby certain travellers endeavour to characterize and distinguish themselves, it alludes at the same time to the progressive transformation of the notion of travel—in terms of ethnicity, gender, and class—during the twentieth century. A term that initially described an essentially colonial practice, access to which was almost invariably restricted to white, middle- or upper-class, educated French males, has been steadily 'decolonized' or prized open to encompass a wider range of journeys and itineraries within and between cultures, voluntary and enforced. Although the opening chapters accordingly reflect a more orthodox, exclusive understanding of travel, the volume as a whole endeavours to track these progressive shifts, and the postface in particular assesses the direct implications of these transformations for the objects of inquiry. Western understandings of travel have, therefore, not been universalized, erasing the specificity of other modes of displacement; instead, other modes such as migration and indenture have forced the renegotiation of such earlier understandings. The catholic understanding of travel that emerges is not, of course, unproblematic. On the one hand, at a time when many French travel writers define themselves in nostalgic terms, it may be seen to diverge even from contemporary understandings of travel; on the other, as James Clifford suggests, if travel is everything then travel is nothing. I use the term—as I use 'diversity' and 'exoticism'—with this tension in mind, aware of the risks inherent in the extremes of inclusiveness and exclusiveness, of celebration and denigration, of ahistorical abstraction and ideological overdetermination. I employ 'travel', therefore, as Clifford suggests it might be adopted in his essay

'Traveling Cultures', i.e. 'as a translation term' that 'get[s] us some distance *and* fall[s] apart'.[14]

These reflections on 'travel' clearly impact on considerations of the relatively hazy textual form in which it is commonly described, 'travel literature'. I use the category as Robyn Davidson uses 'literature of mobility', in contrast with the more documentary or journalistic term 'travel writing'.[15] Defying the critical judgements that customarily divide texts into discrete generic categories, 'travel literature' depends more on a sense of dynamic genericity that presents the material to which the label relates in terms of intergeneric uncertainty or transgeneric voguing between different forms. 'Travel literature' accordingly avoids the prescription attached to fixed notions of genre, and exists as an often unpredictable category in which is assembled a variety of texts. What these share in common is their representation of journeys, actual and/or imagined, through places with which those undertaking them are unfamiliar—or with which they had thought they were familiar, but through travel discover they no longer are. Some have a primarily documentary purpose, but most have been selected for their potential to illuminate evolving attitudes towards travel, towards the intercultural encounters that constitute this practice, and towards the diversity on which these encounters customarily depend.

There is a risk, in the light of the comments made above about the shifting nature of travel, that a focus on travel *literature* excludes a range of voices and spatial practices. Despite some notable exceptions, a number of which are addressed here, this generic category has been, and often still is, defined according to the exclusions applied to travel itself. I am fully aware of these restrictions and attempted prescriptions, and have endeavoured to address them, both implicitly and explicitly, throughout the volume. Moreover, although the principal focus is textual, drawing on a wide range of material (conventional travel writing, reportage, novels) collected under the umbrella term of 'travel literature' I have outlined above, the concern is equally with a wider and associated phenomenon that might be dubbed the 'cultures of travel'—a phenomenon often freighted through literary texts, but equally present in other cultural phenomena and events, ranging from

---

[14] James Clifford, 'Traveling Cultures', in *Routes: Travel and Translation in the Late Twentieth Century* (Cambridge, Mass.: Harvard University Press, 1997), 17–39 (p. 39; emphasis in original).

[15] See Robyn Davidson, 'Introduction', in *The Picador Book of Journeys* (London: Picador, 2001), 1–7.

exotic panoramas and *Expositions coloniales* to photography and guidebooks. My understanding of the 'cultures of travel' converges with Inderpal Grewal's use of the same term in *Home and Harem*, where focus on 'cultural productions that are not strictly seen as travel narratives' permits her to identify contact zones at home as well as abroad, 'contained in particular discursive spaces that embody and control the narratives of encounters with difference'.[16] The term is accordingly to be distinguished from Rudy Koshar's specific understanding of 'travel cultures', inspired by the German term *Reisekultur*, which refers to 'a changing horizon of knowledge and expectation to which individuals were oriented as they traveled for pleasure and interacted with new peoples and environments'.[17]

Although much of the material addressed is predominantly—and in several of the earlier chapters exclusively—drawn from Europe, the corpus remains nevertheless an eclectic one, incorporating a variety of genres and forms from various regions of the French-speaking world, and presenting metropolitan material in a contrapuntal relation to its non-metropolitan equivalent. Indeed, as the postface makes clear, such distinctions in the contemporary period become increasingly difficult to sustain. The focus on travel ensures that national cultures are not understood in terms of exclusion or independence, but presented instead as interdependent: as has been suggested above, the Hexagonal space of France itself is consciously integrated into a wider understanding of 'francophone space'.[18] By this term, I understand the network of regions, societies, and communities linked by their lesser or greater use, as a result of geographical proximity, historical accident, or colonial intervention, of the French language (or localized/creolized forms of it) as a means of communication. Any such space is clearly not static, and it is characterized in its postcolonial form by transplantations and interconnections that the spatial divisions of colonialism endeavoured to prevent. Moreover, the definition of such a field of inquiry along

[16] See Inderpal Grewal, *Home and Harem: Nation, Gender, Empire, and the Cultures of Travel* (London: Leicester University Press, 1996), 4.

[17] Rudy Koshar, *German Travel Cultures* (Oxford: Berg, 2000), 9–10.

[18] Despite sharing reservations with a number of other scholars regarding the epithet 'francophone', I reject any necessary association with an exclusively French understanding of the word (i.e. referring to all French-speaking with the exception of France itself) and favour the decolonization of its semantic field in line with its etymological roots (i.e. referring to all French-speaking cultures including France itself). On this subject, see Roger Little, 'World Literature in French; or Is Francophonie Frankly Phoney?', *European Review*, 9/4 (2001), 421–36.

purely linguistic lines ignores the multilingual and transnational formations of which travel permits exploration. In reading representations
emerging from this space, I engage with comparatist practices such as
Edward Said's counterpoint, and aim to offer a reflection on the
grounds of comparison, with particular reference to contemporary
approaches to travel literature. I do not, however, propose a systematically contrapuntal approach or an attempt to read metropolitan and
non-metropolitan literature in relation to each other. Indeed, the exploration of travel reveals the fallibility of any such clear-cut binaries.
The aim is instead to illuminate the complexity of the field of travel and
the rich potential for future research into it.

   The book has been written, therefore, with a clear awareness of the
selective and subjective exclusions inevitable in the formation of its no
more than broadly representative (as opposed to openly revisionist)
corpus. The progression of the study reveals, therefore, in the texts
addressed, the emergence within travel literature of alternative voices
whose increasingly insistent articulation reflects the definitional shifts
alluded to above. Despite the contemporary policing of generic boundaries described in Ch. 6, the rare African francophone journey accounts
in the inter-war period have been progressively supplemented in the
post-war and post-colonial period as the journey motif became a central
element of the Francophone literary tradition. Some readers may, however, be surprised by the apparently gendered nature of the corpus,
especially given this study's explicit attention to issues of travel and
ethnicity. Although the corpus is not exclusively masculine or male-
authored, the lack of women's travel narratives included reflects issues
relating to gender and genre that I have begun to address elsewhere.[19]
An increasing body of criticism has been devoted both to the gendering
of the travel narrative and to issues relating to women's experience of
travel.[20] In the light of this, it seems that French travel literature,

---

[19] See Charles Forsdick, 'Hidden Journeys: Gender, Genre and Twentieth-Century
Travel Literature in French', in Jane Conroy (ed.), *Cross-Cultural Travel: Papers from
the Royal Irish Academy International Symposium on Literature and Travel* (New York:
Peter Lang, 2003), 315–23.

[20] See e.g. *L'Exotisme au féminin*, *Les Carnets de l'exotisme*, 1 (2000), Susan Bassnett,
'Travel and Gender', in Hulme and Youngs (eds.), *Cambridge Companion to Travel
Writing*, 225–41, Shirley Foster, *Across New Worlds: Nineteenth-Century Women Travellers and their Writings* (Hemel Hempstead: Harvester, 1990), Simone Fullager, 'Narratives of Travel: Desire and Movement in Feminine Subjectivity', *Leisure Studies*, 21 (2002),
57–74, Karen R. Lawrence, *Penelope Voyages: Women and Travel in the British Literary
Tradition* (Ithaca, NY: Cornell University Press, 1994), Bénédicte Monicat, *Itinéraires de
l'écriture au féminin: voyageuses du 19e siècle* (Amsterdam: Rodopi, 1996), Sara Mills,

perhaps more so than its English-language counterpart, seems to resist the inclusion or retention of female voices, a trend that serves to confirm ultimately paradoxical cultural assumptions relating to the feminization of both the domestic space and the field of travel itself.[21] Several women travellers, such as Isabelle Eberhardt, Alexandra David-Néel, and Ella Maillart, have achieved posthumous prominence, but largely because of their perceived exceptionalism. A survey of travel literature produced in French, however, suggests that not only were fewer female-authored texts produced, but also that their work would appear to be even more ephemeral than that of their male-authored counterparts. As the final chapters of this book suggests, this situation is changing rapidly with the emergence of a number of prominent postcolonial women writers such as Assia Djebar and Leila Sebbar producing journey accounts; moreover, despite the heavily gendered nature of the contemporary *Pour une littérature voyageuse* movement, contemporary French women travel writers, such as the late Nicole-Lise Bernheim, have achieved a certain prominence in France itself.[22]

A sensitivity to these issues relating to gender informs this study, especially in its concluding stages, as does an attentiveness to matters concerning travel and social class. As I have explained above, these are two areas of intersection that merit sustained attention in their own right, although had I privileged them the resultant volume would have been an entirely different one. In considerations of cultural diversity, of its decline, and of its persistence, however, I have consciously foregrounded issues of cultural and ethnic origin in the same way as does, for instance, Edward Said in a text such as *Culture and Imperialism*. I am conscious, therefore, that the approach is open to some of the criticisms that Said's work itself has attracted from critics such as Aijaz Ahmad, although I would stress again the existence throughout of what I hope is an apparent if underlying awareness of the issues on which these criticisms rest.[23] What follows presents itself as a 'take' rather

---

Discourses of Difference: An Analysis of Women's Travel Writing and Colonialism (London: Routledge, 1991), and Sidonie Smith, *Moving Lives: Twentieth-Century Women's Travel Writing* (Minneapolis: University of Minnesota Press, 2001).

[21] See Eric Leed, *The Mind of the Traveler: From Gilgamesh to Global Tourism* (New York: Basic Books, 1991).

[22] See Nicole-Lise Bernheim, *Chambres d'ailleurs* (Paris: Payot, 1999 [1986]), *Saisons japonaises* (Paris: Payot, 2002 [1999]), and *Couleur cannelle: une plantation biologique à Ceylan* (Paris: Arléa, 2002).

[23] See Aijaz Ahmad, *In Theory: Classes, Nations, Literatures* (London: Verso, 1992).

than an attempt at a comprehensive survey. Chapters are of differing
lengths, according to the subject matter addressed, and content is, as
has been explained above, deliberately eclectic, ranging from the photographs of Albert Kahn's Archives de la Planète to Édouard Glissant's
postcolonial theories of travel, from accounts of 2CV journeys to
contemporary Polynesian women's writing. The volume is thus inevitably wide-ranging, but given its claimed scope and ambition, I am all
too aware of what it excludes. It has not been possible, given structure
and available space, to develop at any length several aspects that
current gaps in scholarship suggest might be useful, such as a more
detailed study of early twentieth-century photography and the planet-
ary archive, a fuller account of the links between travel writing and
colonial literature, a more sustained reading of postcolonial travel
narratives. All charts or overviews are inevitably subjective and selective, and this one is no exception. I hope, of course, that this volume will
trigger responses, complementary or contradictory, convergent or divergent—and that it might in some way contribute to a further opening
up of the field of studies in travel literature in French.

The volume follows a chronological structure, tracking its subject
matter from the colonial era to our present post-colonial period. In
justifying the timescale of the study, both chronologically and concep-
tually, the Introduction focuses in particular on the two *fins de siècle* by
which this book is framed, the 1890s and the 1990s. It explores in some
detail the role of cultural diversity—and the exoticism through which
this is customarily freighted—at these two centennial moments, but
instead of promoting a cyclical view of history it borrows Raymond
Williams's notion of the 'structure of feeling' to suggest more subtle
shifts associated with transformation and repetition. In the light of this,
subsequent chapters proceed chronologically, but connections between
distinct moments undermine any straightforward linearity this structure may initially seem to perform. In this introductory chapter I also set
out the recurrent themes of decline and persistence of diversity, underlining their convergence and divergence, and stressing the ways in
which, to borrow Robert Young's comments on hybridity, they change
as they repeat, repeat as they change. The focus on the *fin de siècle* is
more, however, than a justificatory emphasis on historical framing; it is
at the same time a reminder that, despite the book's chronological
structure, passing from colonialism to postcolonialism, it makes no
claims to a neat diachrony, for the synchronic slices that constitute
five of the main chapters reveal the complex web of reference, looking

both forwards and backwards, on which reflection on cultural diversity at any given moment depends.

Before progressing to these reflections on travel and diversity at specific moments of the twentieth century, however, the first chapter addresses a theoretical aspect of the introduction already alluded to above that requires further development in its own right, i.e. the status and definition of exoticism as a tool for representing and understanding cultural diversity. Drawing on French-language and English-language criticism from throughout the twentieth century, it charts exoticism's uneven semantic field and challenges the reductive assumptions relating to the term common amongst postcolonial critics. Building on these initial theoretical and conceptual reflections, the remaining chapters of the book offer a series of clearly focused examinations of the dialectical relationship between the imminent collapse of diversity and its salvage, between its disappearance and perpetuation. They do not purport to offer a comprehensive survey of the vast field associated with these issues; instead, through engagement with the varied corpus outlined above, they try to suggest that a key response to the perceived decline of cultural diversity has been a constant 'reinvention of travel'.[24] Chapter 2 presents divergent approaches to the decline of diversity in the very different projects of Victor Segalen and Albert Kahn, considering these approaches in the light of popular science (in the form of entropy) and salvage ethnography. In Ch. 3, the focus shifts to the inter-war period and the rapidly changing cultures of travel associated with such major events as the 1931 Exposition coloniale and the 1936 Front Populaire. In the work of French travellers the chapter identifies an anxiety over the future of travel and over the status of the traveller, an anxiety accentuated by a growing awareness of the links between colonialism and conventional understandings of travel. The chapter also explores the implications of rare early accounts of Francophone African journeys to France itself in the work of Ousmane Socé.

Chapter 4 draws on Lévi-Strauss's threnody for post-war travel in *Tristes Tropiques*, but at the same time explores a hitherto ignored body of texts describing Citroën 2CV journeys to suggest the ways in which the reinvention of journeying developed in the 1950s permitted the persistence of a reconfigured sense of cultural diversity. At the same time, it acknowledges the rapid expansion of the field of travel as, at a

---

[24] I borrow this term from the title of Jean-Xavier Ridon's excellent *Le Voyage en son miroir*.

time when the French empire reached its final stages, travellers from the colonies converged on France to contribute to the country's rapid industrialization. It is a sensitivity to shifts within travel literature that underpins Chapter 5. While the 1960s seem to be characterized by a drift towards the *nouveau roman* and the New Criticism and by a process that has been cast as the 'bracketing off' of the empirical, outside world, the Swiss traveller Nicolas Bouvier developed a fresh understanding of the travel narrative that transforms the world into a mosaic of reassembled fragments. Bouvier's aesthetics of travel, although largely ignored until towards the end of his life, nevertheless suggests connections with travel narratives of Roland Barthes and Michel Butor, whose own texts reflect individual travellers struggling to make sense of those fragments of elsewhere with which travel confronts them.

Chapter 6 focuses on the contemporary period and offers one of the first analyses of the *Pour une littérature voyageuse* movement with which Bouvier himself was associated. Exploring the movement's exclusive processes of self-definition, the chapter studies the imperialist nostalgia and neo-Romantic impulses that inspire many of the authors associated with the group, but then proceeds to investigate parallel, alternative modes of journeying associated with deceleration and the rediscovery of domestic space. This consideration of alternative modes of travel leads to a postface in which the progressive prizing open of contemporary understandings of travel is given full consideration. Underlining the centrality of travel to contemporary Francophone thought, this concluding section focuses on the work of Édouard Glissant and explores the ways in which the Martiniquan's reflections on a dynamic, intercultural 'Relation' [Relating] suggest that travel might have become, in the early twenty-first century, a more generalized means of understanding cultural formations. Drawing on contemporary Polynesian examples, it suggests that a region traditionally seen as the passive destination of French travellers has, through self-articulation, become a dynamic, mobile space that not only replies to the archive of misrepresentations generated by several centuries of French travel narratives, but also uses travel as a means of self-exploration. From the rigid, controlling colonial traveller's gaze with which the study began, the book moves therefore to a more challenging instrumentalization of travel in this concluding exploration of dynamic postcolonial cultures.

A Note on Translation

One of the objectives is to introduce students and readers whose principal interest is in twentieth-century travel literature in English to a parallel French-language corpus. Awareness of this corpus outside French-speaking cultures is often restricted to only those prominent and heavily cited texts (such as Lévi-Strauss's *Tristes Tropiques*) available in English translation. The aim to create connections between traditions, whilst also triggering dialogue between those who study them, is intimately related to the object of study itself. Very few genres exist autonomously within single-language or single-cultural traditions; and travel literature, even more perhaps than the novel to whose emergence it is closely allied, must—as has been explained above—be read as a transnational and transcultural form. Journey narratives themselves travel, in the same way as do the individuals whose itineraries they describe: both literally, as travellers themselves read *en route* and map their own journeys onto those of their predecessors, and metaphorically, as texts are adopted into different traditions.[25] As a result, the study of travel literature—and of travel cultures more generally—is best perceived as part of a wider comparatist project in which interculturality has a paradigmatic rather than merely thematic status. This observation is supported by Peter Hulme and Tim Youngs, in their pioneering *Companion to Travel Writing*. Although the collection of essays it contains aims to focus on post-1500 travel narratives published in Britain, the editors' definition of their corpus is—as is the understanding of the corpus in this study—appropriately non-prescriptive. Hulme and Youngs acknowledge the artificiality of over-restricting a form so dependent on the crossing of borders, and as Rod Edmond makes clear in his fascinating essay on Tahiti and the South Seas, 'to concentrate entirely on Anglophone travel writing would be to distort the picture'.[26]

---

[25] A recent example of this phenomenon involves the elaboration of an imaginary genealogy by authors involved in the predominantly French *Pour une littérature voyageuse* movement: the bibliography included in their manifesto—*Pour une littérature voyageuse* (Brussels: Complexe, 1992)—is an example of self-performative identity and lists works in translation from a series of different literary traditions (pp. 207–11). Also, Loredana Polezzi cites the example of Claudio Magris's *Danube*, transgressing generic boundaries as it transfers between literary cultures. See *Translating Travel: Contemporary Italian Travel Writing in Translation* (Aldershot: Ashgate, 2001), 184–205.

[26] Rod Edmond, 'The Pacific/Tahiti: Queen of the South Sea Isles', in Hulme and Youngs (eds.), *Cambridge Companion to Travel Writing*, 139–55 (p. 139).

Whereas comparatist methodologies once depended on mastery of a range of languages, it has become customary and expedient to provide translations where appropriate. In this volume, I have followed that practice. I acknowledge, however, that the relationship between travel, translation, and the persistence of diversity remains a complex one. Despite James Clifford's suggestion, in the subtitle of *Routes*, that he would address the relationship between translation and travel, the subject has only recently been subject to careful and thorough consideration in the work of critics such as Michael Cronin and Loredana Polezzi. Travel literature, as this book itself will suggest, may indeed usefully be read as a form of translation of the experience of one culture into a form consumable in another. At the same time, however, travel, particularly in its contemporary commercial guise of mass tourism, may—like translation from minority to majority languages—be seen as a major contributor to the perceived transformation of the world into a monocultural and monolingual space. Travel as an entropic process, levelling the degree of diversity between cultures and slowly eroding the effort required to negotiate their divergence, may therefore, when its more apocalyptic implications are underlined, be associated either with utopian monolingualism, in the form of Esperanto, or its dystopian equivalent, an all-pervasive anglophonia. Both of these reduce the energy spent in translation whilst at the same time impoverishing linguistic diversity. It may therefore seem paradoxical that a study whose principal object is the persistence of diversity simultaneously enacts the erasure of diversity by systematically providing translations of material cited in French. These translations are provided for the practical reasons explored above, and original citations have been retained. Where possible, I have used commercially available versions; all other unattested translations are my own.

A Note on Terminology

I follow what are becoming the accepted conventions in relation to two repeated terms. The term 'francophone' is used in an etymological and inclusive sense to mean 'French-speaking', and accordingly refers to all regions, countries, and communities (including France itself) where French is one of the primary means of communication; the epithet 'Francophone' is used, in distinction to a reductively Hexagonal understanding of 'French', to designate the literature, culture, and thought of those non-European French-speaking regions, countries, and communities that were once colonies of or remain constitutionally dependent on France. 'Post-colonial' is used to refer historically or chronologically to what comes after colonialism; 'postcolonial' refers instead to a contemporary assessment of the culture and history of empire from the moment of conquest, with the epithet understood in Jeannie Suk's terms as a 'contractual indicator of a practice of reading that accentuates the commonality of the problems that arise from colonialism'.[27]

C.F.
Liverpool
May 2004

---

[27] Jeannie Suk, *Postcolonial Paradoxes in French Caribbean Writing: Césaire, Glissant, Condé* (Oxford: Clarendon, 2001), 19.

Acknowledgements

I AM most grateful for the support, advice, and comment of former colleagues in Glasgow, where this book began, and to current colleagues in Liverpool, where it was completed, as well as to undergraduates in both institutions who have followed my classes on twentieth-century travel literature.

The Arts and Humanities Research Board granted extended leave, which permitted me to complete the primary research on which the book is based, and I was awarded two overseas conference grants by the British Academy to present papers relating to the project at conferences in Hartford, Connecticut, and Urbana-Champaign, Illinois. This book was also written in parallel with a collaborative, AHRB-funded project on 'New Approaches to Twentieth-Century Travel Literature in French', which I had the privilege to direct. I am indebted to the two postgraduate research fellows attached to that project, Feroza Basu and Siobhán Shilton, with whom I worked closely for three years in Glasgow and Liverpool.

Sections of the book were also presented as conference or seminar papers at the following institutions: University of Cambridge, NUI Cork, Lancaster University, University of Nottingham, Royal Holloway University of London, SOAS, University of Stirling, University of Wales, Swansea, and Trinity College Dublin. I am grateful to colleagues in those institutions for their comments and encouragement.

Since this project has been some time in preparation, I record particular thanks to the many friends and colleagues whose support, encouragement, and generosity have assisted me in the construction of my corpus and subsequent study of it, especially Christine Dutton, David Murphy, François Poirier, Jean-Xavier Ridon, Angela Ryan, and Andy Stafford. I also acknowledge with gratitude the contributions of current or past postgraduate students working in cognate fields: Stef Cadenhead, Catherine McGlennan, Katy Hindson, and Penny Williams.

Early versions of sections of this book appeared as: 'Exoticism in the *Fin de Siècle*: symptoms of decline, signs of recovery', *Romance Studies*, 18/1 (2000), 31–44; 'Travelling Concepts: Postcolonial Approaches to Exoticism', *Paragraph*, 24/3 (2001), 12–29; ' "Le grand danger terrestre": Exoticism and Entropy in the Early Twentieth Century', in David Murphy and Aedín Ni Loingsigh (eds.), *Thresholds of Otherness/Autrement mêmes* (London: Grant & Cutler, 2002), 57–80; 'Sa(l)vaging Exoticism: Travelling Towards the Other in 1930s French Literature', in Charles Burdett and Derek Duncan (eds.), *Cultural Encounters: European Travel Writing in the 1930s* (Oxford: Berghahn, 2003), 29–45; ' "Cette mosaïque encore lacunaire": Nicolas Bouvier, Between Unity and Diversity', in Jan Borm, Jean-Yves Le Disez, Bruce Jackson, and Loredana Polezzi (eds.), *Travel Writing, Mediation and Otherness* (New York: Peter Lang, 2005); and 'À quoi bon marcher: Uses of the Peripatetic in Contemporary Literature in French', *Sites: The Journal of Twentieth-Century/Contemporary French Studies*, 5/1 (2001), 47–62. I am grateful to the editors of these journals and books for granting permission to reproduce this material, which is presented in different versions here.

The book is for John and Sophie, who taught me by example what Segalen meant when he wrote: 'est exotique tout ce que l'enfant veut'.

Contents

Introduction
Exoticism in the *Fin de Siècle*: Decline and Recovery

Like nostalgia, diversity is not what it used to be.[1]

La fusion croissante, la chute des barrières, les grands raccourcis
d'espace, doivent d'eux-mêmes se compenser quelque part au
moyen de cloisons nouvelles, de lacunes imprévisibles, un réseau
d'un filigrane très ténu striant des champs qu'on avait cru tout
d'abord d'un seul tenant.[2]

The increasing fusion, the destruction of barriers, the great short
cuts through space, must of their own accord compensate themselves by means of new partitions and unforeseen lacunae, a system of very fine filigree striated through the fields that one initially
perceived as an unbroken space.[3]

TRAVEL literature is a category into which most of the corpus on
which this study draws might be seen to fall. Despite the convenience
of such classification, however, the body of material to which this label
is applied remains highly amorphous and ill defined. Long dismissed by
critics as a formulaic, documentary, sub-literary body of texts, it has,
however, recently emerged in the light of the rapid expansion of scholarship in the field as a generically complex and creative form; simultaneously it has acquired a privileged role in the exploration of
intercultural relations on which many contrastive or differential aspects
of identity formation depend. Travel literature draws on other forms
and borrows from other genres to such an extent that it might be argued
to lack any formal or generic autonomy; Jean Bessière, avoiding the

---

[1] Clifford Geertz, 'The Uses of Diversity', *Michigan Quarterly*, 5/1 (1987), 105–23
(p. 114).
[2] Victor Segalen, *Essai sur l'exotisme*, in *Œuvres complètes*, ed. Henry Bouiller 2 vols.
(Paris: Laffont, 1995), i. 737–81 (p. 772).
[3] Victor Segalen, *Essay on Exoticism*, trans. and ed. Yaël Schlick (Durham, NC: Duke
University Press, 2002), 57–8 (translation modified).

tautologous observation that 'travel literature is literature about travel', has claimed that a definition is possible 'if we consider travel to be the representation of the mutual knowledge travelers need to elicit from their encounter with the Other'.[4] A further distinguishing feature of the genre on which this study intends to focus is its apparent consciousness of, even desire for, the instability or perishability of the object with which it is concerned. In other words, travel writers seek and even rely on diversity to justify their journeying, but often find themselves chronicling what they perceive as its imminent extinction or decline.

According to certain critical analyses, the novel depends on constant formal crisis for its generic evolution.[5] The same might be said of travel literature, described by Emily Apter as a 'self-hating genre', often 'in danger of teetering on the verge of obsolescence'.[6] Travel literature often takes this association with crisis further, however, by transforming the external crises customarily associated with the declining diversity of its field of inquiry into a strategy of literary self-justification. In the nineteenth century, a statement of the travel narrative's inadequacy and even unreliability became a staple element of the text's preface, not only a *captatio benevolentiae* employed to persuade the sceptical reader of the account's veracity, but also a clear marker of its generic status;[7] by the early twentieth century, in texts such as Victor Segalen's *Équipée* and Henri Michaux's *Ecuador*, such a questioning of textual self-worth had been accentuated and transformed into a more generalized crisis of representation: doubts regarding strategies of transcultural textualization were compounded by fears over the sustainability of the perception of cultural diversity on which these very strategies depended. It is this apparent tension between loss and desire, lack and perpetuation that the current study proposes to explore. A literary form that traditionally relies on the existence (or construction) of an 'elsewhere', the experience of which is to be textualized and translated for consumption by a 'home' audience, seems paradoxically to privilege and incorporate a sense of its own decline. A number of the various forms that this tension seems to take will be explored in their specific historical contexts in the

---

[4] Jean Bessière, 'Retiring President's Address', *ICLA Bulletin*, 21/1 (2002), 4–17 (p. 7).

[5] See e.g. Michel Raimond, *La Crise du roman: des lendemains du naturalisme aux années vingt* (Paris: J. Corti, 1966), and Dominique Viart, *Le Roman français au XXe siècle* (Paris: Hachette, 1999).

[6] Apter, *Continental Drift*, 197, 199.

[7] See Jean-Claude Berchet, 'La préface des récits de voyage au XIXe siècle', in Tverdota (ed.), *Écrire le voyage*, 3–15.

chapters that follow. Although the book does not go so far as to claim that this is a feature distinguishing or defining *all* travel literature in the modern period, it suggests nevertheless that the perceived decline of diversity and its simultaneous, even complementary persistence are sufficiently recurrent as to become a dominant element of any attempt to present an overarching grasp of this body of texts. Moreover, the inextricable decline of diversity, as will be demonstrated below, may be presented as an integral element of the modern condition, associated with the mechanization of transport, the spread of a democracy defined according to internationally recognized standards, and the accelerated displacement of people, goods, and information; yet it is with postmodernity, in concepts such as Baudrillard's radical alterity, and with postcoloniality, in notions such as Glissant's right to opacity and 'Relation', that the sustainability of an albeit fragile diversity seems again to emerge.[8] Again, the progressive erosion of diversity is accompanied by a sense of the exaggeration of reports of its decline.

The implicit sense of erosion that characterizes certain nineteenth- and earlier twentieth-century attitudes to the distinctiveness of individual cultures may, in its more extreme manifestations, have bordered on apocalypticism; but the transfer from generation to generation of such renewed prophecies of entropic decline uncovers the pervasive and conservative tendency according to which transformation is cast crudely as death or loss. This criticism is not to deny the manifest consequences of forces such as imperialism, international capitalism, and the globalized media, claims of whose merely abstract or theoretical existence are undermined by the tangibly shifting relationship of the local and the global, by evidence of language death, by the extinction of species, by the increasing haziness of what we understand by the 'national' and its replacement by more complex transnational formations. There is empirical evidence to corroborate the accuracy of projections relating either to the decline of indigenous languages as a result of language shift triggered by the globalization of English, or to biodiversity loss as a result of global warming. Only half of the 6,000 languages spoken in the world today, for example, are likely to survive until the end of this century; and although estimates of the number of species vary, it is thought that climate change may lead to the loss of a further

---

[8] See Jean Baudrillard, *La Transparence du mal: essai sur les phénomènes extrêmes* (Paris: Galilée, 1990), and Édouard Glissant, *Poétique de la Relation* (Paris: Gallimard, 1990).

million (one in ten of all plants and animals) that appear to be 'committed to extinction' by 2050.[9] In addition, in terms of declining biodiversity, it is of course likely that species will be lost before they are scientifically identified. As the essays in Luisa Maffi's *On Biocultural Diversity* suggest, there are links between these various processes of decline; the editor herself outlines 'the detrimental effects of current global socioeconomic and environmental processes on [...] biological species, the world's ecosystems, and human cultural and linguistic groups and their traditional knowledge'.[10] Yet in relation to individual cultures, whose existence is perhaps not as clear-cut as that of a language or a species, any such notion of a reductively assimilationist encroachment is often challenged by models of resistance, developed or foregrounded in particular by postcolonial critics.

The persistence of much of the world's linguistic and cultural diversity indeed depends on small groups of indigenous people whose distinctiveness is eroded by external contact; travel plays a clear role here as the effects of arrival of those from outside are exacerbated by processes of migration elsewhere. The result is not necessarily, however, a drift towards extinction or increasing moribundity. In Jan Pieterse's terms:

Cultural experiences, past or present, have not been simply moving in the direction of cultural uniformity and standardization. This is not to say that the notion of global cultural synchronization is irrelevant—on the contrary—but it is fundamentally incomplete. It overlooks the countercurrents—the impact non-Western cultures have been making on the West. It downplays the ambivalence of the globalizing momentum and ignores the role of local reception of Western culture—for example the indigenization of Western elements. It fails to see the influence non-Western cultures have been exercising on each other. It has no room for crossover culture—as in the development of 'third cultures' such as world music. It overlooks the fact that many of the standards exported by the West and its cultural industries themselves turn out to be of culturally mixed character if we examine their cultural lineages.[11]

---

[9] See Mark Abley, *Spoken Here: Travels Among Threatened Languages* (London: Heinemann, 2004), and Chris D. Thomas et al., 'Extinction Risk from Climate Change', *Nature*, 427 (2004), 145–8.

[10] See Luisa Maffi, 'Introduction: on the Interdependence of Biological and Cultural Diversity', in *On Biocultural Diversity: Linking Language, Knowledge and the Environment* (Washington: Smithsonian Institution Press, 2001), 1–50 (p. 3).

[11] Jan Nederveen Pieterse, 'Globalization as Hybridization', in Mike Featherstone, Scott Lash, and Roland Robertson (eds.), *Global Modernities* (London: Sage, 1995), 45–68 (p. 53).

A clear example of such alternative narratives of intercultural contact and its unpredictable outcomes can be seen in transculturation, a concept popularized by Mary Louise Pratt in her study of travel writing, *Imperial Eyes*.[12] Transculturation subverts the centre–periphery model of the relationship between 'stronger' and 'weaker', 'dominating' and 'dominated' cultures. The concept challenges notions of influence, claiming that meetings of cultures creates a 'contact zone' in which the culture of the (former) colony may in fact adapt to its own purposes phenomena belonging to the culture of the (former) colonizer.[13] A culture once deemed peripheral may have the potential to reflect back this altered version, and accordingly reverse the vectors of power. In offering a more attenuated version of cultural transformation and exchange, transculturation suggests that in the meetings between cultures the relative diversity that distinguishes them from each other may alter, but that it is not necessarily lost.

This observation is linked to an aspect of globalization theory that challenges the assumption of diversity's progressive erosion with which the notion is customarily associated. Exploring the associated phenomenon of 'glocalization', Roland Robertson claims: 'It is not a question of either homogenization or heterogenization, but rather of the ways in which both of these two tendencies have become features of life across much of the late-twentieth-century world.'[14] In postmodern terms, grand narratives prophesying progressive erosion of convergent differences or their equally progressive but divergent fragmentation are replaced by a more complex and uneven relationship between the global and the local that challenges traditional views of cultures' boundedness and traditional assumptions regarding what happens when such bounds are breached. In the same volume, Jan Pieterse

---

[12] The term 'transculturation' was first proposed by Fernando Ortiz in *Cuban Counterpoint: Tobacco and Sugar*, trans. Harriet de Onís (Durham, NC: Duke University Press, 1995 [1947]). It was given new critical currency by Mary Louise Pratt in her *Imperial Eyes: Travel Writing and Transculturation* (London: Routledge, 1992), see esp. pp. 5–7.

[13] Pratt's 'contact zone' is linked, in spatial terms, to Mann's concept of 'interstitial emergence' (the creation of diasporic sites inhabited by migrants, exiles, and nomads, that are sources of social and cultural renewal), and also reminiscent, in terms of the process it describes, of the Brazilian cannibalist movement. See Michael Mann, *The Sources of Social Power* (Cambridge: Cambridge University Press, 1986), and Randal Johnson, 'Tupy or not Tupy: Cannibalism and Nationalism in Contemporary Brazilian Literature and Culture', in John King (ed.), *Modern Latin American Fiction: A Survey* (London: Faber & Faber, 1987), 41–59.

[14] Roland Robertson, 'Glocalization: Time–Space and Monogeneity-Heterogeneity', in Featherstone, Lash, and Robertson (eds.), *Global Modernities*, 25–44 (p. 27).

seems to push this argument further by describing a multidimensional, open-ended process of globalization: a 'process of hybridization which gives rise to a global mélange'.[15]

Although the final sections of this book will consider in greater detail such a postcolonial persistence of diversity or its reinvention in new forms (and the prizing open of the field of travel on which both of these depend), the opening chapters are more concerned with the ways in which very different strategies of perpetuation of a range of distinctive cultures emerge in earlier travel narratives by Western authors. The frame of the study is chronological, spanning the twentieth century. It tracks the relationship of travel and cultural diversity from, as has been suggested above, the colonial past to the postcolonial present. Despite an appearance of linearity, however, such an approach does not lend itself to any neat vector, with carefully delimited points of departure and arrival; as will become clear, certain travel narratives depend on nostalgia and salvage, and it is equally by the cyclical figure of return that they are characterized. Indeed, not withstanding the comments on postcolonial diversity made above, there are traces of circularity in this study as certain attitudes towards cultural diversity in the 1890s resurface, albeit in altered and often nostalgic forms, in the 1990s.

To provide some texture to the complex and shifting notions central to this study—diversity, exoticism, and travel—this introductory chapter will explore these two chronological extremes, extremes that risk collapsing into each other once the epithet *fin-de-siècle* is applied to them. Such an approach seems apt, for in the popular imagination the decadence of the *fin de siècle* is customarily associated with an 'exoticist' excess. The resurgence of an interest—both popular and academic—in travel literature in 1990s France itself led to the identification of what might be cast as a new *fin-de-siècle* exoticism.[16] Primarily recognized as a publishing phenomenon (evidence of which is clear in the existence of twenty-nine different series devoted to *le travel-writing* published in France in 1992), this literary trend consisted of two distinct strands and encompassed the work of contemporary authors, whilst remaining at the same time reliant on the republication of numerous earlier travelogues.[17] The retrospection inherent in this element

[15] Jan Nederveen Pieterse, 'Globalization as Hybridization', 45–68 (p. 45).

[16] See Jean-Marc Moura, *La Littérature des lointains: histoire de l'exotisme européen au XXe siècle* (Paris: Champion, 1998), 431–4, for a discussion of 'exotisme fin-de-siècle' in a late twentieth-century context.

[17] The twenty-nine series had declined to thirteen in 1998. See 'L'étonnant paradoxe de la littérature de voyage', *Livres de France*, 208 (1998), 36–8.

of repackaging of out-of-print narratives is complex. On the one hand it often implied an element of 1990s imperialist nostalgia; on the other—and these two elements are clearly related—it suggests the exhaustion of the narrative potential of contemporary travel and the resultant need to retrace previous journeys.[18]

A number of contemporary *écrivains-voyageurs* have avoided these twin tendencies, and managed to approach what one of the only French critics to engage actively with postcolonial theory, Jean-Marc Moura, has called 'une littérature de l'ailleurs affranchie du lien colonial, une différence écrite par elle-même et en ses propres termes' [a literature of elsewhere freed from its colonial ties, a difference written by itself and in its own terms].[19] French travellers such as Jean-Luc Coatalem nevertheless produce narratives reliant on a desire for the colonial traces underlying postcolonial space. The bathos and comic insensitivity to indigenous environments of anglophone authors such as Redmond O'Hanlon can be read similarly as marks of self-consciously nostalgic texts that replace anxiety about the decline of global diversity with a parodic remapping of previous, colonial itineraries.[20] The critic Charles Sugnet has suggested that the work of a number of contemporary travel writers linked to the journal *Granta*—on which *Gulliver*, the journal of the *Pour une littérature voyageuse* movement, was modelled—is written as though the former imperial centres still hold: 'A curious fusion of the 1880s and the 1980s is what keeps all those *Granta* travel writers up in the air, afloat over various parts of the globe, their luggage filled with portable shards of colonialist discourse.'[21] Although Sugnet's criticism might equally be applied to certain contemporary French travel writers, such as Coatalem himself, there remains nevertheless a suspicious

---

[18] The term 'imperialist nostalgia' is used and explored by Renato Rosaldo in *Culture and Truth: The Remaking of Social Analysis* (London: Routledge, 1993), 68–87. Rosaldo describes succinctly his concept: 'A person kills someone, and then mourns the victim,' or 'someone deliberately alters a form of life, and then regrets that things have not remained the way they were prior to the intervention' (69–70).

[19] See Jean-Marc Moura, *L'Europe littéraire et l'ailleurs* (Paris: PUF, 1998), 9.

[20] See e.g. *Into the Heart of Borneo* (Edinburgh: Salamander, 1984), and *In Trouble Again: A Journey between the Orinoco and the Amazon* (London: Hamilton, 1988). Translations of O'Hanlon's works have been central to the French *Pour une littérature voyageuse* movement, and are included in the bibliography that concludes its 1992 manifesto.

[21] Charles Sugnet, 'Vile Bodies, Vile Places: Travelling with *Granta*', *Transition*, 51 (1991), 70–85 (p. 85). Michel Le Bris was inspired by *Granta* to set up the review *Gulliver* in 1990 to explore what he called 'une littérature qui dise le monde'. The first series ran for thirteen issues until 1993, and a second series was relaunched by Librio in 1998. For an anthology of articles in the first series, see Michel Le Bris (ed.), *Étonnants Voyageurs: anthologie des écrivains de Gulliver* (Paris: Flammarion, 1999).

neatness to such criticism: the 'curious fusion' of decades a century apart avoids engagement with complex issues linked to questions of belatedness, to the nature of recurrent tropes, and to the relation of such tropes to the context in which they appear. Sugnet sees, on the one hand, a cyclical process in which the ends of centuries seem to fuse; Jean-Marc Moura has, on the other, borrowed the title of Patrice Touchard's collection of essays on this period of 100 years—*Le Siècle des excès*—in order to chart a linear process of radical transformation. Moura alludes to:

ce 'siècle de l'excès', où nous sommes passés de l'apogée de l'impérialisme colonial à une décolonisation quasi-complète selon une mutation si profonde qu'elle paraissait tout simplement inimaginable aux contemporains de Conrad.[22]

this 'century of excess', during which we went from the height of colonial imperialism to an almost complete decolonization according to a process of change so profound that it would have seemed unimaginable to Conrad's contemporaries.

A concern with such issues of linearity and cyclicality in the evolution of representations of the exotic is central to this book, and has motivated these introductory reflections on the meanings of exoticism in the *fin de siècle*. There is a focus on this particular chronological construct as it underpins the frame in which this study will unfold. The book stretches from the 1890s to the 1990s. It thus spans a period that evolved in linear terms, as Moura makes clear, from colonial confidence to post-colonial uncertainty; yet the century in question was nevertheless framed, in an apparently cyclical process, by two moments of apparent malaise during each of which, I shall argue, exoticism played a defining role. Recent critical interest in the *fin de siècle* itself has revealed not only the richness of the term but also its recurrent ambiguity. Its application as an epithet to the end of the twentieth century can be seen to have involved a fusion of distinct endings, a fusion which—as Sugnet's analysis implies—is simultaneously a confusion of two specific historical moments. When first applied to a contemporary moment (i.e. in the 1890s), the *fin de siècle* was self-referential, a neologism coined to describe a specific moment and particular set of circumstances. To evoke the *fin de siècle* in the 1990s involved a more complicated, retrospective process of allusion, for it relied on what Hillel Schwartz

---

[22] See Moura, *La Littérature des lointains*, 10. Moura refers to Patrice Touchard (ed.), *Le Siècle des excès, de 1880 à nos jours* (Paris: PUF, 1992).

calls 'the cumulative experience of the ends of centuries'.[23] Recurrent themes (both local and global) of the decade in question—the French *crise identitaire*, the depletion of natural resources, scientific apocalypse and environmental disaster, threats of terrorism and urban meltdown, news of sudden economic crises, and prophecy of the End of History— suggest that commentators were driven by a sense of expectation or even obligation to diagnose cultural crisis as the century drew to a close. Moreover, at a time when the consensus of commemoration increasingly eclipsed the tensions and contradictions of historical experience, the final decade of the twentieth century was transformed, in an approximate process of déjà-vu, into the centenary of the previous *fin de siècle*: the 1990s, for instance, were marked by the much publicized hundredth anniversaries of works such as Oscar Wilde's *The Importance of Being Earnest*, of the invention of X-rays, cinema, and radio.[24]

Tracey Hill has explored this transformation of the *fin de siècle* into a transferable set of conceptual parameters that obscure the specific historical moment:

Symmetries can be seen to exist between the two fins de siècle, but it is never clear if typically fin-de-siècle phenomena are the inevitable consequence of the end of a century, or whether imminent arrival of the *fin de siècle* prompts us to reiterate apparently suitable behaviours. The latter is more conducive to an historicist interpretation, in that it permits one to take into account *differences* between the two epochs, as well as their similarities.[25]

There is a need to avoid the imaginative if seductive leaps of what one critic has called in this context a 'historiography of convenience'. Such an approach uses the received version of a previous *fin de siècle* as an optic through which to view a current situation, i.e. as a convenient paradigm in which to squeeze understandings of the present.[26] Evoking

---

[23] Hillel Schwartz, *Century's End: An Orientation Manual Toward the Year 2000* (New York: Currency Doubleday, 1996), p. xi.

[24] See Asa Briggs, 'The 1990s: The Final Chapter', in Asa Briggs and Daniel Snowman (eds.), *Fins de Siècle. How Centuries End 1400–2000* (New Haven, Mass.: Yale University Press, 1996), 197–233 (p. 223).

[25] 'Introduction', in Tracey Hill (ed.), *Decadence and Danger: Writing, History and the Fin de Siècle* (Bath: Sulis, 1997), 1–12 (p. 3).

[26] The phrase 'historiography of convenience' is used by William Gallois in his contribution to Anne Frémiot (ed.), *Fin de siècle?* ([Nottingham]: Department of French, University of Nottingham, 1998). For an illustration of this type of imaginative leap, see Shearer West, *Fin de Siècle* (Woodstock, NY: Overlook, 1994): 'what became apparent to me in the course of researching this book was just how chillingly familiar many of the *fin-de-siècle* arguments about gender, politics, society and religion actually are. If, through

the *fin de siècle* is accordingly hazardous, and can imply a conception of history that rejects linear, chronological progression and locks time into cycles of repetition. Although *fin-de-siècle* was first used as an epithet to describe a specific moment in the late nineteenth century, recent considerations of it have extended its use retrospectively to other ends of centuries, whilst at the same time providing us with a convenient vantage point from which to consider our own recent situation. Such wide-ranging notions as *fin de siècle*, *fin des voyages*, and even *fin du roman* can become, therefore, products of academic or critical discourses whose aim is to impose taxonomy and form onto what tends to be amorphous (i.e. aesthetic production) or what, moreover, is subversively unclassifiable as a result of its worrying proximity (i.e. contemporary literature and culture).

As has already been suggested, in such a hazy understanding of the *fin de siècle* (as this type of attitude of mind or portable set of themes rather than as a unique chronological moment), reference to what is perhaps an even hazier notion of exoticism is commonplace. A positive response to decadence at home can be chronic extroversion, a search for renewal elsewhere—renewal in as radically different or exotic a context as possible; but at the same time, a symptom of such ennui can be an obsessive concern with artificial constructed worlds at home in which exoticized elements of elsewhere become escape routes from domesticity. The title of this Introduction conceals the tensions outlined here, tensions of decline and recovery, of erosion and perpetuation that will inform the successive chapters of which this book consists. The term 'exoticism' itself, as will be made clear in Ch. 1, is an aesthetic and ideological glory-hole. Disparaging or laudatory by turns, its fluid meanings tend to indicate more about the stance of its user than about the nature of the object to which it is applied. The semantic field of 'fin de siècle' is similarly complex. Its commonly pejorative overtones of decadence and degeneration supplemented not only by the 1890s neutral understanding of the term as meaning 'modern' or 'up-to-date', but also by a more positive sense which sees the end of one century as a hopeful moment of transition into the next—as Eugen Weber claims: 'il sert à désigner tout' [it can be used to mean everything].[27] By assessing attitudes and strategies relating to the decline and

---

reading this book, anyone feels that their understanding of the 1990s is enhanced by an exploration of the 1890s, I will feel that my work was worthwhile' (p. viii).

[27] See Eugen Weber, *France: Fin de Siècle*, Belknap Press (Cambridge, Mass.: Harvard University Press, 1986), 9. As David Mendelson suggests, the *fin-de-siècle* years of the

the preservation of diversity at two centuries' ends—those of the nineteenth and twentieth—this introductory chapter underlines the complexity and ambiguity of these two terms whilst considering how they relate over the gap of a century.

To read exoticism in the light of our own recent *fin de siècle* is inevitably to evoke a diverse body of figures, images, and cultural references. To allude to exoticism in a contemporary context is to provoke a range of responses and interpretations that range from the expiatory to the nostalgic, from postcolonial dissection of colonial discourse to nostalgic analysis of a spirit of adventure strangely detached from any firm grounding in contemporary intercontinental history.[28] After years of apparent redundancy, when the word was seen as the embarrassing cultural by-product of a shameful expansionist enterprise, exoticism has nevertheless been resurrected, over the past two decades, as an often-repeated term of critical currency in a variety of disciplines ranging from postcolonial studies and anthropology to musicology and art history.[29] This resurgence has accompanied—and has undoubtedly been in part provoked by—the major return both in the popular imagination and in academic discourse to the figure on which exoticism traditionally depends and which this book takes as its principal object of enquiry: what Victor Segalen classes as 'l'épisode périmé d'un voyage' [the weary interlude of a journey].[30]

In 1990, the first number of the *Carnets de l'exotisme* proposed a revisionist *défense et illustration* of exoticism. The often-nostalgic overtones of this manœuvre focus primarily on the work of nineteenth- and early twentieth-century authors and artists.[31] From the journal's opening issue there was a clear attempt, along the predictable lines of French resistance to the body of thought cast as 'postcolonial', at an anti-Saidian recuperation of authors who had fallen out of favour following

1890s can be seen as a period of transition or renewal when the 'génération de 1885'— Valéry, Proust, and Gide—came to maturity. See Mendelson, 'Le "Voyage en Orient" et le renouvellement de l'écriture fin-de-siècle', in Gwenhaël Ponnau (ed.), *Fins de siècle: Terme–Évolution–Révolution* (Toulouse: Presses universitaires du Mirail, 1989), 295–301 (p. 295).

[28] For a varied selection of essays considering contemporary approaches to exoticism, see Isabel Santaolalla (ed.), *'New' Exoticisms: Changing Patterns in the Construction of Otherness* (Amsterdam: Rodopi, 2000).

[29] For a consideration of the contemporary critique of exoticism, see Moura, *La Littérature des lointains*, 11.

[30] See Victor Segalen, *Équipée*, in Œuvres complètes, ii. 261–320 (p. 265).

[31] The *Carnets* were published by Éditions Torii in Poitiers for twenty-one numbers until 1998; a new series was launched by Torii and Kailash in 1999.

the upheavals of decolonization.[32] To this is linked a sense that the exotic belongs to a literary tradition that has reached its conclusion and can be approached, in Alain Buisine's terms, only: 'comme objet historique daté, comme utopie "périmée" de la différence' [as a historically dated object, as an 'obsolete' utopia of difference].[33] Although this turn to the past in order to measure (often in the writings of previous travellers) the extent of our current loss could be seen as a marked example of Rosaldo's 'imperialist nostalgia', nevertheless current attitudes to exoticism are less clear-cut than any such denial of the contemporary might imply. There is, for instance, a common contemporary response to globalization that interprets the exchange of cultural products as part of an inevitable process of levelling, inherent in which are the triumph of *cocacolonisation* and the collapse of 'elsewhere'. According to such entropic versions of the present, the recent *fin de siècle* is distinguished by a marked post-exoticism—a concept explored in particular by Antoine Volodine in the grim futuristic vision of his 1998 novel *Le Post-exotisme en dix leçons leçon onze*.[34] This sense of the exhaustion of 'elsewhere' as a potential source of otherness—or what Claude Reichler has called 'deuil ethnographique' [ethnographic mourning]—is countered and problematized, however, both by responses to the *Carnets de l'exotisme* survey on contemporary exoticism (which suggest an ongoing engagement with notions of the geographically exotic) and by references to contemporary French literature of travel (and more specifically to the work of the *Pour une littérature voyageuse* group).[35]

---

[32] For a discussion of the French reaction to Said, see David Murphy, 'De-centring French Studies: Towards a Postcolonial Theory of Francophone Culture', *French Cultural Studies*, 13/2 (2002), 165–85 (pp. 179–81).

[33] See 'Prière d'insérer', *Carnets de l'exotisme*, 1 (1990). This sense of belatedness is seen in particular in some of the responses to the 'Enquête sur l'exotisme' distributed to a number of contemporary authors, responses to which were published subsequently in the *Carnets*.

[34] Antoine Volodine, *Le Post-exotisme en dix leçons leçon onze* (Paris: Gallimard, 1998). Volodine's text is a prison novel in which he describes a group of dissident authors. The novel represents a break with any previous tradition and, despite its eccentric location, is far removed from any 'exotic' strand in French fiction.

[35] See Claude Reichler, 'Le deuil du monde', *Traverses*, 41–2 (1987), 134–45. The responses to the *Carnets* survey reveals the complex semantic field currently covered by 'exoticism'. Claude Ollier claims that any 'genre exotique' is 'caduc' [obsolete] (*Carnets*, 5 (1991), 49), whereas Pélégri argues, for instance, that: 'Les lieux n'étonnent plus, mais l'exotisme subsiste dans l'esprit' [Places are no longer sources of astonishment, but exoticism persists in the mind] (*Carnets*, 2–3 (1990), 61). These references to contemporary French literature of travel include a 1991 article by Michel Le Bris that serves as an apology

In contemporary French travel literature, there is therefore profound anxiety triggered by perceived threats to the integrity of the fields of the journey, whether these be symbolic or actual. Yet there remains a residual emphasis on the potential of geographical displacement to allow a neo-exoticism, or what Jacques Lacarrière classes as a search for 'ce qui est différent, ce qui est dissemblable' [what is different, dissimilar].[36] There is an obvious tension between this continuation of a tradition and any parallel commentary on its demise. The writing of travel literature in French, however, persists and even flourishes. The principal grouping of contemporary French traveller writers is assembled under the title *Pour une littérature voyageuse* and has met annually since 1989 for an increasingly successful festival in Saint-Malo. The choice of 'Étonnants voyageurs' as the title for this annual meeting of their movement is a clear reference to Baudelaire's 'Le Voyage'. What is perplexing is the ambivalence of this Baudelairean epithet describing the contemporary travellers as 'étonnants': for is the poet astonished by the travellers' conclusions about the human depravity they witness, or instead, surprised to see them at all, amazed that they continue to travel despite the disappointment of their inevitable reward: 'Amer savoir, celui qu'on tire du voyage' [Bitter knowledge acquired from travel]?[37] In their writings, Le Bris and his fellow travellers seem to explore this ambivalence while refusing to offer any definite resolution of it. However, some authors associated with the *Pour une littérature voyageuse* group, such as Alain Borer and Eric Poindron, turn quite deliberately to previous travellers in order to discover ways of engaging with space (as well as ways of representing such engagements) that avoid the tourist practices of contemporary, industrialized travel.[38] Indeed, the anti-tourism apparent, for instance, in the group's 1992 *livre-manifeste* suggests an aristocratic concern for self-distinction. The implication is that any contemporary exoticism depends on practices of exclusion; it is consequently inspired by anxiety about the decline of the field of the

---

for late twentieth-century exoticism. See Michel Le Bris, 'Le Grand Retour de l'aventure', *Carnets de l'exotisme*, 5 (1991), 51.

[36] Jacques Lacarrière, 'Nous ne sommes plus des paramécies', *Gulliver*, 11 (1993), 31–3 (p. 32).

[37] For a discussion of this ambivalence in Baudelaire's use of the phrase, see Walter Putnam, 'Myth, Metaphor, and Music in "Le Voyage" ', in William J. Thompson (ed.), *Understanding 'Les Fleurs du mal': Critical Readings* (Nashville, Tenn.: Vanderbilt University Press, 1997), 192–213 (pp. 205–6).

[38] See Alain Borer, *Rimbaud en Abyssinie* (Paris: Seuil, 1984), and Eric Poindron, *Belles étoiles: avec Stevenson dans les Cévennes* (Paris: Flammarion, 2001).

exotic, as well as about the resultant extinction of travellers them-selves.[39] In his excellent 1994 survey of contemporary notions of travel literature, Adrien Pasquali summarizes this paradoxical situation:

Dans un monde et un temps où les questions liées aux communications et à la communication sont l'objet d'une inflation discursive, où les facilités de trans-port ont favorisé une généralisation des pratiques voyageuses, pouvons-nous cerner les motifs de cet engouement pour les voyages et les récits de voyage?[40]

In a world where and at a time when questions linked to communication and means of communication trigger a flood of words, when opportunities for travel have encouraged a spread of practices linked to travel, can we determine the reasons for this craze for travel and travel writing?

The proliferation of anti-touristic discourse as a means of self-preser-vation is an important source for any investigation of *fin-de-siècle* exoticism, 1990s style. For anti-tourism links contemporary travel writing to the nostalgic repackaging and republishing of earlier, now out-of-print travel narratives that have accompanied it. As Jean-Didier Urbain has illustrated in *L'Idiot du voyage*, anti-tourism emerged in parallel with mass travel in the mid-nineteenth century.[41] It reached a height in the 1890s, when it represented a response to the perceived erosion of cultural diversity on which exoticism depends. As a result, the prophecy of an end of travel—an integral element of contemporary ecological discourse—has a long history and complex genealogy. The purported decline of diversity cannot be situated at a specific moment, but must be seen as a recurrent element constitutive of exoticism (and, I shall argue, of a certain understanding of travel) itself. The apocalyp-ticism underpinning contemporary jeremiads about 'la domestication totale de la planète, la mort de l'exotisme et la généralisation du Même' [the complete domestication of the planet, the death of exoticism and the spread of sameness] accordingly brings to mind Raymond Williams's comments on the erosion of rural England in the opening section of *The Country and the City*.[42] As Williams traces back into the

---

[39] The term 'traveller' is gendered deliberately. Amongst the *Pour une littérature voyageuse* group, there are currently no contemporary women travellers and only several female antecedents, most significantly Ella Maillart and Anita Conti.

[40] Pasquali, *Le Tour des horizons*, 9.

[41] See Jean-Didier Urbain, *L'Idiot du voyage* (Paris: Payot, 1993).

[42] For this analysis of contemporary accounts of the decline of the exotic, see Pasquali, *Le Tour des horizons*, 61. The link between discourses of the erosion of the exotic and Williams's account of the decline of the pastoral is discussed by James Clifford in *The Predicament of Culture: Twentieth-Century Ethnography, Literature, and Art* (Cam-bridge, Mass.: Harvard University Press, 1988), 4.

past the constant displacement of notions of rural decline and conse-
quent urban encroachment, he claims: 'what seemed like an escalator
began to move'.[43] What Williams identifies is pertinent for several
reasons, not least of which is that the erosion of a national rural culture
is often seen as an element of wider processes inherent in the decline of
diversity.[44] The notion of the moving escalator, or of what might be
dubbed backward referencing, becomes a useful model for tracking
accounts of the decline of exoticism, a decline that shifts into the past
from a current moment when, in James Clifford's terms:

The 'exotic' is uncannily close. Conversely, there seem no distant places left on
the planet where the presence of 'modern' products, media and power cannot be
felt. An older topography and experience of travel is exploded. One no longer
leaves home confident of finding something radically new, another time or
space. Distance is encountered in the adjoining neighbourhood, the familiar
turns up at the ends of the earth.[45]

From the present, the 'escalator' shifts through the Francophone critique in the works of Césaire and Fanon, via Paul Morand's early 1930s
cosmopolitanism and Victor Segalen's early twentieth-century diagnosis of global entropy, back to Chateaubriand's 1841 claims in the
conclusion to *Mémoires d'outre-tombe*: 'Si je compare deux globes
terrestres, l'un au commencement, l'autre à la fin de ma vie, je ne les
reconnais plus. [...] Il n'y a pas un coin de notre demeure qui soit
actuellement ignoré. [...] Les distances s'abrègent' [If I compare two
terrestrial globes, one at the beginning of my life and the other at the
end, I can no longer recognize them. [...] There is no corner of our
abode that is currently left unexplored. [...] Distances are being shor-
tened].[46] Williams concludes that his escalator stops at Eden, and, with
its reliance on myths of the Noble Savage, it is possible that the discourses of the decline of the exotic and of elsewhere are themselves also
rooted in that same 'well-remembered garden'.[47] Chateaubriand's comments represent, however, a striking stage in this tradition since they
predate by three years the first attested use of *exotisme* in France in

---

[43] Raymond Williams, *The Country and the City* (London: Hogarth 1985), 9.

[44] This was certainly the perception in early twentieth-century France where Albert
Kahn's response to *fin-de-siècle* fears about the decline of the exotic, *Les Archives de la
Planète*, involved photographic recording at home and abroad. On this subject, see Ch. 1.

[45] Clifford, *The Predicament of Culture*, 13–14.

[46] Chateaubriand, *Mémoires d'Outre-Tombe*, ed. J.-C. Berchet, 4 vols. (Paris: Garnier,
1998 [1849–50]), iv. 597–8.

[47] Williams, *The Country and the City*, 12.

1844.[48] Before the term was even coined, therefore, its demise was being outlined. The decline of exoticism could, then, be usefully classed as what Williams himself called a recurrent 'structure of feeling'.

This designation is particularly useful as it brings us back to the concerns over the conflations inherent in a 'historiography of convenience' with which this introductory chapter began. There can clearly be no seamless chronological tradition in which *fins de siècle* recur; it must be their differences rather than glibly imposed similarities that are of interest. For Williams, the 'structure of feeling' describes an emergent pattern of general experience that characterizes a particular generation of creative artists.[49] It is always the individuality of each moment that is striking: the decline of the exotic means different things at different times, and in different contexts quite different values are being brought into question. What is striking here is the paradoxical interpretation of entropy as a recurrent element of the *fin-de-siècle* imagination, for whereas the erosion of distinctiveness inherent in entropy implies an inexorably linear decline, its association with the *fin de siècle* ties it into a cyclical pattern of recurrence. Hence, for its perpetuation or recurrence, the decline of diversity must contain recovery encoded within it. As Chris Bongie has stated, a repeated element of this 'disappearing world' strand of exoticism is the recurrent belief in the individual's privileged status as last observer, in the deferral of the collapse of elsewhere: ' "In theory" there are no more horizons, but "in reality" they still exist.'[50]

No claim is made here that there is necessarily anything unique about the crisis of exoticism at the *fin-de-siècle* moment. The perceived decline of diversity is instead accentuated as a result of a specific set of contemporary circumstances and subsequent interpretations, combination of which has served to amplify the status of such instability and transform it into a central plank of the centurial moment. Close analysis of context remains, therefore, paramount. Not surprisingly, the narratives of displacement that emerge within French literature towards the end of the nineteenth century suggest a marked tension surrounding

---

[48] For a discussion of the evolution of the term, see Vincenette Maigne, 'Exotisme: évolution en diachronie du mot et de son champ sémantique', in R. Antonioli (ed.), *Exotisme et création: actes du colloque international de Lyon, 1983* (Lyons: Hermès, 1985), 9–16.

[49] For a discussion of Williams's notion of the 'structure of feeling', see Alan O'Connor, *Raymond Williams: Writing, Culture, Politics* (Oxford: Blackwell, 1989), 83–5, and Raymond Williams, *Politics and Letters* (London: New Left Books, 1979), 156–65.

[50] Bongie, *Exotic Memories*, 4.

attitudes towards exoticism and travel. Certain elements of this tension remain, however, specific to the 1880s and 1890s. In his book *Mad Travellers*, Ian Hacking describes the *fin de siècle*—or a period roughly circumscribed by that term—as an 'ecological niche' in which travel, with transport increasingly mechanized and the journey democratized, could still become pathological. Max Nordau had warned in *Degeneration* against the risks of 'railway spine', a physical hazard linked to increasingly mechanized travel. What Hacking foregrounds, however, is 'the fugue epidemic of the 1890s', a clinical diagnosis of obsessive, uncontrollable journeying that was given the name of dromomania by a group of turn-of-the-century psychiatrists in Bordeaux, a number of whom taught Victor Segalen during his time at medical school there.[51] According to Hacking, such a transient diagnosis was triggered by a specific cultural polarity, with fugue situated 'between two social phenomena that loomed very large in contemporary consciousness: romantic tourism and criminal vagrancy, one virtuous, one vicious'.[52] The feasibility of this linking of tourism with virtue is questionable, as the violent attacks by numerous contemporary anti-tourists make clear. Moreover, discussion of the implications of this proposed Manichean opposition is beyond the scope of this introduction. What is pertinent for current purposes is the fact that 1890s anxiety about travel had led not only to this clinical intervention in the field, but also to clear uncertainty surrounding the status of journeys elsewhere and one of the customary aesthetic responses to them, exoticism itself.

The slow rise of tourism in the second half of the nineteenth century gained new momentum in the *fin de siècle* as a result not only of a series of technological and geographical advances, but also of the implications for the provision of new fields of travel of colonial expansion itself.[53] As Porter and Teich outline, the 1890s represent a watershed, for the rise at that time of giant corporations, of mass production, and of mass consumption allowed the subsequent spread of motor vehicles and aviation, and the acceleration of everyday life these entailed.[54] This view of the *fin de siècle* as a moment of technological progress adds to

---

[51] See Ian Hacking, *Mad Travellers: Reflections on the Reality of Transient Mental Illness* (London: Free Association Books, 1999), 12.

[52] Hacking, *Mad Travellers*, 81.

[53] See Richard Overy, 'Heralds of Modernity: Cars and Planes from Invention to Necessity', in Mikulás Teich and Roy Porter (eds.), *Fin de siècle and its Legacy* (Cambridge: Cambridge University Press, 1990), 54–79.

[54] See Teich and Porter, 'Introduction', ibid. 1–9 (p. 3).

the ambiguous layering of the term and counters the often associated traditionalist bemoaning of European decline: 'Driving cars and flying planes endorsed the rejection of a decaying Europe and asserted commitment to a constructive modernity that was specific to neither class nor nation, but had dimensions that were ultimately global.'[55]

The implications of such progress for the traditional field of the exotic are clear. Not only, on a collective level, did technological modernity suggest the creation of globally standardizing networks of influence, shored up by the geopolitical expansion of Empire; but also, on a level of individual experience, the former association of the exotic with the inaccessible broke down. Peripheral spaces were opened up, and either reproduced in the metropolitan centre or had a transformative version of that centre imposed upon them. In his provocative and illuminating study of *fin-de-siècle* exoticism, Chris Bongie summarizes these implications: 'no part of the world will be exempt from this fin de siècle insight into the dissolution of "unknown" alternative worlds and the repetitive appearance in their place of "our" world, which for the decadentist imagination seems caught up in a process of irreparable decline'.[56] Responses to the crisis in exoticism that Bongie describes are nevertheless complex, and cannot be reduced to a single vector or strategy. A recurrent *fin-de-siècle* theme was, for instance, that of the Yellow Peril. *Le Péril Jaune* depended on images of entropic levelling, but reversed the usual centrifugal vector causing the levelling of differences as a result of the spread of Western influence. It was all-encompassing radical otherness itself—the so-called 'marécage asiatique' [Asian quagmire]—which appeared to be resurrected as a threatening alterity that would engulf the European and reverse the actual vectors of New Imperialism.

This underlying sense of ill-ease was thus related to the spread of sameness, whatever the source of such a spread, and focused especially on the implications of the European journey out towards a rapidly disappearing exotic periphery. For some, fear of the instability or imminent collapse of 'home' leads to a desire for escape and an irrepressible desire for displacement elsewhere; for others, the uncertainty of the present is linked to a fear of foreignness (rooted either in the threat of its radical otherness or of its imminent collapse into sameness). This obsessive introversion leads either to the exclusion of elsewhere, or even to its reconstruction closer to home in stage-managed forms. The

---

[55] See Overy, 'Heralds of Modernity', 74.   [56] Bongie, *Exotic Memories*, 19.

fin de siècle is perhaps more likely to be associated with this second response and with the sceptical notion of a 'fin des voyages',[57] as is made clear by the over-privileging of des Esseintes as the (non-)traveller emblematic of such malaise. In an extreme response to these intimations of decline, Huysmans's hero concludes that the only possible access to an approximate experience of otherness is situated in the refusal to leave, in the reconstruction of an elsewhere at home. Making an un-doubted allusion to the proliferation of exotic sideshows in the heart of late nineteenth-century Paris alluded to below, the sedentary protagonist asks: 'à quoi bon bouger quand on peut voyager si magnifiquement sur une chaise?' [what is the point of moving when you can travel so magnificently in a chair?], claiming to achieve, without actual travel, 'l'éreintement physique et la fatigue morale d'un homme qui rejoint son chez soi après un long et périlleux voyage' [the physical and moral exhaustion of a man coming home after a long and dangerous journey].[58] On the one hand (and initially at least), his question seems to perpetuate the age-old quarrel between the traveller and the stay-at-home;[59] on the other (and perhaps more subtly), the stasis to which des Esseintes resigns himself is part of the steady transformation of travel throughout the nineteenth century and, in particular, of its progressive mechanization. Des Esseintes's chair remains ambiguous, therefore, for although it reflects the domestication of travel and the dispersal of the exotic into the everyday, it suggests at the same time the domestication of the *means of* travel. In subsequent studies of the effects of speed and its relation to the cinematic, Paul Virilio also describes the transformation of the passenger's seat in a train, plane, or automobile into a 'fauteuil', and Saint-Pol-Roux (to whom Virilio's reflections are greatly indebted) claims about car travel in *Vitesse*: 'On est si bien assis qu'on se demande si ce n'est pas le paysage qui voyage' [We are so comfortably seated that we wonder whether it is not the landscape itself that is travelling].[60] In the light of these subsequent analyses, Huysmans can be seen to problematize the definition of travel at a moment when the space that surrounded the traveller began in-creasingly to resemble the domestic interior. Mechanization removed the body from direct, active contact with space and turned travel into a

---

[57] See J. Przybos, 'Voyage du pessimisme et pessimisme du voyage', *Romantisme*, 61 (1988), 67–74.

[58] J.-K. Huysmans, *À Rebours* (Paris: Garnier-Flammarion, 1978 [1884]), 174.

[59] See Pasquali, *Le Tour des horizons*, 31.

[60] Saint-Pol-Roux, *Vitesse* (Mortemart: Rougerie, 1973), 39.

passive event. Walking—the most common form of direct, non-mech-
anized, active contact—does not, of course, become obsolescent; it is
nevertheless seen as problematic as if the peripatetic body, especially of
the vagrant, the dromomaniac, or the prostitute, is somehow treated as
physically excessive and in need of control.

It is striking that the conclusions of *A Rebours* were mirrored in
popular culture in what Vanessa Schwartz describes as 'fin-de-siècle
panoramania': i.e. an early form of armchair tourism whereby the
experience of the exotic was reproduced in the heart of Paris.[61] This
trend seems to have culminated in the 'Tour du monde—panorama-
diorama animé', presented at the Exposition universelle in 1900. Three
floors of panoramas incorporated multisensory effects, animated motion, and indigenous performers; visitors would leave Marseilles to tour
Spain, Greece, Istanbul, Syria, Egypt, Ceylon, Cambodia, China, and
Japan, accordingly enjoying a whistle-stop tour of exotic locales.[62]
Multiple forms were juxtaposed—painted panoramas, early film foot-
age, actors, and indigenous performers—to create a 'realistic' effect.
Departure was no longer necessary since a domesticated, tamed, safe
version of the exotic was readily available in the heart of Paris. A similar
desire for the presence of 'elsewhere' at home was also serviced by a
new generation of post-Romantic exoticists, epitomized perhaps by
Pierre Loti and Claude Farrère, who reacted to the decline of the exotic
in face of colonial culture with a centrifugal yet aristocratic manœuvre.
They claimed that an apolitical, aesthetic approach to the authentic
cultures of colonized countries was not only feasible, but also both a
possible source of renewal for a jaded national literature and a potential
'contrepoids à la décadence métropolitaine' [counterbalance to metropolitan decadence].[63]

This sense of a struggle against declining diversity (and a parallel
inadequacy perceived in the means of accessing any traces of that
diversity still extant) is perhaps accentuated by the range of terms
with which *fin de siècle* is associated: *fin de race*, *fin du monde*, *fin de
règne*, *fin de globe*, and *fin des voyages*. Of these, it is the myth of a *fin
des voyages* that haunts literature of the nineteenth century. It is this

---

[61] See Vanessa R. Schwartz, *Spectacular Realities: Early Mass Culture in Fin-de-Siècle
Paris* (Berkeley: University of California Press, 1998), 150.

[62] Ibid. 173–6.

[63] See Jacques Chévrier, 'L'esprit "fin de siècle" dans quelques romans coloniaux des
années 1890–1910. Le cas de l'Afrique noire', in Ponnau (ed.), *Fins de siècle*, 495–508
(p. 496).

myth that has become a theme of increasing urgency in the twentieth, and accordingly an integral element of the aesthetics of *fin-de-siècle* France. What motivates me in this introductory chapter is not, however, a re-rehearsal of a series of late nineteenth-century myths of endings; I am interested instead in an investigation of how fears and responses to those fears in the 1890s can operate as an introduction to consideration of similar issues a century later—as well as during the intervening hundred years. As I have already suggested in the book's preface, Victor Segalen remains central to understandings of *fin-de-siècle* exoticism: not only because his work illustrates (and, to a certain extent, attempts to resolve) the tension between the twin movements of exoticism—death and rebirth, loss and recovery—particularly acute at the centennial moment;[64] but also because his exploration of the notion of exoticism has provided a contemporary conceptual framework in which to consider the representation of cultural diversity. Segalenian exoticism avoids previously reductive notions of the field of the exotic as artificial or colonial, or both. It was especially in the 1990s that Segalen's work emerged as a central yet problematic contribution to considerations of intercultural contact: central because of the conceptual and terminological sophistication it offers; problematic because of the associations with colonial literature and the seemingly radical rejection of hybridity that Segalen's work inevitably involves. Indeed, divergent critical responses to his work suggest not only its complexity, but also its potential contribution to an understanding of contemporary *fin-de-siècle* exoticism that rejects any movement towards reductivity.

Whilst Edward Said has woven Segalen into a Western Orientalist tradition of exoticizing hegemony, the Martiniquan Édouard Glissant has presented him as central to his own elaboration of a *fin-de-siècle* poetics of diversity, alluded to above, which he dubs 'la Relation'.[65] Glissant has developed Segalen's notion of cultural impenetrability into the contemporary idea of a 'right to opacity' that serves as a bulwark against all-encroaching neo-imperial axes of power. Glissant's work

[64] According to J. M. Goulemot, J. Lecuru, and D. Masseau, the *fin de siècle* is customarily associated with 'à la fois terme et naissance' [simultaneously ending and beginning]. See 'Les siècles ont-ils une fin?', in Pierre Citti (ed.), *Fins de Siècle: colloque de Tours 4–6 juin 1985* (Bordeaux: Presses universitaires de Bordeaux, 1990), 17–33 (p. 20).

[65] For Edward Said's comments on Segalen, see *Orientalism* (Harmondsworth: Penguin, 1991 [1978]), 252, *Culture and Imperialism* (London: Chatto & Windus, 1993), 222, and 'Afterword to the 1995 Printing' in *Orientalism*, rev. edn. (Harmondsworth: Penguin, 1995), 329–54 (p. 341). See also Glissant, *Poétique de la Relation*, 35–48.

represents what is perhaps the most coherent, attenuated response to recent claims of the advent of a progressive monoculture. It can be seen as perhaps the most sustained expression of what Moura calls an 'exotisme de ce siècle finissant encore attaché à l'irréductible différence des autres cultures' [exoticism of this century's end still attached to the irreducible difference of other cultures].[66]

Between the *fins de siècle* at stake here, the symbolic and actual territory of the exotic has shifted radically. As Charles Townshend suggests, for instance, there was a substantive transformation between the 1890s and the 1990s in ecological attitudes towards the physical threat of radically different environments:

Where turn-of-the-century explorers pitted their frail bodies and boats against the terrifying might of the Antarctic, children of the 1990s have worrisome wall displays of the fragile wilderness loaded with ever-lengthening lists of endangered species.

We go into our *fin de siècle* with plenty of *fin-de-siècle* anxieties still in place; but the exciting side of angst seems to have been lost on the way.[67]

This loss of 'adventure' is caused not only by the increasing spread of tourism, but also by the ever-increasing mechanization of travel itself. The transformation of space is supplemented, moreover, by the erasure of space as a result of ever-increasing speed that, in Paul Virilio's terms, will ultimately lead to the annihilation of spatial difference.[68] Hence there is a definite recurrence of tensions (identified already at the previous *fin de siècle*) between the inexorable decline of diversity and its appearance in newly emergent forms. However, although the spread of commodity culture, the industrialization of travel, and the expansion of the mass media may lead to the erosion or at best radical alteration of authentic human differences, there is a growing awareness that narratives of loss and entropic decline are too geometric, too neat. Not least, such narratives are seen increasingly to impose a post-colonial unification of human histories in which local specificities are absorbed into a Westernized monoculture.

In the later twentieth-century engagement with exoticism, new perspectives emerged. As James Clifford describes in the introduction to his

---

[66] Moura, *La Littérature des lointains*, 434.

[67] See Charles Townshend, 'The Fin de Siècle', in Alex Danchev (ed.), *Fin de Siècle: The Meaning of the Twentieth Century* (London: Tauris Academic Studies, 1995), 198–216 (p. 213).

[68] See e.g. *Vitesse et Politique* (Paris: Galilée, 1977).

Predicament of Culture, there is an alternative version of global culture which can be distinguished from the discourse of entropic decline, especially in the work of Édouard Glissant: 'Alongside this narrative of progressive monoculture a more ambiguous "Caribbean" experience may be glimpsed.'[69] Clifford's whole study is an inspired response to an ethnographic truth that he proceeds to state as follows: 'It is easier to register the loss of traditional orders of difference than to perceive the emergence of new ones.' *Fin-de-siècle* exoticism in the 1990s was a complex notion, dependent itself on the reinvention of diversity, based less on competing autonomous traditions and more on constant inter-relations. Clifford returns to the two vectors of this introduction's subtitle—decline and recovery—but instead of creating a tension be-tween them, interprets them as complementary aspects of a complex cultural situation: 'modern ethnographic histories are perhaps con-demned to oscillate between two metanarratives: one of homogeniza-tion, the other of invention. In most specific conjunctures, both narratives are relevant, each undermining the other's claim to tell "the whole story", each denying to the other a privileged, Hegelian vision.'[70] Exoticism—as well as the diversity on which it depends—is a protean, constantly recontextualized concept that quite simply refuses to die. In its current manifestations, self-consciously aware of its customary as-sociation with the *fin de siècle*, it even appears to challenge the pertin-ence of this temporal epithet with which it is customarily coupled. For encoded in certain contemporary, *fin-de-siècle* considerations of exoti-cism is a questioning of the notion of the *fin de siècle* itself.

In a section of his *Traité du Tout-Monde* entitled 'Rhétoriques de fin de siècle', for instance, Glissant describes the disorientating effects of imposing Eurocentric divisions of time—such as the century—on Caribbean history: 'La division du temps linéaire occidental en siècles [est] capable même d'avaler, de digérer peut-être les intrusions des histoires des peuples, de les inscrire de force dans sa linéarité' [The division of linear Western time into centuries is capable even of swal-lowing, perhaps of digesting the intrusions of indigenous histories, of forcibly inscribing them in its linearity].[71] It is the emergence of alter-native histories and competing vectors of influence—of a version of the French Revolution, for instance, which places the hub of action in

---

[69] Clifford, *The Predicament of Culture*, 15. [70] Ibid. 17.
[71] Édouard Glissant, 'Rhétoriques de fin de siècle', in *Traité du Tout-Monde* (Paris: Gallimard, 1997), 105–15 (p. 105).

Haiti as opposed to Paris—that challenges such patterns and has contributed to the identity crisis perceived in French society throughout the 1990s:

En vérité, s'il est un sentiment de déréalisation dans l'Europe actuelle, au moment où elle tente de se faire, cela ne tient pas aux affres bien repérées qu'on éprouve à une fin de siècle, mais à l'énorme multiplicité dans laquelle l'Histoire désormais se dévoie, et au lancinement de la perte de puissance ou de pouvoir sur cette Histoire, chez ceux qui l'avaient conçue comme une origine projetant dans une fin.[72]

To tell the truth, if there is a sense of a lack of fulfilment in contemporary Europe at a time when it is attempting to construct itself, this is not as a result of the well-documented agonies experienced at a *fin de siècle*, but a result of the great plurality of histories towards which History is henceforth being led and of the nagging loss of power or authority over that History for those who had understood it as an origin pointing towards an ending.

Glissant's conclusion points to the precarious status of terms such as 'fin de siècle'; and their precariousness is accentuated as a result of newly emergent patterns of diversity understood, in Segalenian terms, as dependent on the possibility of shifting yet resistant patterns of distinctive if interdependent cultures:

Si la fin de siècle (et la fin de ce siècle) apparaît significative, c'est qu'en même temps, si l'on peut dire, elle a gardé sa fonction de pendule de la linéarité temporelle mais que, surprise déjà dans la multiplicité des temps et des histoires qui ont surgi du fond du monde et qui se rejoignent enfin, elle ne fait plus signe avec autant d'absolu.[73]

If the *fin de siècle* (and the end of this century) appears to be significant, it is because, one might say, it has retained its function as a pendulum of linear chronology, whilst simultaneously—already caught out by the multiplicity of times and histories that have appeared suddenly from the ends of the earth and are, at last, meeting—it no longer expresses a meaning quite so absolutely.

Exoticism, traditional staple of *fin-de-siècle* culture and identity, re-emerges radically renewed in certain strands of contemporary thought; and in re-emerging, as the following chapter will go on to suggest, it challenges the concepts of travel and declining cultural diversity with which it is customarily associated.

---

[72] Glissant, 'Rhétoriques de fin de siècle', 105–6.
[73] Ibid. 106.

I

Travelling Concepts: Postcolonial Approaches to Exoticism and Diversity

L'exotisme est un piège parce qu'on le croit facile, alors qu'il est d'une épuisante difficulté. Ce qui est vrai pour le critique, autant que pour le conquérant et le romancier.[1]

Exoticism is a trap because whereas people believe it to be an easy concept it is actually exhaustingly difficult. This is true for the critic as much as it is for the conqueror and the novelist.

Dénoncer [l'exotisme], c'est persister dans un discours vague mélangeant les divers niveaux de sens que recouvre en fait la notion; ignorer le terme ou s'en servir d'une manière myope à l'occasion de travaux précis mais limités dans leur vocation définitionnelle, c'est renoncer à comprendre un fait littéraire qui a toutes les chances d'être extrêmement important dans l'histoire de la littérature européenne.[2]

Denouncing exoticism means perpetuating a hazy discourse which confuses the various different meanings actually encompassed by the notion; ignoring the term or using it in a restrictive way in focused studies with few ambitions in terms of providing definitions is to refuse to come to terms with a literary phenomenon that is most likely to become extremely important in the history of European literature.

---

[1] Denise Brahimi, 'Enjeux et risques du roman exotique', in Alain Buisine and Norbert Dodille (eds.), *L'Exotisme: actes du colloque de Saint-Denis de la Réunion, 1988*, Cahiers CRLH-CIRAOI, 5 (Paris: Didier-Érudition, 1988), 11–18 (p. 18).

[2] Moura, *L'Europe littéraire et l'ailleurs*, 36

THE aim of this opening chapter is to explore the relationship between exoticism and diversity, and to track shifting twentieth-century attitudes to the concept of exoticism. The theoretical issues it explores will underpin the more practical analyses of texts and contexts with which subsequent chapters are concerned. The chapter will explain how the recent theoretical elaboration of exoticism as an item of critical currency, developed in particular by scholars concerned with French-language materials, challenges the postcolonial denigration of the term whilst permitting a more attenuated approach to the contact between cultures emerging from the practices of travel. Any such renewal of interest in exoticism and a more cautious approach to its field of reference are not, however, immediately apparent to readers of postcolonial theory and criticism, fields in which the term is more likely to be subject to a pejorative approach. Unease associated with deployment of the term is not a new phenomenon. In a fragment of the *Essai sur l'exotisme* written in Tientsin in May 1913, for instance, Victor Segalen comments on his surprisingly stubborn retention of the title word, exoticism itself: 'compromis et gonflé, abusé, prêt d'éclater, de crever, de se vider de tout' [a bloated and compromised word, abused, ready to explode, to burst, to empty itself of everything].[3] Refusing to resort to 'l'aigreur et l'acidité' [sourness or acidity] of neologisms in order to encapsulate the subject of his study, he proposes an exercise in semantic spring-cleaning for a term coined in the 1840s and not yet three-quarters of a century old.[4] As Segalen was well aware, however, the concept of exoticism and the processes it entails are rooted in early modern (and, arguably, even medieval) contact between radically different cultures.[5] Indeed, the version of exoticism that emerges from his *œuvre*, a reaction to the entropic decline of various forms of diversity, was itself more retrospective than projective, recovering traces of pre-contact Tahiti or imperial China in a present eroded by tourism, colonialism, and others forces of modernity. Segalen's would-be prophetic vision of exoticism's decline, reflecting a 'structure of feeling' that can be tracked back (as has been suggested in the introductory chapter) at least to the early nineteenth century, suggests a progressive exhaustion of the exotic understood in quantative terms and a dependence on a process of aestheticization that recasts diversity in qualitative terms:

---

[3] Segalen, *Essai sur l'exotisme*, 771; *Essay on Exoticism*, 56.
[4] Segalen, *Essai sur l'exotisme*, 765; *Essay on Exoticism*, 47.
[5] See Vincenette Maigne, 'Exotisme: évolution en diachronie du mot et de son champ sémantique', and Todorov, *Nous et les Autres*.

those truly sensitive to its persistence can 'se réfugi[er] sur des sommets plus glaciaires' [true exots can take refuge on more glacial peaks].[6]

RETHINKING THE EXOTIC

Such an early application of a quasi-ecological teleology to the depletion of radical otherness was accelerated by the reassessment of exoticism in the light of decolonization and postcoloniality. By the 1960s, the equation of 'exotic' and 'colonial'—a conflation resisted, it should be added, by Segalen himself—had become an orthodoxy. Ethnography attempted to break its historical links with colonialism, not only creating a new relationship with its traditional subject, but also seeking new subjects. Georges Condominas's study of the Mnong Gar (or Moï) people in Central Vietnam claimed that 'l'exotique est quotidien' [the exotic is everyday].[7] In this key expression, he reflected both a growing reflexivity in understandings of exoticism and a recognition of the (now commonplace) idea that what for one person is exotic is for another banal: as Jean Genet would claim, cultural geography is always provisional, and France as a result potentially 'utterly exotic'.[8] This generalization of the exotic and attempted stripping of its ideological overtones indicated a return to the term's initial, sixteenth-century neutral usage as a shifter simply suggesting relative foreignness; combined, however, with lexical malaise in the wake of Empire, this generalization resulted in a progressive reduction in use, with the result that the British Anthropological Society has recently claimed that the exotic is 'no more'.[9]

Such a claim is not only prematurely celebratory, but also fails to account for the resurgence of interest in the exotic that became particularly apparent in the 1990s.[10] In the light of the foregrounding, in both postcolonial and postmodern thought, of otherness and alterity, this re-emergence of exoticism as an item of critical currency was in itself not surprising; what has been striking, however, is the terminological laxity emerging from a relatively restricted theoretical problematization of the

---

[6] Segalen, *Essai sur l'exotisme*, 762; *Essay on Exoticism*, 39.

[7] Georges Condominas, *L'Exotique est quotidien* (Paris: Plon, 1965).

[8] Hughes, *Writing Marginality in Modern French Literature*, 7. The reflexivity of the exotic was initially explored in the contemporary period by Segalen and Henri Michaux, and given a subsequent domestic, endotic spin by authors such as Georges Perec.

[9] See Jeremy MacClancy (ed.), *Exotic No More* (Chicago: University of Chicago Press, 2002).

[10] See Michel Panoff, 'Une valeur sûre: l'exotisme', *L'Homme*, 26/1–2 (1986), 287–96.

term. There has been, as is suggested in the Preface, a clear bifurcation between francophone and anglophone understandings and approaches, with English-language scholarship on the exotic heavily reliant on notions of colonial discourse derived largely from Edward Said's work, and with its French-language counterpart offering less ideologically committed readings of colonial literature.[11] Moreover, as is demonstrated below, amongst postcolonial critics in particular, exoticism is customarily dismissed as an outmoded, essentializing, and objectifying process, as if this pejorative understanding of the word reflected a widespread orthodoxy unworthy of further exploration. In relation to this, Ron Shapiro has identified what he calls 'postcolonialism's puritanical fumigation of language', according to which 'terms like exotic [...] are all subject to a merciless grinding down to a single ideological edge, thereby sharply reducing the range of different contexts in which such words might retain some usefulness and some flexibility of meaning'.[12] There are notably exceptions to this under-theorization and a related reliance on received understandings of the term, but thorough exploration of the field of the exotic—and the plurality of exoticisms it encompasses—remains ongoing.[13]

   In highlighting these laxities and blind spots, Terry Eagleton has characterized postcolonial theory as the 'pretentiously opaque' product of a 'gaudy, all-licensed supermarket of the mind', and proceeded to develop this criticism into a more wide-ranging and acerbic attack on 'Post-Modernism's enduring love-affair with otherness'.[14] Claiming that this subject is 'not the most fertile of intellectual furrows', he continues: 'once you have observed that the other is typically portrayed

---

[11] Contrast e.g. Graham Huggan, *The Postcolonial Exotic: Marketing the Margins* (London: Routledge, 2001), with recent French-language engagements such as Henri Copin, *L'Indochine dans la littérature française des années vingt à 1954: exotisme et altérité* (Paris: L'Harmattan, 2000), and Patrick Laude, *Exotisme indochinois et poésie: étude sur l'œuvre poétique d'Alfred Droin, Jeanne Leuba et Albert de Pouvourville* (Paris: Sudestasie, 2000).

[12] Ron Shapiro, 'In Defence of Exoticism: Rescuing the Literary Imagination', in Santaolalla (ed.), *'New' Exoticisms: Changing Patterns in the Construction of Otherness*, 41–9 (p. 43).

[13] See e.g. Santaolalla (ed.), *'New' Exoticisms*, Bongie, *Exotic Memories*, Roger Célestin, *From Cannibals to Radicals: Figures and Limits of Exoticism* (Minneapolis: University of Minnesota Press, 1996), Huggan, *The Postcolonial Exotic*, and Renata Wasserman, *Exotic Nations: Literature and Cultural Identity in the United States and Brazil, 1830–1930* (Ithaca, NY: Cornell University Press, 1994).

[14] Terry Eagleton, 'In the Gaudy Supermarket', *London Review of Books*, 21/10 (1999), 3–6 (p. 3); and 'A Spot of Firm Government', *London Review of Books*, 23/16 (2001), 19–20 (p. 19).

as lazy, dirty, stupid, crafty, womanly, passive, rebellious, sexually rapacious, childlike, enigmatic and a number of other mutually contradictory epithets, it is hard to know what to do next apart from reaching for yet another textual illustration of the fact'.[15] Yet the links between otherness, diversity, and exoticism remain close but relatively unexplored. Although Eagleton is perhaps right to be wary about the tendency of certain work in the field to back itself into a self-referential, self-perpetuating impasse, the project for those committed to moving beyond reductively dismissive and pejorative understandings of exoticism is, with inevitable overlap between these elements, fourfold: first, an exploration of the complex semantic field covered by the expression, paying special attention to the ways in which an initially colonial term has 'travelled' to become a common item of postcolonial usage; secondly, a cautiously diachronic approach to exoticism, considering not only how the concept has evolved, but also how exotica have been received and represented in a variety of historical contexts; thirdly, a systematic theorization, underlining the complexity of the processes of exoticism and their contribution to an understanding of intercultural contact; and finally, an elaboration—albeit speculative or tentative—of applications of exoticism to contemporary contexts, attenuating the customary reduction of exoticism to a nostalgic, retrospective practice.[16] Such a programme is multidisciplinary, involving scholars from philosophy, history, sociology, cultural studies, and literary studies; and individual studies are inevitably inter- or transdisciplinary, revealing an intellectual hybridization that eschews the respect of clear boundaries on which exoticism regularly depends.

In tracking the semantic shifts of exoticism and of the practices the term encompasses, the work of Edward Said is invaluable. In *Orientalism* he offers a regionally specific account of the exoticization of one region by another, but it is another, lesser-known text that provides the key. In his 1982 essay 'Traveling Theory', Said adopts the figure of travel to propose a persuasive model for analysing the evolution of twentieth-century critical theory.[17] Developing the initial commonplace idea that

---

[15] Eagleton, 'A Spot of Firm Government', 19.

[16] A number of recent studies have begun to fulfil this project. See e.g. A. James Arnold, 'Perilous Symmetry: Exoticism and the Geography of Colonial and Postcolonial Culture', in Freeman G. Henry (ed.), *Geo/graphies: Mapping the Imagination in French and Francophone Literature and Film* (Amsterdam: Rodopi, 2003), 1–28.

[17] See Edward W. Said, 'Traveling Theory', in *The World, the Text and the Critic* (London: Vintage, 1991), 226–47. (First published 1983.)

'[l]ike people and schools of criticism, ideas and theories travel—from person to person, from situation to situation, from one period to another',[18] Said proceeds to elaborate a more complex analysis of the four stages inherent in this process: (1) departure from a point of origin, (2) passage through different contexts, (3) transplantation into a new context, with its own conditions of acceptance, and (4) re-emergence of the initial idea, transformed by its displacement and new uses. Through the example he cites (the shift of Lukács's theory of 'reification' from early twentieth-century Hungary via Goldmann in Paris to the work of Raymond Williams in later twentieth-century Cambridge), Said initially suggests that theories' travels lead to the diffusion of their impact and their progressive depoliticization, decontextualization, and even domestication. A later revision of this thesis in 'Traveling Theory Reconsidered' suggests that the opposite is also possible and that reinterpretation in a new political or historical context can in certain circumstances (such as those of Fanon's radical reappropriation of Lukács in the context of the Algerian War) lead to a theory's reinvigoration.[19]

Although Said accepts that any fully comprehensive account of the shifts he describes would be an enormous task, he nevertheless sketches a paradigm whose more generalized uses have been explored by subsequent critics.[20] The discussion of Fanon in Said's own reconsideration of his initial ideas suggests that, as a development of this brief essay, accounts of postcolonial theory itself would benefit from similar scrutiny. Postcolonialism is the result of contemporary theory's ongoing travels, with one possible version of its genesis involving the transatlantic journey of an eclectic range of French and Francophone thought and its reinterpretation and re-emergence on North American campuses.[21] Indeed, one critical response to postcolonial theory sees it as

---

[18] See Edward W. Said, 'Traveling Theory', in *The World, the Text and the Critic* (London: Vintage, 1991), (226–47).

[19] See Edward W. Said, 'Traveling Theory Reconsidered', in Robert M. Polhemus and Roger B. Henkle (eds.), *Critical Reconstructions* (Stanford, Calif.: Stanford University Press, 1994), 251–65.

[20] For an application of Said's ideas, with particular attention to the emergence of American poststructuralist thought, see Ieme van der Poel and Sophie Bertho (eds.), *Traveling Theory: France and the United States* (Madison, NJ: Fairleigh Dickinson University Press; London: Associated University Presses, 1999). See also James Clifford, 'Notes on Travel and Theory', *Inscriptions* 5 (1989), 177–88, and Caren Kaplan, *Questions of Travel: Postmodern Discourses of Displacement* (Durham, NC: Duke University Press, 1996).

[21] This model of transatlantic displacement has a wider application in understandings of the construction of Critical Theory in the North American academy. See Jean-Philippe

excessively reliant on metropolitan theory, with a tendency to decontextualize and absorb non-metropolitan voices into discourses centred on the Western academy.[22] As a result of the proximity and constantly contested nature of the object of study, we do not perhaps yet enjoy a sufficient critical distance to make full sense of the implications of these complex trajectories. What is clear, however, is that postcolonialism depends not only on the travels of contemporary theory—on, for example, the re-emergence of Foucault in Said or Lacan in Bhabha—but also on the displacement, recycling, and reinterpretation of colonial concepts (and, more controversially, of the language used to describe them). Robert Young's *Colonial Desire: Hybridity in Theory, Culture and Race* explores a striking (and, for the author, troubling) example of this: the nineteenth-century term 'hybridity', used initially to describe a biological or more specifically physiological and racialized phenomenon, but reactivated in later twentieth-century terminology to describe a cultural one. Stuart Hall criticizes Young for what he sees as his conflation of two radically different concepts that happen to share, in very different contexts, the same label, and focuses on 'the inexplicably simplistic charge [...] that the post-colonial critics are "complicit" with Victorian racial theory *because both sets of writers deploy the same term—hybridity—in their discourse!*'[23]

Young's study does not operate as reductively as Hall suggests. It attempts instead, more circumspectly, to prompt questions about the extent to which contemporary theorizations have broken absolutely with the formulations of the past, and suggests that: 'There is a historical stemma between the cultural concepts of our own day and those of the past from which we tend to assume we have distanced ourselves. [...] There is no simple or correct notion of hybridity: it changes as it repeats, it also repeats as it changes.'[24] At the core of this chapter is

Mathy, 'The Resistance to French Theory in the United States: A Cross-Cultural Inquiry', *French Historical Studies*, 19 (1995), 331–47, and Claire Goldberg Moses, 'Made in America: "French Feminism" in Academia', in Roger Célestin, Eliane DalMolin, and Isabelle de Courtivron (eds.), *Beyond French Feminisms: Debates on Women, Politics and Culture in France, 1981–2001* (New York: Palgrave Macmillan, 2003), 261–84.

[22] See e.g. Aijaz Ahmad, 'The Politics of Literary Postcoloniality', *Race and Class*, 36/3 (1995), 1–20.

[23] Stuart Hall, 'When was "The Post-Colonial"? Thinking at the Limit', in Iain Chambers and Lidia Curti (eds.), *The Post-Colonial Question: Common Skies, Divided Horizons* (London: Routledge, 1996), 242–60 (p. 259).

[24] Robert J. C. Young, *Colonial Desire: Hybridity in Theory, Culture and Race* (London: Routledge, 1995), 27.

a similar assumption about exoticism, another persistent term whose originally colonial overtones were slowly transformed until it re-emerged as a common yet contested item of currency in a postcolonial context: exoticism itself also changes as it repeats, repeats as it changes.

This seemingly cursory reference to Young's work serves as more, however, than a reminder that words travel as much as the concepts and theories for which they are vehicles, that there is a resultant need for sensitivity in postcolonial studies to shifting semantic fields and to associated issues of translation. In addition, Young's subject—colonial hybridity—forms an integral part of the context in which exoticism itself must be considered. It may even be represented as exoticism's other, for whereas hybridity refers to uneven syntheses and the emer-gence of new, transcultural forms, colonial exoticism tends to perpetu-ate perceptions of the discrete cultures inherent in diversity, to accentuate the polarities of difference, and to deny the implications of contact. Note, however, the epithet 'colonial' that is applied to exoticism here as a necessary qualification. Such attenuation, and the resultant implication that exoticism is not necessarily a monolithic, ahistorical process, suggest that there has been a marked under-theorization of the exotic in postcolonial studies and a tendency to employ the term without the same (often controversial) attention to detail that marks discussion of other terms recuperated or coined for postcolonial purposes.[25] In the 1998 Routledge *Key Concepts in Post-colonial Studies*, for instance, the complex evolution of exoticism is eclipsed by a more restricted understanding, and no account is taken of the phenomenon's re-emergence in ambivalent postcolonial forms. Since *exotisme* (and its English equivalent 'exoticism') were coined in the first half of the nineteenth century, the term has been subject to steady semantic shifts between two poles, one signifying an exotic-ness essential to radical otherness, the other describing the process whereby such radical otherness is either experienced by a traveller from outside, or translated, transported, and represented for consumption at home.

It is this final sense of translation, transportation and representa-tion—of exoticism as process—on which contemporary critics have focused. The editors of *Key Concepts in Post-Colonial Studies* describe,

---

[25] The clearest example of this lexical controversy that characterizes much postcolonial criticism is the epithet 'post(-)colonial' itself. For a useful discussion of this issue, see Bill Ashcroft, 'On the Hyphen in Post-colonial', *New Literatures Review*, 32 (1996), 23–32. There are some notable exceptions to this under-theorization: see n. 13 above.

for instance, the shift in the field of the exotic from objective signification of relative indigeneity to connoting, in a nineteenth-century context, 'a stimulating or exciting difference, something with which the domestic could be (safely) spiced'.[26] What the Routledge exploration of this 'key concept' omits—and what any definition of exoticism that fails to go beyond metropolitan displays of empire ignores—is the constant contestation that has marked twentieth-century uses of this term, especially in its French-language context. From the early attempts of Victor Segalen (mentioned above) to redefine the concept in his *Essai sur l'exotisme* to the more recent efforts in a variety of fields—narratology, anthropology, historiography, postmodern sociology, and studies in contemporary travel—to forge positive contemporary usages, 'exoticism' has constantly defied any such reduction.[27] Whereas in contemporary critical currency, the term has almost universally pejorative overtones and is restricted by its coupling to colonial discourse, close analysis reveals a need for a more nuanced understanding that encompasses not only the potential reflexivity or reciprocity within exoticism, but also the implicit challenge it may pose to the reductive overtones outlined above.

In his study of *fin-de-siècle* exoticism, Chris Bongie has emphasized a central element on which such ambivalence depends: exoticism's stubborn persistence in the face of prophecies of the collapse of its symbolic field, i.e. of the erosion of difference by sameness, of the encroachment of globalization on indigenous specificity. Exoticism is characterized by a twin yet contradictory movement—by a cycle of decline and regeneration—as a result of which *exotisme*, a term dismissed as obsolescent by French colonial authors in the inter-war period, has re-emerged as an increasingly cited postcolonial concept. The now largely unequivocal

---

[26] Bill Ashcroft, Gareth Griffiths, and Helen Tiffin, *Key Concepts in Post-Colonial Studies* (London: Routledge, 1998), 94.

[27] See Francis Affergan, *Exotisme et altérité* (Paris: PUF, 1987), Jean Baudrillard, *La Transparence du mal*, Michel de Certeau, *L'Écriture de l'histoire* (Paris: Gallimard, 1975), Gérard Genette, *Palimpsestes: la littérature au second degré* (Paris: Seuil, 1982), and Jean-Didier Urbain, *Secrets de voyage*. Urbain reclaims the term 'exoticism' to describe shifting patterns of cultural diversity resistant to contemporary globalization, suggesting that it is a quality inherent in perception and dimension. Focusing on travellers undertaking interstitial journeys, he describes them as 'les découvreurs d'un nouvel exotisme' [discoverers of a new exoticism], seeking 'des mondes très proches, la *terra obscura* et la *terra prohibita*—des univers exotiques pour des voyages au regard desquels la distance géographique n'est plus un critère décisif' [worlds that are very close, *terra obscura* and *terra prohibita*—exotic universes for journeys with regard to which geographical distance is no longer a conclusive criterion] (p. 104).

and unquestioning Anglo-Saxon use of 'exoticism' results perhaps from the predominance of Said's *Orientalism* as a point of postcolonial reference. This text's perceived status as a foundational work has focused attention on a geographically specific (although notoriously fluid) tradition of exoticism, although not necessarily to the detriment of wider-ranging considerations of the representation of otherness: Said's conceptual framework seems to have transcended its initially fixed spatial parameters in order to achieve a more generalized resonance. Peter Mason, in describing exoticism as a representational effect dependent on decontextualization and recontextualization, claims to see a radical divergence from Orientalism since such a process is 'indifferent to ethnographic or geographic precision and tends to serve imaginative rather than concretely political ends'.[28] Not only does this overemphasize Orientalist interest in any accurate representation of its subject; but it also downplays the latently ideological intentions of many products of colonial exoticism. The distinction between exoticism and Orientalism is perhaps linked more to differing epistemological traditions and the terminology on which they depend.

There is a need to avoid the careless conflation of exoticism and Orientalism found in some scholarship on the representation of otherness. Many of the points raised by the more perceptive early readers of *Orientalism* are certainly applicable to exoticism itself: the need to view questions of Orientalist misrepresentation in relation to issues of the (un)reliability of representation in general; the recognition of the polyphony inherent in Orientalist accounts and evident in texts right back to the twelfth-century Franco-Italian travel account of Marco Polo; or an awareness of the heterogeneity of Orientalist discourses and their progressive transformation according to historical circumstances.[29] As Santaolalla has argued, however, there is a need to distinguish between the two: Orientalism and exoticism are not synonymous and do not follow the same patterns.[30] Not only is exoticism less geographically determined; but also, often disrupting the monodirectional and

---

[28] Peter Mason, *Infelicities: Representations of the Exotic* (Baltimore, Md.: Johns Hopkins University Press, 1998), 3.

[29] See Clifford, 'On *Orientalism*', in *The Predicament of Culture*, 255–76, Dennis Porter, '*Orientalism* and Its Problems', in Patrick Williams and Laura Chrisman (eds.), *Colonial Discourse and Post-Colonial Theory: A Reader* (New York: Columbia University Press, 1994), 150–61, and Lisa Lowe, *Critical Terrains: French and British Orientalisms* (Ithaca, NY: Cornell University Press, 1991).

[30] Santaolalla, 'Introduction: What is "New" in "New" Exoticisms?', in *'New' Exoticisms*, 9–17 (pp. 10–11).

essentially colonial nature of Orientalism with what Santaolalla casts as its 'multidirectional and polyvalent' potential, exoticism provides a much more versatile means of understanding intercultural contact and the mutual implications of the interaction of cultures.[31]

REHABILITATING EXOTICISM

The rehabilitation of *exotisme* in a variety of contexts and disciplines is, in various ways, witness to the long-standing French resistance to any thorough and active engagement with postcolonial thought.[32] French versions of exoticism do not necessarily indicate an insensitivity to the condition of postcoloniality itself, but suggest instead that there is a need to open up understandings of terms used in a postcolonial context and take account of (un)translatability as these terms travel between contexts. Positive uses of exoticism in de Certeau's historiography, Affergan's anthropology, or even Genette's narratology indicate a se-mantic reinvestiture of terms that would be rendered difficult by an acceptance of the common usage of central postcolonial terms. The 'postcolonial', often perceived in France as an Anglo-Saxon invention emerging from an obsession with the 'politiquement correct', is held at bay, however, despite—or even as a result of—the potential illumin-ation it offers to the culture and institutions of contemporary France.[33] Ideological attempts to exclude the other range from the radical cen-tralization of Republicanism to the desire for ethnic homogenization on the Far Right, but Frenchness has never successfully been constructed as a core, seamless identity.[34] However, the postcolonial problematic

[31] Santaolalla, 'Introduction: What is "New" in "New" Exoticisms?', in *'New' Exoti-cisms*, 13.

[32] Two of Edward Said's texts have been translated, but have attracted little critical attention: *L'Orientalisme: l'Orient créé par l'Occident* (Paris: Seuil, 1980), and *Culture et impérialisme* (Paris: Fayard/Le Monde diplomatique, 2000). Homi Bhabha and Gayatri Spivak remain unavailable in French translation, but James Clifford's *The Predicament of Culture* has appeared as *Malaise dans la culture: l'ethnographie, la littérature et l'art au XXe siècle* (Paris: École nationale des Beaux-Arts, 1996).

[33] See Alec G. Hargreaves and Mark McKinney, 'Introduction: The Post-Colonial Problematic in France', in Alec G. Hargreaves and Mark McKinney (eds.), *Post-Colonial Cultures in France* (London: Routledge, 1997), 3–25.

[34] See e.g. on the tracing of French identity to two distinct ethnic groups, the Franks and the Gauls, L. Poliakov, *Le Mythe aryen: essai sur les sources du racisme et du nationalisme* (Paris: Calmann-Lévy, 1971); for a reflection on the role of border identities in the construction of French identity, see Peter Sahlins, *Boundaries: the Making of France and Spain in the Pyrenees* (Berkeley: University of California Press, 1989).

rarely emerges from the French discourses of politics or culture. In a challenging article exploring such exclusion, Antoine Compagnon has described the 'isolement de l'université française' [isolation of the French university] and the resulting 'silence théorique qui semble s'être épaissi en France' [silence surrounding theory that seems to have deepened in France].[35] It is only in the recent work of Jean-Marc Moura that there has been a co-ordinated attempt to engage actively with postcolonial theory and sketch out a coherent theoretical framework for reading francophone literature.[36] Emily Apter focuses on this marginalization to suggest how its reversal (and the creation of what she calls 'postcolonial studies *à la française*') would have two major implications, national and international:

it could pose a healthy challenge to ideological universalism, metropolitan narcissism, cultural 'pasteurization', and the critically underexamined institutional tenets of national language and literature; [...] postcolonial criticism could foster the inclusion of francophone studies within a framework other than that of 'enlightened' assimilationism, thus leading to a broader interest in French studies abroad.[37]

Exoticism is one point of postcolonial intersection and controversy whose study would facilitate the active dialogue Apter advocates and would permit a prizing open of academic and intellectual cultures. Far from being an exclusively French phenomenon, it emerges in all cultures when there is contact with radical otherness; however, by noting in his *Essai sur l'exotisme*: 'Exotisme en littérature française. Très fécond. Nécessaire, car les Français n'inventent pas' [Exoticism in French

---

[35] See Antoine Compagnon, 'L'Exception française', *Textuel*, 37 (2000), 41–52 (p. 41). For a specific comment on the absence of engagement with postcolonialism, see p. 45.

[36] Michel Beniamino, *La Francophonie littéraire: essai pour une théorie* (Paris: L'Harmattan, 1999) signals the lack of any overarching theoretical apparatus for discussion of postcolonial literature in French, but does not engage extensively with material from outside the French-language tradition. Moura's main work on postcolonial theory is to be found in 'Francophonie et critique postcoloniale', *Revue de littérature comparée*, 1 (1997), 59–87, and *Littératures francophones et théorie postcoloniale* (Paris: PUF, 1999). Despite the use of 'postcolonial' in their title, the various essays collected by Moura and Jean Bessière in *Littératures postcoloniales et représentations de l'ailleurs: Afrique, Caraïbe, Canada* (Paris: Champion, 1999) reveal that a coherent approach has not yet been achieved and that the shift in the Anglo-Saxon academy from 'Commonwealth Literature Studies' to 'Postcolonial Studies' has not yet been re-enacted in the French-language context. On the French resistance to postcolonial thinking, see also Alec G. Hargreaves, 'The Challenges of Multiculturalism: Regional and Religious Differences in France Today', in William Kidd and Siân Reynolds (eds.), *Contemporary French Cultural Studies* (London: Arnold, 2000), 95–110.

[37] Apter, *Continental Drift*, 3–4.

literature. Very rich. Necessary because the French do not invent],
Segalen signalled the concept's perhaps quintessentially French overtones.[38] Segalen's essay is a major contribution to an ongoing debate on
exoticism's symbolic field and contested meanings that reached a height
with the rise of French New Imperialism. It is here that a fuller understanding of postcolonial uses of exoticism must begin.

Contemporary analyses of the cultures of Empire linking exoticism to
the propagandist mechanisms of the colonial novel or of colonial exhibitions depend on a turning of the terminological tables, for the extensive
critical apparatus written to justify French colonial literature and culture is centred on their would-be 'post-exoticist' tendencies. *La littérature coloniale* emerged largely unnoticed in the early twentieth century,
when its authors were most likely to be associated with Pierre Loti and
Claude Farrère, representatives of an earlier, post-Romantic, exoticist
tradition. With the inter-war rise in public awareness of Empire, however, colonial authors began to understand the pedagogical potential of
their texts and set about producing a distinctive literary history and an
associated genealogy (as well as often explicit hierarchy) of contemporary and earlier representations of otherness. This active and widespread
theorization of the relationship between literature and Empire was not
reproduced in Britain, and was indeed partly related to the French sense
of inferiority about the absence of a francophone Kipling.[39] For these
theorists of colonial literature, *exotisme* was understood mainly in a
pejorative sense, dismissed as precursory, superficial, subjective, and
detached from its object in terms of both ideology and geography:
'l'exotisme selon la vieille formule, impressionisme superficiel, qui ne
tient compte que du décor, du costume, de ce qu'il y a d'extérieur et
d'étrange dans les mœurs du pays' [exoticism according to the old
formula, superficial impressionism, that only takes into account backcloth, costume, what is exterior or strange in a country's customs].[40]
Whereas Roland Lebel rejected such an earlier tendency as one of
'faux exotisme' (a clear tautology, in terms of certain contemporary

[38] Segalen, *Essai sur l'exotisme*, 760; *Essay on Exoticism*, 38.

[39] On this subject, see Yaël Schlick, 'The "French Kipling": Pierre Mille's Popular
Colonial Fiction', *Comparative Literature Studies*, 34/3 (1997), 226–41.

[40] Roland Lebel, *Histoire de la littérature coloniale en France* (Paris: Larose, 1931), 79.
For a fuller account, see Jean-Marc Moura, 'Littérature coloniale et exotisme. Examen
d'une opposition de la théorie littéraire coloniale', in Jean-François Durand (ed.), *Regards
sur les littératures coloniales*, 2 vols. (Paris: L'Harmattan, 1999), ii. 21–39, and Yaël
Schlick, 'Re-Writing the Exotic: Mille, Segalen, and the Emergence of *littérature coloniale*',
Dalhousie French Studies, 35 (1996), 123–34.

understandings of the concept), Cario and Régismanset claimed in 1911 that colonial literature would offer in its place a seemingly oxymoronic 'exotisme nouveau'.[41] Distanced from what Robert Randau classed as 'littérature d'escale' [stopover literature] or 'littérature de tourisme colonial' [colonial tourist literature], colonial literature would exploit authors' closer links to and knowledge of the colonial space and their ethno-psychological sensitivities.

This attempt to salvage exoticism by presenting colonial literature as the legitimate heir to an exoticist tradition met contemporary resistance in the work of Victor Segalen, despite the colonial movement's paradoxical efforts to hijack *Les Immémoriaux* as an epitome of the *roman colonial*. Segalen's fragmented reflections that constitute the unfinished *Essai sur l'exotisme* are as critical of colonial literature as they are of the earlier tradition from which the colonial authors attempted to distance themselves. To the manifest exoticism of the nineteenth century, he adds the latent exoticism of these early twentieth-century contemporaries. Whereas the colonial theorists from Régismanset to Lebel suggested some form of historical continuity and the replacement of one movement by its natural successor, Segalen's project is more radical and disruptive. The essay is in many ways a definitional enterprise, with its repeated redefinition of 'exotisme' allowing Segalen to sketch out his personal understanding of the aesthetics of diversity. His critique of the French exoticist tradition contains many parallels with more recent analyses: Segalen emphasizes the domestication and assimilation inherent in representations of otherness that depend on stereotype and cliché in order to diffuse the disorientation inherent in contact with alterity; moreover, in dubbing exoticists 'Proxénètes de la Sensation du Divers' [Panderers of the Sensation of Diversity],[42] he underlines the potential narcissism associated with stage-management of otherness, describing contemporary exoticism as a self-generating tendency, bearing little or no relation to its purported object. However, the essay performs a recuperative gesture, rejecting a certain understanding of exoticism on the one hand, whilst, on the other, attempting to endow it with new significations:

Malgré son titre exotique, il ne peut y être question de tropiques et de cocotiers, ni de colonies ou d'âmes nègres, ni de chameaux, ni de vaisseaux, ni de grandes

---

[41] Louis Cario and Charles Régismanset, *L'Exotisme: la littérature coloniale* (Paris: Mercure de France, 1911), 285.

[42] Segalen, *Essai sur l'exotisme*, 755; *Essay on Exoticism*, 29.

houles, ni d'odeurs, ni d'épices, ni d'Îles enchantées, ni d'incompréhensions, ni de soulèvements indigènes, ni de néant et de mort, ni de larmes de couleur, ni de pensée jaune, ni d'étrangetés, ni d'aucune des 'saugrenuités' que le mot 'Exotisme' enferme dans son acceptation quotidienne. [...] Il eût été habile d'éviter un vocable si dangereux, si chargé, si équivoque. En forger un autre; en détourner, en violer de mineurs. J'ai préféré tenter l'aventure, garder celui-ci qui me paraît bon, solide encore malgré le mauvais usage [...]. Exotisme: qu'il soit bien entendu que je n'entends par là qu'une chose, mais immense: le sentiment que nous avons du Divers.

Despite its exotic title, it cannot be about such things as the tropics or coconut trees, the colonies or Negro souls, nor about camels, ships, great waves, scents, spices, or enchanted islands. It cannot be about misunderstandings and native uprisings, nothingness and death, colored tears, oriental thought, and various oddities, nor about any of the preposterous things that the word 'Exoticism' commonly calls to mind. [...] It would have been wiser to avoid such a dangerous term—a term so charged and yet so ambiguous—and to forge another one in order to reroute or break with these lesser meanings. But I preferred to take the risk and keep this term, which still seemed good and solid to me despite the bad uses to which it had been put. [...] Exoticism. It should be understood that I mean only one thing, but something immense by this term: the feeling which Diversity stirs in us.[43]

Unlike a number of more recent critics, for whom exoticism is historically tainted and irredeemably pejorative,[44] Segalen refuses therefore to dismiss the term out of hand, despite what he sees as its chronic ill-health. Preferring to use it as the basis of his personal aesthetics of diversity, Segalen explores the meanings and etymological limits of exoticism to signify an anti-assimilationist project whereby the Western traveller not only experiences (and represents) elsewhere as radically other, but is also himself exoticized in the eyes of the indigenous travellee.[45] Segalen has been celebrated for the implicitly anti-colonial nature of his work, and there is undeniably a striking divergence between his texts and those of his pro-imperial contemporaries.[46] Yet any anti-colonialism perceptible in Segalen's work is more the result of an aesthetic logic than of a specifically ideological stance. Indeed, the

---

[43] Segalen, *Essai sur l'exotisme*, 765; *Essay on Exoticism*, 46–7.

[44] See e.g. Jennifer Yee, *Clichés de la femme exotique* (Paris: L'Harmattan, 2000), 22.

[45] On the concept of the 'travellee', see Pratt, *Imperial Eyes*, and Loredana Polezzi, 'Did Someone Just Travel All Over Me? Travel writing and the travellee...', in Jan Borm (ed.), *Seuils et Traverses: enjeux et écriture du voyage* (Brest: CRBC; Versailles: Suds d'Amériques, 2002), 303–12.

[46] See Forsdick, *Victor Segalen and the Aesthetics of Diversity*, 58–80.

ideological underpinnings of Segalenian exoticism—and the *droit à la différence* on which it depends—reveal a complex interaction of what more critical versions of his work read as nostalgia and conservatism: in response to an all-encroaching entropy (an early twentieth-century version of globalization), the exotic is located at a distance not only in terms of space but also of time. The pre-colonial Tahiti of *Les Immémoriaux* and the pre-Revolutionary China of *Le Fils du Ciel* reveal a yearning for an intact otherness, the impossibility of whose existence these texts simultaneously rehearse. Segalen's response in the *Essai*, in *Stèles*, and in *René Leys* is to propose counter-entropic strategies in order to arrest what he saw as the homogenization of different cultures, not so much denying the tensions of hybridity or the co-existence of different cultures, but resisting their fusion or actual hybridization.

Despite the apparent pitfalls in this poetics of hybridity, critics have paid little attention to the ethnic aspects of Segalen's work, perhaps because they are only fleetingly made explicit. The unfinished text of *Le Maître-du-Jouir*, however, reveals an explicit aversion to miscegenation and a rejection of Gobineau's ultimately ambivalent attitude to racial admixture as a simultaneously degenerative and regenerative process of cultural interaction.[47] In his efforts to regenerate Polynesian culture and react to the degeneration charted in his earlier Tahitian novel *Les Immémoriaux*, Segalen's protagonist 'Gauguin' rejects the character of mixed ethnicity, Sara, dismissed as 'étrangère à tous les sangs, vagabonde entre tous les langages, [...] pire que la bâtarde d'un serpent et d'un oiseau' [foreign to all kin, straying between all languages, [...] worse than the cross-bred offspring of a snake and a bird].[48] This dismissal of a character situated between cultures reflects the reliance of Segalen's aesthetics on polarized differences, but there is no evidence that such an aversion to miscegenation is triggered by an overwhelming desire to protect ethnic hierarchies. Instead, Segalen's exoticism is predicated on the contrasts between cultures and on the tensions inherent in their initial contact. The refusal to assimilate the exotic through language and its devices leads to the structures of the *stèle*, juxtaposing Chinese characters and French text in a sealed space of the page, forcing them to coexist whilst denying their fusion.

Segalen's exoticism—and its clear aversion to hybridity—is an undeniable product of the ideological discourses of his time. However,

---

[47] On Gobineau's ambivalence, see Robert J. C. Young, *Colonial Desire: Hybridity in Theory, Culture and Race* (London: Routledge, 1995), 99–109.

[48] Segalen, *Le Maître-du-Jouir*, in *Œuvres complètes*, i. 293–348 (p. 331).

because of its problematization of cultural diversity and of its challenge to the reductive and ultimately assimilative mechanisms of colonial representation, this early twentieth-century attempt to theorize the exotic has itself travelled to be incorporated into postcolonial francophone reflection in this field.[49] What Segalen foreshadows, in particular in his uses of the apocalyptic figure of entropy, is the centrality of exoticism to a problematic series of later twentieth-century issues: hybridity, globalization, multiculturalism, and the changing configurations of Self and Other. His almost mathematical understanding of the decline of the exotic and of its progressive marginalization towards 'des sommets plus glaciaires' may suggest that cultural diversity is an exhaustible, endangered resource, threatened by the levelling effects of modernity; but Segalen's thought constantly shifts between fear of homogeneity and a desire for heterogeneity. His subsequent claim, used in the introductory chapter's epigraph, that the entropic erosion of distinctions will be compensated for by newly emergent patterns of diversity—'de cloisons nouvelles, de lacunes imprévisibles, un réseau d'un filigrane très tenu striant des champs qu'on avait cru tout d'abord d'un seul tenant'—reflects a resurgence of residual traces of distinctiveness perceived within contemporary cultural shifts, as described by contemporary thinkers such as Édouard Glissant. A mark of (neo)colonial commodification or an element of more nuanced understandings of global cultures, exoticism in postcolonial thought plays a complex role, therefore, and for a full understanding of uses of the term there is a need to explore its more recent fortunes as an item of critical currency.

POSTCOLONIAL EXOTICISM: THE FORTUNES OF A TERM

In any genealogy of postcolonial criticism, the work of Aimé Césaire and his one-time pupil Frantz Fanon plays a foundational role. As a result, postcolonialism could be seen to be rooted in their critique of colonial exoticism, for both authors' political writings are reliant on an anti-exoticist analysis of the relationship between European representations of otherness and colonial power. Aimé Césaire suggests in *Discours sur le colonialisme* that the misrepresentation of colonized

---

[49] See Charles Forsdick, 'L'Exote mangé par les hommes', in Charles Forsdick and Susan Marson (eds.), *Reading Diversity* (Glasgow: Glasgow French and German Publications, 2000), 1–20.

cultures by 'amateurs d'exotisme'—a category of accomplices of Empire included in one of the author's rhetorical catalogues—is central to the wider preparation of colonial space for domination and exploitation.[50] Describing the new society that would emerge from anti-colonial struggle, he rejects a return to the pre-colonial moment: 'Ce n'est pas une société morte que nous voulons faire revivre. Nous laissons cela aux amateurs d'exotisme' [It is not a dead society that we want to bring back to life. We will leave that to the lovers of exoticism].[51] Exoticism is accordingly associated in Césaire's analysis with what Rosaldo has dubbed 'imperialist nostalgia', the Western desire to resurrect what colonial contact has destroyed. In 'Racisme et culture', Fanon moves beyond Césaire's fleeting references that absorb exoticism into wider processes of colonial 'chosification' to explore its role in deculturation. Exoticism is seen as a means of simplifying, objectifying, neutralizing, and ultimately mummifying the colonized culture:

L'exotisme est une des formes de cette simplification. Dès lors, aucune confrontation culturelle ne peut exister. Il y a d'une part une culture à qui l'on reconnaît des qualités de dynamisme, d'épanouissement, de profondeur. Une culture en mouvement. En perpétuel renouvellement. En face on trouve des caractéristiques, des choses, jamais une structure.[52]

Exoticism is one of the forms of this simplification. It allows no cultural confrontation. There is, on the one hand, a culture in which qualities of dynamism, of growth, of depth can be recognized. A culture in motion. Perpetually renewing itself. And on the other, there are characteristics, things, never a structure.

The denial of coevalness that Fanon describes here suggests that exoticism depends on a complex twin process of geographical *rapprochement* and chronological displacement to a distant past.[53] For whilst the colonial is brought—tamed and fixed—to the metropolitan centre, it is simultaneously displaced into a pre-modern (or even primitive) moment.

The Fanonian understanding of the violence implicit in exoticism continues to influence more recent considerations of the phenomenon.

---

[50] Aimé Césaire, *Discours sur le colonialisme* (Paris: Présence Africaine, 1955), 31.

[51] Ibid. 29.

[52] Frantz Fanon, 'Racisme et culture', in *Pour la révolution africaine* (Paris: Maspero, 1964), 33–45 (p. 36).

[53] 'Denial of coevalness' is a mechanism of Western anthropological representation, the first systematic study of which is to be found in Johannes Fabian, *Time and the Other. How Anthropology Makes its Object* (New York: Columbia University Press, 1983).

Deborah Root, for instance, in her study of Western commodification of difference, writes: 'Exoticism, then, works through a process of dismemberment and fragmentation in which objects stand for images that stand for a culture or a sensibility as a whole. Exoticism is synecdochal, and fragments of culture work to exemplify a larger whole'.[54] Such a polarized understanding served a clear purpose in the post-war context of decolonization when the exoticist misrepresentations of colonial stereotypes were integral to the binary oppositions of any post-colonial self-definition. As René Ménil states in his 1959 article 'De l'exotisme colonial', there was once a neutral understanding of 'exotisme normal' that results from a moment of contact between different cultures:

Je suis pour lui étranger comme il est pour moi étranger: il a de moi une vision exotique et j'ai de lui une vision exotique. Il n'en peut être autrement. [. . .] La vision exotique est une vue de l'homme prise 'de l'autre côté', du dehors et par-dessus les frontières géographiques.[55]

For him I am foreign as he is foreign for me: he sees me as exotic and I see him as exotic. It cannot be any other way. [. . .] The exotic gaze is a perspective 'from the other side', from outside and across geographical boundaries.

With colonialism, however, this neutral understanding was replaced by a form of exoticism that is dictated by the relative power of the representer and represented. The resultant falsification of the colonized's self-image creates a cycle of dependency from which an ultimately self-referential 'exotisme contre-exotique' [counter-exotic exoticism] offers no exit. Ménil concludes: 'il faut dépasser l'expression poétique contre-exotique qui est contaminée par cela même contre quoi elle veut se dresser' [We must move beyond a mode of poetic expression that is counter-exotic for this is contaminated by what it is supposed to be reacting against].[56]

Ménil describes the paradoxical situation that must be faced by any poetics of postcolonial representation for which the understanding of exoticism is dictated by a residually colonial grasp of the term.[57] As the reliance of nineteenth-century Haitian literature on metropolitan

---

[54] Deborah Root, *Cannibal Culture: Art, Appropriation and the Commodification of Difference* (Boulder, Col.: Westview Press, 1996), 42.

[55] René Ménil, 'De l'exotisme colonial', in *Antilles déjà jadis* (Paris: Jean-Michel Place, 1999), 20–7 (p. 20).

[56] Ibid. 24, 26.

[57] On this subject, see Susan Hawthorne, 'The Politics of the Exotic: The Paradox of Cultural Voyeurism', *Meanjin*, 48 (1989), 259–68, and Roland Survélor, 'Folklore, exotisme, connaissance', *Acoma*, 2 (1971), 21–40.

models makes abundantly clear, a chronologically post-colonial Francophone culture does not automatically or necessarily break away in its self-images from earlier French exoticization. However, an element central to the reappropriation of voice that has characterized postcolonial literature in French is the disruption of exoticism's one-way vector and the growing adoption of a relativized, Segalenian understanding of the term. Mildred Mortimer has explored the reliance of African literature in French on the journey to France, in which the country itself is transformed as a result into a site of exoticism, and Romuald Fonkoua has developed a range of *exotismes* to describe the reaction of the postcolonial traveller to the exotic metropolitan space.[58] It would be prematurely celebratory to claim that a postcolonial exoticism, dependent on processes of reciprocity and exchange, has replaced colonial exoticism. It is increasingly clear that postcolonial mobility has opened up previously unimagined spaces of heterogeneity, cultural interaction, and diversity. However, the generalized concept of exoticism most apparent in debates relating to the description of these spaces and in postcolonial theory itself remains dependent on a colonial model and takes little account of the more complex postcolonial model with which this coexists.

For Homi Bhabha, for example, the persistence of exoticism is anathema to postcolonial hybridity and the associated processes of creolization, *mestizaje*, in-betweenness, diaspora, and liminality. Like multiculturalism or notions of cultural diversity, exoticism depends on 'a radical rhetoric of the separation of totalized cultures that live unsullied by the intertextuality of their historical locations, safe in the utopianism of the mythic memory of a unique collective identity'.[59] What Bhabha fears is the exoticist tendency of Western theory to foreclose on the other, to use it as a passive illustration rather than an active participant in efforts to make sense: 'forever the exegetical horizon of difference, never the active agent of articulation'.[60] Such instrumentalization of otherness—illustrated by Bhabha with 'Montesquieu's Turkish Despot, Barthes's Japan, Kristeva's China, Derrida's Nambikwara Indians, Lyotard's Cashinahua pagans'—is a pitfall of which

---

[58] See Mildred Mortimer, *Journeys through the French African Novel* (Portsmouth, NH: Heinemann; London: James Currey, 1990), and Romuald Fonkoua, 'Le "voyage à l'envers": essai sur le discours des voyageurs nègres en France', in Romuald Fonkoua (ed.), *Les Discours des voyages* (Paris: Karthala, 1998), 117–45.

[59] Homi Bhabha, *The Location of Culture* (London: Routledge, 1994), 34.

[60] Ibid. 31.

postcolonial critics are increasingly aware. Bhabha attempts to negotiate this risk by proposing as a postcolonial paradigm: 'an *inter*national culture, based not on the exoticism of multiculturalism or the *diversity* of cultures, but on the inscription and the articulation of culture's hybridity'.[61]

Here, Bhabha sees exoticism as essentialization, as an integral element of neocolonial representations. Such dismissal of exoticism by anglophone postcolonial theory, or its reduction to a purely colonial understanding, restricts the term, fails to distinguish it from earlier processes of exoticization, and ignores recent, more disparate French developments in its use. Rethinking exoticism acknowledges the versatility of the term, the evolution of the concepts it describes, and its suitability for exploring and contextualizing the diverse complexities of postcolonial literature and culture. Critics of Bhabha have focused on parallels between, on the one hand, his understanding of free-floating hybridity and, on the other, postmodern celebrations of fluid, dislocated, and depoliticized diversity. Such a notion focuses on structures and relations rather than the actual interaction of discrete objects that constitutes meetings in the 'contact zones' between cultures. Gerry Smyth has pointed to its hegemonic recuperability, underlining the possible absorption of the notion of hybridity 'by those with an interest in denying the validity of a coherent discourse of resistance'.[62]

There is a risk that hybridity understood this way deflects attention from the often imbalanced dynamics inherent in intercultural contact and discourages the dense contextualization that the complexity of each situation demands. This is not to say that postcolonial critics must return to the strictly delineated, antithetical groups—centre/periphery, self/Other, colonizer/colonized—in which (approximate) knowledge of the second is only possible through the representations of the first, but instead that there is a need for more open models of cultural interaction in which all actors are valorized, cast as both representer and represented, knower and known. Édouard Glissant's model of 'Relation', for example, posited on a 'droit à l'opacité' [right to opacity], protects specificity whilst exploring the discontinuous meetings between cultures, and the renegotiation and reconfiguration of relations between

---

[61] Ibid. 38.
[62] Gerry Smyth, 'The Politics of Hybridity: Some Problems with Crossing the Border', in Ashok Bery and Patricia Murray (eds.), *Comparing Postcolonial Literatures: Dislocations* (Basingstoke: Macmillan, 2000), 43–55 (p. 43).

them. Non-hierarchical and non-reductive, it deflects any nostalgia for clear-cut, binary oppositions, refusing any sense of pure otherness by maintaining that the logic of hybridity operates both within and between cultures.

Although Glissant becomes increasingly hesitant in his references to certain aspects of Segalen's exoticism, he continues to acknowledge his debt to the early twentieth-century author, as the title of *Introduction à une poétique du divers* makes clear. In terms of 'traveling theory', Glissant's privileging of diversity and of the irreducible difference of the other represents the resurgence and re-employment of these central aspects of Segalen's thought in a Caribbean context. Although Glissant resists using the word *exotisme* himself, he recognizes the paradoxical Segalenian understanding of the term, describing this as 'un système de pensée de l'exotisme tel qu'il combat à la fois tout exotisme et toute colonisation' [a system of thinking about exoticism that counters simultaneously all exoticism and all colonization].[63] This thinking-through of exoticism in order to study the meetings of different cultures in non-reductive ways, avoiding lopsided analyses and straightforward binaries, is integral to recent French-language uses and explorations of the term *exotisme*. As a result, it is currently perhaps most appropriate to talk of exoticisms, the plural reflecting the uncertainty over what exoticism may signify. The term still suggests the unevenness of relations between cultural differences, and its recent attenuation does nothing to diffuse the fact that the colonial project deployed as a strategy of power the right to dub the other 'exotic'. However, acceptance of the complexity of the term and of the processes it describes reflects a postcolonial shift, an acknowledgement that there is a need to qualify and refine our understanding of representations of otherness, to accept that the epithet 'exotic' can operate as a shifter, and even that exoticism itself as a form of radical otherness can accordingly function, in phenomena such as cultural opacity, transculturation, and contrapuntal approaches to interculturality, as a mode of resistance.

This is clearly not to suggest that nostalgic overtones have been erased: as has been suggested in the introductory chapter, a number of issues of the *Carnets de l'exotisme*, founded in 1990, reflect a yearning for a sense of cultural diversity linked to former (colonial) modes of travel. However, from recent French-language explorations of *exotisme*

---

[63] Édouard Glissant, *Introduction à une poétique du divers* (Paris: Gallimard, 1996), 76.

emerge two principal ideas, both of which are linked to a wider process of unthinking colonial exoticism: first, the need for attenuation of the term and of the processes it describes; secondly, the possibility of understanding the notion in terms of reciprocity. Western exoticism is not a monolithic process, but operates according to a scale of representations ranging (in Roger Célestin's terms) from 'exemplification' to 'experimentation', the former characterized by disappearance of the exotic object into controlling strategies of representation elaborated for and by the centre, the latter characterized at its extreme by the absence of text since the traveller-subject sheds all marks of affiliation with the centre and is absorbed into the radical otherness of the exotic periphery.[64] However, whereas Célestin's analysis operates within these poles, seeing these extremes as models rather than working examples, Jean-Marc Moura develops a similar scheme to qualify textual representations of otherness, borrowing the terms *alter* and *alius* to distinguish two actual and radically different approaches to the exotic in Loti and Segalen, appropriative and distancing:

ALTER est l'autre d'un couple, pris dans une dimension étroitement relative où se définit une identité et donc son contraire. *ALIUS* est l'autre indéfini, l'autre de l'identité et de tout élément qui s'y rattache, mis à distance de toute association facile, l'autre utopique. *ALTER* est intégré dans une conception du monde dont le centre est le groupe; *ALIUS* est éloigné, excentrique, et atteint au prix d'une errance hors de ce groupe. *ALTER* est un reflet de la culture du groupe; *ALIUS* un refus radical.[65]

ALTER is the other in a binary relationship, understood in terms of a narrow relativity by which one identity is defined—and, accordingly, its opposite is defined as well. *ALIUS* is understood as the undefined other, the other of identity and of any element linked to identity, a distancing of any simplistic association, the utopian other. *ALTER* is integrated into an understanding of the world of which the group is at the centre; *ALIUS* is distant, eccentric, only reached as a result of restless wandering outside this group. *ALTER* is a reflection of the group's culture; *ALIUS* its radical refusal.

Whilst accepting that these two modes of representation may coexist and interact, Moura nevertheless suggests—as does Bernard Mouralis in his 1975 study *Les Contre-littératures*—that exoticism can have a subversive purpose in forcing the author and reader somehow to negate or at least to suspend the values, assumptions, and ideologies of their

---

[64] See Célestin, *From Cannibals to Radicals*, 5–7.
[65] *L'Europe littéraire et l'ailleurs*, 53.

respective cultures.[66] The challenge of exoticism is consolidated by the emergence of postcolonial literature, one of whose effects is the exoticization or defamiliarization of the languages, spaces, cultures, and modes of representation of the former metropolitan centres. As Vincennette Maigne claims in her article on the etymology of the exotic, the epithet was originally characterized by a 'réversibilité possible', a possibility temporarily eclipsed by its Eurocentric appropriation in the processes of colonial expansion.[67] In a concrete sense, as Romuald Fonkoua has suggested, African and Caribbean travellers in Europe sent back to France an exoticized image of itself. Postcolonial exoticism, understood in these senses, may be used to explore texts from the former centre and periphery and may even operate to erase this division, allowing a truly inclusive understanding of the francophone space.

The aim of this chapter has been to expand and consolidate understandings of exoticism and, while accepting the pertinence of recent anglophone uses of the notion, to suggest that the interest in *exotisme* in French-language literature and thought is not simply an instance of recuperation and recycling of the term, but also of its redemption and renewal. Peter Mason claims that: 'as a field of forces in which Self and Other constitute one another in a lopsided relation, [the exotic] is always open to contestation', and it has become clear that colonial and postcolonial uses of exoticism are interrelated, the latter both repeating and contesting the former.[68] As a result, in identifying exoticism as a blanket term covering a range of representational possibilities and practices, there is no attempt to dismiss the ever-present dangers of (neo)colonial exoticism. Indeed, in coining the expression 'the postcolonial exotic', Graham Huggan has claimed to identify a troubling ambivalence in the term 'postcolonial', that functions 'not merely as a marker of anti-imperial resistance, but as a sales tag for the international commodity culture of late (twentieth-century) capitalism'.[69] Although Huggan's prime target is the 'alterity industry' of World Fiction (epitomized by the workings of the Booker Prize, and, by extension perhaps, those of the Prix Goncourt), he extends his critique of contemporary exoticization to include certain aspects of postcolonial

---

[66] See Bernard Mouralis, *Les Contre-littératures* (Paris: PUF, 1975).
[67] Maigne, 'Exotisme: évolution en diachronie du mot et de son champ sémantique', 11.
[68] Mason, *Infelicities*, 2.
[69] Graham Huggan, 'The Postcolonial Exotic', *Transition*, 64 (1994), 22–9 (p. 24).

studies itself. Such fear of exoticism indicates clear reasons for the blanket dismissal of the term described above.[70]

However, exoticism is not—or is not exclusively—an adjunct of colonial discourse whose late twentieth-century re-emergence merely reflects the persistent workings of 'imperialist nostalgia'. Instead, it is part of a subtle process of imbrication with a range of concepts central to postcolonial thought, concepts whose ongoing redefinition in the theories and practices of postcolonial literature and culture is witness to the fundamentally unfinished nature of postcolonialism itself. This book explores the idea that exoticism, as a site of contested meanings, is an element inevitably central to any widening of postcolonial studies that will permit more active dialogue with francophone material (with 'francophone' again understood in its most inclusive senses). It also suggests that the exoticism inherent in travel narratives—and more generally in the cultures of travel—is more likely to cast light on the instability of intercultural encounters than would any reductive reading of such narratives in the light of a monolithic colonial discourse. Exoticism and *exotisme* are not synonymous; understandings of the terms overlap, but their implications can at times be radically divergent; in certain uses, both remain compromised terms. But such ambiguities are linked closely to exoticism's persistence as a concept reflecting the inevitable ambiguities of contact between different cultures. It is perhaps more appropriate, therefore, to speak of postcolonial exoticisms, although there is a risk that this plural suggests not only the density of the problematic to which the term alludes, but also to the potential exhaustion threatened by the constant recycling and swelling of its semantic field. Whatever exoticism's future, as a term or as a concept, in theory or in practice, for understandings of postcolonial literature and theory—and for understandings of their relationship to a colonial legacy—it remains a double-edged notion, both retrospective and projective: a means of examining colonial (and neocolonial) representations of otherness, as well as a tool for exploring postcolonial reconfigurations of global culture. As Huggan suggests most clearly, analysing a situation that many other of his peers would perhaps rather

---

[70] See Huggan, 'The Postcolonial Exotic', 27. Simon During describes a similar notion of 'global popular' in which 'exoticism, normality and transworld sharedness combine' to obscure clear analysis of globalization. See 'Postcolonialism and Globalization', *Meanjin*, 51/2 (1992), 339–53 (pp. 342–3). Panoff explores the persistence of an earlier sense of exoticism in 'Une Valeur sûre: l'exotisme'.

ignore, colonial and postcolonial studies inevitably engage with and depend on a degree of diversity; it is awareness of this diversity and its careful negotiation, as opposed to fetishization, that should be the critic's aim. As such, it is exoticism understood as a means of understanding the complex reconfigurations of diversity as well as the equally complex interactions of different cultures and their travelling representatives that underpins the subsequent stages of this study.

2

Le Grand Danger Terrestre: Early Twentieth-Century Exoticism and the Decline of Diversity

Il y a une formule terrible, venue je ne sais plus d'où: 'L'entropie de l'Univers tend vers un maximum'.[1]

There is a dreadful expression, I no longer know where it comes from: 'The Entropy of the Universe tends towards a maximum.'[2]

BEFORE the work of Victor Segalen became a common item of critical currency, attracting interdisciplinary and increasingly transatlantic attention, critics often struggled in their efforts to underline its worth. With the appearance of a two-volume edition of the *Œuvres complètes* in 1995 and a *Cahier de l'Herne* devoted to Segalen in 1998, the entry of *Stèles* and *Equipée* onto the French *Agrégation* syllabus in 1999, the publication of an American translation of the *Essai sur l'exotisme* in 2002, and the appearance of his complete correspondence in 2004, the author's canonization now seems well under way.[3] Before Segalen's wider recognition, however, a common and recurrent critical strategy deployed to reassert the value of the 'neglected' author was to elaborate networks of affiliations whereby proximity to canonical figures suggested not only a measure of respectability, but also an intimation of undiscovered worth. Segalen flits, therefore, through a series of meetings, leaving passing textual traces: he crops up as a student visiting Huysmans at Ligugé; as a young author on his return from Polynesia, he is traced collaborating with Debussy on two ultimately aborted librettos, or corresponding with Pierre Loti; at the same time, he emerges briefly from Jules Renard's diary in 1907 as 'souffreteux, pâle, rongé,

---

[1] Segalen, *Essai sur l'Exotisme*, 766.   [2] Segalen, *Essay on Exoticism*, 48.
[3] See Victor Segalen, *Correspondance*, 2 vols. (Paris: Fayard, 2004).

trop frisé, la bouche pleine d'or qu'il aurait rapporté de là-bas avec la tuberculose' [his mouth full of gold that he appears to have brought back from there along with TB];[4] and Paul Léautaud's diary records its author as similarly unimpressed, commenting on the field for the Prix Goncourt (for which Segalen's *Les Immémoriaux* was considered): 'Le Mercure [de France] a déjà trois candidats: moi, [Edmond] Jaloux, et un M. Ségalen, qui n'a d'ailleurs aucune chance' [The *Mercure* has already got three candidates: me, Jaloux, and a M. Segalen who does not stand a chance].[5] These meetings were not, therefore, always fruitful, and this lack of success can be seen in particular in his dealings with two French diplomat-poets to whom his official position in China gave him access: Paul Claudel and Saint-John Perse. The problematic nature of his relations with the former has been explored at length elsewhere, especially by Gilles Manceron in his comprehensive biography of Segalen, and the latter's denial of having met Segalen or even of having read any of his work suggests a marked anxiety of influence.[6] Claudel was equally evasive, despite his more regular contact with the poet and his acceptance of the dedication of *Stèles*. On these foundations, Manceron proceeds to construct a complex conspiracy theory—also involving Jean Paulhan at Gallimard—according to which Segalen was silenced posthumously. Any positive uses of the network of affiliations were effectively blocked.

Critics focus, therefore, on the meetings that never were, emphasizing whilst regretting Segalen's belatedness, but nevertheless speculating on hypothetical exchanges that might have occurred had circumstance and premature death not prevented them. Having arrived at Hiva-Oa three months after Gauguin's death, Segalen acts as impromptu literary executor and early apologist for the painter and, at a now legendary auction, attempts to save fragments of the painter's final work from ridicule and dispersal.[7] This precursory interest in Gauguin is mirrored

---

[4] Jules Renard, *Journal*, ed. Léon Guichard and Gilbert Sigaux (Paris: Gallimard, 1960), 1142.

[5] Paul Léautaud, *Journal littéraire*, 19 vols. (Paris: Mercure de France, 1954–6), i. 362.

[6] See Gilles Manceron, *Segalen* (Paris: Lattès, 1992), 482. For a consideration of relations between Segalen and Perse, see Robert Condat, 'Quelques points de repère dans les rapports entre Segalen et Saint-John Perse', *Littératures*, 9–10 (1984), 299–308, Jean-Louis Joubert, 'Poétique de l'exotisme: Saint-John Perse, Victor Segalen et Edouard Glissant', in Buisine and Dodille (eds.), *L'Exotisme*, 281–91, and Catherine Mayaux, 'Victor Segalen et Saint-John Perse: deux poètes en Chine', *Europe*, 696 (1987), 117–25.

[7] On Segalen and Gauguin, see Manceron, *Segalen*, 158–83, and 'Koké et Tépéva: Victor Segalen dans les pas de Gauguin', in *Gauguin—Tahiti: l'atelier des tropiques* (Paris: Éditions des Musées nationaux, 2003), 322–33. The auction is described by Alain

by an early appreciation of Rimbaud who re-emerges as a spectre throughout Segalen's work. Segalen even became one of the earliest Rimbaldian scholars, since his research for 'Le Double Rimbaud' took him to interview the poet's associates in Abyssinia—arriving over ten years late this time—as well as his sister and brother-in-law in France. It is one of these non-existent meetings, cast by James Clifford as 'significant missed rendez-vous',[8] that I intend to use as the opening focus of this chapter: the meeting-that-never-was between Victor Segalen (1878–1919) and the banker, collector, philanthropist, and utopian Albert Kahn (1860–1940).

ENTROPY AND THE DECLINE OF DIVERSITY

To reflect the bridge between centuries' endings to which I referred in the introductory chapter, an exploration of the links between the posthumous itineraries of these two early twentieth-century figures is particularly striking. The individual responses of Kahn and Segalen to the perceived decline of geographical diversity in the 1890s both received close attention a century later in the 1990s. A consideration of the very different bodies of work of these two men and of their individual responses to entropy is perhaps timely, for the recent resurgence of attention given to Segalen and Kahn has been central to contemporary reconsiderations, in France and elsewhere, of cultural diversity. Their 'rediscovery' is an essential element of our own *fin-de-siècle* interest in issues relating to the exotic. Moreover, despite the divergence of their responses, the two figures also share a common starting point: in many ways they may be seen as adjacent travellers on the same 'escalator', inspired simultaneously by shared fears about the absorption of cultural diversity into global sameness, a steady erosion of the exotic reflected in particular in Segalen's adoption of the physical figure of entropy.[9] Kahn

Buisine and Norbert Dodille as both a 'pure fable ségalenienne' and foundational myth of a modern aesthetics of diversity which illustrate the nature of exoticism as a pervasive 'désir de la différence'. See 'Introduction', in Buisine and Dodille (eds.), *L'Exotisme*, 5–7 (p. 7).

[8] Clifford uses the phrase in relation to Segalen and Gauguin. See *The Predicament of Culture*, 152.

[9] Segalen's comments on entropy are included in his *Essai sur l'Exotisme*, 766. For a discussion of late nineteenth- and early twentieth-century uses of the figure of entropy, see Stephen G. Brush, *The Temperature of History: Phases of Science and Culture in the Nineteenth Century* (New York: Burt Franklin, 1978), and 'Thermodynamics and History', *Graduate Journal*, 7 (1967), 477–566, Greg Myers, 'Nineteenth-Century

states as the inspiration for his utopian archive of cultural differences (observed in France itself, as well as elsewhere) the desire to arrest, with the aid of technology, the effects of the passage of time. By the time of Kahn's bankruptcy in 1931, his Archives de la Planète contained 72,000 photographic plates and 140,000 metres of film, an admittedly vast resource, yet patchy fulfilment of its founder's initially utopian goal: 'une sorte d'inventaire photographique de la surface du globe occupée et aménagée par l'Homme, telle qu'elle se présente au début du XXe siècle' [a sort of photographic inventory of the surface of the globe inhabited and developed by humans as it appears at the beginning of the twentieth century].[10]

After decades of neglect, Kahn's 'jardins exotiques' (at Boulogne in the Paris suburbs) and the archives themselves have recently been renovated and made more accessible.[11] By reducing an understanding of the exotic to the archival, however, there is a risk that any historical dimension is eclipsed and that the notion of cultural diversity is fixed

Popularizations of Thermodynamics and the Rhetoric of Social Prophecy', in Patrick Brantlinger (ed.), *Energy and Entropy: Science and Culture in Victorian Britain* (Bloomington: Indiana University Press, 1989), 307–38, Pierre Thullier, 'Qui a peur de la thermodynamique?', in *Le Petit Savant illustré* (Paris: Seuil, 1989), 13–17, and Eric Zencey, 'Entropy as Root Metaphor', in Joseph W. Slade and Judith Yaross Lee (eds.), *Beyond the Two Cultures: Essays on Science, Technology and Literature* (Ames: Iowa State University Press, 1990), 185–200, and 'Some Brief Speculations on the Popularity of Entropy as Metaphor', *North American Review*, 271/3 (1986), 7–10.

[10] Letter from Emmanuel de Margerie to Jean Brunhes, 26 January 1912, quoted in Mariel Jean-Brunhes Delamarre and Jeanne Beausoleil, 'Deux témoins de leur temps: Albert Kahn et Jean Brunhes', in Jeanne Beausoleil (ed.), *Jean Brunhes autour du monde: regards d'un géographe / regards de la géographie* (Boulogne: Musée Albert Kahn, 1993), 91–107 (p. 91).

[11] The Archives are now housed at the Jardins exotiques d'Albert Kahn. On the 'jardins exotiques d'Albert Kahn', see Pascal de Blignières, *Albert Kahn, les jardins d'une idée* (Paris: Éditions la Bibliothèque, 1995), Marie Bonhomme, 'Les jardins d'Albert Kahn: une hétérotopie?', in Jeanne Beausoleil and Pascal Ory (eds.), *Albert Kahn 1860–1940: réalités d'une utopie* (Boulogne: Musée Albert Kahn, 1995), 97–105, and Olivier Choppin de Janvry, 'Exotisme et jardins historiques ouverts au public (L'Isle-Adam, Jardins A. Kahn, Désert de Retz). Vers la destruction ou la restauration d'un mythe', *Carnets de l'Exotisme*, 13 (1994), 85–92. For a selection of photographs in the Archives, see Jeanne Beausoleil and Mariel J.-Brunhes Delamarre (eds.), *Les Archives de la Planète*, 2 vols. ([n.pl.]: Cuénot, 1978–9). A number of volumes focused on specific regions, both within and outside France, are also available. See e.g. *Visage de l'Auvergne: collections Albert Kahn autochromes 1911–1926* (Paris: Presses Artistiques, 1984), and *Chine 1909–1934*, 2 vols. (Boulogne: Albert Kahn Musée et Collections, 2001, 2003). In addition, some material is now available on CD-ROM. Kahn continued a tradition of exploiting advances in photographic technology to present geographical diversity to the French public. Such a tradition dates back to *Excursions daguerriennes: vues et monuments les plus remarquables du globe*, 2 vols. (Paris: Lerebours, 1841).

firmly in the distant past. Kahn's archives can accordingly, as will be demonstrated below, be seen simultaneously as a site of salvage and as a museum for any meaningful notion of exoticism. Despite its similar starting point, the scope of Victor Segalen's project was radically different. Segalen claimed to refuse a strand of *fin-de-siècle* exoticism—epitomized by authors such as Pierre Loti—that identified the decline of diversity, but then proceeded to draw melancholic, aesthetic pleasure from the perceived inevitability of such a process. As Chris Bongie has stated and as this study has explored in its introductory chapter, a repeated element of this 'disappearing world' strand of exoticism is the belief in the individual's privileged status as last observer, on the deferral of the collapse of elsewhere:

Dire visions such as these [those of Claude Lévi-Strauss in *Tristes Tropiques*], however, most often resemble each other not only in their pessimism but also in their propensity for deferring the very thing that is being affirmed: although humanity is settling into a 'monoculture', it is at the same time still only *in the process of*, or *on the point of*, producing a 'beat-like' mass society.[12]

Whereas Kahn responded to this privileged moment in a predominantly reactive fashion, by attempting to salvage what fragments of diversity were left, Segalen's response is proactive, exploring the ambiguities of such a notion of perishability and laying the foundations for an understanding of the exotic that transcends the reduction of the concept to the merely geographical and non-European.

Segalen arrived in Beijing in June 1909, to prepare for the first of two major archaeological expeditions he would carry out in China.[13] Six months previously, Kahn had spent three weeks in the same city, a pause on his own journey around the world.[14] By 1909, Kahn's fortune acquired from banking and international speculation allowed him to devote himself entirely to a philanthropic concern for the social and an awareness of the educational value of cultural diversity. Having set up his 'jardins exotiques' in 1895 and inaugurated the important 'Bourses Autour du Monde' in 1898, the experience of his circumnavigation led

[12] Bongie, *Exotic Memories*, 4.
[13] Perhaps the best account of this first Chinese journey is included in Segalen's letters to his wife, published as *Lettres de Chine* (Paris: Plon, 1967).
[14] On Kahn's circumnavigation, see Marie Mattera Corneloup, 'Albert Kahn autour du monde, 1908–1909', in Beausoleil and Ory (eds.), *Albert Kahn 1860–1940*, 59–72. The major source of information on this journey is the *Journal de route de mon voyage autour du monde, du 13 novembre 1908 au 11 mars 1909*, kept by Kahn's driver and travelling companion, Albert Detetre (Archives Raymond Dutetre, Archives du musée Albert Kahn).

him to found in 1909 the 'Archives de la Planète'.[15] Segalen and Kahn's arrival in Beijing predated the outbreak of the Chinese Revolution by two years, but the remnants of the imperial system that they discovered were rickety and largely dependent for their survival on the foreign powers who had carved the city into concessions after the Boxer Rebellion of 1900. Nevertheless, for two French travellers particularly sensitive to the perishability of what was to them the exoticism of Chinese imperial culture, this brief pre-revolutionary moment became a privileged one. The object of observation may have been in a process of hopelessly rapid transformation, but the possibility of one last glimpse was temporarily permitted. The pre-revolutionary moment encapsulates what Chris Bongie, cited above, considers to be essential to late nineteenth- and early twentieth-century exoticism: i.e. a sense of final access to an increasingly endangered otherness, and a simultaneous deferral of its erasure. It is this sense of urgency surrounding the progressive erasure of local differences that leads Kahn to devote a substantial part of his fortune to the photographic and cinematic collection of traces of global diversity. The 1908–9 journey around the world represents, as Marie Mattera Corneloup has claimed, the 'creuset de maturation pour le projet naissant des *Archives de la Planète*' [context from which the emergent Archives de la Planète project was to develop].[16]

That this decision should have emerged from a journey around the world is striking, for Segalen suggests that the geometric figure of circumnavigation is central to his own diagnosis of the decline of diversity—which he casts elsewhere as 'le grand danger terrestre'.[17] In his pataphysical text 'Sur le voyage de Magellan', Michel Leiris would claim to disrupt geometric logic by reasserting the possibility of infinite journeys: 'La terre n'est peut-être pas sphérique. Elle est peut-être plate, et infinie,—du moins très grande—avec reproduction périodique des mêmes objets' [The earth is perhaps not spherical. It is perhaps flat, and

---

[15] On the *bourses*, see *Autour du Monde par les Boursiers de Voyage de l'Université de Paris* (Paris: Alcan, 1904), and Nathalie Clet-Bonnet, 'Les bourses Autour du Monde. La fondation française, 1898–1930', in Beausoleil and Ory (eds.), *Albert Kahn 1860–1940*, 137–52.

[16] See Corneloup, 'Albert Kahn autour du monde, 1908–1909', 65.

[17] Segalen writes: 'Le Divers décroît. Là est le grand danger terrestre. C'est donc contre cette déchéance qu'il faut lutter, se battre—mourir peut-être avec beauté' (*Essai sur l'Exotisme*, 775) [Diversity is in decline. Therein lies the great earthly threat. It is against this decay that we must fight, fight amongst ourselves—perhaps die with beauty] (*Essay on Exoticism*, 63).

infinite,—or at least very big—with periodical reproduction of the same objects].[18] In the *Essai sur l'Exotisme*, Segalen similarly had alluded to Magellan, leader of the first circumnavigatory voyage; yet accepting the inevitable closure of the geometric figure, he remembered him in a selective fashion for not having completed his journey and for having accordingly (and unwittingly) maintained an understanding of elsewhere as inexhaustible:

Le premier voyage autour du monde dut en être le plus désenchanté. Fort heureusement Magellan mourut avant le retour. Son pilote, lui, accomplit simplement son métier sans se douter de l'effroyable chose: il n'y avait plus d'Extrême Lointain![19]

The first voyage around the world must have been the most disenchanting. Luckily, Magellan died before his return. As for his pilot, he simply completed his task without worrying about the horrific thing: there was no longer an utter Remoteness in the world![20]

That circumnavigation is proof of the perishability of the exotic is a constant theme in the *Essai* where Segalen describes '[l]a rupture, le désenchantement du monde sphérique au lieu du monde plat' [the upset, the disenchanting quality of the spherical world as opposed to the flat world].[21] The modern traveller is condemned to retracing steps, to re-enacting the discovery of 'l'effroyable chose' of which Magellan remained ignorant: cultural diversity is not only finite, but also on the decline. Every journey not only involves a vector, according to which starting point and goal seem to merge, but also depends on modes of travel dictated by the steady cartographic unification of a diverse world: 'Sur une sphère, quitter un point, c'est commencer déjà à s'en rappro-cher! La sphère est la Monotonie. Les pôles ne sont que fiction. [...] [C]'est là que le tourisme a commencé! Dès que l'on sut le monde-boule' [On a spherical surface, to leave one point is already to begin to draw closer to it. The sphere is Monotony. The poles are but a fiction. [...] This is where tourism began! From the moment man realized the world was a sphere].[22] The traveller post-Magellan is condemned to a pes-simistic process whereby the exotic other is steadily transformed into the same. In describing Phileas Fogg's journey, for instance, Jules Verne echoes Segalen's analysis of this transformation of the field of travel: 'ce

---

[18] Michel Leiris, *Zébrages* (Paris: Gallimard, 1992), 117.
[19] Segalen, *Essai sur l'Exotisme*, 776.   [20] Segalen, *Essay on Exoticism*, 64.
[21] Segalen, *Essai sur l'Exotisme*, 764; *Essay on Exoticism*, 43.
[22] Segalen, *Essai sur l'Exotisme*, 764; *Essay on Exoticism*, 43.

gentleman ne demandait rien. Il ne voyageait pas, il décrivait une circonférence. C'était un corps grave, parcourant une orbite autour du globe terrestre, suivant les lois de la mécanique rationnelle' [this gentleman required nothing. He was not travelling, he was following a circumference. He was a weighty body, tracing an orbit around the earth, according to the rational principles of mechanics].[23]

Segalen's critical engagement with exoticism, like that of Kahn himself, is grounded therefore in an experience not only of physical travel, but also of the threat of closure inherent in specifically circumnavigatory travel. It was as he completed his own journey around the world in 1904, off Java on the return from Tahiti, that he first noted his intention to: 'Écrire un livre sur l'Exotisme' [Write a book on Exoticism], to undertake a major and yet ultimately unachievable project that would preoccupy him for the next fourteen years.[24] What began, however, as the elaboration of a personal aesthetic and concern with literary form was slowly transformed into the exploration of what he calls a more generalized 'théorie de l'Exotisme' [theory of Exoticism] to which he eventually attaches the status of a general law in its own right.[25] An important point in this shift from the personal to the general is the emergence in Segalen's writing of the notion of entropy. It is significant that its first appearance, in a marginal note in October 1911, coincides almost exactly with the outbreak of the Chinese Revolution:

Il y a une formule terrible, venue je ne sais plus d'où: 'L'entropie de l'Univers tend vers un maximum'. Ceci a pesé sur ma jeunesse, mon adolescence, mon éveil. L'Entropie: c'est la somme de toutes les forces internes, non différenciées, toutes les forces statiques, toutes les forces basses de l'énergie. [...] [J]e me représente l'Entropie comme un plus terrible monstre que le Néant. Le néant est de glace et de froid. L'Entropie est tiède. Le néant est peut-être diamantin. L'Entropie est pâteuse. Une pâte tiède.[26]

There is a dreadful expression, I no longer know where it comes from: 'The Entropy of the Universe tends towards a maximum.' This notion has weighed upon me—in my youth, my adolescence, my awakening. Entropy: it is the sum of all internal, nondifferentiated forces, all static forces, all the lowly forces of energy. [...] I imagine entropy as a yet more terrifying monster than

[23] Jules Verne, *Le Tour du monde en quatre-vingts jours*, cited in Moura, *La Littérature des lointains*, 401.

[24] Segalen, *Essai sur l'Exotisme*, 745; *Essay on Exoticism*, 13.

[25] Segalen, *Essai sur l'Exotisme*, 774; *Essay on Exoticism*, 61.

[26] Segalen, *Essai sur l'Exotisme*, 766.

Nothingness. Nothingness is made of ice, of the cold. Entropy is lukewarm. Nothingness is diamond-like, perhaps. Entropy is pasty. A lukewarm paste.[27]

What is presented as the emergence of a vague recollection—this 'formule terrible' is in fact Clausius's 1865 abbreviated version of the Second Law of Thermodynamics—becomes an all-consuming concern, with entropy serving as the principle figure of what he calls the 'Dégradation du Divers' [the decline of Diversity].[28]

Segalen borrows a popularized concept from theoretical physics to describe the impetus behind a series of contemporary developments whose spread is contingent upon the shrinking of the symbolic field of the exotic. Such developments are represented as 'les moyens d'Usure de l'Exotisme à la surface du Globe' [the means of Wearing Down Exoticism on the surface of the globe]: mechanization of travel, increased tourism, the reaching of the poles, the opening of the Panama canal, and various shifts towards democratic process.[29] There is clear evidence here of resignation to the levelling implicit in entropy when that figure is adapted and adopted as a metaphor for global transformations; yet at the same time, Segalen continues to engage with and draw upon debates in turn-of-the-century physics in order to investigate the nature of matter—and by extension, it seems, ethnic and cultural diversity—in order to discover whether it is essentially homogeneous or fragmented:

Je demande donc au support étendu de tout ce qui existe si le fond de tout est l'homogène ou le divers. Il semble qu'une réponse soit décisive. Si l'homogène prévaut dans la réalité profonde, rien n'empêche de croire à son triomphe dans la réalité sensible, celle que nous touchons, palpons, étreignons et dévorons de toutes les dents et de toutes les papilles de nos sens. Alors peut venir le Royaume du Tiède; ce moment de bouillie visqueuse sans inégalités, sans chutes, sans ressauts, figuré d'avance par la dégradation du divers ethnographique.[30]

I ask therefore the extensive support of all that exists, whether this heart of everything is the homogenous or the diverse. It seems that one answer is certain. If the homogenous prevails in the deepest reality, nothing prevents one from believing in its eventual triumph over sensory reality, that which we touch,

---

[27] Segalen, *Essay on Exoticism*, 48.

[28] Segalen, *Essai sur l'Exotisme*, 770; *Essay on Exoticism*, 54. On Clausius's coining of the term 'entropy', see Brush, *The Temperature of History*, 31. I have already discussed in greater detail the role of the Second Theory of Thermodynamics in Segalen's work in *Victor Segalen and the Aesthetics of Diversity*, 184–8. It seems essential, however, to outline the issues again in the context of this study, as the figure of entropy is central to the book's more general consideration of the decline and persistence of diversity.

[29] Segalen, *Essai sur l'Exotisme*, 775; *Essay on Exoticism*, 62.

[30] Segalen, *Essai sur l'Exotisme*, 771–2.

finger, clutch, and devour with all our teeth and all the buds of our senses. Then the way will be cleared for the Kingdom of the Lukewarm; that moment of viscous mush without inequalities, falls, or reboundings, was prefigured grotesquely by the disappearance of ethnographic diversity.[31]

Citing the recent research of Lord Kelvin, Einstein, Wilhelm Ostwald, and the Curies, Segalen proposes an understanding of matter founded on notions of discontinuity and granular structures, both of which will act as a support for his own search for a negentropic resistance of diversity to the dynamics of global change.

With this dabbling in the theories of physics or Laws of Thermo-dynamics and in their metaphorical use in an aesthetic context, it may appear that Segalen was a precursory intellectual imposter. However, his own engagement with entropy must be seen as part of a much wider process of popularization of this scientific metaphor in the second half of the nineteenth century. The Second Principle of Thermodynamics emerged when Carnot's experiments on the efficiency of steam engines in the 1820s led him to believe that there was an inevitable homogen-ization of differing levels of energy within a closed system. Generalized in the mid-nineteenth century by Lord Kelvin, it was used to describe a general dissipation of mechanical energy. It was this understanding that was eventually finally popularized in the neologism 'entropy'. This brought to an end what to outsiders seemed the esoteric circumlocu-tions of scientific theory, and such simplification of nomenclature had an undeniable influence on the subsequent history and transformation into metaphor of this aspect of thermodynamics, of which Eric Zencey has provided a succinct definition:

In one of its more accessible guises, the second law of thermodynamics holds that energy spontaneously degrades from more useful to less useful forms, even if it accomplishes no work in the process, and that in any transformation of energy (such as those by which we turn the energy of coal into electricity, and thence into heat, or light or motion) some part of the energy is irretrievably lost to us.[32]

These key features of degeneration, homogenization, and steady level-ling of all gradations of difference led in the late nineteenth century to the adoption of entropy as a popular point of reference. In a context of perceived decline in ethnographic and cultural diversity, this notion of transformation and irretrievable loss clearly struck a chord. It is

---

[31] Segalen, *Essay on Exoticism*, 57.   [32] Zencey, 'Entropy as Root Metaphor', 188.

perhaps unsurprising that the figure of entropy has acquired fresh relevance in contemporary debates surrounding globalization.

In a celebrated passage of his *The Two Cultures*, C. P. Snow seems to ignore such wider application and non-scientific adoption: 'Once or twice I have been provoked and have asked the company how many of them could describe the Second Law of Thermodynamics. The response was cold: it was also negative. Yet I was asking something which is about the scientific equivalent of: *Have you read a work of Shakespeare's?*'[33] Had he resorted to the language of popular science and the term 'entropy', he might have received a more positive response, for in the second half of the nineteenth century the disorganizing principle of the second law had struck the popular imagination and led to the development of what Pierre Thullier describes as a generalized thermodynamics.[34] As Zencey has commented, the seemingly paradoxical notion of a 'Law of Chaos' permitted discussion of processes that often otherwise had a tendency to remain abstract or anecdotal: the perceived loss of cultural distinctiveness, the apparent growth of global (dis)order, the threatened spread of sameness.[35] Moreover, it lent a positivist authority to what remained essentially the anecdotal foundations of cultural or ethnographic speculation, although it must be stressed in its translation and popularization—i.e. in the transformation from principle to buzzword—a physical law became a metaphorical figure.[36] However, far from dissipating its impact, this meant that when the scientific foundations of thermodynamics—understood initially as an irreversible, universal system—were challenged both by the possibilities of reversibility inherent in such theories as that of Maxwell's demon, and by the implications of advances relating to atomic theory and radiation, the cultural currency of entropy persisted.

The widespread adoption and popularization of the Second Law of Thermodynamics to non-scientific contexts did not, therefore, lend themselves to the accusations of intellectual imposture that contemporary

[33] C. P. Snow, *The Two Cultures and a Second Look* (Cambridge: Cambridge University Press, 1964), 14–15.

[34] Thullier describes 'une thermodynamique généralisée, valable entre autres pour les forces intellectuelles et les forces spirituelles, pour les forces réactionnaires et les forces révolutionnaires' [a generalized thermodynamics, valid for, among others, intellectual and spiritual movements, reactionary and revolutionary ones] ('Qui a peur de la thermodynamique?', 13).

[35] See Zencey, 'Some Brief Speculations on the Popularity of Entropy as Metaphor', 10.

[36] For a discussion of this point, see Myers, 'Nineteenth-Century Popularizations of Thermodynamics and the Rhetoric of Social Prophecy', 331.

theorists' metaphorical borrowing from scientific discourses would provoke.[37] In the *fin-de-siècle* period, the interpretative flexibility of entropy reached new degrees of suppleness as it was adopted variously by the decadents and the anarchists, the former turning fear of entropic decline into an aesthetic pursuit, the latter exploiting the imminent collapse of a decadent society in a dialectical fashion in order to ground hopes of a new beginning.[38] However, perhaps the most widespread use of entropy—of which Segalen's *Essai* is the clearest expression—is in contemporary concerns over the decline of exoticism.

As Segalen admits in the *Essai*, his comments on the decline of exoticism are neither original nor rooted specifically in the contemporary moment.[39] Emphases and interpretations differ, and Segalen's notion of a progressive, almost mechanical levelling of differences of diversity as different cultures meet is contested by an alternative reading that emphasizes a fragmented, chaotic outcome of such encounters in which initial distinctiveness is still lost, but the outcome of such loss is less predictable. In such divergent responses can clearly be seen the tension between monoculture and hybridity. His reaction is certainly part of a more generalized perception—or, to borrow again, Raymond Williams's term, 'structure of feeling'—in early twentieth-century France.[40] Albert Kahn's reaction to *fin-de-siècle* fears about the decline of the exotic, for instance, Les Archives de la Planète, involving what he hoped would be photographic recording at home and abroad, similarly reveals a growing awareness of the interrelationship of imperialism, tourism, and urbanization.[41] This generalized prophecy of the decline

---

[37] See Alan Sokal and Jean Bricmont, *Impostures intellectuelles* (Paris: Jacob, 1997).

[38] On this subject, see Catherine Coquio, 'Le Soir et l'aube: décadence et anarchisme', *Revue d'Histoire Littéraire de la France*, 99/3 (1999), 453–66 (p. 458).

[39] See Segalen, *Essai sur l'Exotisme*, 777.

[40] See e.g. the attention to the perceived corrosion of indigenous cultures in the work of André Chevrillon, discussed by Jean-François Durand, 'Regards sur la culture arabo-musulmane dans le récit de l'ère coloniale (1890–1912)', in David Murphy (ed.), *Remembering Empire* ([n.pl.]: Society for Francophone Postcolonial Studies, 2002), 13–36.

[41] Parallels between imperialism and urbanization were central to Ernest Gellner's critique of Said's *Culture and Imperialism*. See 'The Mightier Pen?', *Times Literary Supplement*, 19 February 1993, 3–4. Kahn's Archives contain several series of photographs of regions in early twentieth-century France, such as those of the Auvergne. In its desire to collect traces of domestic diversity, Kahn's enterprise was not unique. His contemporary Benjamin Stone conceived a similar project of salvage in Britain, the aims of which were outlined by W. Jerome Harrison in *Proposals for a National Photographic Record and Survey* (London: Harrison & Sons, 1892): 'Be ours the task to fix the fleeting features of the epoch in which we live, and to hand down to posterity the "outward and visible" state of things as they existed fin de siècle, at the close of the nineteenth century' (p. 14). On Stone,

of exoticism suggests that an aesthetic of cultural diversity regularly depends on a statement of the fragility of its object, the exotic itself. However, the incorporation of a notion of entropy into these dynamics—epitomized, for instance, in the theoretical writings of Segalen, or in the obsessive collecting of Albert Kahn—represents an important shift, for the logic of entropy implies not the delicate (yet on the whole stable) fragility in which the processes of erosion are almost imperceptible, but an inexorable process of decline. It is no coincidence that the incorporation of such a mathematical model occurred at a moment of crisis in exoticism when, in Chris Bongie's terms, 'the exotic comes to seem less a space of possibility than one of impossibility'.[42] Although the geopolitical expansion implicit in New Imperialism was central to this dissolution of elsewhere, the crisis in exoticism spilt beyond exclusively colonial considerations and was linked to a fundamental questioning, explored in the introductory chapter, of the activity on which exoticism traditionally depended: i.e. travel itself. For in parallel to the scramble to possess elsewhere was a scramble to visit elsewhere before its difference evaporated. Associated with this was a struggle to defend the rights of the traveller against those of a growing and threatening mass of tourists.

TRAVEL, SALVAGE, AND THE ARCHIVE OF 'ELSEWHERE'

In the late nineteenth-century exoticization and domestication of the practices of travel, exoticism was harnessed to three principal uses: national propaganda, popular entertainment, and the popularization of 'elsewhere' for general consumption. As soon as such domestication of the exotic was incorporated into an entropic worldview, the decline of cultural diversity it implied appeared to become inexorable for, despite its association with chaos, entropy remains an uninterruptible linear process of steady homogenization. Thomas Richards explores this inevitability in his study of *The Imperial Archive*: 'As a myth of knowledge, entropy, like evolution, would seem to place history outside the domain of human activity. Because it transfers agency

see *Sir Benjamin Stone's Pictures: Records of National Life and History* (London: Cassell, [n.d.]), and *Sir Benjamin Stone, 1838–1914, and the National Photographic Record Association, 1897–1910* (London: National Portrait Gallery, 1974).

[42] Bongie, *Exotic Memories*, 17.

from human beings to physical principles, it ostensibly represents a pessimistic relinquishing of all the possibilities of social control.'[43] In other words, according to an entropic worldview, history and geography are shaped by the laws of physics and not by human activity, and can only be influenced by imaginary, superhuman elites who possess the technology to manipulate physical laws.

Despite his wealth at the height of his success, Albert Kahn did not belong to such an elite. Nevertheless, as a result of his wealth, he had power to intervene technologically—through the processes of photography and cinema—in what he saw as the decline of exoticism in order to create an archive of cultural diversity:

Les structures figées protégaient les peuples. Les mutations technologiques, morales, politiques, ont commencé. Albert Kahn, les pressentant, voulait rendre compte de la diversité des peuples de la terre avant l'abolition de l'ordre ancien du monde, pensant que l'uniformisation culturelle allait les balayer.[44]

Fixed structures used to protect people. Now technological, moral, and political changes have begun. Albert Kahn had a premonition about such change and wanted to provide a record of the diversity of the different peoples on earth before the old order of the world was replaced, thinking that cultural levelling was going to sweep these different peoples away.

The mechanization of travel was seen to threaten the integrity and authenticity of elsewhere, but the technologization of representation provided a bulwark against such perceived decline. In the late 1830s, Fox Talbot had claimed that photography had a special aptitude for recording the 'injuries of time', by which he meant the erosion of buildings and monuments.[45] It was this desire to arrest the progression of time and accordingly to freeze the effects of entropy that led Kahn to state the negentropic aim of his Archives: 'fixer, une fois pour toutes, des aspects, des pratiques et des modes de l'activité humaine dont la disparition fatale n'est plus qu'une question de temps' [to fix, once and for all, aspects, practices, and forms of human activity whose fatal disappearance is only a question of time].[46] For Kahn, still photography would capture colour, cinema would capture movement.

[43] Thomas Richards, *The Imperial Archive: Knowledge and the Fantasy of Empire* (London: Verso, 1993), 103.

[44] See Michel Lesourd, 'L'appropriation du monde', in Beausoleil (ed.), *Jean Brunhes autour du monde*, 15–47 (p. 34).

[45] See Susan Sontag, *On Photography* (London: Allen Lane, 1977), 69.

[46] Letter from Emmanuel de Margerie to Jean Brunhes, 26 January 1912, quoted in Delamarre and Beausoleil, 'Deux témoins de leur temps', 92.

Photography's power to 'fix' in this way not only made it an attractive prospect for early ethnographers, but also granted the camera such a privileged role in the production of anthropological data. As Fatima Tobing Rony explains, contemporary anthropologists tended to view the indigenous figure 'as a patient, often as pathological and near death (if not already dead)', and the camera permitted a 'decomposition' of such processes so that transformations imperceptible to the naked eye could be recorded.[47] The teams of photographers dispatched by Kahn over a period of about twenty years did not have explicitly ethnographic pretensions, but, having been trained by the human geographer and Collège de France professor Jean Brunhes, they nevertheless form part of a collective endeavour of salvage and often reductive classification that marked the nascent human sciences in the early twentieth century.[48] The utopian scope and exhaustive archival ambition of Kahn's project—encyclopedic in its aim to offer 'une sorte d'inventaire photographique de la surface du globe'—were limited only by his bankruptcy and personal ruin in 1931, but by that date he had collected an already substantial resource.

Arlette Farge describes the experience of visiting the archive as one of drowning—'celui qui travaille en archives se surprend souvent à évoquer ce voyage en termes de plongée, d'immersion, voire de noyade...' [people who work in archives often catch themselves conjuring up this journey in terms of diving, sinking, even drowning...].[49] It is as if an abundance of material overwhelms the individual consulting it, and consultation is followed by the subsequent shock of the 'retour d'archives' as one attempts to process such a proliferation of material: 'au plaisir physique de la trace retrouvée succède le doute mêlé à l'impuissance de ne savoir qu'en faire' [the physical pleasure of finding traces of the past is followed by the sense of doubt and powerlessness associated with not knowing what to do with them].[50] Nearly seventy years after the last photograph of Kahn's *Archives* was taken, this is the bewilderment that faces a contemporary visitor. The cultural diversity

---

[47] Fatima Tobing Rony, *The Third Eye: Race, Cinema and Ethnographic Spectacle* (Durham, NC: Duke University Press, 1996), 46–8. Rony discusses the work of Félix-Louis Regnault, one of the first photographers to advocate the collection of images into an archive that would preserve 'vanishing races' in celluloid (pp. 62–5).

[48] Kahn sent out the first teams of photographers to Algeria, Morocco, Sweden, and Norway in 1910. See Jeanne Beausoleil, 'Albert Kahn', in Beausoleil and Mariel Delamarre (eds.), *Les Archives de la Planète*, i. 6–19 (p. 15).

[49] Arlette Farge, *Le Goût de l'archive* (Paris: Seuil, 1989), 10.

[50] Ibid. 19.

they represent is marked, and, as source material on individual cultures, they are undoubtedly invaluable. Moreover, in the light of recent interest in the archive in the work of Arlette Farge and Jacques Derrida, new means of approaching such banks of data have emerged. Derrida has emphasized, for instance, their twin purpose, both institutive and conservative, revolutionary and reactionary; James Clifford, in a striking comparison between Segalen's *Peintures* and the photograph of an 'Igorot Man' brought to the 1904 World's Fair in St Louis, alludes to the potential disturbances latent in the superficially neutral and objective classifications of an ethnographic archive.[51] In the imperial context of Kahn's collecting, the reduction of the exotic to a photographic archive remains, however, problematic, and tends towards the conservative and even taxidermic.[52] Although alluding to the policing of chapbooks in nineteenth-century France, Michel de Certeau's notion of the 'beauty of the dead' is appropriate here, for the process of taxidermy to which he refers seeks to aestheticize what is dead in an attempt to reinfuse it with life. De Certeau suggests that, in the second half of the nineteenth century, the threat of popular culture was transformed and assimilated, via folklore in particular, into 'un musée désormais rassurant' [a henceforth reassuring museum].[53] This 'exotisme de l'intérieur' [internal exoticism], although different from a reductive exoticization of elsewhere, depends nevertheless on analogous processes.[54] Any effect of radical alterity is lost as fragments are standardized in format and appearance, fed into a potentially inexhaustible dossier, and drawn into a network of control or, in Michel Lesourd's terms, of 'appropriation du monde' which—paradoxically—participate in the decline of diversity by bringing the exotic closer to home.[55] In Rony's terms, 'Kahn made the planet into a series of snapshot jewels.'[56] Moreover, their value as an objective representation of a salvaged

---

[51] See Jacques Derrida, *Archive Fever: A Freudian Impression* (Chicago, Ill.: University of Chicago Press, 1996), 7, and Clifford, *The Predicament of Culture*, 163.

[52] On the taxidermic mode of ethnographic cinema, see Rony, *The Third Eye*, 79.

[53] See Michel de Certeau, 'La beauté de la mort', *La Culture au pluriel* (Paris: Seuil, 1993 [1974]), 45–72 (p. 53); 'The Beauty of the Dead', in *Heterologies: Discourse on the Other*, trans. Brian Massumi (Manchester: Manchester University Press, 1986), 119–36 (p. 124).

[54] See de Certeau, 'La beauté de la mort', 48; 'The Beauty of the Dead', 121.

[55] See Lesourd, 'L'appropriation du monde'. In *On Photography*, Susan Sontag claims that the 'most grandiose result of the photographic enterprise is to give us the sense that we can hold the whole world in our heads—as an anthology of images. To collect photographs is to collect the world' (p. 3).

[56] Rony, *The Third Eye*, 81.

diversity is problematized not only because photography—like travel literature more generally—inevitably interprets cultural diversity through the frames (technological or otherwise) of the interpreting culture, but also because of more practical (yet associated) concerns: there is, for instance, a definite sense of stage management in a number of photographs, particularly the *autochrome* colour plates which demanded a longer (two-second) pose and accordingly tended to lack spontaneity as they were taken at quiet periods and lack specific local detail.[57]

However, in the Archives de la Planète, global and not merely local pretensions persist. When considered as a whole, they allow consideration of a more generalized response to perceived entropy that I shall identify—by analogy with the contemporary practice of 'salvage ethnography'—as 'salvage exoticism'. 'Salvage exoticism' allows attenuation of the traditionally polarized view that divides early twentieth-century exoticism into an imperialist aesthetic (whose aim is the extension of Western hegemony) and its exoticizing counterpart (privileging elsewhere as a refuge from overbearing modernity).[58] The tradition of salvage permeates nineteenth-century anthropology and is one of the principal modes of relating to non-Western cultures. Rooted in earlier non-scientific practices of collection and compilation, it places the burden on the present generation of travellers, scientists, and scholars to preserve for posterity traces of rapidly disappearing diversity. In early anthropology, the urgency inherent in a discourse of salvage was used to justify investment in fieldwork, to generate disciplinary credibility, and to legitimize its institutional support. It is encoded in the observations and justifications of such foundational figures of Malinowski and Boas. Salvage remains a useful ethnographic ploy, even when comments on the vanishing primitive or lamenting the passing of 'traditional' society have become banal rather than insightful. The resistance of diversity is witnessed, for instance, in the current popularity of documentaries focused on the ' "disappearing world" phenomenon', which depend on the extinction they are supposed to lament.[59]

---

[57] Marie Bonhomme and Mariel Jean-Brunhes Delamarre, 'La méthode des missions des *Archives de la Planète*', in Beausoleil (ed.), *Jean Brunhes autour du monde*, 194–219 (p. 212).

[58] This binary categorization is explored by Bongie, *Exotic Memories*, 16.

[59] See Annie E. Coombes, 'The Recalcitrant Object: Cultural Contact and the Question of Hybridity', in Francis Barker, Peter Hulme, and Margaret Iversen (eds.), *Colonial Discourse/Postcolonial Theory* (Manchester: Manchester University Press, 1994), 89–114 (p. 106).

However, the notion of salvage tends to skew research, since it directs attention to disorganization and stresses the pathology of cultural loss instead of engaging with the actually existing everyday operation of small communities. As Jacob W. Gruber has noted: 'the very notion of salvage insisted on investigation of those sociocultural systems already in an advanced state of destruction'.[60]

In the indiscriminate processes inherent in any such scramble to accumulate material, there is a risk that it is not so much data that is assembled as a collection of exotica whose only common feature is its perceived imminent disappearance. Accordingly, salvage is a practice well suited to exoticism, which is often focused precisely on the extremes of radical difference and whose existence as a practice is constantly threatened by the erosion of these extremes.[61] In the light of Kahn's archive, indications of the ambiguity of photography, an essential tool in such processes of salvage, begin to emerge. Elizabeth Edwards analyses the collapse of objectivity inherent in photographic salvage: 'It could be argued that photography [...], which was conceived as "salvage ethnography" documenting traditional cultures in the face of irreversible change, is not necessarily purely "documentary". It evokes feelings of nostalgia at the passing of cultures and an aestheticized "nobility" which transcends the "realist" or "documentary" mode.'[62] As both Susan Sontag and Roland Barthes have suggested, each photograph is a *memento mori*, a testimony to 'time's relentless melt'; yet, at the same time, it is a reaction to such passing of time in its

---

[60] See Jacob W. Gruber, 'Ethnographic Salvage and the Shaping of Anthropology', *American Anthropologist*, 72 (1970), 1289–99 (p. 1297). On the foundations of 'salvage' as methodology, see also Alfred Cort Haddon, 'The Saving of Vanishing Knowledge', *Nature*, 55 (1897), 305–6.

[61] On this subject, see Panoff, 'L'exotisme: une valeur sûre'.

[62] Elizabeth Edwards, 'Introduction', in Elizabeth Edwards (ed.), *Anthropology and Photography, 1860–1920* (New Haven, Conn.: Yale University Press, 1992), 3–17 (p. 10). For Edwards's account of the uses of photography in Alfred Cort Haddon's expedition to the Torres Straits in 1898, see 'Performing Science: Still Photography and the Torres Straits Expedition', in Anita Herle and Sandra Rouse (eds.), *Cambridge and the Torres Straits: Centenary Essays on the 1898 Anthropological Expedition* (Cambridge: Cambridge University Press, 1998), 106–35. Haddon's expedition represented the first major enterprise of salvage ethnography and can be seen as such as the institutional foundation of the practice. It was well reported in France, and Segalen used the initial findings of the expedition as the inspiration for his short story 'Dans un monde sonore'. On this subject, see Charles Forsdick, 'Sight, Sound, and Synesthesia: Reading the Senses in Victor Segalen', in Michael Syrotinski and Ian Maclachlan (eds.), *Sensual Reading: New Approaches to Reading and Its Relation to the Senses* (Lewisburg, Pa.: Bucknell University Press; London: Associated University Presses, 2001), 229–47 (pp. 238–41).

slicing out and freezing of a single moment.[63] In the context of exoticism, this freezing of time—or freezing of a culture in time—becomes problematic for it enacts and reinforces what Johannes Fabian has called the pervasive tendency in Western representations of other cultures to situate the non-Western in a temporally distinct moment and to supplement geographical displacement with chronological distance.[64] Along these lines, Kahn's archive of elsewhere endeavours to present elements of other cultures deemed 'traditional', untainted by Western contact; as a result, it presents these cultures as outside the processes of history. This is an example of what Renato Rosaldo has called the pervasive tendency of 'imperialist nostalgia', a form of mystification whereby the implications of imperial and economic expansion are disguised in a yearning for pre-imperial forms of culture. Salvage exoticism depends on this impulse, at once nostalgic and obfuscatory, but at the same time, in its adherence to and reliance on the inexorable processes of entropy, such an approach to otherness suggests its own partiality and even perishability as a means of recovering diversity.

In his important essay 'On Ethnographic Allegory', James Clifford looks more closely at the mechanisms of such nostalgia and the recovery it involves. His conclusion is that the identification of 'disappearance' is part of a recurrent narrative structure: 'Ethnography's disappearing object is, then, in significant degree, a rhetorical construct legitimating a representational practice: "salvage" ethnography in its widest sense. The other is lost, in disintegrating time and space, but saved in the text.'[65] Clifford is not claiming that cultures do not change radically on contact with others; nor is he questioning the value of recording specific phenomena that may be considered to be vanishing. His point is that the salvage paradigm is itself an allegory of a certain type of Western intervention in other cultures that refuses to see those other cultures as dynamic or capable of self-representation. He questions the moral and scientific authority associated with such practices of salvage as well as the assumption, which often accompanies this, that with rapid change cultural 'essence' is irretrievably lost. This is the very understanding of culture that undergirds Kahn's Archives and characterizes the salvage exoticism they represent. Their response to the decline of diversity is a desire for recovery—but recovery is understood

[63] Sontag, *On Photography*, 15.   [64] See Fabian, *Time and the Other*.
[65] James Clifford, 'On Ethnographic Allegory', in James Clifford and George Marcus (eds.), *Writing Culture* (Berkeley: University of California Press, 1986), 98–121 (p. 112).

in the sense of a complex, almost museological recuperation of difference that ultimately denies any such difference by treating diversity either as a stage-managed spectacle or as a static element in an archive.

In Segalen's response to cultural entropy, there is an emphasis on the uses of the museum and on the importance of the collection.[66] However, despite an initial interest in the figure of salvage, he rapidly distances himself from any response dependent on that trope. As Rosaldo has outlined, bringing culture into writing is a form of sacrifice, for its transformation into a book destroys its existence as primarily oral. As such, Segalen's *Les Immémoriaux* can be read as a complex allegory of the processes of Western representation, for it tracks—in a text—the implications of the advent of literacy for a previously oral culture. It would be reductive, however, to cast the novel as a work of 'imperialist nostalgia'. Despite its prelapsarian starting point in precolonial Tahiti, the work is not characterized by a longing for some untainted Polynesian tabula rasa, but is instead a self-conscious re-enactment of salvage exoticism that not only reveals its own shortcomings but also ultimately undermines itself.

Far from being obscured, issues of writing difference become the subject of the text. The transformative power of literacy on cultural forms is reflected in the evolution in the text of lexicon, idiom, syntax, and narrative voice. The novel concludes, in colonial Tahiti, with the death of Paofaï, member of the indigenous priesthood on the pre-colonial island and seemingly last remaining repository of the island's oral traditions. Readings of the novel that conclude with this image of erasure and fixity and proceed to analyse it as a pessimistic account of the encroaching effects of entropy miss, however, subtle suggestions in the text of a cultural diversity that goes beyond the formal conceit (of a Tahitian narrator creating a Tahitian discourse) on which the novel depends. The text contains clear traces of resistance and transculturation, and these disrupt the entropic vision of the decline of the local. Hybrid forms emerge such as the 'himine', the missionaries' hymns transformed into Tahitian forms; and as the Tahitian nationalist Henri Hiro observed, on the death of Tupua, although the sleeping Terii may miss the oral cosmographies the dying priest recites, a young boy (largely ignored by the adults) does hear and remember them. His presence suggests the survival of a living archive of difference, defying

---

[66] On this subject, see Charles Forsdick, 'Victor Segalen and Museology: Stage-Management of the Exotic in an Age of Entropy', *French Cultural Studies*, 6 (1995), 385–412.

the pragmatic complicity of Terii in processes of evangelization and Westernization.

Such appropriation of voice, although highly innovative and contrary to contemporary trends in colonial literature, nevertheless created an exotic effect that not only rapidly subsided in reading (and risked becoming a literary conceit), but also re-enacted the progressive erosion of difference to which Segalen's work was supposedly a response. The second stage of Segalen's elaboration of an aesthetic of diversity denies the conceit on which *Les Immémoriaux* depends. He writes in the *Essai sur l'Exotisme* in 1908, the year after the publication of his Tahitian novel: 'Partons donc de cet aveu d'impénétrabilité. Ne nous flattons pas d'assimiler les mœurs, les races, les nations, les autres; mais au contraire réjouissons-nous de ne le pouvoir jamais; nous réservant ainsi la per-durabilité du plaisir de sentir le Divers' [Let us proceed from this admission of impenetrability. Let us not flatter ourselves for assimilat-ing the customs, races, nations, and others who differ from us. On the contrary, let us rejoice in our inability ever to do so, for we thus retain the eternal pleasure of sensing Diversity].[67] Segalen's mature aesthetic depends on a restated belief in the impenetrability—or in Glissant's terms, the opacity—of the other, and his work is a search for a series of negentropic strategies to combat the decline of diversity. He explores new ways of representing the exotic (in, for example, the elaboration of forms such as the *stèle*), as well as new ways of perceiving it, of discovering sensitivity to new configurations of diversity that will com-pensate for the effects of entropic levelling.

As I have argued, in its account of evangelization and the imposition of literacy, *Les Immémoriaux* only appears to reflect an entropic vector of the absorption of local specificity into global monoculture. Such a neat pattern is disrupted by Segalen's awareness of the complexity of intercultural contact. The ultimately ambivalent attitude of the Tahitian novel towards the erasure of exoticism leads to what its author de-scribes in his Chinese texts as an 'éclatement de la formule' [explosion of the formula], as if he recognizes the pitfalls inherent in the allegory of writing contained in *Les Immémoriaux*.[68] The details of the novel that emphasize the potentially reciprocal nature of exoticism and underline its status as a bipolar process are developed further. In the juxtaposition

---

[67] Segalen, *Essai sur l'Exotisme*, 751; *Essay on Exoticism*, 21.
[68] Henry Manceron and Victor Segalen, *Trahison fidèle*, ed. Gilles Manceron (Paris: Seuil, 1985), 134.

of Roman characters with ideogrammes in *Stèles*, a tension is created as the French reader struggles to make sense of a poem part of which (i.e. the Chinese characters) remains opaque. On the printed page, Segalen illustrates what he describes in the *Essai* as 'la perception aiguë et immédiate d'une incompréhensibilité éternelle' [the keen and immediate perception of an eternal incomprehensibility] that triggers 'la perdurabilité du plaisir de sentir le Divers' [the eternal pleasure of sensing Diversity].[69]

Considering this textual strategy, Chris Bongie describes a 'modern' Segalen for whom the refuge of the exotic is *écriture*. In a 'salvational turn to language', the latter seems to respond to the irresoluble nature of the exotic crisis by shifting the symbolic terrain of diversity from the field of travel to the page itself, and salvaging what remains of the exotic in the text.[70] Although Segalen's Chinese texts involve such Mallarmean experimentation, they remain none the less a sustained reflection on the actual experience of exoticism in a period of rapidly transforming cultural diversity. The narrator of *René Leys*, faced with the inaccessibility of the Forbidden City in Beijing and offered access to the exotic experience of it only through the (undoubtedly) mythomaniac imagination of the novel's young eponymous hero, suffers not from the disappearance of another culture, but from the destabilizing effects of early twentieth-century cultural transformation on any integral notion of the Western subject. The fantasy of exotic possession is constantly thwarted.

As a response to what James Clifford has cast as the 'linear, relentless progress leading nowhere certain and permitting no pause or cyclic return' characterizing the post-Darwinian experience of time, there is a 'persistent prelapsarian appeal' to cultural islands outwith time.[71] In *René Leys*, access to one of these—the Forbidden City itself—is constantly prevented, and when the traveller-narrator of *Equipée* chances upon the community of Trous de Sel Noir, closed to the outside world for three centuries, access is only temporary and the whole episode reduced to 'un rêve de marche'.[72] The narrator is plunged back into the 'Voyage au Pays du Réel' (described in the work's subtitle) and forced back into engagement with the terrain. The landscape of *Equipée* is complex, a 'monde discontinu', with a fragmented, shifting surface,

---

[69] Segalen, *Essai sur l'Exotisme*, 751; *Essay on Exoticism*, 21.
[70] Bongie, *Exotic Memories*, 109.
[71] See Clifford, *The Predicament of Culture*, 111.
[72] Victor Segalen, *Equipée*, in *Œuvres complètes*, ii. 261–320 (p. 306).

but it is also a place where rivers are absorbed into the sink of the ocean and where statues are subject to the entropic processes of weathering. It is the encounter with such a statue that provides an allegory for the aesthetics of diversity that emerges from *Equipée*. Faced with a worn lump of sandstone, Segalen does not resort to photography to fix an image of steady decline. Instead, relying on what he calls in *Feuilles de Route* 'des yeux non photographiques' [non-photographic eyes], he begins to trace the residual contours of the stone on to paper with a pencil until suddenly: 'le phénomène fut' [the phenomenon appeared] and the statue is restored on the sketched page.[73]

Despite the text's initially pejorative attitude towards travel, *Equipée* consists of a series of confrontations such as this: 'corps à corps' with the force of water, 'face à face' with the landscape of the *Terre Jaune*, 'nez à nez' with the stump of sandstone, 'nez à nez' with his autoscopic double.[74] Exoticism is accordingly dynamic, dependent on contact and not restricted to a residual essence. The result is a re-exploration of cultural diversity, a redefinition of exoticism, and its transformation into an unstable encounter in which the identities of both parties are at risk; 'exotic' even becomes a shifting epithet, applicable to the self in a process of 'exotisme à l'envers' [reverse exoticism].[75] The Chinese cycle of Segalen's work is accordingly a struggle against the repeated threat of entropy described in the essay, an illustration of the author's resolve to defy the laws of physics to tease out new patterns of diversity.

Whereas Kahn took literally the implications of entropic discourse and responded to what he saw as the inexorable decline of cultural diversity by confining the exotic to an archive, Segalen's reaction is more complex. Ultimately, in his aesthetic practice if not in his 'theoretical' comments, he seems to reject as excessively neat the grand narrative of entropy. He then questions the privileged role in observing the decline of other cultures that such a narrative seems to grant the West. Segalen sketches out an aesthetic in which exoticism is no longer dependent on observation of pathological states of decay, but gestures instead towards newly emergent patterns of diversity. Segalen's recognition of the risks of uneven cultural expansion—simultaneous with his ultimate conviction that monoculture is more a recurrent spectre than a concrete reality—has led to his adoption by a number of contemporary

---

[73] See Victor Segalen, *Feuilles de route*, in *Œuvres complètes*, i. 961–1249 (p. 1071), and *Equipée*, 311.
[74] Segalen, *Equipée*, 287, 306, 310, 314.
[75] See ibid. 304.

Francophone Caribbean thinkers and writers. For Édouard Glissant, for instance, Segalen is one of the 'premiers poètes de la Relation' [first poets of Relating];[76] in the various volumes of his *Poétique* and in *Le Discours antillais*, Glissant explores and develops Segalen's thought, adopting and adapting various Segalenian notions such as 'le Divers' whilst insisting on the distinction between cultural diversity and civilizational hierarchy. Glissant has faced the contemporary threat of monoculture, but challenges this with a specific account of the Caribbean experience which is encapsulated in a positive understanding of chaos:

[C]haos ne veut pas dire désordre, néant, introduction au néant, chaos veut dire affrontement, harmonie, conciliation, opposition, rupture, jointure entre toutes ces dimensions, toutes ces conceptions du temps, du mythe, de l'être comme étant, des cultures qui se joignent, et c'est la poétique même de ce chaos-monde qui, à mon avis, contient les réserves d'avenir des humanités d'aujourd'hui.[77]

Chaos does not mean disorder, nothingness, preparation for nothingness, chaos means confrontation, harmony, conciliation, opposition, break-up, connection of all these dimensions, all these conceptions of time, myth, of fixed identity as identity in process, of cultures that meet, and it is the very poetics of this world-as-chaos that, in my opinion, contains the future reserves of today's branches of humanity.

The processes Glissant outlines here—what he calls, in deference to Segalen, 'une poétique du divers', encompassing new, complex patterns of diversity, shifting in non-hierarchical relationships and challenging the threat of standardization—resonate with Segalen's own definition of 'de cloisons nouvelles, de lacunes imprévisibles'. Segalen's response to entropy is thus linked suggestively to Glissant's evocation of 'le chaos-monde', suggestively not least since their interrelation implies a more complex, post-national genealogy of literature in French than is often admitted—a genealogy in which a genuinely non-hierarchical notion of diversity plays a defining role and to which Segalen (together with his traditional adversary Saint-John Perse) is emerging as a key.[78]

---

[76] See Glissant, *Poétique de la Relation*, 39.
[77] Édouard Glissant, 'Le chaos-monde, l'oral et l'écrit', in Ralph Ludwig (ed.), *Écrire la parole de nuit: la nouvelle littérature antillaise* (Paris: Gallimard, 1994), 111–29 (p. 124).
[78] See Mary Gallagher, *La Créolité de Saint-Jean Perse* (Paris: Gallimard, 1998).

3

Sa(l)vaging Exoticism: New Approaches to 1930s Travel Literature in French

> Le quotidien de l'un peut désorienter jusqu'à la mort l'homme de l'autre quotidien, c'est-à-dire l'étranger, ce quotidien fût-il le plus banal, le plus gris, le plus monotone pour l'indigène.
>
> What is everyday for one person can confuse to death someone whose idea of the everyday is different, that is the foreigner, even if for the local population this everyday is as banal, as grey, and as monotonous as can be.[1]

HENRI MICHAUX'S early life was one spent in motion as he struggled to distance himself from his native Belgium. He served twice as a sailor on board French ships, travelling to North and South America; he moved from his native Belgium to Paris in 1924; he set sail for South America in 1927, undertaking a long journey there the following year, an account of which would form the basis of *Ecuador*; and he also spent a considerable period travelling through Asia.[2] Attempting to explain the motivation for the restlessness that characterizes much of his early life, he coined the expression 'voyager contre', travelling against, to describe these 'voyages d'expatriation'.[3] Although this slogan might be used in association with the general escapism that is alleged to underpin much travel or may even be seen as one of the alibis or 'secrets de voyages' employed to disguise its true motives,[4] it seems a particularly apt characterization of the triggers for the inter-war journeys of many

---

[1] Henri Michaux, *Ecuador* (Paris: Gallimard, 1929), 159–60.
[2] For an excellent biography, see Jean-Pierre Martin, *Henri Michaux* (Paris: Gallimard, 2003).
[3] See Michaux, *Ecuador*, and Robert Bréchon, *Michaux* (Paris: Gallimard, 1959), 20–1.
[4] See Urbain, *Secrets de voyage*.

of Michaux's contemporaries.[5] Michel Leiris, for instance, joining Marcel Griaule's trans-African mission from Dakar to Djibouti, was impelled by a desire to break with Surrealism, to flee the growing tensions (both personal and political) of early 1930s Europe, and to discover an alternative vocation in practising the emerging discipline of ethnography.

What Leiris discovers, however, as many travellers had before him, is the persistence of home. Although moving away from the spectacle to which his compatriots were flocking and that his erstwhile Surrealist colleagues were endeavouring to attack—i.e. the Exposition coloniale—the events in Vincennes continue to dog him.[6] The 'travellees' he meets, characters traditionally relegated in the colonial travel account (such as that of the Croisière noire) to the static role of indigenous onlooker (present, in Loredana Polezzi's terms, to be 'travelled over'), have a tendency to become travellers in their own right, as it is Leiris himself who is condemned to the sessility of colonial and ethnographic routine: 'Journée purement bureaucratique. Classement. Courrier. Visites' [Purely bureaucratic day. Filing. Post. Visits]; 'Jamais en France je ne fus aussi sédentaire' [I was never as sedentary in France].[7] The journey initially perceived as an escape from a futile Parisian existence itself descends into futility; even when, at the end of the first part of the text, as he prepares to cross the border into Abyssinia, the narrator has claimed to be 'enfin au seuil de l'exotisme' [on the threshold of exoticism at last], travel continues to be subject to political machination and delicate negotiation with the indigenous authorities, finally progressing at a rate similar to that of 'un omnibus incommensurablement lent' [an incommensurably slow bus].[8] The Africa he anticipates on the cruise from France, similar to that imagined by Céline's Bardamu in *Voyage au bout de nuit*, fails to materialize, and as a result does not provide the stark change for which Leiris seems to long. As the word 'monotone'

---

[5] A similar point about British travel writing in the same period underpins Paul Fussell, *Abroad: British Literary Travelling Between the Wars* (New York: Oxford University Press, 1980).

[6] For an account of the Surrealist critique of the Exposition, and their counter-exhibition, see Panivong Norindr, *Phantasmatic Indochina: French Colonial Ideology in Architecture, Film and Literature* (Durham, NC: Duke University Press, 1996), 59–71. The Surrealists published two tracts in 1931, 'Ne visitez pas l'Exposition coloniale' and 'Premier bilan de l'Exposition coloniale', both of which are included in José Pierre (ed.), *Tracts surréalistes et déclarations collectives 1922–1939*, i. *1922–1939* (Paris: Le Terrain vague, 1980), 194–5, 198–200.

[7] Michel Leiris, *L'Afrique fantôme* (Paris: Gallimard, 1934), 52, 93.

[8] Ibid. 281, 601.

slowly pervades the early stages of the account—'vie [. . .] au fond très monotone' [fundamentally very monotonous life]; 'parcours spéciale-ment monotone' [particularly monotonous route]—it is in fact the indigenous characters he meets who seem not only to long to travel themselves, but also actually acquire the status of travellers.[9] This happens either reluctantly, in the case of the furious group of young people 'envoyés à l'Exposition Coloniale pour la danse' [sent as dancers to the Colonial Exhibition], or nonchalantly, in that of the Sultan of Garoua, who has recently returned from Vincennes where: 'Il est monté en aéroplane et le monument qu'il préfère est le Palais de Versailles' [He went up in a plane, and his favourite monument is the palace of Versailles].[10] In a 1933 reportage, 'Cargaisons humaines', Georges Simenon had unsettled conventional understandings of travel by chal-lenging the assumption that only those metropolitans with first-class tickets could claim the title of 'voyageur': 'Deux humanités voyagent côté à côté, sur le même bateau, à quelques mètres de distance. Rien ne les sépare, sinon, d'un seul côté, un écriteau qui dit: *Défense de circuler sur le pont des premières classes*'[11] [Two forms of humanity travel side by side, on the same boat, a few metres apart. Nothing separates them except that on one side there is a sign that says: *No access to the first class decks*]. Whereas Simenon prized open the term on the grounds of class, Leiris's *Afrique fantôme* suggests that understandings of travel should also not be restricted in terms of ethnicity.

INTER-WAR TRAVEL AND THE RECONCEPTION OF DIVERSITY

In aesthetic and epistemological terms, Leiris's diary—as well as the scientific Mission on which it offers a subversively subjective 'take'—reflects evolving inter-war attitudes to exoticism and cultural diversity. An increasingly fragmented Surrealism sought new direction in the recognition of an Other visible in the emergent fields of ethnography and psychoanalysis. *Documents*, the journal on which Leiris had been an editorial assistant to Georges Bataille in the two years leading to the

---

[9] Ibid. 56, 63. The cobbler in Tamba Counda, for example, 'veut se faire emmener à l'exposition coloniale' [longs to be taken to the Colonial Exhibition] (p. 47).

[10] Ibid. 134, 202.

[11] Georges Simenon, 'Cargaisons humaines', in *A la recherche de l'homme nu*, ed. Francis Lacassin (Paris: 10/18, 1976), 23–44 (pp. 23–4). (First published in *Police et Reportage*, 1933.)

departure of the Dakar-Djibouti expedition, had been underpinned by a predominantly ethnographic objective. It had attempted to illustrate in its juxtapositions the resistant heterogeneity of cultural phenomena. The collection and categorization central to Griaule's Mission, linked in part to the salvage exoticism explored in Ch. 1, represented therefore an important development as an exoticist approach to diversity was replaced by a scientific and culturally relativist analysis of ethnic and cultural diversity.[12] In *The Predicament of Culture*, James Clifford has tracked the complex network of affiliations that link Surrealism and ethnography during the period in question. Part of Clifford's study focuses on a series of authors (including Segalen, Leiris, and Césaire) associated with what he dubs a 'poetics of displacement' characterized by 'more troubling, less stable encounters with the exotic'.[13] For the author, the inter-war years in particular represent a period of major upheaval in the evolution of attitudes towards cultural diversity. Traditional orders of difference were challenged by new understandings of cultural interconnectedness that would come to predominate in the post-war and postcolonial period. The anxiety with which these transformations are associated challenges understandings of the 1930s that present this decade, for which the Vincennes exposition often assumes metonymic status, as one of colonial consolidation about to be frustrated by the humiliation of French defeat in 1940. It is true that the 1931 event, introducing the French public to the benefits of 'la Plus Grande France' [Greater France] on a much larger scale than any previous exhibition, was undoubtedly a success in propagandist terms, and achieved its principal purported aim: 'Donner aux Français conscience de leur Empire' [to make the French aware of their Empire].[14] Indeed, as Pierre Mille commented the following year, the Exposition's impact encouraged the opportunist editors of *littérature coloniale* to exploit this upturn in interest: 'Commercialement, [les éditeurs] ont dû penser que, puisque trente millions de visiteurs avaient franchi les portes de cette Exposition, il y en aurait bien quelques milliers pour éprouver la curiosité de lire quelque chose sur les colonies.

---

[12] On salvage ethnography and the Mission Dakar-Djibouti, see Jean Jamin, 'Objets trouvés des paradis perdus: à propos de la Mission Dakar-Djibouti', in Jacques Hainard and Roland Kaehr (eds.), *Collections passion* (Neuchâtel: Musée d'ethnographie, 1982), 69–100 (p. 80).

[13] Clifford, *The Predicament of Culture*, 152

[14] Quoted by Charles-Robert Ageron, 'L'Exposition coloniale de 1931: mythe républicain ou mythe impérial?', in Pierre Nora (ed.), *Les Lieux de mémoire*, 3 vols. (Paris: Gallimard/Quarto, 1997), i. 493–515 (p. 502). (First published 1984–92.)

Ça "se vendrait" ' [Commercially, publishers must have thought that, because 30 million visitors went through the gates of this Exhibition, there must be a few thousand curious enough to want to read something on the colonies. It 'would sell'];[15] and even Robert Ageron, contesting Brunschwig's rarely questioned transformation of the Exposition into the 'apogee of Empire', concedes that the event may have contributed to an increase in the number of applications for the École coloniale.[16]

At the same time, however, as the stage-management of Empire-as-theme-park at Vincennes catered for a superficially generic exoticism, increasing numbers of observers began to question the 'exhibitionary order' that controlled the event and reflected wider patterns of representation of otherness.[17] A series of assumptions underpinning the Exposition persisted—i.e. that indigenous cultures must be represented by the French alone, that indigenous characters may people these representations (but only on French terms), and that those *évolués* invited to Vincennes would be confirmed by their journey to France in their belief in French superiority and the benefits of continued colonial interventionism (and hence continue to proselytize in favour of these causes on their return); but such assumptions proved to be major miscalculations, ignoring rumbling and sporadically explosive post-colonial discontent whilst failing to foresee what Christopher Miller considers to be the 'boomerang effect of bringing a colonized elite to France'.[18] Already, the first major displacement of 200,000 colonial 'travellers' to France, that of the *tirailleurs sénégalais* or *indigènes* during the First World War (when 31,000 of them died), had triggered a similarly ambiguous outcome: African and Indochinese troops led by colonial propaganda to assume the civilizational superiority of Europe, had travelled to France to discover Europeans slaughtering each other with newly found mechanical barbarism.[19] As two recent novellas by

---

[15] Pierre Mille, *Barnavaux aux colonies, suivi d'Écrits sur la littérature coloniale*, ed. Jennifer Yee, Autrement mêmes (Paris: L'Harmattan, 2002), 188. (First published in *Les Nouvelles littéraires*, 1932.)

[16] Ageron, 'L'Exposition coloniale de 1931', 510.

[17] See Timothy Mitchell, 'Orientalism and the Exhibitionary Order', in Nicholas B. Dirks (ed.), *Colonialism and Culture* (Ann Arbor: University of Michigan Press, 1992), 289–317.

[18] Christopher Miller, *Nationalists and Nomads: Essays on Francophone African Literature and Culture* (Chicago, Ill.: University of Chicago Press, 1998), 59.

[19] For a discussion of the *tirailleurs*, see Myron Echenberg's *Colonial Conscripts: the 'Tirailleurs Sénégalais' in French West Africa, 1857–1960* (Portsmouth, NH: Heinemann; London: James Currey, 1991) and *Tirailleurs en images*, special issue of *Africultures*, 25 (2000). For a first-hand account by a French woman closely associated with the colonial

Didier Daeninckx[20] have made clear, colonial subjects brought to France in 1931 suffered a similarly powerful shock: not only, in the most extreme cases, were they expected to perform in some of the final 'zoos humains' to operate on French soil; but also they were faced with a view of their indigeneity that bore no relation to the current state of the colonies and the everyday lives of many of their inhabitants.[21]

In an article marking the seventieth anniversary of the Exposition, the ACHAC (Association pour la Conaissance de l'Histoire de l'Afrique Contemporaine) historians Nicolas Bancel, Pascal Blanchard, and Sandrine Lemaire comment on the French amnesia in relation to the event, seen as surprising given its sheer size.[22] Although French attitudes remain ambivalent, such uneasiness seems to be encapsulated in the disassociation from its imperial past of one of the few remaining vestiges of the Exposition, the former Musée des colonies et de la France extérieure (1931–5) and subsequently the Musée de la France d'Outre-Mer (1935–60) at the Porte Dorée. The colonial friezes by Janniot, the tropical aquarium, and the period salons remain, but what was until recently the Musée des arts africains et océaniens now houses the less historically tainted Cité de l'architecture et du patrimoine.[23] Yet in recent years, interest in the Exposition has increased rapidly, mainly,

troops, see also Lucie Cousturier, *Des inconnus chez moi*, ed. Roger Little, Autrement mêmes (Paris, L'Harmattan, 2001 [1920]).

[20] See Didier Daeninckx, *Cannibale* (Paris: Verdier, 1998), and *Le Retour d'Ataï* (Paris: Verdier, 2002).

[21] For a comprehensive and long-overdue account of 'human zoos', see Nicolas Bancel, Pascal Blanchard, Gilles Boetsch, Eric Deroo, and Sandrine Lemaire (eds.), *Zoos humains: de la vénus hottentote aux reality shows* (Paris: La Découverte, 2002). See also Olivier Razac, *L'Écran et le Zoo: spectacle et domestication, des expositions coloniales à Loft Story* (Paris: Denoël, 2002).

[22] See Nicolas Bancel, Pascal Blanchard, and Sandrine Lemaire, '1931! Tous à l'Expo...', *Polémique sur l'histoire coloniale, Manière de voir*, 58 (2001), 46–9. The historians associated with the Association pour La Connaissance de l'Histoire de l'Afrique Contemporaine have been instrumental in popularizing an awareness of French colonial history. For details of the group's exceptional work, see Nicolas Bancel, Pascal Blanchard, and Sandrine Lemaire, 'De la mémoire coloniale à l'histoire', *Francophone Postcolonial Studies*, 1/1 (2003), 8–24.

[23] Note, however, that the ties between the building and its colonial past have not been entirely severed: the first exhibition to be held in the Cité de l'architecture was 'Alger, paysage urbain et architectures', a survey of the expansion of the Algerian capital from colonial conquest in 1830 to the present day. See Emmanuel de Roux, 'Comment s'est bâtie Alger la Blanche', *Le Monde*, 19 August 2003, 20. On the earlier museum, see Dominique Taffin, 'Le Musée des Colonies et l'imaginaire colonial', in Nicolas Bancel, Pascal Blanchard, and Laurent Gervereau (eds.), *Images et Colonies: iconographie et propagande coloniale sur l'Afrique française de 1880 à 1962* (Nanterre: Bibliothèque de documentation internationale contemporaine; Paris: ACHAC, 1993), 140–3.

it must be admitted amongst English-language scholars, for whom the event has achieved an emblematic status: Panivong Norindr sees the 1931 reconstruction of Angkor Wat as a key to the construction of what he dubs the 'phantasmatic Orient'; Herman Lebovics grants the Exposition a central role in the reconfiguration of French identity in the first half of the twentieth century; Christopher Miller sees it as the site of colonial tensions surrounding the emergence of hybridity in inter-war France; and Patricia Morton observes in the architecture of the Vincennes site a large-scale example of hybrid modernity.[24] In this study of attitudes to cultural diversity in 1930s France, the Exposition—and the paradoxes and tensions it appears to crystallize—is granted an ambivalent status; it is seen as a watershed creating a division in the often undifferentiated two decades of inter-war attitudes to elsewhere and otherness.[25] For there is a need to distinguish between the now well-documented exoticism of post-Great War, jazz-age France, returned to the *années folles* of peacetime and seeking release and renewal in often exuberant engagement with colonial—and more particularly black—culture;[26] and the more anxious attitudes to otherness that begin to characterize the economically depressed, pre-war 1930s.[27]

---

[24] Norindr, *Phantasmatic Indochina*; Herman Lebovics, *True France: The Wars over Cultural Identity, 1900–1945* (Ithaca, NY: Cornell University Press, 1992); Christopher Miller, *Nationalists and Nomads*; Patricia A. Morton, *Hybrid Modernities: Architecture and Representation at the 1931 Colonial Exposition, Paris* (Cambridge, Mass.: MIT Press, 2000). See also Nicola Cooper, *France in Indochina: Colonial Encounters* (Oxford: Berg, 2001). Among French studies of the Exposition, the most notable is the small volume by Catherine Hodeir and Michel Pierre, *L'Exposition coloniale* (Brussels: Complexe, 1991).

[25] Steve Ungar similarly underlines this ambivalence, seeing in the *Exposition* the statement of 'une culture coloniale aboutie' [an accomplished colonial culture] as well as 'l'entropie de la vision d'une culture impériale qui cède [...] aux mutations politiques et sociales que provoquera la décolonisation' [the entropy of the vision of an imperial culture yielding to political and social changes triggered by decolonization]. See 'La France impériale en 1931: une apothéose', in Pascal Blanchard and Sandrine Lemaire (eds.), *Culture coloniale: la France conquise par son empire, 1871–1931* (Paris: Autrement, 2003), 201–11 (p. 211). On the 1930s, see especially Elizabeth Ezra, *The Colonial Unconscious: Race and Culture in Interwar France* (Ithaca, NY: Cornell University Press, 2000).

[26] See e.g. Petrine Archer-Straw, *Negrophilia: Avant-Garde Paris and Black Culture in the 1920s* (London: Thames & Hudson, 2000), and Brett A. Berliner, *Ambivalent Desire: The Exotic Black Other in Jazz-Age France* (Amherst: University of Massachusetts Press, 2002).

[27] Like the *Exposition coloniale*, the seemingly serious undertaking of the Mission Dakar-Djibouti is a similarly ambivalent marker, preceded by the fund-raising spectacle of a boxing match involving the African-American Al Brown and attended by Josephine Baker. On this subject, see Jean Jamin, 'De l'humaine condition de Minotaure', in *Regards sur Minotaure: La Revue à tête de bête* (Geneva: Musée d'art et d'histoire, 1987), 79–87. A similar juxtaposition occurs in relation to the contemporaneous Croisière jaune, whose

This chapter further explores the growing dissatisfaction, examined in particular in Ch. 1, both with uses of the term 'exoticism' in post-colonial criticism and with the tendency to conflate colonial and post-colonial uses of the term. As Ch. 1 has suggested, exoticism is a complex, controversial, and even contradictory term that certainly cannot be reduced to the purely geographical although it is most commonly used to describe an aesthetic by-product of travel. It is, however, the link between the symbolic field of the exotic and the geographical field of travel, specifically in French-language texts of the 1930s, that this chapter explores. Between the First and Second World Wars, France witnessed a complete renewal in the field of travel and of its writing. The 1930s in particular became a privileged moment for considerations of this body of texts, for that decade witnessed rapidly multiplied contact between Europe and elsewhere before the post-war collapse of colonial dependency. This contact resulted not only from new opportunities for travel (by air, road, and rail) and new means of transferring information (such as the radio, or mass-circulation illustrated magazines, such as *L'Illustration*, both of which phenomena favoured the emergence of fresh genres such as *reportage* and new fictional characters such as Tintin) but resulted also—if travel writing is to be understood in a much wider sense as travel literature—from a crisis in European civilization that caused many intellectuals and authors to travel elsewhere. Such expansion and reassessment of the potentials of the journey beyond the geographical boundaries of Europe occurred against the backdrop of a series of growing threats to the traditional field of travel itself: intimations, in indigenous challenges to colonial rule such as that at Yen Bay in 1930, of the failure of the colonial system; increasing evidence of the rise of what would later be called globalization, in a variety of forms; and a increasingly vehement anti-exoticism which meant that a hitherto staple element of travel writing was undergoing radical change.

Since it was coined just over 150 years ago, the term 'exotisme' has been subject to steady semantic shifts between two poles: one signifying an exoticness essential to radical otherness, the other describing the process whereby such radical otherness is either experienced by the traveller from outside or translated, transported, and finally represented

scientific objectives are accompanied by the voice of Baker, a selection of whose records are taken by the travellers on their journey. See Georges Lefèvre, *La Croisière jaune: expédition Citroën centre-Asie* (Paris: L'Asiathèque, 1990 [1933]), 175.

for consumption at home. It is this final sense of translation, transportation, and representation—all three of which depend on the metaphor of travel, since they imply not only distance but also the bridging of distance—on which contemporary critics have focused. The authors of the 1998 Routledge *Key Concepts in Post-Colonial Studies*, for instance, see exoticism as a process of domestication, of transforming phenomena that are potentially threatening into what Renata Wasserman calls 'innocent signifiers of an otherness which was simply exotic, that is, nonsystematic, carrying no meaning other than that imposed by the culture in which they were exhibited'.[28] Responding to this analysis, the authors of these *Key Concepts* conclude: 'Isolated from their own geographical and cultural contexts, they represented whatever was projected onto them by the societies into which they were introduced. Exotics in the metropoles were a significant part of imperial displays of power and the plenitude of empires.'[29] The idea of 'imperial displays of power' is perhaps most manifest in the European tradition of competing colonial exhibitions, and as has been explained above, any consideration of 1930s exoticism in the French tradition must take into account the 1931 Paris *Exposition coloniale*. The event represents a logical culmination of a long tradition of colonial contributions to Universal Exhibitions, a peak not only of French colonial exoticism but also (when seen in relation to the 150th anniversary celebrations of the 1830 French conquest of Algeria the previous year) of French colonial ideology or what the colonial historian Raoul Girardet calls the 'idée coloniale' [the idea of an Empire].[30]

The commonly accepted meanings of 'exoticism' in post-colonial criticism are therefore, pertinent for considerations of 1930s France. However, what exploration of this 'key concept' often omits—and what any consideration of 1930s exoticism which fails to go beyond metropolitan displays of empire seems to ignore—is the constant contestation which has marked twentieth-century uses of the term, and the ways in which it has constantly eschewed reduction and triggered a sense of anxiety. In contemporary critical currency, the term has almost universally pejorative overtones and is restricted by its coupling to colonial discourse. Close analysis, however, reveals a need for more attenuated

---

[28] Renata Wasserman, 'Re-inventing The New World: Cooper and Alencar', *Comparative Literature*, 36/2 (1984), 130–45 (p. 132).

[29] Ashcroft, Griffiths, and Tiffin, *Key Concepts in Post-Colonial Studies*, 95

[30] See Raoul Girardet, *L'Idée coloniale en France de 1871 à 1962* (Paris: La Table Ronde, 1972).

understandings which, avoiding pan-European generalizations, explore specific cultural traditions, and not only encompass reflexivity but also propose a potential challenge to the reductive overtones implied above.

If one were to take a diachronic approach to 1930s travel literature and attempt to situate it in a wider context of twentieth-century exoticism, the privileged status of this corpus of texts is immediately apparent. It was produced in the decade leading up to the Second World War, whose impact on attitudes to otherness cannot be underestimated, and accordingly predates (whilst simultaneously heralding) the effects of post-war cultural shifts: the rapid modernization of France; the equally rapid decline of Empire; and the growing awareness of the changing nature and implications of travel. This decade represents, therefore, a key period before the rapid changes brought about by the war and by the effects of its aftermath—the principal amongst these being the sudden reconfiguration of relations between Europe and its (soon to be decolonized) others, particularly in the light of the severing of direct colonial links and the forging of new patterns of cultural interrelations that either undermined or refuted Western hegemony. Travel literature of the 1930s is to be positioned, therefore, before the critical assaults—implicit in particular in the immediately post-war work of Aimé Césaire and Frantz Fanon discussed above—on this hazily defined genre and on the exoticism with which it is invariably allied; as the exoticist critique explicit in the travel texts of Michaux and Leiris suggests, it is to be situated also before the term 'exoticism' (and the set of ideas it encompasses), so closely linked to Empire, had fallen into several decades of obsolescence.

It is not necessarily this chronological approach, however, that the idea of a 'structure of feeling' invites. To tease out the implications for studies of contemporary travel literature inherent in 1930s uses of the concept of exoticism, a synchronic approach is perhaps a more effective means of exploring the tensions and contradictions becoming particularly acute in this decade. Material presented as representative is inevitably selective, but will reveal how the decline—as a result of rejection or violent critique—of a certain strand of colonial exoticism encapsulated, in embryo, the foundations of a more positive, less reductive understanding of the term. It is such an understanding that has achieved renewed critical currency—particularly in the French tradition—in the later twentieth century. What will emerge from this brief reflection is an awareness of the need, when exploring exoticism and travel writing, to balance its two elements, described by Jean-Marc Moura as 'littérarité' (its textual nature) and 'culturalité' (its links with dominant contemporary ideologies and intellectual movements).[31]

BRINGING EMPIRE HOME

It is not the intention in this chapter—nor, as I have made clear above, in this study more generally—to deny or even simply downplay the clearly damaging and pejorative overtones of exoticism (whose justified presence in certain contexts is irrefutable), but instead to place the notion of a specifically colonial exoticism within a much wider contextual frame. In early 1930s France, some of the most vociferous criticism of exoticism emerged from the colonial propagandists whose work is, in retrospect, most likely to be characterized by the very term they attempted to reject. Roland Lebel, leading apologist for and first would-be 'theorist' of French colonial literature, categorizes exoticism in his *Histoire de la littérature coloniale en France*: 'c'est l'attirance des pays beaux où nous situons instinctivement les personnages du rêve édénique, c'est le mirage des îles fortunées, c'est le parfum du voyage et de l'inconnu' [it is the lure of those beautiful countries where we instinctively locate characters belonging to the dream of Eden, the mirage of islands blessed by the gods, the aroma of travel and of the unknown]. He insists, in the light of this definition, on a distinction between 'le touriste colonial' [the colonial tourist] and 'l'écrivain colonial proprement dit' [the colonial author in the true sense], between 'exotisme' and 'colonialisme'.[32] Colonial literature is presented as 'une réaction contre le faux exotisme, contre le cliché, contre les préjugés et les sottes prétentions' [a reaction against false exoticism, against clichés, against prejudices and foolish conceits].[33] Pierre Mille articulates similar reservations, but having questioned the existence of colonial literature in 1909 ('La littérature coloniale *française* n'existe pas' [*French* colonial literature does not exist]), seems to suggest that there emerged two decades later, after the Exposition, a 'littérature coloniale—vraiment coloniale, non pas seulement exotique, ou de tourisme,

---

[31] On this subject, see Moura, *La Littérature des lointains*, 37.

[32] Lebel, *Histoire de la littérature coloniale en France*, 8, 79, 86.

[33] Ibid. 82. Such accusations of falsehood, implying the existence of a more 'authentic' representation of exotic cultures, are repeated in Robert de la Sizeranne's review article on the visual arts at the Exhibition, 'Le bon et le mauvais exotisme', *Revue des deux mondes*, 51/5 (1931), 597–616.

ou d'aventures' [colonial literature—truly colonial, not simply exotic,
dependent on tourism or adventure].[34] The earlier tradition of exoticist
literature, rooted in the nineteenth century and epitomized perhaps by
the work of Loti, was seen to lack the qualities of colonial literature: a
depth of analysis, a wealth of documentary detail, and an authenticity
offered by an author either born in the colonies or at least posted there
for most of their career.[35] Whilst the *littérature coloniale* movement
attempted to define itself negatively and chronologically in distinction
from the previous benchmarks of a exoticist tradition perceived to have
failed, its exponents and apologists failed to recognize that it served in
many ways as an extension of nineteenth-century exoticism and as a
recurrence of its representational practices. Colonial propagandists
nevertheless found in the 1931 *Exposition* an overemphasis on the
picturesque, as well as on the stage-management with which this is
associated. Pierre Mille claimed:

Partout on a fourré des palmiers, [. . .] des aloès, des cactus. Afin que le public
dise: 'Comme c'est ressemblant!' Au contraire, si on lui avait montré une vraie
forêt équatoriale ou tropicale d'Afrique ou d'Asie [. . .], il aurait trouvé que ce
n'était pas ressemblant.[36]

They stick palm trees, aloe trees, cacti everywhere. So that people say: 'It's a
really good likeness!' But if they had been shown a real equatorial or tropical
forest in Africa or Asia, they would have found it was not a very good likeness
at all.

On the one hand, in a mechanism similar to that customarily employed
by travellers seeking to distinguish themselves from tourists, the experienced colonial traveller claims knowledge of the colonies to which the
metropolitan stay-at-home cannot pretend; yet on the other, there is an
uneasy awareness of the transformation of a purportedly pedagogical
event into what General Messimy, President of the Association sciences-
coloniale, called a 'feria colossale' [huge festival].[37]

It was the aim of the principal organizer of the *Exposition*, Field
Marshal Lyautey, to avoid such exoticizing overtones of an 'exhibition
foraine' [travelling fairground exhibition] and to present a 'foyer
d'enseignement pratique' [source of practical instruction].[38] Yet as

---

[34] See Mille, *Barnavaux aux colonies*, 171, 188.
[35] For a discussion of this colonial critique of exoticism, see Moura, *L'Europe littéraire
et l'ailleurs*, 112–19.
[36] Mille, *Barnavaux aux colonies*, 186
[37] Ageron, 'L'Exposition coloniale de 1931', 508.
[38] Ibid. 497.

Panivong Norindr has claimed in his *Phantasmatic Indochina*, the result of the *Exposition*—crystallized in particular in the reconstruction as its centrepiece of the temple of Angkor Wat—was to suppress politics, to erase historical forces, and to counter the threat of contemporary insurrection by presenting the French colonies in South East Asia as a kingdom at peace.[39] Pierre Mille's otherwise sympathetic account of the Exhibition site—and his imaginary meeting with Barnavaux—underlines the panoptic mastery provided by the reconstructed temple, and it was a denunciation of the policing of the 'exotic' that the first Surrealist tract, 'Ne visitez pas l'Exposition coloniale!', begins.[40] According to Norindr's analysis, Indochinese students and workers holding demonstrations in the grounds of the *Exposition* were removed since their protests revealed not only the false nature of the indigenous characters required for the exhibition's living diorama, but also the ideological implications of the very colonial exoticism on which the event depended: 'Because they contested the representations elaborated at the Exposition, these unruly natives had to be removed from this new colonial Eden. Otherwise they could have exposed the whole exoticising project of the fair.'[41] These indigenous extras were required to be docile, compliant, and above all silent, marvelling at what Mille dubs the 'miracle' of Western technology.[42] The myth of the Noble Savage that they were supposed to perpetuate was threatened, however, by a number of discordant voices among their ranks, challenging visitors' right to photograph them or to address them—like animals or children—with the familiar 'tu'.[43]

The French colonial historian Raoul Girardet confirms the fears and observations of Mille, Messimy, and their peers. Despite the lip-service paid to pedagogic intentions by the event's organizers, visitors in 1931 were drawn more by the 'émerveillement de l'exotisme' [wonder of exoticism] than by any overwhelming desire to discover or understand the colonial other.[44] And this attraction to a tamed, alluring, titillating exotic other was seemingly catered for by the *Exposition* itself, during

[39] Norindr, *Phantasmatic Indochina*, 7. On the restorative function of the Exhibition, and the pervasive creation of a sense of colonial order countering indigenous disorder, see also Ungar, 'La France impériale en 1931', 207.

[40] See Pierre Mille, 'A l'Exposition coloniale: vue d'ensemble', *Revue des deux mondes*, 51/3 (1931), 265–87 (p. 266), and 'Ne visitez pas l'Exposition coloniale!', 194.

[41] Norindr, *Phantasmatic Indochina*, 33.

[42] Mille, 'A l'Exposition coloniale', 268.

[43] Ageron, 'L'Exposition coloniale de 1931', 508.

[44] Girardet, *L'Idée coloniale en France*, 134.

which 'authentic' indigenous performers (brought to France for the duration) were included in an often inauthentic decor whose detail was dictated by aesthetic and ideological concerns more than by a desire for ethnographic accuracy.[45] There were camel races, canoe trips, and regular opportunities to sample suspiciously generic 'gastronomie coloniale' [colonial cuisine] and 'boissons exotiques' [exotic beverages]. The marketing of the event depended heavily on an illusion of colonial travel, offering 'le tour du monde en quatre jours' [a journey round the world in four days] and underlining the potential efficiency of a visit to the exhibition site: 'Pourquoi aller en Tunisie quand vous pouvez la visiter aux portes de Paris?' [What is the point of going to Tunisia when you can visit it at the gates of Paris?].[46] An article in a special issue of the periodical *L'Illustration* makes the advantages of this opportunity for vicarious travel explicit. In 'Promenade à travers les cinq continents', Paul-Émile Cadilhac claims:

Je conseille aux voyageurs qui redoutent les traversées de parcourir la planète en passant par l'Exposition. Là, ni roulis, ni tangage; le mal de mer y est inconnu; et l'on va par rail ou par autocar de Madagascar à l'Océanie et de la Martinique aux Indes néerlandaises. Les distances sont abolies, les océans supprimés, et ce n'est pas le moindre des miracles réalisés par le Maréchal Lyautey.[47]

I advise those who dread sea crossings to travel the planet by visiting the Exhibition. There is no rolling or pitching on a ship; seasickness is unheard of; you go by train or coach from Madagascar to Oceania and from Martinique to the Dutch East Indies. Distances are abolished, oceans swept away—and these are not the least of the miracles performed by Field Marshal Lyautey.

Yet other texts inspired by the *Exposition* similarly insist on the stage-managed nature of the event, underlining not only its artificiality but also the domesticating mechanisms of the exoticism on which much of it was posited: 'A côté, d'effroyables Canaques, tout de peau noire et de raphia volant, vous séchaient le sang de terreur avec leurs danses guerrières, mais ils faisaient ensuite la quête, et cette pratique de civilisés avait un caractère intime et rassurant' [Nearby, terrifying Kanak, all black skin and swirling raffia, made your blood curdle with their war

---

[45] The prefabricated nature of the site is commonly observed in contemporary accounts. Jeanne Ramal-Cals, for instance, describes a father telling his son that a rock is 'entièrement fait à la main' [entirely handmade]. See 'Souvenir de l'Exposition coloniale', *Les Œuvres libres*, 126 (1931), 7–22 (pp. 9, 18).

[46] Ageron, 'L'Exposition coloniale de 1931', 502.

[47] P.-É. Cadilhac, 'Promenade à travers les cinq continents', *L'Illustration*, 23 May 1931, 73–6 (p. 73).

dances, but then they queued up—and this civilized practice had a cosy and reassuring feel to it].[48] It was indeed the New Caledonian visitors to the Exposition who seem to have attracted close attention—and who, with Didier Daeninckx's recent novellas—continue to do so.[49] As Joël Dauphiné explains in his meticulously presented account of the recruitment and travel of the Kanak to 1931 Paris, even at the time of the Exhibition the organizers found the New Caledonian delegation too sensitive to handle, seeing the inhabitants of the islands too closely associated with the primitivist exoticism this display of colonial propaganda endeavoured to avoid. The account of their journey is a harsh one, involving unkept promises, the group's separation when half their number were sent to perform in a German zoo, and a steadily rising sense of indignation on the part of the Kanak and their few French supporters. Displayed in the *jardin d'acclimatation* in the Bois de Boulogne, apart from the main exhibition, they were nevertheless a popular fringe attraction, catering for the desire for controlled and domesticated fear inherent in a certain strand of popular exoticism. Journalists, however, ridiculed this metropolitan construction of indigeneity, and Alin Laubreaux describes a visitor to the *jardin* who recognizes Prosper, a well-educated printworker whom he had known a decade previously, masquerading as a cannibal in order to make the journey to Paris.[50]

Unlike Ousmane Socé's *Mirages de Paris*, an account of a Senegalese protagonist's experiences in 1931 France (to be discussed below), texts with such a metropolitan focus cannot perhaps be integrated into a traditional understanding of 1930s 'travel writing'. The *Exposition* and those texts that emerged from it provide an essential context within

---

[48] Ramal-Cals, 'Souvenir de l'Exposition Coloniale', 9.

[49] See n. 20 above. Daeninckx has become one of the most active and prominent critics of French amnesia regarding the country's colonial past. His *Meurtres pour mémoire* (Paris: Gallimard, 1984) was instrumental in directing popular attention to the Bataille de Paris massacre (17 October 1961), and *Cannibale*, re-released in a recent pedagogical edition, has been central to recent attempts to commemorate the 1931 Exposition.

[50] See Joël Dauphiné, *Canaques de la Nouvelle Calédonie à Paris en 1931: de la case au zoo* (Paris: L'Harmattan, 1998), 150–4. The article was originally published in *Candide* (14 May 1931), a right-wing publication, 'de tendance maurrassienne', whose customary support for the Exposition was tempered here by clear reservations about excessive stage-management. On *Candide*, see Pascal Blanchard, 'L'union nationale: la "rencontre" des droites et des gauches à travers la presse et autour de l'exposition de Vincennes', in Blanchard and Lemaire (eds.), *Culture coloniale*, 213–31 (p. 227). The transformation of the educated *évolué* into would-be 'primitive' reflects the tendency of ethnography, discussed in Michel Leiris's 'L'ethnographe devant le colonialisme', to deny coevalness and to present colonial societies as exclusively 'non mécanisées'. See *Cinq études d'ethnographie* (Paris: Denoël; Gonthier, 1969), 84–5.

which such travel writing can be considered. Moreover, ironically or not, these texts often adopt the devices of travel literature to constitute virtual travel narratives. Accounts of circumnavigation on the exhibition site, for instance, continue an earlier tradition of vicarious travel, epitomized (as has been suggested above) by the eleventh chapter of Huysmans's *À Rebours*, and are to be read as part of a wider network of the cultures of travel. Des Esseintes's parodic exoticism in this decadent journey is a literary variation on a popular late nineteenth-century phenomenon, discussed in the introduction to this volume, that Vanessa Schwartz has summed up in her *Spectacular Realities* as 'fin-de-siècle panoramania'. Schwartz describes the 1880s and 1890s craze for dioramas and virtual journeys that allowed a whistle stop tour of exotic locales without leaving Paris itself. Read in the light of this wider historical context, the *Exposition coloniale* is to be seen both as a further stage in the erasure of elsewhere foreseen by Huysmans and as an integral part of the 1930s reassessment of the symbolic and actual fields of travel. Contemporary commentators on the *Exposition*, observing the potential contact zone the site represents, describe a process of mutual exchange or reciprocity. Such a 'phénomène de compénétration' [phenomenon of co-penetration] ignores the stark asymmetries that the colonial situation generates and on which it depends. In Mille's terms, 'c'est l'Européen qui devient un peu Asiatique, l'Asiatique un peu Européen' [the European becomes slightly Asian, the Asian slightly European].[51] The shortcomings of the assimilative impulse of French colonial policy had certainly, by this stage, been revealed by colonial practice, and, as Christopher Miller demonstrates, the Exposition was 'designed to exhibit *authentic* differences': ' "Solidarity" did not mean blending or mixing; it was predicated on segregation and specificity', i.e. the exhibition was concerned with the perpetuation of a hierarchical diversity in a colonial context, and not its erosion.[52] On the one hand, its staging of colonial cultures represents a conquest and reorganization of space—France is not only the centre of the world, but is also even

---

[51] Pierre Mille, 'A l'Exposition coloniale', 272–3. Lyautey spoke in similar terms of having 'l'œil constamment ouvert sur ce qu'il peut y avoir, chez ces frères différents, de meilleur que chez nous; de garder le souci incessant de nous adapter à leurs statuts, à leurs traditions, à leurs coutumes, à leurs croyances, en un mot, de les comprendre' [being constantly on the look out for those things which, in the different cultures of these our brothers, might be better than in our own culture; constantly taking care to adapt ourselves to their statutes, traditions, customs, beliefs, in a word, to understand them]. Cited in Hodeir and Pierre, *L'Exposition coloniale*, 90–1.

[52] Miller, *Nationalists and Nomads*, 69 (emphasis in the original).

transformed into a self-contained representation of the world: the site accordingly perpetuates the tension between ethnic or cultural diversity (and the hierarchies underpinning this) and a political unification or (more accurately) centralization; on the other, it stood as a clear indication of what was seen to be implied by the growing mechanization of travel and in particular the rapid growth of transport by air, i.e. technology would soon render geographical travel obsolete as the exotic would be available *à domicile*.

SPEED, DECELERATION, AND INTER-WAR TRAVEL

The inter-war period, and in particular the 1930s, was marked by the first regular flights between France and Africa and by a series of transcontinental car journeys—such as the Citroën Croisières noire and jaune, in 1924–5 and 1931–2 respectively. These well-publicized itineraries combined in particular public longing for speed with the lure of exoticism, commercial concerns with a projection of national identity.[53] The official account of the trans-Asian expedition relies on the language of conquest and assault in order to describe 'ce grand périple qui devait tracer en Asie un immense sillon de propagande française' [this great voyage whose aim was to trace across Asia a huge furrow of French propaganda].[54] The Citroën journeys are marked by an ambivalent rapport with elsewhere that can be seen in their participants' self-performance as a group of 'aventuriers' (as opposed to 'voyageurs') united by what Jacques Wolgensinger calls a 'fraternité virile' [virile fraternity].[55] Conscious that the success of their journeys will signal mechanical travel's potential to facilitate and hence democratize access to previously remote spaces, accordingly rendering them accessible, they nevertheless underline their pioneer status. The journey account is characterized by the image of the

---

[53] On the Croisière jaune, see Denis Baldensperger, 'Il y a 50 ans: Citroën lance "la Croisière jaune"', *Historia*, 413 (1981), 93–101, J.-P. Dauliac, *La Croisière jaune 1931–32* ([Mougins]: Éditions de l'automobiliste, 1986), and Jacques Wolgensinger, *L'Épopée de la Croisière jaune* (Paris: Laffont, 1970). For an account of the Croisières noire and jaune, as well as of two lesser-known expeditions using Citroën-Kégresse vehicles in the American Rockies (1934) and in Antarctica (the so-called Croisière blanche; 1933–4), see John Reynolds, *André Citroën: The Man and the Motor Cars* (Stroud: Sutton, 1996), 85–141. The leader of the Croisière jaune, Georges-Marie Haardt, who died of pneumonia shortly after the expedition's completion, planned a further but unrealized Croisière indochinoise. See Wolgensinger, *L'Épopée de la Croisière jaune*, 232.

[54] Lefèvre, *La Croisière jaune*, 8.

[55] Wolgensinger, *L'Épopée de la Croisière jaune*, 217.

'chemin vierge' [unsullied path] along which they travel, the implicit salvage in their scientific activity (the expedition returned with 5,000 photographs, 50,000 metres of film, as well as numerous geological, cultural, and scientific artefacts), and the stark contrast between their vehicles of modernity and the pre-industrial cultures with which they come into contact.[56] Scott Berliner claims that the Croisières encapsulate 'the contradiction of postwar exoticism: the search for Eden and the desire to put a road through it'.[57] Such rapid acceleration and expansion of travel brought with it a blurring of cultural diversity and an erosion of radically different cultures, access to which was often seen in terms of the spread of global sameness.

One of the authors in the period to draw almost exclusively on the theme of travel and on a fascination with speed was Paul Morand, whose cosmopolitanism can be read as the antithesis of an earlier exoticism—and accordingly, in Sartre's terms, as 'le glas de l'exotisme' [the death knell of exoticism].[58] Morand's travel writing is a sustained commentary on the effects of the inter-war mechanization of travel whose implications he explores in the aphoristic 1927 text *Le Voyage*: 'Pauvre géographie: au cours du dernier siècle, les atlas changeaient tous les vingt ans. Aujourd'hui, il faudrait les sortir en éditions spéciales, heure par heure' [Poor old geography: last century, atlases changed every twenty years. These days, we ought to bring them out hourly as special editions].[59] In his 1932 text, *Flèche d'Orient*, Morand describes the journey across Europe by air of an expatriate Russian prince. As the text progresses, there emerges not only a new aesthetics of space triggered by the fresh perspectives allowed by air travel, but also a radically different experience—particularly in terms of time—of the space crossed in travel. What can be seen is 'un univers quadrillé, compartimenté, géométrique' [a cross-ruled, partitioned, geometric universe] in which speed erases contour and colour to impose a universal greyness.[60] Morand had certainly claimed in a 1924 interview that his purpose was to 'démoder l'exotisme, cette photographie en couleur', to render outmoded an exoticism dependent on superficial aspects of

---

[56] See Lefèvre, *La Croisière jaune*, 72.

[57] Berliner, *Ambivalent Desire*, 200.

[58] Jean-Paul Sartre, 'D'une Chine à l'Autre', in *Situations V* (Paris: Gallimard, 1964), 7–24 (p. 8). For a full discussion of Morand and the ideological/aesthetic implications of his analysis of inter-war travel, see Bruno Thibault, *L'Allure de Morand: du Modernisme au Pétainisme* (Birmingham, Ala.: Summa, 1992).

[59] See Paul Morand, *Le Voyage* (Monaco: Éditions du Rocher, 1994 [1927]), 30.

[60] Paul Morand, *Flèche d'Orient* (Paris: Gallimard, 1932), 41.

local colour.[61] His own textual response appears paradoxical, however, for he often embraces the exhilarating sensation of speed whilst bemoaning its implications for access to (and, he claims, erosion of) the visible cultural diversity on which travel depends.

As such, Morand's texts can be associated with those of his contemporaries such as Saint-Pol-Roux (on whose work such modern theorists of speed as Paul Virilio have drawn) who combine a post-Futurist attraction to speed with a growing awareness of its destructive properties. In the aphorisms of his later work, especially *Vitesse* (written 1932) and *La Randonnée* (an account of a return car journey in the early 1930s from Camaret to Brest), for example, Saint-Pol-Roux considered the implications of an ever-accelerating experience of travel: i.e. a sense of immobility—'Fauteuil d'auto: fauteuil de cinéma' [Car seat = cinema seat]; 'Notre vitesse mécanique n'est qu'une immobilité motorisée' [Mechanized speed is no more than motorized motionlessness]—and a radical alteration of any notion of dimension: 'La vitesse humaine rapetisse la Terre. Vitesse: cécité' [Human speed reduces the dimensions of the Earth. Speed = blindness].[62] Morand's response to this apparent redundancy of the experience of travel and to the transformation of the journey into little more than a geometric vector is contained in the 1937 text, *Éloge du repos* (initially entitled: *Apprendre à se reposer*). This text, written shortly after the adoption by the Front Populaire of the universal right to paid holidays, develops Morand's comments in earlier works on the effects of speed, emphasizing its destructive implications: 'La vitesse tue la forme. D'un paysage vu à cinq cents à l'heure, que reste-t-il? [...] La terre perd sa variété; en avion, il n'y a plus, sous nos pieds, de peupliers et de châtaigniers; il y a l'Arbre ... ' [Speed eradicates form. What is left of a landscape seen at 500 kilometres an hour? [...] The earth loses its variety; when you are in a plane, there are no longer poplars and chestnuts beneath you; there are simply Trees].[63] The distinctions associated with different varieties are reduced to purely generic categories. Criticizing any cult of speed and counselling slowness, he claims that the erosion of radical otherness previously located elsewhere can be compensated for by the discovery of a new sense of

[61] Paul Morand, 'Exotisme et cosmopolitisme', *Carnets de l'exotisme*, 10 (1992), 79–80 (p. 79). (First published 1924.)

[62] Saint-Pol-Roux, *Vitesse*, 25, 30, 53. See also *La Randonnée* (Mortemart: Rougerie, 1978).

[63] Paul Morand, *Éloge du repos* (Paris: Arléa, 1996), 118. (First published as *Apprendre à se reposer* (Paris: Flammarion, 1937).)

exoticism within France itself: 'il y a, plus près de nous, des rivières connues seulement des grenouilles et des pagayeurs; l'automobiliste pressé les ignore, car il faut être sur l'eau pour découvrir soudain l'autre aspect d'une France invisible de la terre ferme' [closer to home, there are rivers that are known only by frogs and canoeists; as he rushes past, the motorist is not aware of them, for you need to be on the water to discover another side of France invisible from dry land].[64] Morand echoes the beginnings of the demonization of the car inherent in Saint-Pol-Roux's critique, linking speed to the evaporation of diversity and suggesting a paradoxical aristocracy of the gaze associated with the velocity of means of transport selected. Morand's apparently positive attitude to the reforms of 1936 must be attenuated, however, by his realization that paid holidays and greater mobility presented yet another threat to the field of cultural differences that permits travel.

The reconstructed temple of Angkor Wat stood in 1931 as an icon for the brief interlude of the Exposition (during which an illusion of travel was permitted for all). The image of a working-class couple on a tandem in 1936—and of bottles of Ambre solaire or Orangina, both launched in the same year—represented the possibility of actual if more modest travel for all and even the dawning of an age of mass tourism.[65] The colonial exoticism of the Exposition raised questions about the aesthetic or symbolic field of cultural diversity, the practical implications of which would only become apparent after the Second World War; the democratization of travel became a challenge to its actual, geographical field, albeit initially on a more humble domestic scale, encapsulated perhaps in the phrase: 'the Riviera for all'.[66] The 1930s

---

[64] Morand, Éloge du repos, 106.

[65] Eugen Weber, The Hollow Years: France in the 1930s (London: Sinclair-Stevenson, 1995), 162.

[66] See Julian Jackson, The Popular Front in France: Defending Democracy, 1934–38 (Cambridge: Cambridge University Press, 1988), 134. On the implications of the Popular Front for leisure and tourism, see L. Bodin and J. Touchard, Front Populaire, 1936 (Paris: Armand Colin, 1976), 136–45, Julian Jackson, ' "Le temps des loisirs": Popular Tourism and Mass Leisure in the Vision of the Front Populaire', in M. S. Alexander and H. Graham (eds.), The French and Spanish Popular Fronts: Comparative Perspectives (Cambridge: Cambridge University Press, 1989), 226–39, Jackson, The Popular Front in France, 131–8, and C. B. Lavenir, La Roue et le stylo: comment nous sommes devenus touristes (Paris: Odile Jacob, 1999), 337–61. As Eugen Weber makes clear in his study of fin-de-siècle France, popular aspirations to paid holidays—and opposition to such aspirations— emerged in the late nineteenth century (Weber, France Fin de Siècle, 190–4). The year 1936 represents, therefore, more a symbolic stage in the democratization of travel than an actual turning point. Most travellers benefiting from the Popular Front's congés payés stayed relatively close to home as 'the first paid holidays represented less a "discovery of France" than a "retour au pays" ' (' "Le temps des loisirs" ', 236).

also saw the introduction of cheap rail travel, but the choice of the bicycle is striking; the car, to the nascent threat of which Morand seems to allude, was not yet as accessible to the masses as it would become, in the form of vehicle such as the Citroën 2CV (whose impact on the cultures of travel is explored in the following chapter), in the post-war period; but two-wheeled transport (bicycle ownership increased from 7 million in 1936 to nearly 9 million in 1937) still represented the threat of democratized mobility, in however modest a form.[67] From the mid-nineteenth century onwards, anti-tourism had become a common defence used by certain travellers to protect their privileged access to traces of cultural difference.[68] As a human, the tourist is classed as a mediocre spectator whose vision is limited to a superficial, kaleido-scopic exoticism.[69] The traveller's vision is distinguished then from the tourist's gawping, and the field of the exotic seems to remain intact.

In his *Le Flâneur sous la tente*, for instance, Maurice Constantin-Weyer perpetuates this tradition when he creates an anti-touristic col-lusion with his reader: 'Le mouvement des glaciers échappe à l'œil du simple touriste. Nous savons pourtant qu'ils sont loin d'être inertes' [The movement of glaciers escapes the notice of the tourist's untrained eye. However, we know that they are far from being inert].[70] Such aristocratic attempts to elaborate hierarchies of the perception of other-ness, and accordingly to ensure its perpetuation, were eclipsed, how-ever, by a number of texts that foregrounded instead the all-encroaching erasure of cultural diversity. These texts at the same time refused any sense of exoticism understood as a quest for radical difference. This refusal of exoticism is particularly marked in a number of French 1930s novels set in Tahiti, such as Georges Simenon's *Touriste de bananes*, in which a tracking of the decline of a French exoticist myth of several centuries' standing reveals the swallowing of local specificity by a spectre of global entropy.[71] For Simenon, the *homme-nature*—or Westerner in search of a utopian lifestyle in an exotic locale—is an

---

[67] On the increase in bicycle ownership, see Jackson, *The Popular Front in France*, 132.

[68] On anti-tourism, see James Buzard, *The Beaten Track: European Tourism, Literature and the Ways to Culture* (Oxford: Clarendon, 1993), and Urbain, *L'Idiot du voyage*.

[69] See Segalen, 'Essai sur l'exotisme', 750, for a version of this critique made two decades earlier.

[70] Maurice Constantin-Weyer, *Le Flâneur sous la tente* (Paris: Stock, 1941), 159.

[71] For a discussion of Simenon's *Touriste de bananes* (Paris: Gallimard, 1936), see Sonia Faessel, 'Simenon, Gary: deux lectures du mythe de Tahiti. *Touriste de bananes* et *La Tête coupable*', *Travaux de littérature*, 10 (1997), 379–95, and Daniel Margueron, *Tahiti dans toute sa littérature: essai sur Tahiti et ses îles dans la littérature française de la découverte à nos jours* (Paris: L'Harmattan, 1989), 184–7.

anachronism or a zoological curiosity. The quest of such characters inevitably founders as they discover an exotic culture, stage-managed for outsiders, in which traces of past 'authenticity' are either imported or acted out. The indigenous characters in *Touriste de bananes*, for instance, are by day taxi-drivers and prostitutes; it is only by night that they don the trappings of a supposedly pre-colonial Polynesia to create an artificial version of their island for tourist consumption.

Already in a series of reports entitled 'L'Afrique vous parle' written for the magazine *Voilà* in 1932, Simenon's exasperation at the impact on indigenous culture of colonial expansion had led him to conclude: 'Elle nous dit merde!' [It says balls to us!]. This idea of former colonial or exotic subjects talking back in a manner likely to shock the European listener is integral to the decline or critique of the dominant strand of colonial exoticism described above.[72] Although two of the major French novels of the decade, *Voyage au bout de la nuit* and *La Nausée*, both articulate a disillusionment with travel and a rejection of the traps of exoticism, Simenon's recognition of the emergence of indigenous voices suggests an approach to 1930s travel and exoticism that qualifies any foretelling of its total decline. Céline's journey to the end of the night, for instance, is a voyage of confirmation and not of discovery; the horror of circumnavigation that characterizes it emerges from the narrator's sense of interminable progress through a series of situations that differ in superficial detail rather than in substance. The American stage of the journey is initially in tune with the technological exoticism that characterized other contemporary texts, as diverse as *Bécassine voyage* and André Maurois's *L'Amérique inattendue*, about transatlantic travellers. Even this section of Céline's narrative, however, eventually leads beneath the façade of concrete and steel to the seamy underside of the American dream.[73] The contemporary topos of the journey is subverted and, especially in the character of Robinson, the ideal of adventure entirely negated.[74] As such, Céline's portrayal of the end of travel resonates with Simenon's model of a linear and geometrical decline of a culture only residually 'exotic', in the non-pejorative sense of this

---

[72] Simenon, 'L'heure du nègre', in *A la recherche de l'homme nu*, 45–106 (p. 106). (First published in *Voilà*, 1932.)

[73] See Caumery and J. P. Pinchon, *Bécassine voyage* (Paris: Gautier-Languereau, 1921), and André Maurois, *L'Amérique inattendue* (Paris: Mornay, 1931).

[74] For a consideration of uses of travel in Céline's *Voyage*, see Andrea Loselle, *History's Double: Cultural Tourism in Twentieth-Century French Writing* (New York: St Martin's Press, 1997), 127–57.

epithet. However, as my introductory remarks to this chapter suggested, travel literature in French of the 1930s marks the decline of a certain understanding of exoticism and not of exoticism *per se*. In a concluding consideration of a selection of travel accounts, it will be suggested that a more complex notion of intercultural contact begins to emerge. This notion remains permanently conscious of the risks of a domesticating exoticism, whilst nevertheless maintaining a focus on cultural specificity and a belief in the existence of diversity as the raw material on which travel literature depends. This salvaging of exoticism does not so much emerge from individual texts as from the interplay of a number of texts that—to borrow Edward Said's terms in *Culture and Imperialism*—can be brought together in contrapuntal arrangements. Such an understanding reveals the intertwined and overlapping histories of metropolitan and formerly colonized societies and avoids the destructive expiation for empire that the rapid descent into obsolescence of the term 'exoticism' often seems to suggest.[75]

It is useful to begin looking at such an attenuation of previous understandings of 1930s exoticism in the early travel narratives of Henri Michaux, *Ecuador* and *Un barbare en Asie*. The first is an anti-travel text which defines itself generically as the antithesis of previous travel accounts,[76] and the second similarly marks a break with any previous tradition of travel writing for it describes—in Sartre's terms—'la Chine sans lotus ni Loti' [China without lotus plants and without Loti].[77] The text is marked by a stubborn refusal of diversity, a discovery of monotony, and a loss of any sense of dimension that leads its exasperated narrator to exclaim: 'Cette terre est rincée de son exotisme' [The earth's exoticism has been rinsed out].[78] Refusing to become an 'amateur d'exotisme' [dabbler in exoticism], the narrator constantly questions the value of his journey, seeing individuals in those he meets rather than ethnotypes and discovering the 'quotidien' instead of the anticipated 'exotique'.[79] It is in such a reflection on the everyday, however, that a

---

[75] See Said, *Culture and Imperialism*.

[76] For a fuller consideration of Michaux's travel accounts and their implications for contemporary 1930s exoticism, see Didier Alexandre, 'Henri Michaux, le barbare', *Revue d'Histoire Littéraire de la France*, 95/2 (1995), 199–217, Peter Broome, 'Henri Michaux and Travel: From Outer Space to Inner Space', *French Studies*, 39 (1985), 285–97, and Bruno Thibault, ' "Voyager contre": la question de l'exotisme dans les journaux de voyage d'Henri Michaux', *The French Review*, 63 (1990), 485–91.

[77] Sartre, 'D'une Chine à l'Autre', 8.

[78] Michaux, *Ecuador*, 35.

[79] Ibid. 98.

renegotiation of the exotic begins to emerge: 'le quotidien de l'un peut désorienter jusqu'à la mort l'homme de l'autre quotidien' [what is every-day for one person can confuse to death somebody for whom the every-day is situated elsewhere].[80]

This exploration of the everyday is developed in *Un barbare en Asie*, in which Michaux's focus on 'l'homme dans la rue' [the man in the street] leads to a series of reflections on radical otherness in which he refuses to render the exotic neutral, inoffensive, or domesticated.[81] However, as the title of the work itself suggests, the text also implies a reversal, an exoticization of the European travelling self that grants the narrator an ambiguous position as outsider. For Michaux, the exotic is perhaps exhausted or redundant as a geographically fixed essence, but exoticism itself is reinterpreted as a potentially reciprocal process of negotiating the experience of the new or unknown. André Gide de-scribes in a 1935 diary entry this foregrounding of selectivity and subjectivity in considerations of contact between radically different cultures: 'Ce qui fait le charme et l'attrait de l'Ailleurs, de ce que nous appelons exotisme, ce n'est point tant que la nature y soit plus belle, mais que tout nous y paraît neuf, nous surprend et se présente à notre œil dans une sorte de virginité' [What constitutes the charm and lure of the *Ailleurs*, of what we call exoticism, is not so much that nature is more beautiful there as that everything seems to us so new, surprises us, and is presented to our gaze with a sort of virginity].[82] It is a new approach to exoticism such as this that is implicit in Michaux's narra-tor's response to those surprised by his failure to write about his native Belgium:

Comment n'écrirait-on pas sur un pays qui s'est présenté à vous avec l'abon-dance des choses nouvelles et dans la joie de revivre?

Et comment écrirait-on sur un pays où l'on a vécu trente ans, liés à l'ennui, à la contradiction, aux soucis étroits, aux défaites, au train-train quotidien, et sur lequel on ne sait plus rien.[83]

How on earth could you not write about a country whose appearance to you was characterized by an abundance of new things and by the joy of being able to breathe again?

And how on earth could you write about a country where you have lived for thirty years, thirty years associated with boredom, contradictions, petty

---

[80] Michaux, *Ecuador*, 159–60.
[81] Henri Michaux, *Un barbare en Asie* (Paris: Gallimard, 1933), 12.
[82] André Gide, *Journal, 1889–1939* (Paris: Gallimard, Pléiade, 1951), 1236.
[83] Michaux, *Un barbare en Asie*, 99

concerns, failures, daily routine—a country about which you no longer know anything.

The Barbarian-narrator is even granted a privileged position: 'un passant aux yeux naïfs peut parfois mettre le doigt sur le centre' [the naive gaze of a passer-by can sometimes pin down the essential]. It is the traveller, resigned to outsider status and intent on seeking experience of elsewhere rather than confirmation of preformed impressions, who can avoid being a passive, superficial observer and can present in textual form the experience of being faced with a radically different, even inassimilable culture.[84]

MIRAGES DE PARIS, AFRIQUE FANTÔME: EXCHANGED GAZES, COMPLEMENTARY JOURNEYS

Because of the context from which it emerges, Michaux's innovation of seeing the travelling self as other goes beyond the conceit of an earlier tradition of a metamorphosed or reversed ethnographic gaze. The exoticization of Europe no longer depends on literary games with mirrors, but becomes in 1930s France an integral element in an emergent traveller's self-reflexivity, a development that logically leads to the appearance of journey accounts representing the autonomous voices of formerly silenced exotic subjects. My conclusions to this chapter will centre on the implications of these initial French stages of what has now come to be known as the Empire Writing Back. The 1930s saw the growth of a newly prominent black culture rooted in Paris whose importance can be seen in a series of journals and reviews set up in that decade.[85] Far from being simply the creator of mythical universes elsewhere, France found itself to be the centre of a mythical universe and, for many Africans and Caribbeans, a stage in a journey of apprenticeship or even initiation. One of the first novels in which these aspects are apparent is the Senegalese author Ousmane Socé's *Mirages de Paris*. Inspired by and structured around a journey from Africa to Europe, it is an account of the protagonist Fara's stay in Paris during the Exposition

---

[84] Ibid. 101.
[85] On the role of the journey to and stay in Paris as a key element in the emergence of the Francophone literatures of Africa and the Caribbean, see Romuald Fonkoua, 'Le "voyage à l'envers" ', and Belinda Jack, ' "Mirages de Paris": Paris in Francophone Writing', in Michael Sheringham (ed.), *Parisian Fields* (London: Reaktion 1996), 150–61.

coloniale.[86] The text focuses on the processes of recuperation of the exotic, considering how the trappings of Empire—from the imposition of town planning right down to pencils, exercise books, and women's shoes—are radically other for the Senegalese child who develops what Christopher Miller has dubbed a 'pathological francocentrism', and for whom Paris becomes a longed-for 'El Dorado': 'un dangereux amour de l'exotisme prenait corps dans son âme d'enfant encline aux illusions dorées' [a dangerous love of exoticism was taking shape in his youthful consciousness, already inclined to believing in gilded illusions].[87]

For the French reader, the adult Fara's journey from Africa entails distinct defamiliarization, as it depends on the traditional devices of the travel narrative to describe France itself: demonization of white characters; use of a catalogue of exotic-sounding names—'Angoulême... Poitiers... Tours... Blois... Orléans...'—to give an impression of space crossed;[88] and disappointment at the moment of arrival. However, Socé does not simply replicate or reverse these aspects of the European text. His work is a critique of the superficiality of literary exotic, a superficiality that emerges in particular in descriptions of the *Exposition* itself, the duping of visitors which is one of the novel's recurrent themes: 'Il marcha le long de la grande avenue des Colonies françaises. Sur sa droite, la Martinique, la Réunion, la Guadeloupe, évoquaient les Îles selon les traits classiques qu'en donnent [*sic*] la littérature' [He walked along the main avenue of the French Colonies. On the right were Martinique, Réunion, and Guadeloupe, conjuring up images of these islands according to the classical features that literature grants them].[89] The meaning of the 'mirages' of the title is, therefore, double-edged. The term refers not only to Fara's expectations of Europe generated by the partial view of France propagated through French colonial education, but also to France's own imaginary projection of elsewhere, encapsulated in the *Exposition* itself, but perpetuated by an immense archive of colonial stereotypes. The protagonist's disappoint-

---

[86] Socé's novel has received little critical attention. See, however, F. Joppa, 'Situation de *Mirages de Paris* d'Ousmane Socé dans le roman néo-africain', *Présence Francophone*, 1 (1970), 219–32, Roger Little, 'Death by Water: Socé's Fara and Lacrosil's Cajou', *ASCALF Bulletin*, 23 (2001), 6–22, Christopher Miller, *Nationalists and Nomads*, 55–89, and Aedín Ní Loingsigh, 'Exil et perception du temps chez Tilli et Socé', *ASCALF Bulletin*, 16–17 (1998), 3–21.

[87] See Miller, *Nationalists and Nomads*, 62, and Ousmane Socé, *Mirages de Paris* (Paris: Nouvelles Éditions Latines, 1964 [1937]), 15.

[88] Socé, *Mirages de Paris*, 27.

[89] Ibid. 35.

ment at slippage between the imagined and the discovered is accentuated by his growing awareness of metropolitan ignorance regarding
cultures outwith Europe: one character asks if Dakar is the capital of
Madagascar,[90] colonial journalists and lecturers, growing numbers of
whom profited from the popularity of reportage, are cast as 'fabricants
d'exotisme' [manufacturers of exoticism],[91] and in a conversation over
dinner with the parents of his would-be fiancée Fara describes in detail
the mechanisms of colonial exoticism:

> Il dit l'ignorance des habitants d'ici sur les Noirs. Leurs amis qui sont en
> Afrique, pour la plupart, ne parlent que des petits travers des Noirs et de leurs
> drôleries sur lesquels ils s'appesantissent longuement, en font les traits domin-
> ants de leur caractère. [...] Le cinéma et la littérature viennent à la rescousse,
> produisent de 'l'exotisme' et de la 'documentation' pour des effets préconçus.
> De sorte que ceux des Européens qui croyaient connaître les Noirs étaient ceux
> qui les connaissaient le moins. [...] Le résultat paradoxal est que, devant un
> Noir, le monsieur pense avoir affaire à un grand enfant et le Noir croit se trouver
> en présence d'un grand enfant blanc.[92]

> He spoke about the French ignorance of Africans. On the whole, their friends in
> Africa only talked about the Africans' little failings and their funny actions, and
> they dwelt on these at length and turned them into dominant character traits.
> [...] Cinema and literature come to the rescue and produce preconceived effects
> with 'exoticism' and 'documentation'. As a result, those Europeans who
> thought they knew Africans well were those who in fact knew them the least.
> [...] The paradoxical result was that a Frenchman faced with an African
> thought he was dealing with a big child whilst the African thought he was in
> the presence of a big white child.

Fara's failure to fit in to Parisian society—and his parallel inability to
return to Senegal—result in his ultimate death, with the tragedy of his
suicide becoming the protagonist's only means of freeing himself from
exile. This concluding sense of the black traveller's alienation from
metropolitan France accentuates the sense of ethnic division that permeates the text. Such alienation was already apparent during Fara's
boat journey to France, during which, 'dans les cabines des troisièmes',
he becomes part of Simenon's anonymous 'cargaisons humaines' (although it is significant that an additional and unofficial ethnic segregation exists among the third class passengers 'pour éviter une
promiscuité peut-être déplaisante' [to avoid a potentially disagreeable
intermingling]).[93] Fara's death suggests that the colonial subject cannot

---

[90] Ibid. 41.   [91] Ibid. 66.   [92] Ibid. 90–1.   [93] Ibid. 20.

survive contact with the colonizing culture whilst maintaining the integrity of his own identity. The text includes what is for French-language literature an early exploration of hybridity from a non-con-demnatory viewpoint, and the protagonist's conversation with the phil-osopher Sidia encapsulates the tensions between an extreme position reliant on continued segregation (although it must be stressed that Sidia's comments are essentially biological) and Fara's apology for *métissage* in all its forms. Although the *métis* child of Fara and Suzanne survives the text's conclusion, the latter's death suggests that the zone of contact between cultures is neither abstract nor utopian, but, in Chris-topher Miller's terms, the space of a 'risky voyage with an uncertain outcome'. Fara's journey to France is a reminder of the asymmetries and ideals that can undermine processes of hybridization.[94]

The apparent pessimism with which this text concludes can, however, be attenuated. It may even be seen to conceal traces of a more positive model of meetings of cultural differences when read in the light of contemporary French texts offering a similar critique of and a similar challenge to the mechanisms of exoticization. The 'Parisian mirages' of the novel's title refer not only to the version of a colonial elsewhere projected by the *Exposition coloniale* and the exoticist discourses this event encapsulates, but also to the version of France hallucinated and desired by Fara himself. From a French perspective, in *L'Afrique fan-tôme*, Leiris describes and critiques similar processes. As 'l'étiage de l'exotisme' [the level of exoticism] reduces according to the travellers' increasing familiarity with their surroundings, so the diarist resorts to photographs to prove to himself that he has been—and by extension, still is—in Africa: 'Drôle de mirage'.[95] Leiris sketches out an ethnog-raphy of the ethnographer, reliant on the emergent traveller's self-reflexivity described above. Michel Leiris's *L'Afrique fantôme*, with reference to which this chapter opened, falls therefore into the category of travel texts that problematize the construction and representation of cultural diversity whilst criticizing works that continue to peddle colo-nial exoticism.[96] A contrapuntal reading of this text together with Socé's would form a substantial chapter in its own right, with the contradictory vectors of the two authors' journeys illuminating each other. For present purposes, however, *L'Afrique fantôme* can only be

---

[94] Miller, *Nationalists and Nomads*, 89.
[95] Leiris, *L'Afrique fantôme*, 212–13.
[96] For a critique of conventional travel writing, see Leiris, *L'Afrique fantôme*, 266.

referred to as a concluding illustration of the complex understanding of 1930s exoticism this chapter has begun to outline, as a means of pulling together a number of strands.[97] Leiris's account of the Dakar-to-Djibouti ethnographic expedition, the principal aim of which was the collection of artefacts for the Musée de l'Homme, is problematic because of the dependence of its narrative on repeated acts of salvage, recuperation, or theft.[98] There is a slippage, however, between such description of the institutional practice of 1930s ethnography and Leiris's personal exploration of the failings of colonial exoticism. Leiris eschews accounts of landscape or description of specific scenes, and seems to prefer everyday, sedentary situations—such as transcribing oral narratives in a railway depot—to the actual progress of travel. In his own terms: 'C'est la grande guerre au pittoresque, le rire au nez de l'exotisme' [It is a major war against the picturesque, a laughing in the face of exoticism].[99] In *Mirages de Paris*, Fara suffers from the denial of coevalness: both his own dreams of Parisian progress and his reception in the French capital relegate him to an imaginary past on which the primitivist overtones of a colonial exoticism can depend. Repeatedly in his African journey, Leiris also finds traces of such denial—not only in the expectations of the Western traveller, but also in the expedient African response to these very touristic expectations: at one point, the narrator decries the artificiality of exchanges, and claims that the only link between him and Dogon informants is 'une commune fausseté' [a shared duplicity], constituting what Christopher Miller might describe as 'the fog of intercultural space'.[100]

What is apparent in both of these texts—from their titles onwards—is their authors' wariness about the (to borrow Norindr's term) 'phantasmagoric' versions of elsewhere that can emerge from reliance on an exoticism that is itself dependent on an earlier tradition, drawing on recurrent tropes and stereotypes. As such, they seem to undermine the

[97] For a fuller account of Leiris's attitude to conventional exoticism, see J. Pierrot, '*L'Afrique fantôme* de Michel Leiris ou le voyage du poète de l'ethnographe', in Jean Mesnard (ed.), *Les Récits de voyage* (Paris: Nizet, 1986), 189–241.

[98] For recent readings of Leiris's account which consider the inherent contradictions of 'salvage ethnography', see R. Larson, 'Ethnography, Thievery and Cultural Identity: A Rereading of Michel Leiris's *L'Afrique fantôme*', *PMLA*, 112 (1997), 229–42, and M.-D. Shelton, 'Primitive Self. Colonial Impulses in Michel Leiris's *L'Afrique fantôme*', in E. Barkan and R. Bush (eds.), *Prehistories of the Future: The Primitivist Project and the Culture of Modernism* (Stanford, Calif.: Stanford University Press, 1995), 326–38.

[99] Leiris, *L'Afrique fantôme*, 89.

[100] Ibid. 131; Miller, *Nationalists and Nomads*, 59.

belief in authenticity and the associated desire for documentary realism
both employed by the *littérateurs coloniaux*, in their rejection of exotic
literature. Socé's text emphasizes, however, the potential reciprocity—
and even mutual incomprehension—inherent in the encounter represented by exoticism. His narrator's exoticization of metropolitan
France is echoed by Leiris's own emphasis, in a preparatory article for
the Mission Dakar-Djibouti, on the need for the traveller to be aware of
his status—and representation—as the other's other.[101] This is one of
the contemporary paradoxes of Leiris's ethnographic text, for any
academic aspirations to objectivity are eclipsed by an overwhelming
sense of subjectivity: 'écrivant subjectivement j'augmente la valeur de
mon témoignage' [writing subjectively, I add value to my account].[102]
The texts of Leiris and Socé both mark the demolition of a certain form
of exoticism dependent on superficial differences of climate, pigmentation, and landscape; in their exploration of the profoundly problematic
nature of journeys between cultures, they endeavour to point to a newly
self-reflexive understanding of travel that is focused on sustained consideration of more radical and persistent differences between cultures.

What has emerged from this chapter—and in particular from these
beginnings of a contrapuntal reading of two 1930s travel texts—are the
foundations of a new understanding of the concept of exoticism, entirely independent of Segalen's thought, since the *Essai sur l'exotisme*
was published for the first time only in 1955. The term 'exotic' is
recovered as a linguistic shifter, no longer describing a restricted series
of fixed locales and a bank of often jaded images; the notion of exoticism becomes dependent on reflexivity and reciprocity, and develops
into a potential tool for considerations of intercultural contact and of
travel itself. With this understanding of exoticism as a form of interaction or exchange, there is a further shift from the notion's pejorative
overtones of cliché and control to a potentially more complex understanding of the interaction between individual and place. There is an
emphasis on experience and in particular on the negotiation and interplay with the real and the imaginary inherent in meetings with radical
otherness. Exoticism is salvaged and reasserted not simply as a literary
theme or device, but also as a means of reading and understanding
texts; it is no longer exclusively a 'non-systematic marker of imperial

---

[101] Michel Leiris, 'L'œil de l'ethnographe. (À propos de la Mission Dakar-Djibouti)', in
Zébrages (Paris: Gallimard, 1992), 34. (First published 1930.)

[102] Leiris, *L'Afrique fantôme*, 263.

displays of power', but becomes instead a means of exploring such displays, the context from which they emerged, and the competing, contradictory yet complementary journeys to which they inevitably relate.

4

Around the World in a 2CV: Post-War French Travel Writing and the Reordering of 'Elsewhere'

[Q]uoi de plus humble, de plus domestique qu'une 2CV? L'un des sujets interviewés, au cours d'une démonstration brillante, réussit cependant à en faire une voiture sportive. [...] Les mythes sont à la fois mobiles et infinis.[1]

What is more humble, more domestic than a 2CV? Yet one of the interviewees, during a brilliant demonstration of his vehicle, managed to turn it into a sports car. [...] Myths are at the same time mobile and infinite.

IN the Musée de l'Automobile de la Sarthe, two unique vehicles are almost hidden, with little explanatory material accompanying them, among the collection of cars associated with the neighbouring Le Mans 24-hour circuit. Whereas the racing cars represent sporting endurance at home, la Scarabée d'or [The Golden Scorpion, Georges-Marie Haardt's half-track Citroën from the *Croisière jaune*] and the 2CV used by Baudot and Séguéla almost three decades later in their circumnavigation of the globe signal something very different, a chronic extroversion. Both vehicles reflect a desire for displacement that is nevertheless equally reliant in each case on French industrial innovation. This seemingly effortless juxtaposition of journeys, one inter-war, the other post-war, disguises the marked contrasts that distinguish them: the adventure—or, more accurately, official *mission*—of the Croisière jaune represents both nationalistic expansionism and commercial hubris, the latter of which would contribute to the collapse of

---

[1] Roland Barthes, 'Mythologie de l'automobile', in *Œuvres completes*, ed. Eric Marty, 3 vols. (Paris: Seuil, 1993), i. 1136–42 (p. 1141). (First published, as 'La voiture, projection de l'ego', in *Réalités*, October 1963.)

André Citroën's empire and its subsequent nationalization; the 2CV journey, a private undertaking equally reliant on early traces of the mediatization of travel, reflects instead the democratization of travel at which André Citroën himself had aimed and the ready availability of a simple but robust vehicle to those of modest means. Whilst the Croisière jaune stands for professional adventure and scientific endeavour, circumnavigation using a 2CV represents an at times foolhardy amateurism and the desire to manufacture personal exploits in the extremes of travel. With the technical, diplomatic, and financial back-up of the Croisière jaune contrasts the meagre self-sufficiency of the 2CV travellers. From the apogee of imperialism with which the Croisière was associated,[2] the culture of travel passes to the more troubled relationship with Empire and the sense of its instability that characterizes these more humble journeys beginning in the 1950s.

The Citroën croisières, not only the trans-Asian jaune but also its predecessor the trans-African noire, reflect the confidence of France returned to peacetime: the specially adapted vehicles on which they depended, using tank tracks in the place of rear wheels, harnessed recently introduced military technology for ostensibly non-military purposes. Scott Berliner, in one of the few analytical accounts of the Croisière noire, claims: 'Freed from the muck and horrors of the western front, the French sought adventure and tests of spirit in Africa. The film [of the journey] allowed all Frenchmen to live the "great adventure" vicariously.'[3] There is a need to distinguish between the two journeys, which Jacques Wolgensinger perceptively casts as 'post-war' and 'pre-war': 'Si la Croisière jaune appartient à notre temps, la Noire appartient au passé' [If the Croisière jaune belongs to our era, the Croisière noire belongs to the past].[4] For although both refer in their epithets to the pigmentation of those through whose countries they travel, the two journeys differ in their assumptions and discursive underpinnings: the African journey is marked by imperialist nostalgia, a yearning for what Christopher Miller has cast as the 'blank darkness'

---

[2] Its confident departure coincided, after all, with the Exposition de Vincennes, and the meeting of its two groups of travellers in Northern China was originally scheduled for 14 July. See Jacques Wolgensinger, *La* 2CV: *Nous nous sommes tant aimés*, Découvertes 270 (Paris: Gallimard, 1995), 137. Moreover, the journey benefited from the post-exhibition fascination with elsewhere to disseminate and publicize its findings.

[3] Berliner, *Ambivalent Desire*, 204. Léon Poirier's 1926 film of the journey, *La Croisière noire*, was subsequently and most successfully projected throughout France.

[4] Jacques Wolgensinger, 'Préface', in Fabien Sabatès, *La Croisière Noire Citroën* ([n. pl.]: Eric Baschet, 1980), 7–10 (p. 7).

of a purportedly primitive sub-Saharan continent unaffected by the disequilibrium triggered by Western intervention;[5] the Asian itinerary is similarly marked by a sense of loss, but in this context associated with the decline of civilizations that—almost in the same terms as those of Segalen's 'loi d'ascendante beauté'—have slowly degenerated to reach a final stage of post-revolutionary decay.[6] Both, however, project a heroic individualism grounded in physical endurance and a belief in the technological future of modern France, aspects that, as a result of the asymmetries generated not least by the power of the travelling Western gaze, tend to consolidate the perceived fixity of the cultures these journeys cross.[7] Yet this conventional exoticism is at the same time challenged by an emerging awareness of the implications for the field of travel inherent in the travellers' intervention: photography is seen to 'écras[er], en voulant les saisir, les impondérables de l'art' [crush the imponderable aspects of art as it attempts to grasp them], an indigenous guide is disorientated by the experience of mechanized speed, and the text concludes with a warning note of creeping entropy: 'Le vieux monde étouffe: pour conquérir l'espace, il supprime la distance—et le charme de l'inconnu' [The old world is suffocating: in order to gain mastery over space, it does away with distances—and the charm of the unknown].[8] Although there are continuities between the *croisières* and the post-war Citroën journeys on which this chapter will primarily focus—Jacques Wolgensinger alludes, for instance, to Louis Audouin-Dubreuil, Haardt's deputy on all three inter-war journeys, continuing to

---

[5] The extent of the Croisière's impact in the Belgian Congo can be seen e.g. in the reference to the rapid development of roads for its passage. See Georges-Marie Haardt and Louis Audouin-Dubreuil, *La Croisière noire: expédition Citroën Centre-Afrique* (Paris: Plon, 1927), 184. Although the official account of the journey acknowledges its intention to 'consecrate' France's civilizing mission (*La Croisière noire*, 4), it is more hesitant about the role played in André Citroën's (ultimately aborted) plans to develop a tourist infrastructure linking North and West Africa. Ho Chi Minh (in a 1923 article in *La Paria*, signed Nguyen Ai Quoc) denounced the preliminary Citroën trans-Saharan expedition (December 1922–January 1923) as a ' "chenille" civilisatrice [lancée] à travers le Sahara' [a civilizing 'caterpillar' hurled across the Sahara]. See 'Ménagerie', in Ho Chi Minh, *Textes 1914–1969*, ed. Alain Ruscio (Paris: L'Harmattan, 1990), 46–9 (pp. 47–8).

[6] See Philippe Postel, *Victor Segalen et la statuaire chinoise: archéologie et poétique*, Bibliothèque de Littérature générale et comparée, 31 (Paris: Honoré Champion, 2001), 162–64.

[7] The Croisières played a role at the same time in Anglo-French colonial rivalries. See James B. Wolf, 'Imperial Integration: The Car, the British and the Cape-to-Cairo Route', in Robert Giddings (ed.), *Literature and Imperialism* (Basingstoke: Macmillan, 1991), 112–27 (p. 115).

[8] Haardt and Audouin-Dubreuil, *La Croisière noire*, 35, 47, 315.

explore the Sahara in his 2CV in the 1950s—the world in which they travelled was a radically different one, necessitating a rapid reconfiguration of the expectations required of travellers who negotiate a way through that world.[9]

RETHINKING TRAVEL IN POST-WAR FRANCE

Before beginning the main body of this chapter, a relatively long preamble will situate within a wider conceptual frame these issues of 1950s travel and anxiety about the possibility of travel. For this, I draw on the cultural, political, and economic history of post-war France, considering in particular the intersection of decolonization and modernization (or Americanization). These are two key shifts that—as Kristin Ross has suggested in *Fast Cars, Clean Bodies*—are closely intertwined and, once considered together, mutually illuminating.[10] Moving from the Citroën-Kégresse 'autochenilles', of which 5,795 were constructed between 1920 and 1937 (although by the 1930s their use was restricted to a military one), the chapter focuses on the Citroën 2CV, a vehicle that has achieved iconic status as a mythologized signifier of what is perceived—both inside and outside France—as quintessentially French. This mythologization has occurred not least as a result of the car's recurrent representation in a series of novels, *bandes dessinées*, and films, ranging from Louis Malle's *Les Amants* (1958) to Claude Chabrol's *La Cérémonie* (1995), passing via English-language productions such as *American Graffiti* (1973), *For Your Eyes Only* (1981), and *Indecent Proposal* (1992). Discussing the symbolic value of the car in relation to national identity, Len Holden reiterates the now standard comparison of the sophisticated DS with the utilitarian 2CV, claiming that the latter:

symbolises an entirely different aspect of Gallic culture—the plain simplicity of style in a populist and cheap vehicle. The 'deux chevaux' is a car that represents the values of the alternative; the Left Bank (Rive Gauche), the bereted and corduroyed artist with his bottle of *vin de table* and French stick. The romance of the poverty stricken artist. Style without affluence.[11]

---

[9] See Wolgensinger, 'Préface', 9.

[10] See Kristin Ross, *Fast Cars, Clean Bodies: Decolonization and the Reordering of French Culture* (Cambridge, Mass.: MIT Press, 1995).

[11] Len Holden, 'More than a Marque. The Car as Symbol: Aspects of Culture and Ideology', in David Thoms, Len Holden, and Tim Claydon (eds.), *The Motor Car and Popular Culture in the 20th Century* (Aldershot: Ashgate, 1998), 28–40 (p. 35).

This external, widely disseminated perception, elements of which are shared by French attitudes towards the vehicle, was shored up by Citroën's sophisticated marketing department that progressively underlined the car's counter-cultural overtones and its associations with creativity, austerity, and a degree of levity.

The myth of the 2CV is, however, a complex one. Although Barthes's vehicle of choice in *Mythologies* is its sleek, rapid, and futuristic antithesis, the Citroën DS, it is to the 2CV that he turns in a lesser-known text from 1963, 'Mythologie de l'automobile', part of which is cited as this chapter's epigraph. Designed for domestic and primarily rural journeys,[12] the vehicle became rapidly associated with an urban counterculture as well as a younger generation's actual flight from France; seen in gendered terms as a women's car (contrasted with the masculine DS), it nevertheless became a vehicle for the attempted reinvigoration of post-war French male identity; criticized at its launch for its functional ugliness, a refutation of Ilya Ehrenburg's claim that the 'poor, but vainglorious' French 'would put up with a feeble engine, but not ugly proportions', the car was soon presented as 'a serious attempt to poeticize the everyday'.[13] This chapter is, therefore, the study of a domestic myth, the Citroën 2CV, a vehicle whose mythologization was actively encouraged by its manufacturer. Humble, austere, economical, 'domestique', it is these qualities that made the 2CV a popular car at home and contributed to its exoticism abroad. Developing Barthes's final comment in this chapter's epigraph, however—'les mythes sont à la fois mobiles et infinis'—the chapter will explore not the introverted domesticity but the extroverted mobility of the 2CV, underlining its emblematic role in a series of important shifts regarding attitudes to national identity and cultural diversity occurring in France in the long decade of the 1950s, stretching from the Liberation in 1944 to the Evian Accords in 1962.[14]

As one of the first mass-produced and relatively inexpensive cars on the French market, the 2CV primarily reflects in French national terms the pan-European democratization of motoring in 1950s and 1960s

---

[12] Patrick Keiller claims, for example, that the 2CV 'did not offer the [...] long-distance travel possibilities that came to be expected of the car in the post-war era'. See 'Sexual Ambiguity and Automotive Engineering', in Peter Wollen and Joe Kerr (eds.), *Autopia: Cars and Culture* (London: Reaktion, 2002), 342–53 (p. 349).

[13] See Ilya Ehrenburg, *The Life of the Automobile*, trans. Joachim Neugroschel (London: Pluto, 1985 [1929]), 27, and Keiller, 'Sexual Ambiguity and Automotive Engineering', 345.

[14] On the 1950s, see Susan Weiner (ed.), 'The French Fifties', *Yale French Studies*, 98 (2000).

France, and the reconfiguration of everyday, domestic journeys that this allowed.[15] For the 2CV was designed by Pierre Boulanger as a 'voiture-outil de travail' [car-as-tool], a utilitarian vehicle in whose production considerations of aesthetics and speed gave way to the primacy of economy and efficiency. Boulanger summed up this objective—'L'esthé-tique et la vitesse, je ne veux pas en entendre parler' [I want to hear no talk of aesthetics and speed].[16] With development disrupted in 1939 by the outbreak of war, production could only begin ten years later, on a very modest scale and with the sparse materials available in a carefully planned post-war economy. Although the Pons Plan privileged manu-facturers who concentrated on commercial vehicles and smaller private cars, by this time the 2CV looked outmoded in relation not only to American cars (slowly permeating national consciousness, especially through their representation in popular culture), but also to its nearest rival, the Renault 4CV. In a climate of post-war austerity, however, practicality and efficiency won over pragmatic French consumers, and production leapt from 876 in 1949 to 16,288 in 1951, rising steadily every year to reach a peak of nearly 250,000 in 1964. A contemporary commentator sums up how the vehicle managed to encapsulate the *esprit du temps* of the late 1940s:

La 2CV n'est pas une signe extérieure de richesse; ses propriétaires n'en tireront pas davantage vanité que d'un instrument de travail quelconque, d'une machine à écrire ou d'un bureau. La 2CV n'éveillera ni la fierté ni l'orgueil de son propriétaire, ni sa honte non plus. Moyenne, médiocre d'apparence, elle s'insère à la perfection dans notre époque.[17]

The 2CV is not an exterior sign of wealth; its owners will gain no more status from it than they would from any utilitarian object such as a typewriter or a desk. The 2CV will not awaken in its owner any sense of pride or any shame. An average vehicle with a mediocre appearance, it fits perfectly into our period.

---

[15] The Citroën 2CV is accordingly to be interpreted as part of a wider automotive history that includes other vehicles such as the British Austin Mini and the German Volkswagen Beetle.

[16] Quoted by Wolgensinger, *La 2CV*, 21. The car's 1948 British reviewer in *Autocar* claimed: 'The designer has kissed the lash of austerity with almost masochistic fervour', and a second road tester, in *The Motor*, added in 1953 (several years after production had begun) that this was a 'vehicle with almost every virtue except speed, silence and good looks'. Quoted in Matt White, *Citroën 2CV: the Complete Story* (Ramsbury: Crowood Press, 1999), 50.

[17] *Revue automobile suisse*, 14 October 1948. Quoted in Jean-Louis Loubet, *Histoire de l'automobile française* (Paris: Seuil, 2001), 256.

So popular was the car that on its official launch in 1949, potential owners had to apply for a vehicle. With a three-year waiting list, which was alleviated only once production increased in the 1950s, there was even prioritized distribution according to the applicant's profession.[18]

The popularity was despite (and, at the same time, because of) a number of objections: the car had a low maximum speed (and hence a low fuel consumption), its coachwork was slab-sided (and hence easy to repair), its finish was uniformly grey (and hence easy to touch in). The original designer's remit—supposedly triggered by a moment of illumination in the trying terrain of the Massif Central—reflects this stark simplicity and utilitarian nature: it was to be powerful enough to carry 'deux cultivateurs en sabots, 50 kg de pommes de terre ou un tonnelet' [two farmers in clogs, a sack of potatoes, and a barrel], rugged enough to 'transporter à travers un champ labouré un panier d'œufs sans les casser' [carry a basket of eggs over a ploughed field without breaking them].[19] The car's affordability and adaptability led the largely unstudied group of travel writers with whom this chapter is concerned to test these capacities far from the rural France for which it had originally been designed. Before addressing this particular strand of 1950s and 1960s French travel, however, there is a need to recognize other journeys, for the itineraries of the 2CV travellers across and between continents depended on other, preceding journeys, those of thousands of immigrants (many from North and West Africa) drawn to what was then perceived as mainland France by the car manufacturers' need for cheap and abundant labour at a time of demographic deficit and rapid economic growth. Affordable motoring depended above all on both an affordable workforce and an accelerated shift to the working practices associated with Fordism.[20] The 2CV contributed to the rapid motorization and mobilization of rural France, and there is still a history of this vehicle to be written similar to that produced about the Model T Ford and its impact on grass-roots America by Henry Wik.[21]

The 2CV was accordingly—and, for some perhaps, improbably— part of the 'Speed Revolution', the progressive replacement of slower

---

[18] Priority professions included farmers, nurses, midwives, country priests, doctors, and vets. See Loubet, *Histoire de l'automobile française*, 279.

[19] Wolgensinger, *La 2CV*, 21, and Bob MacQueen and Julian McNamara, *The Life and Times of the 2CV* (Cambridge: Great Ouse, 1982), 8.

[20] See Yamina Benguigui, *Mémoires d'immigrés* (Paris: Pocket, 2000 [1997]), 15–22.

[21] Henry Wik, *Henry Ford and Grass-Roots America* (Ann Arbor: University of Michigan Press, 1972).

local cultures by an accelerated global monoculture.[22] In the French case, the car was central to the democratization of speed (albeit of relative speed). As Edgar Morin makes clear in *Commune en France*, mechanized transport and the freedom it allowed were increasingly available to women, the young, and those of more modest means.[23] What this discourse of confident modernization *at best* treats as independent or *at worst* simply spirits away, however, are the conditions of production and their implications. Susan George has coined the phrase 'fast castes' to imply that those with the greatest prestige, wealth, and power also have access to the highest velocities.[24] By extension, speed can be seen as a tool of social analysis alongside the traditional trio of ethnicity, class, and gender, in other words as 'a vehicle which allows us to explore the complex ways in which different phenomena interact, without becoming frustrated by the constraints imposed by some forms of cultural analysis'.[25] French car workers created speed for others, whilst their own slowness was perpetuated; in Kristin Ross's terms, 'France made use of her colonies "one last time" in order to resurrect or maintain its national superiority over them—a superiority made all the more urgent by the ex-colonies' own newly acquired nationhood'.[26]

The car workers on whom 2CV production depended created the means of speed and mobility for others, therefore, without having access to them themselves. The accounts of their journeys to, from, and within France remain, for the most part, unwritten, although scattered traces are available. Claire Etcherelli's 1967 novel *Élise ou la vraie vie* offers a fictional account of an Algerian car worker in late 1950s Paris and, more recently, Yamina Benguigui's 1997 documentary *Mémoires d'immigrés* salvages traces of this often occluded aspect of

[22] On this subject, see Jeremy Millar and Michiel Schwartz, 'Introduction—Speed is a Vehicle', in *Speed: Visions of an Accelerated Age* (London: The Photographers' Gallery; Whitechapel Art Gallery, 1998), 16–21.

[23] See Edgar Morin, *Commune en France: la métamorphose de Plozevet* (Paris: Fayard, 1967), 376–8.

[24] See Susan George, 'Fast Castes', in Millar and Schwartz (eds.), *Speed: Visions of an Accelerated Age*, 115–18.

[25] Miller and Schwartz, 'Introduction—Speed is a Vehicle', 17.

[26] Ross, *Fast Cars, Clean Bodies*, 9. For a concrete illustration of this idea, see Robert Linhart, *L'Etabli* (Paris: Minuit, 1978), p. 66: '[Notre agent de secteur] est, comme c'est souvent le cas, un ancien militaire colonial qui a pris sa retraite à l'armée et du service chez Citroën. Alcoolique rougeaud, il traite les immigrés comme des indigènes du bon vieux temps: avec mépris et haine' [the administrator of our area, as is often the case, is a former colonial soldier who has retired from the army and taken a job with Citroën. A ruddy-cheeked alcoholic, he treats immigrants like he used to treat the natives: with contempt and hatred].

recent French history.[27] However, it is Robert Linhart's 1978 text *L'Établi*, recounting his experience in the Citroën factory at Choisy in the immediate post-May 1968 period, that is of particular interest. In this text is a stark account of the human cost specifically of 2CV production. Linhart, a Maoist *normalien*, provides a case study account of the Gauche Prolétarienne's strategy of *établissement*, as he enters (almost as a *voyageur clandestin* or stowaway) and politicizes a world of work traditionally closed to the young intellectual.[28] By gaining access in this way to what Marguerite Duras called, in her *Libération* review of the book, 'les divers ateliers de la section *des charmantes, universellement délicieuses* 2CV *Citroën*' [the various workshops of *the charming, universally loved Citroën* 2CV*'s* department] (my emphasis), he manages to subvert the official image of the car at a time when production—already at over 200,000 vehicles a year—had not yet reached a peak.[29] In a text reminiscent of Céline's accounts of the Ford factory forty years earlier, Linhart describes the humiliating selection procedure of workers and the company's racist recruitment policies that, taking no account of individual experience, automatically treat the French as semi-skilled workers (OS2) and African immigrants as unskilled (M1 or M2). The smell, sound, and overwhelming greyness of the production line so dominates his life that 2CVs begin to fill his nightmares.

Linhart's account serves as a corrective. It forces the reader not only to reassess the mythology of the 2CV, but also (and by association) to rethink the definitions of travel and adventure with which by the late 1960s it was closely and customarily associated. Implicit in the text are the thousands of individual journeys to and from France undertaken by the author's displaced co-workers. Such an approach inevitably illuminates the context for the travel accounts to which this vehicle is central, whilst at the same time offering a violent reversal of the official versions of the car, projected by its manufacturer and dominating most of the literature devoted to the 2CV. For 'travel', in the post-war period, began to become a consciously contested concept whose instability was caused in particular by the emergence of competing narratives of displacement from the contexts of decolonization. In his

---

[27] See Etcherelli, *Élise ou la vraie vie*, and, e.g., the account of the Tunisian worker Khémaïs's forty years' service at Renault, in Benguigui, *Mémoires d'immigrés*, 23–33.

[28] For an account of *établissement*, see Virginie Linhart, *Volontaires pour l'usine: vie d'établies 1967–1977* (Paris: Seuil, 1994).

[29] The relevant section of Duras's review is available at <http://www.liberation.com/livres/25ans/jankelevitch.html> (accessed 17 March 2004).

important essay, 'Traveling Cultures', James Clifford writes in relation to this prizing open of the notion of travel: 'if contemporary migrant populations are not to appear as mute, passive straws in the political-economic winds, we need to listen to a wide range of "travel stories" (not "travel literature" in the bourgeois sense)'.[30]

Without developing an explicitly contrapuntal reading of these journeys to and from the metropolitan centre, which would be beyond the scope of this chapter, it is nevertheless with both these 'travel stories' and a comparatist sensitivity in mind that the corpus of 2CV travel accounts is approached. For this influx of guest workers not only emphasizes the complex field of travel in which post-war travellers journeyed, criss-crossed by complementary trajectories that were forced to coexist whether those undertaking them acknowledged this or not; it also highlights the often hidden ideological backcloth to the travel writing under consideration, and points to the major reordering of 'home' and 'elsewhere' rapidly triggered by decolonization and accelerated by the former colonies' independence. The 1950s witnessed the consolidation of a soon-to-be post-colonial literature in French produced by Francophone authors whose point of origin was outside France. It is significant that a number of these—such as Ousmane Sembene and Camara Laye—were employed in car factories. More striking than this biographical detail, however, is the predominant interest in travel, and in particular travel to and in France itself, that characterizes much of this 1950s literature written in the period of rapid decolonization. Emblematic of this emphasis is the work of Bernard Dadié, whose 1959 'novel' *Un nègre à Paris* makes explicit what was implicit in a series of earlier texts: henceforth, not only was France a legitimate object of the ethnographic or travelling gaze, but also those doing the travelling or gazing would increasingly be former colonial subjects, asserting their will to write back.[31] This is a direct challenge to the literary conceit on which *Les Lettres persanes*, the text to which Dadié's narrative is customarily and often patronizingly compared, depends.[32] In Elisabeth Mudimbe-Boyi's terms, Dadié's text

---

[30] Clifford, 'Traveling Cultures', 38.

[31] For a study of the central role of travel in post-war French-language literature from outside France, see Mortimer, *Journeys through the French African Novel*. Dadié wrote two other travel narratives recording journeys, respectively, to Rome and New York: *La Ville où nul ne meurt* (Paris: Présence Africaine, 1968) and *Patron de New York* (Paris: Présence Africaine, 1969).

[32] For such an intertextual reading, see e.g. Jean Dérive, '*Un nègre à Paris*: intertexte et contexte', *Komparatistische Hefte*, 15–16 (1987), 177–95.

makes an assertion echoed in a few other contemporary travel narratives such as Édouard Glissant's *Soleil de la Conscience*: 'The narrative techniques adopted by the author of *Un Nègre à Paris* are essentially irony and humour. Behind the tame and ironic tone of this travel narrative, however, there is a subtext that projects a vision of the West that no longer originates within the West, but comes from elsewhere and discloses the West as an Other.'[33]

The need to reassess post-war French culture and history in the light of postcolonial considerations is evidently not restricted to the definitions and practices of travel. As Kristin Ross has made clear, commodities and cultural artefacts must also be situated in relation to the twin historiographical discourses of modernization and decolonization. These can no longer be seen as separate and geographically limited, the first linked with France, the second with a conveniently dislocated 'elsewhere'. Had Pierre Nora selected the 2 CV as a 'lieu de mémoire', its status as a site of collective and individual memory and counter-memory would have proved a rich subject of inquiry. Had, in addition, such an article followed the pattern of other contributions to this monumental work, it is unlikely that the full implications of the car's complex production history—i.e. the backcloth hidden by its mythical status—would have been fully teased out. For Nora's concept of Frenchness is nation-centred, tied closely to the geography of the Hexagon; there is only a fleeting recognition of the role played by colonial expansion in the formation of national and Republican identity.[34] In this way, Nora's volumes reflect trends that have until recently dominated French historiographical and commemorative practice. Certain aspects of twentieth-century colonial history—the 1931 Exposition coloniale at Vincennes (explored in the previous chapter), the massacre of North African demonstrators by the Parisian police on 17 October 1961, the independence won by Algeria in 1962—have been remembered in France only reluctantly, with attempts at commemoration (or, perhaps more accurately, recovery from amnesia) marked with controversy that

---

[33] Elisabeth Mudimbe-Boyi, 'Travel, Representation, and Difference, or How Can One Be a Parisian?', *Research in African Literatures*, 23/3 (1992), 25–39 (p. 31). See also Michael Syrotinski, ' "When in Rome …": Irony and Subversion in Bernard Dadié's Travel-Writing', *The Journal of African Travel Writing*, 7 (1999), 66–79.

[34] On this subject, see Richard L. Derderian, 'Algeria as a lieu de mémoire: Ethnic Minority Memory and National Identity in Contemporary France'. *Radical History Review*, 83 (2002), 28–43, and Hue-Tam Ho Tai, 'Remembered Realms: Pierre Nora and French National Memory', *History Cooperative*, 106/3 (2001), 38 pars. (http://www.historycooperative.org/journals/ahr/106.3/ah000906.html, accessed 1 Nov. 2004).

has been presented by some commentators as being the result of an active suppression of colonial memory.[35] These uneven processes of recollection and amnesia are symptomatic of more general questions relating not only to contemporary France and other French-speaking cultures, but also to the ways in which knowledge about them is constructed.[36] In the wake of the French Empire there remains a complex network of French-speaking (or, in certain cases, partially French-speaking) regions, countries, and communities that together form a loosely-bounded francophone space; the study of the various journeys taking place within this space, creating uneven connections and uneasy alliances, is central to our understanding of it.

With Citroën preparing to open a *conservatoire* to house its archives, there is a possibility that the company's role in and contribution to this alternative history may begin to emerge in a more sustained manner. Understandings of the 2CV may move beyond the comprehensive insider and occasionally hagiographic view of its official historian, Jacques Wolgensinger. As has been explained above, a now commonplace reflection on Nora's construction of the 'lieu de mémoire' concerns the geographically limited—and limiting—version of Frenchness it perpetuates. Like any other dynamic or colonizing culture, France has always been a site of transit and exchange; however desirable a clean-break settlement may have seemed in the context of inevitable decolonization, Empire did not come to an abrupt and tidy end in 1962. The end of the Algerian War did not permit sudden autonomy and self-sufficiency for the former colonizer, but led instead to the transformation of France into an increasingly porous, dynamic postcolonial space—in Clifford's terms, a 'traveling culture'—in which the consequences of Empire would become increasingly apparent: France's history and culture were no longer its own, or, more accurately, there was (and there remains) an urgent need to renegotiate the definitions of 'Frenchness', to re-explore those objects, concepts, and sites through which this is customarily freighted. Which brings attention back to the 2CV.

Seen solely in the light of French industrial history, the car reflects the growing prosperity and mobility with which the 'Trente Glorieuses' are

---

[35] Anne Donadey, ' "Une certaine idée de la France": the Algeria Syndrome and Struggles over "French" Identity', in Steven Ungar and Tom Conley (eds.), *Identity Papers: Contested Nationhood in Twentieth-Century France* (Minneapolis: University of Minnesota Press, 1996), 215–32.

[36] See Pierre Tévanian, *Le Racisme républicain: réflexions sur le modèle français de discrimination* (Paris: L'Esprit frappeur, 2001), 109–33.

characterized.[37] It is not by chance, for instance, that the dust jacket of Edgar Morin's *Commune en France*, his 1960s study of the transformation of a marginal Breton community, shows a coiffe-wearing *bigoudenne* filling her 2CV with fuel. Here is a striking image of the traditional interacting with the modern, resulting in the hybridized situation of this contemporary rural community. Yet the modernity of the 2CV remains relative, as both Roland Barthes and Jean Rouaud have made clear in their comparisons of Citroën's extremes of luxury and utility, the DS and the 2CV, comparisons which seem to deny the two vehicles' coevalness and even to relegate the latter to the sphere of artisanal, proto-industrial austerity.[38] The 2CV is an overdetermined object, a site of competing discourses, which Barthes claims is the only French vehicle truly to attain mythologized status: 'tout le parc français semble ainsi se réduire à une opposition signifiante entre la 2CV et "le reste": "reste" dans lequel les sujets n'éprouvent nul besoin, en dépit des différences de prix, d'introduire des différences de signes, c'est-à-dire de standing' [French cars thus seem to be reduced to a meaningful opposition between the 2CV and 'the rest'—and as far as 'the rest' are concerned, there appears to be no need, despite price differences, to introduce symbolic differences relating to standard of living].[39] Citroën actively capitalized on this singular character that Barthes identified, and en-sured—through forthright advertising and the adoption of the slogan: 'Plus qu'une voiture, c'est un style de vie' [More than a car, it's a lifestyle]—the consolidation of a 'mythe 2CV'. In 1962, a 32-page colour brochure about the vehicle, entitled *Liberté*, was published, launching a publicity campaign masterminded by a team devoted to the 'défense et illustration de la 2CV'.[40]

What are missing from considerations of the car as a purely domestic myth or as a commercial object, however, are traces of its lived context, of the overlapping and asymmetrical journeys I have outlined above. As an icon, the 2CV has been included in the history of France's transition from imperial power to postcolonial state: forced to leave Laos in 1961, for instance, the expat Jacques Pochon-Davignon drove to France over-land with his family in a 2CV van in what has been transformed into an

---

[37] On this period of post-war prosperity, see Jean Fourastié, *Les Trente Glorieuses: ou, La Révolution invisible de 1946 à 1975* (Paris: Fayard, 1979).

[38] See Roland Barthes, 'La nouvelle Citroën', in *Mythologies* (Paris: Seuil, 1957), 150–2, and Jean Rouaud, *Les Champs d'Honneur* (Paris: Minuit, 1990), 32–6.

[39] Barthes, 'Mythologie de l'automobile', 1137.

[40] See Wolgensinger, *La 2CV*, 41–3.

emblematic journey of return;[41] and yet as Baudot and Séguéla discover in Cambodia, the car is also one of the signifiers of a persistently residual French culture in the former colonies.[42] Both of these examples contribute to the 2CV myth, transforming the car into a privileged vehicle of Frenchness. What emerges from the 'travel stories' of car workers, or from the accounts of 2CV journeys is what David Miller has described, in a seemingly paradoxical phrase, the 'humanity of the car'—i.e. the extent to which the vehicle has become an integral element of the cultural environment according to which we define ourselves as human.[43] This is an aspect ignored by much secondary literature relating to the vehicle, which seems to perpetuate a perceived dualism of, on the one hand, science or technology, and, on the other, nature, accordingly eschewing the sociological or anthropological approaches from which studies of food, clothing, and the house have benefited.[44] As Miller makes clear, literature on the car seems to fall into two principal categories: either abstract histories of automobile production and design, or transport studies that focus on the vehicle's consequences. To these I would add works particularly common for vehicles (such as the 2CV) that have achieved cult status: amateur histories in which an enthusiasm for often-recycled detail overshadows any rigour of analysis.

Whether literature on the car demonizes or fetishizes, whether it treats the car as a statistical abstraction or as a myth, what often remains absent is any analysis of the way in which humans interact with vehicles—as drivers, passengers, or workers—of the way in which vehicles shape individual lives: i.e. Miller's 'humanity of the car'. Kristin Ross's *Fast Cars, Clean Bodies* is a notable exception to this rule, and Miller omits to mention it in his study. Ross includes the automobile in her study of those major consumer durables that reflect important changes in individual lives. In the rest of this chapter, which, for reasons that will become apparent when the practical conditions of 2CV travel are considered, might have been subtitled: 'Slow Cars, Dirty Bodies', the intention is precisely to include the driver or traveller in the social history of the car, to consider how those journeys undertaken cast light

---

[41] Ibid. 50.

[42] Jean-Claude Baudot and Jacques Séguéla, *La Terre en rond* (Paris: Flammarion, 1960), 200. (The journey was undertaken: 9 October 1958–11 November 1959.)

[43] Daniel Miller, 'Driven Societies', in Daniel Miller (ed.), *Car Cultures* (Oxford: Berg, 2001), 1–33 (p. 2).

[44] There are, of course, notable exceptions such as Wolfgang Sachs, *The Love of the Automobile: Looking Back in the History of our Desires*, trans. Don Reneau (Berkeley: University of California Press, 1992).

on the complex field of post-war travel—and of identities freighted through that travel.

RUGGED SIMPLICITY, ABUSE, AND NEGLECT: THE 2CV AROUND THE WORLD

It was what some perceived as the disadvantages of the 2CV's mechanical austerity, combined with its low price, that made the vehicle particularly suited to post-war travel. A water-cooled engine tested in prototypes could not start below 5 °C, whereas the eventual air-cooled system was suitable for temperature extremes; its lightness—and capacity, in extreme situations, to be dismantled and carried—was appropriate for a range of difficult terrains; its low fuel consumption allowed access to areas not yet serviced by petrol stations. The only major difficulty was the vehicle's low power—the earliest models had only a 375cc engine—which made mountain climbing extremely difficult. A 1949 British reviewer in *Motor* summed up these (dis)advantages, hinting already at the car's future status as world traveller and praising 'that rugged simplicity of mechanical and electrical detail that will allow it to withstand extremes of abuse and neglect in any part of the world'.[45] In other words, this was an affordable vehicle that could transport those willing to tolerate a degree of discomfort to areas hitherto inaccessible to them.

It is significant that such a car should become available in the immediate post-war period, for it becomes a symptom of and response to two crises—both identified by Lévi-Strauss in the opening chapter of *Tristes tropiques*—characterizing that moment: crises of travel and of masculinity.[46] The anthropologist's text is a paradoxical one: a rejection of travel literature that ultimately belongs to that hazy genre, and an account of the end of travel that takes a series of journeys as its structuring device. Lévi-Strauss's entropic vision of global diversity drifting inexorably towards monoculture—a restatement of the decline already prophesied by Chateaubriand, Loti, Segalen, and others—continues to encapsulate the sense of immediacy and perishability that characterizes salvage exoticism, the desire to see and capture difference

---

[45] The review appeared on 19 October 1949. Quoted in R. M. Clarke (ed.), *Citroën 2CV Gold Portfolio: 1949–1989* (Cobham: Brookland Books, [n.d.]), 5.

[46] See Claude Lévi-Strauss, *Tristes tropiques* (Paris: Plon, 1955), 35–44.

before it is engulfed by sameness. In the post-war period, it was the 2CV that allowed the final access for which each generation seems to long. Lévi-Strauss acknowledges this situation, identifying the vogue for a 1950s travel literature that provides 'les épices morales dont notre société éprouve un besoin plus aigu en se sentant sombrer dans l'ennui' [the moral spices of which our society feels an increasing need as it is conscious of sinking further into boredom].[47] Seeking an anthropological explanation for what he perceives as a gratuitous phenomenon—for these are not authentically '*vrais* voyages' with some commercial or scientific purpose—he identifies elements of a rite of passage, of a need for young travellers to return 'nanti[s] d'un pouvoir' [endowed with a power] that they would otherwise be unable to possess.[48]

Seen in these terms, the post-war scramble for otherness emerges in part at least from a post-war crisis of masculinity, and the 2CV, far from being the feminized vehicle it is often assumed to be, becomes the vehicle for self-projection or self-performance to which Barthes alludes in his 1963 essay 'Mythologie de l'automobile'. Affordable motoring offered not only to activate the full impact of those 1936 Front Populaire reforms to legislation regulating leisure, the logical development of which had been stalled by war; it also put individuality back into travel at a moment when such a possibility of mass tourism began to emerge, and offered to rejuvenate an exhausted and confused masculinity in a post-war and increasingly post-imperial era. As the historian Eric Leed has suggested in *The Mind of the Traveler*, travel can be seen as a 'gendering activity', motion as a masculinized practice that allows men to achieve distinction through self-defining experience away from home.[49] The draft of a 1948 publicity brochure, ultimately deemed too austere, warned potential purchasers: 'La 2CV n'est pas une voiture pour faire le jeune homme' [the 2CV is not the car in which to act the young man],[50] but the vehicle permitted the construction of young masculinity in other ways. In his road texts, Kerouac examined what Sidonie Smith has dubbed the 'unmanning of America returned to peacetime', and attempted to write new narratives of masculinity.[51]

---

[47] Ibid. 37; *Tristes tropiques*, trans. John and Doreen Weightman (London: Cape, 1973), 38.
[48] Lévi-Strauss, *Tristes tropiques*, 42, 40; trans. Weightman, 43, 41.
[49] See Leed, *The Mind of the Traveler*.
[50] Quoted by Wolgensinger, *La 2CV*, 34.
[51] See Smith, *Moving Lives*, 177.

The timid US journeys of 2CV travellers suggest that their planned trajectories had no equally subversive, unruly intent, nor were they on a par with the angst-ridden mobility of James Dean. However, their trigger was similar, and related to a need to salvage masculinity from domestic repetition: in the narrative of his second journey, Jacques Cornet justifies his departure: 'la vie sédentaire pesait' [sedentariness was weighing me down], and the fear of emasculation by bandits in Guy Viau's *Tour d'Afrique* seems to be related to a more general fear of unmanning that underpins and inspires the whole journey.[52] That this need for self-assertion might be associated with a wider crisis of national uncertainty can be seen in the constantly asserted Frenchness of the 2CV journey: the point of departure is often Parisian—the square of Notre-Dame, for example, for Cornet's two journeys, the first of which began on 8 May 1953, the eighth anniversary of VE Day; and the choice of vehicle is often presented chauvinistically: 'une initiative française réalisée avec du matériel français' [a French initiative made with French materials].[53]

The small corpus of texts on which the remainder of this chapter will focus represents only part of a wider, sub-generic category that emerged, with its own conventions and favoured practitioners, to characterize a certain type of French travel writing in the immediate post-war period. What may be dubbed the 'récit de voyage en 2CV' [Citroën 2CV travelogue] was launched by two texts in 1954: *Deux hommes, 2CV, deux continents* and *En 2CV vers les hauts lieux de l'Asie*.[54] Both these accounts, subverting the utilitarian and domestic purposes of

---

[52] Jacques Cornet, *Deux hommes, 2CV, en Asie* (Lyons: Jacques Cornet, 1957), 11 (the journey was undertaken: 2 August 1956–19 April 1957), and Guy Viau, *Le Tour d'Afrique en 2CV de quatre jeunes Français* (Paris: Amiot-Dumont, 1956), 85 (the journey was undertaken: 22 November 1953–9 June 1954). There are, to the best of my knowledge, only two 1960s texts by women travellers that contribute to this sub-genre of travel narratives: Marthe Broutelle, *Paris–Cap Nord en 2CV* ([n.pl.]: Scorpion, 1965), and Caroline Gazaï and Geneviève Gaillet, *Vacances en Iran* ([n.pl]: Berger-Levrault, 1961). A rare (and much later) British contribution to the sub-genre by Nicola Earwaker—*Travels with a 2CV: An Epic Journey by Citroën 2CV from London to Karachi* (London: Javelin Books, 1988)—is the account of a journey by a married couple and belongs to a later period when the vehicle, with rapidly declining production, was becoming an antiquated, cult object.

[53] Viau, *Le Tour d'Afrique en 2CV*, 9.

[54] Jacques Cornet and Henri Lochon, *Deux hommes, 2CV, deux continents* (Paris: Pierre Horay, 1954) (the journey was undertaken: 8 May 1953–10 May 1954), and Robert Godet, *En 2CV vers les hauts lieux de l'Asie* (Paris: Amiot-Dumont, 1954) (dates of journey unknown).

their vehicle of choice, were based on ambitious motorized journeys undertaken over the previous year. Theirs were the first published traces of this as yet largely unstudied phenomenon, which seems to have begun with a circumnavigation of the Mediterranean by Michel Bernier and Jacques Huguier in 1952—13,588 km in 37 days—to develop over the following two decades into a national obsession.[55] It was only the progressive institutionalization and corporate control of these journeys (transformed by Citroën into mass *raïds* [motorized treks] in the early 1970s), coupled with other more radical changes in the practices of tourism, that led to the demise of transcontinental and intercontinental travel in the 2CV. The solitary, pioneering journeys of Cornet and Lochon, who had managed their exploits with minimal technical support, few financial resources, and little regard for speed, would— despite their relative proximity in time—be viewed with nostalgia and envied for their privileged access to a rapidly disappearing world.

There was, of course, nothing new in this envious retrospection. As this study has explained, a recurrent link between generations of twentieth-century travel writers is the announcement, yet simultaneous deferral, of the collapse of elsewhere. It was nostalgia for an earlier mode of travel, emerging from a post-war fear of the entropic decline of cultural diversity, that had triggered the first 2CV journeys themselves and, more importantly, suggested this choice of a means of transport. In a history of Citroën's contribution to French automobile travel, the 2CV journey may be situated at a transitional moment between two poles: on the one hand, the Croisières noire and jaune of the 1920s and 1930s, and, on the other, the already mentioned *raïds* of the early 1970s.[56] The military overtones of the nomenclature applied to both of these suggest the aggressive assertion of national or corporate identity underpinning them. Despite their scientific and ethnographic objectives, the croisières across Africa and Central Asia coincided with the heyday of French colonial propaganda and served to showcase French technology in an international frame. The croisière noire, reminiscent in many respects (down to the detail of the leader Haardt's little white dog, Flossie) of the near contemporary *Tintin au Congo*,[57] presents Africa as a deregulated space in which one of the travellers' principal activities remained enthusiastic hunting; the later *raïds*, openly sporting and

---

[55] For an account of Bernier and Huguier's journey, see Wolgensinger, *La 2CV*, 48.

[56] On the latter, see ibid. 54–60.

[57] This point is made in Sabatès, *La Croisière noire Citroën*, 8.

dependent on careful planning and thorough support mechanisms, had more commercial objectives linked ultimately to corporate publicity. They emphasized collective speed over individual endeavour, and were as such precursory to the contemporary Paris–Dakar road race, during which, in Jacques Meunier's terms, time and space are erased as Africa is not seen, but viewed through a windscreen that is little more than a monitor.[58]

The early 2CV travellers were certainly inspired by the Croisières (and references to them pepper their accounts), but the motivations behind their choice of vehicle were very different. The conquest of geographical space in the 1920s and 1930s was allied to mechanical progress in terms of power and speed, and contemporary critics, such as Saint-Pol-Roux, were already aware of the implications of this for the traveller's relationship to their journey. As Paul Virilio's work has made clear, with the improvement of mechanized transport and the expansion of mass tourism, this analysis was well founded. Yet the 2CV journeys of the 1950s are situated in-between. Neither part of corporate or national identity projection nor a direct reflection of shifts in the leisure industry, they suggest a desire for individualism that depends on the greater flexibility and accessibility a personal car allowed. Young travellers of modest means, hitherto restricted to the railway, bicycle, or foot, could now escape from the reduced distances or narrowly defined itineraries these imposed. The 2CV journeys rely on figures of ascension or extremity, as the car is taken to previously unattained heights, driven over improbable distances (including, in Cornet and Lochon's first account, from Canada to Tierra del Fuego, or, in Baudot and Séguéla's account, around the world), forced to reach previously inaccessible locales. What is striking in each account is the lack of mechanical adaptation. The vehicles used are *voitures de série* [production line vehicles], the implication being that this is an anti-aristocratic activity, open to all. Such democratization of adventure carried the seeds of its own demise, for a steady increase in 2CV travel led to its rapid banalization. What begins in the 1950s as a common topos of auto-referentiality—the few initial 2CV travel writers discover rare traces of each other on their respective journeys—had become, by the 1960s, a trend

---

[58] See Jacques Meunier, 'Paris–Dakar', in *Le Monocle de Joseph Conrad* (Paris: La Découverte, 1987), 116–19 (pp. 116–17). See also Alain Buisine, 'Nuages de poussière dans le Paris–Dakar', in *L'Orient voilé* (Cadeilhan: Zulma, 1993), 15–18, and David Le Breton, *Passions du risque* (Paris: Métailié, 1991), 158–61.

in which self-distinction was impossible.[59] Citroën's inauguration of the *Prix du tour du monde en 2CV* in 1957 not only reflected the increasing number of departures, but also, by further increasing popularity, inevitably contributed to the genre's demise.

READING THE 2CV JOURNEY NARRATIVE

The corpus of early texts represents a discrete sub-genre in its own right, with its own stars and its own conventions, some of which (preparation, focus on indigenous reaction, the 'rite' of passing customs) are shared with travel writing in general, others of which are more specific. The texts are all perhaps strictly speaking travel writing as opposed to travel literature. By this, it is suggested not only that they have a primarily documentary purpose—far removed, for instance from an equivalent Swiss text, Nicolas Bouvier's *L'Usage du monde*, in which the narrator travels from Geneva to Sri Lanka in a Fiat Topolino, the Italian equivalent of the 2CV—but also that the journeys they describe were often undertaken solely with such textualization in mind. The real end result is not, for example, the pseudo-ethnographic account of the Tarahumara people that Lochon promises or the thesis on pharmacy and cultural difference on which Baudot claims to work, for these are the justifications obscuring what Jean-Didier Urbain describes as the 'secrets de voyage', alibis behind which journeys' true motives are disguised. The real end result is the journey as a marketable phenomenon, with what David Le Breton calls a 'dimension publique',[60] presentable in books, slides, film shows, and lectures. A principal accessory to their marketability is the gradually foregrounded central character—the 2CV

---

[59] The meeting with another travel-writer has become a topos of this literature, with perhaps the most commonly cited example being the respective accounts, by Jonathan Raban, in *Coasting* (London: Collins Harvill, 1986), and Paul Theroux, in *The Kingdom by the Sea* (London: Hamilton, 1983), of the intersection of their two journeys around the coast of Great Britain in 1982. Baudot and Séguéla discover traces of Cornet and Khim's stay in the same place three years previously while in Singapore in 1959 (*La Terre en rond*, 178–9). Claude Layec, travelling almost a decade later, meets a series of other 2CV travellers. See *Au Long Cours en 2CV* (Paris: Presses de la Cité, 1968), 141, 295 (the journey was undertaken: 8 August 1966–16 September 1967). He even mentions 'une 2CV accidentée [...] sur la route entre la frontière et Katmandou' [a damaged and abandoned 2CV on the road between the border and Katmandu] (p. 141), an example surely of Lévi-Strauss's 'ordure lancée au visage de l'humanité' [filth thrown into the face of humanity] (*Tristes tropiques*, 36; trans. Weightman, 38).

[60] Le Breton, *Passions du risque*, 136.

itself—that distinguishes these narratives from the inter-war *croisières* (in which the vehicles and problems relating to them play a very minor role) and also causes the reader to focus on the relationship between the means of transport and the poetics of the travel account.[61] In the final section of this chapter there is an exploration of four of the generic or thematic characteristics of 2CV journeys, and a suggestion that these aspects might be used to illuminate what Kristin Ross calls, in the title of her study cited above, the post-war 're-ordering of elsewhere': anthropomorphism; slowness; breakdown and *bricolage*; and domestic ritual.

The humanization of the 2CV is a common feature of literature devoted to it. Jean Rouaud's description of the grandfather's car, the 'boîte cranienne' [cranium], in *Les Champs d'Honneur* is a succinct indication of links between the vehicle's front view and human physiognomy. In the travel accounts, this resemblance is developed to such an extent that the car is seen as organic rather than mechanical. This is particularly apparent in descriptions of physical damage, for the language of corporeal suffering is used to describe the cars' mechanical fatigue, with damage to the bodywork described in terms of proudly worn scars.[62] The cars show human functions: coughing when water is found in the petrol, becoming 'essoufflée' [breathless] when faced with a steep mountain climb, lurching drunkenly, 'complètement ivre' [completely drunk], when conventional fuel is replaced with tequila.[63] Parts of the vehicle become parts of the organic and not mechanical body, human or otherwise: in Viau's account, a car travelling over corrugated iron risks spilling its innards 'comme un cheval ses entrailles pendant une course de taureaux' [like a horse spills its entrails during a bullfight], Baudot and Séguéla describe burst tyres as 'pattes brisées' [broken paws], for Layec the engine becomes a stomach, and, in the same account, a diagnostic search for the cause of breakdown is seen as an autopsy.[64] By the end of the journeys, the vehicle becomes a character in its own right—sharing celebratory tequila, for instance, in Layec's text—and ultimately transcends its identity as a standard,

---

[61] On this subject, see Pasquali, *Le Tour des horizons*, 23.

[62] See e.g. Henri Lochon, *En 2CV chez les primitifs de la Sierra mexicaine* (Lyons: Vinay, 1956), 58. (The journey was undertaken: 4 June 1955–7 November 1955.)

[63] Cornet and Lochon, *Deux hommes*, 125, 107, and Lochon, *En 2CV chez les primitifs de la Sierra mexicaine*, 75.

[64] Viau, *Le Tour d'Afrique en 2CV*, 53, Baudot and Séguéla, *La Terre en rond*, 237, and Layec, *Au Long Cours en 2CV*, 192, 212.

production-line vehicle to acquire, through the journey and the process of return, an individuality and degree of self-distinction: 'Elle [the car] a vraiment piteuse mine. Boueuse, avachie, sa carosserie cabossée, la suspension inexistante depuis bien longtemps, elle n'a que peu de ressemblance avec ses consœurs qui sillonnent les routes de France'[65] [She really has a pitiful expression. Muddy, shapeless, with battered bodywork and her suspension long gone, she looks only vaguely like her sisters driving around the roads of France].

The purpose of this progressive anthropomorphism becomes clear in the repeated paralleling of the car with the body of the traveller: this is a common device in Cornet, who claims, for instance, that 'la voiture va, comme nous, inexorablement vers la ruine' [the car travels, like us, inexorably towards ruin].[66] As Midas Dekkers explains, such a comparison is ultimately flawed: 'If cars wear out, together with houses and lampposts, then so do people. How could it be otherwise? But there's one big difference: people are alive, which means that what wears out gets repaired. Certainly, a person can be compared to a car, but then it must be a car full of car mechanics.'[67] But the parallel serves another purpose here, linked to the travellers' own self-performance. For the vehicle is not seen as a prosthetic, shutting the driver in, transforming him into (what David Le Breton calls) 'un œil hypertrophié' [a hyper-trophic eye] or what Saint-Pol-Roux calls 'un cul-de-jatte aux bottes de sept lieues' [a double amputee with seven-league boots].[68] Instead, the traveller's identity is displaced onto the vehicle, which becomes a *mise-en-abîme* of the physical aspects of travel, itself returned to its etymo-logical roots of 'tripalium' or instrument of torture. At a moment when the traditional traveller is rapidly becoming a compromised individual (in relation to revised attitudes to the imperial project) or an endangered species (in relation to the emergence of mass tourism), the focus on the car allows a salvaging of heroism and is, as such, central to the nostalgic procedures on which these texts depend.

Another element of this nostalgia is to be found in the creative use of slowness. Whereas the confident civilizing and colonizing zeal

---

[65] Layec, *Au Long Cours en 2CV*, 297, and Cornet, *Deux hommes, 2CV en Asie*, 195. See also Baudot and Séguéla, *La Terre en rond*, 259.

[66] Cornet and Lochon, *Deux hommes*, 45.

[67] Midas Dekkers, *The Way of All Flesh: a Celebration of Decay*, trans. Sherry Marx-Macdonald (London: Harvill, 2000), 82. (First published 1997.)

[68] David Le Breton, *Éloge de la marche* (Paris: Métailié, 2000), 82; Saint-Pol-Roux, *La Randonnée*, 24.

underpinning the Croisière noire seems embarrassed by the delays that difficult terrain imposes on the journey, and stoically reduces these to cryptic references in the text—'Allure moyenne: quinze kilomètres par jour' [Average progress: ten miles per day]—this is the detail that the 2CV journey relishes.[69] Unimpeded progress merits little attention, and for this reason European legs of the journey are generally glossed over. Compared to other more powerful contemporary vehicles, the 2CV cannot compete (except in extreme circumstances, such as on American black ice). It is when the vehicle transgresses, i.e. when it leaves the conventional road network and would normally be expected to grind to a halt, that the 2CV distinguishes itself and disrupts the logic of speed. Millar and Schwartz claim: 'To possess speed is to be modern; to control speed rather than to be controlled by it is perhaps the most important form of contemporary power', but the 2CV travellers privilege imposed slowness and focus on the vicissitudes of deceleration, once more to salvage an understanding of travel that is rapidly becoming obsolete.[70] The promotional blurb on *Deux hommes, 2 CV, en Asie* highlights this feature, claiming that the travellers have ' "grignotée" [l'Asie] kilomètre par kilomètre, parfois même mètre par mètre, luttant des journées entières sur des pistes de désert où aucune voiture ne s'était jamais aventuriée' ['conquered' Asia a kilometre at a time, sometimes a metre at a time, struggling for days on end on desert tracks where no other car had ever ventured]. The focus would appear to be on hitches rather than surroundings, revealing a self-absorbed interest in travellers and their vehicles rather than an attention to the microscopic dimension of nature that deceleration or a peripatetic mode of travel potentially reveals. There is often even an indifference to place and the transformation of elsewhere into little more than the space in which travel occurs.

When deceleration reaches its limit, the vehicle grinds to a halt and breaks down. These moments of *panne* punctuate the journeys and, while disturbing the progress of the travellers, create the rhythm of the account. Breakdown brings contingency back into travel and disrupts established itineraries; it undermines the image of travellers as sovereign individuals, but at the same time allows them to turn misfortune into episodes of ingenious escape.[71] The rudimentary nature of the 2CV lends itself to this paradoxical movement, revealing vulnerability whilst

---

[69] Haardt and Audouin-Dubreuil, *La Croisière noire*, 291.

[70] Millar and Schwartz, 'Introduction—Speed is a Vehicle', 17.

[71] On the theme of breakdown in travel, see Jacques Meunier, 'Vive la panne!', in *Le Monocle de Joseph Conrad*, 87–91.

containing its own restoration: on the one hand, whilst not being unreliable, car and driver are inevitably vulnerable to extremes of climate and terrain; on the other, however, the vehicle is sufficiently straightforward to allow mechanical intervention in the field and a dependence on constant *bricolage*. The travellers resort to a variety of ruses to maintain mobility: tequila replaces petrol, soap seals an engine casing, sand fills a burst tyre inner tube, bananas are used to lubricate a dry gear box, sections of a roof rack replace engine mountings, and a brick on the accelerator becomes an improvised cruise control.[72] The car that would become a recurrent character in the francophone *bande dessinée* already shows—in these travel accounts—comic book qualities. Regularly incapacitated, it constantly springs back to life and continues its progress. Baudot and Séguéla's car collides with a tiger in India, but is 'rapidement redressée à la main' [rapidly straightened by hand], and the caption of a picture taken following this event sums up the car's comic elasticity: 'LA VOITURE PLIE MAIS NE ROMPT PAS' [the car bends but does not break].[73]

The car's faults—slowness, lightness, lack of power, austerity of design, simplicity of mechanics—are transformed into evidence of rugged persistence as this 'petite voiture française' manages to return to France.[74] In a process of domestic ritual, the travelling car is transformed into what Barthes terms ' "un petit coin de France" portatif' [a portable 'little corner of France'], not only equipped with French material—the inventories of Baudot and Séguéla and of Viau reveal a chauvinism reflected in all the other accounts—but also containing explicit trappings of French civilization: red wine, Gauloises cigarettes, Kronenbourg, French books, and even photographs of de Gaulle to distribute to the grateful indigenous populations.[75] It is in Africa in particular that the car operates as a vehicle of Frenchness. It is a marker of mechanical modernity presented in a process of inverse exoticism as still foreign to the cultures crossed, but at the same time a fetishized object to which the indigenous populations aspire.[76] Despite their context, published for the most part in the few years between Dien

---

[72] Lochon, *En 2CV chez les primitifs*, 75, Baudot and Séguéla, *La Terre en rond*, 253, 238, 94, Viau, *Le Tour d'Afrique en 2CV*, 63, and Baudot and Séguéla, *La Terre en rond*, 115.

[73] Baudot and Séguéla, *La Terre en rond*, 220.

[74] Ibid. 259.

[75] Barthes, 'Mythologie de l'automobile', 1140; Cornet, *Deux hommes, 2CV, en Asie*, 25, 37.

[76] Baudot and Séguéla, *La Terre en rond*, 42.

Bien Phu and the referendum on African independence, the travel accounts tend to eschew contemporary narratives of de/colonization and to reveal a repeated flight from current concerns. Cornet and Lochon, en route for Bamako, claim: 'Que la guerre de Corée, le plan Marshall et la bombe atomique sont loin!' [How far away the Korean War, the Marshall Plan, and the A-Bomb seem!], and Viau seems more concerned in North African traces of the last war, 1939–45, than the signs of the coming war with Algeria that in 1953 were already apparent.[77] In fact, as the purported goal of Lochon's text suggests—'A la recherche des hommes primitifs' [in search of primitive people]—the texts are characterized by an imperialist nostalgia, a desire to turn back the clock, to erase the implications of colonialism whilst enacting what Lévi-Strauss calls 'la comédie d[']anoblir [les primitifs] au moment où elle achève de les supprimer' [investing them with nobility at the very time when it is completing their destruction].[78]

Parading an image of French post-war modernity yet obscuring the backcloth against which this image is projected, the 2CV journeys enact an identity crisis that is accentuated and rendered yet more complex once the spectre of Americanization is factored in. For the 2CV is a shifter, modern in a Third World context and even mistaken as a marker of Americanness, yet antiquated and even primitive once compared to US automotive engineering.[79] The inverse exoticism that served to accentuate the pre-industrial conditions of African and South American observers has the opposite effect in the USA. Once the car crosses the Atlantic, it is described as 'un engin bizarre qu'ils ont fabriqué sans doute eux-mêmes avec de la tôle ondulée' [a strange machine they probably built themselves with corrugated iron], and greeted with a series of questions: 'What is that?' or 'C'est vous qui l'avez construite?' [Did you build it yourselves?].[80] Such humiliation over appearance is compounded by the vehicle's inability, once in the USA, to reach the minimum speed limit on major roads—'On est prié de ne pas flâner, la route n'est pas pour les fainéants' [We are asked to refrain from dawdling, the road is not for layabouts].[81] This threat to French modernity of an all-engulfing American hypermodernity is given concrete form in the

---

[77] Cornet and Lochon, *Deux hommes*, 229, and Viau, *Le Tour d'Afrique en 2CV*, 36.
[78] Lévi-Strauss, *Tristes tropiques*, 40; trans. Weightman, 41.
[79] Cornet, *Deux hommes, 2CV, en Asie*, 20.
[80] Cornet and Lochon, *Deux hommes*, 21, Layec, *Au Long Cours en 2CV*, 265, and Baudot and Séguéla, *La Terre en rond*, 132.
[81] Baudot and Séguéla, *La Terre en rond*, 126.

image of Baudot and Séguéla's vehicle awaiting customs clearance in Rio de Janeiro: 'Notre pauvre 2CV est là, sur le quai, perdue parmi ses grandes sœurs, quelques trois ou quatre mille voitures américaines, longues et magnifiques' [Our poor 2CV is there, on the quay, lost amongst its big sisters, three or four thousand sleek and splendid American cars].[82]

The American automobile industry had overtaken the technology of its French counterpart in the period following the First World War, and by the 1950s the gap between the two was increasingly marked: the French effort to achieve affordable motorization in a climate of initial austerity contrasted with the peak of US automobile size and fantastic styling. The car came to symbolize what for many French was the hubris of post-war American culture. Aragon, for instance, in an extreme outburst of anti-Americanism when angered by the replacement with a new Ford car of a missing sculpture from a square that honoured Victor Hugo, claimed in *Les Lettres nouvelles*:

A Ford automobile, the civilization of Detroit, the assembly line [...] here is the symbol of this subjugation to the dollar applauded even in the land of Molière; here is the white lacquered god of foreign industry, the Atlantic totem that chases away French glories with Marshall Plan stocks.[...] The Yankee, more arrogant than the Nazi iconoclast, substitutes the machine for the poet, Coca-Cola for poetry, American advertising for *La Légende des siècles*, the mass-manufactured car for the genius, the Ford for Victor Hugo![83]

Although the 2CV travellers fail to take their cultural chauvinism to such limits and resist on the whole any explicit anti-Americanism, their accounts nevertheless reveal an implicit competitiveness, especially when their vehicles are dismissed as 'tacots' [old bangers] and they are told that even a Jeep would fail where they dare to venture.[84] The 2CV tends, however, to outstrip the general-purpose vehicle, by now symbolic of the American presence in France. A jeep can prove 'caho-tante' [bumpy] on rough territory or even becomes 'embourbée' [stuck

[82] Ibid. 69. The US market responded to foreign imports of small cars with a series of changes in legislation: a rise of the minimum speed limit ensured that a fully laden 2CV would never be able to reach this; compulsory crash tests made import even more difficult. American engine oil was not suitable for DS engines and damaged seals so badly that the cars broke down. See Loubet, *Histoire de l'automobile française*, 303–4.

[83] Louis Aragon, 'Victor Hugo', *Les Lettres françaises*, 28 June 1951. Cited (in translation) in Richard Kuisel, *Seducing the French: The Dilemma of Americanization* (Berkeley and Los Angeles: University of California Press, 1996), 41.

[84] Viau, *Le Tour d'Afrique en 2CV*, 83.

in the mud] in conditions through which the 2CV merely struggles to progress.[85] During Cornet and Lochon's attempt in Bolivia to take the 2CV to over 5,000 metres, the accompanying American vehicle is forced to renounce—'La voiture américaine n'ira pas plus loin!'—whereas their vehicle, even though emptied of luggage and stripped of doors and wings, manages the climb.[86] Similarly, as Viau and his fellow travellers prepare to cross the Sahara they meet two Chevrolet drivers: 'ils [the latter] ne peuvent réprimer des sourires moqueurs' [they fail to suppress mocking smiles], yet the 2CVs manage the journey with several minor breakdowns and the customary *bricolage*; the Chevrolet suffers a major breakdown, and its driver and passenger nearly die of dehydration. Viau's conclusion makes explicit the projection and protection of national identity that these journeys allow: 'Nous avons posé un label de garantie sur une fabrication mécanique française. Et nous avons aussi montré que l'esprit d'audace n'avait pas déserté la jeunesse française' [We have placed a guarantee of quality on a French mechanical product. And we have also shown that the spirit of daring has not deserted French young people].[87] Faced with American mechanical hubris, French simplicity and minimalism become a virtue.[88]

Diminutive, deceptively simple, thriving on a combination of crisis and ruse, able to bounce back after even the most serious mishap, torn between conformity to its humble, stay-at-home peers and the individualism granted by travel, reflecting both a sense of tradition and a simultaneous taste for modernity, an advocate of *demos* (the power of the people) not *dromos* (the power of speed), the 2CV—as it emerges from these travel accounts—is an automotive Astérix. It is a projection of post-war French contradictions, desires, and anxieties, offering, in the challenges of travel, the possibility of wish-fulfilment and identity formation—both individual and collective—unavailable at home.[89] Journeys by 2CV reflect a series of shifts in post-war travel and travel writing—practical and generic shifts triggered not least, as I suggested at the beginning of this chapter, by the new found ability of (soon to be former) colonial subjects to write and travel *back*. They reveal in particular the rapidly changing status of the travelling subject and the

---

[85] Cornet, *Deux hommes, 2CV, en Asie*, 88; Cornet and Lochon, *Deux hommes*, 67.

[86] Cornet and Lochon, *Deux hommes*, 118.

[87] Viau, *Le Tour d'Afrique en 2CV*, 149, 182.

[88] See Baudot and Séguéla, *La Terre en rond*, 169.

[89] On this subject, see Alain Duhamel, *Le Complexe d'Astérix: essai sur le caractère politique des Français* (Paris: Gallimard, 1985).

resultant quest for projects or strategies that might allow continued self-distinction and a salvaging of the notion of 'travel'. But the paradoxical choice of such an improbable vehicle is also evidence of continued French politico-cultural protectionism. It is the *exception française* on wheels, an indication of the French struggle to reconfigure national identity in the light of rampant Americanization and the collapse of Empire. In however a humble way, the 2CV journeys cast light on a post-war and soon to be post-colonial nation renegotiating its way through a radically reordered elsewhere.

5

Between Unity and Diversity: Rubbish, the Mosaic, and the Fragments of Travel Literature

[C]omment la prétendue évasion du voyage pourrait-elle réussir autre chose que nous confronter aux formes les plus malheureuses de notre existence historique? [...] L'ordre et l'harmonie de l'Occident exigent l'élimination d'une masse prodigieuse de sous-produits maléfiques dont la terre est aujourd'hui infectée. Ce que d'abord vous nous montrez, voyages, c'est notre ordure lancée au visage de l'humanité.

[W]hat else can the so-called escapism of travelling do than con-front us with the more unfortunate aspects of our history? [...] The order and harmony of the Western world demand the elimin-ation of a prodigious mass of noxious by-products which now contaminate the globe. The first thing we see as we travel round the world is our own filth, thrown into the face of mankind.[1]

THIS chapter's epigraph, one of the most commonly cited passages from Lévi-Strauss's *Tristes tropiques*, appears in the opening chapters of the text and encapsulates the post-lapsarian doom that characterizes the text from its title onwards. The anthropologist's notion of filth thrown in the face of humanity, of 'ordure lancée' is, on the one hand, a modern version of the discourse of disappointment that characterizes much travel literature. This is disappointment triggered—in particular at places such as the Niagara Falls—when expectation is deflated by the

---

[1] Lévi-Strauss, *Tristes Tropiques*, 36, trans. Weightman, 38.

domesticated, humanized sight that meets the traveller's eyes. Yet on the other hand, in continuing to write a substantial travel narrative, Lévi-Strauss gestures towards travel literature's restorative or transformatory potential; he acknowledges the ways in which the successful writer of the journey, in the textualization of travel, can translate the uneven, unexpected, unstable, and often fragmented experience of place into the successful literary work. I foreground at this stage these associated ideas of translation and transformation because they are essential to the elaboration of a critical discourse on travel literature in the post-war period that manages both to address inflated claims relating to the genre's perceived need to represent 'authenticity' and to grasp the almost Mallarmean aspects of a form of writing that tends increasingly to reflect on its own impossibility.

This chapter looks specifically at several French-language travel texts published primarily from the early 1960s to the early 1970s. Its analysis is divided into two related parts: the first eschews a particular focus on rubbish to consider a more general privileging and exploration of fragmentation in post-war travel writing; the second develops these observations in a specific study of fragmentation and the mosaic in the work of the Swiss traveller Nicolas Bouvier, and relates this to an exploration of what strikes me as a more generally staple element of the twentieth-century travel narrative: rubbish. In what might be seen as a *mise-en-abîme*, travel literature may be read as a genre itself previously dismissed by critics as a pulp form, seen at best as the paraliterary and biographical source material useful in the consideration of an author's more serious work. Travel literature itself, however, focuses regularly on the debris with which previous travellers or even the inhabitants of a place themselves have strewn the landscape. In focusing on this aspect of travel literature, I react in relation to my reading of this particular genre to the claim of the garbologists Rathje and Murphy, in their excellent study *Rubbish! The Archaeology of Garbage*, that 'if we can come to understand our discards [. . .] then we will better understand the world in which we live'.[2]

---

[2] William L. Rathje and Cullen Murphy, *Rubbish! The Archaeology of Garbage* (New York: HarperCollins, 1992), 4.

NEW TRAVEL LITERATURE, OR, 'BRACKETING OFF THE
WORLD'?

The rise of academic interest in travel literature has been accompanied—some might claim triggered—by the increasing public popularity
of this genre in the 1980s and 1990s. In France, the salvaging from the
library stacks and subsequent republication of numerous earlier travel
accounts was accompanied and facilitated by the emergence of a new
travel writing movement, *Pour une littérature voyageuse*. Launched in
the late 1980s, this movement asserted itself as a literary school in 1992
by producing a 'livre-manifeste'. The eleven individual contributions to
this volume suggest a diversity that the volume's editor—and the movement's principal *animateur*—Michel Le Bris attempts to control by the
elaboration of an imaginary genealogy. In the preface, he locates the
movement's emergence in the post-Marxist, chronologically poststructuralist 'années charnières' of the mid-1970s; and in a self-
performatively selective bibliography, he constructs a retrospective
pedigree by blending a list of travel narratives from the 1970s, 1980s,
and early 1990s with a series of earlier texts republished in the same
period. The hazily termed banner under which these texts are assembled—'une littérature qui dise le monde'—is contrasted with an apparently contradictory manœuvre, dubbed a ' "mise entre parenthèses" du
monde', that for Le Bris is seen to characterize French literature in the
1960s and 1970s.[3] This 'bracketing-off of the world', a dislocation of
the literary text from the external world it once purported to signify, is
interpreted above all as the cause of the decline of travel literature, and
Le Bris tends to indict a loosely assembled grouping of structuralists and
nouveaux romanciers whom he accuses of imposing on the French
literary establishment what he calls 'l'Empire du signe'.[4]

Self-definition accordingly depends on the selective destruction of a
series of targets associated with what, in his personal 'Manifeste (désabusé) pour une littérature (un peu plus) aventureuse', Le Bris calls 'le
terrorisme structuraliste des années soixante' [structuralist terrorism
of the 1960s]; yet, in a parallel process, a number of earlier travel

---

[3] See Michel Le Bris, 'La vie, si égarante et bonne', in *Le Vent des routes: hommages
à Nicolas Bouvier* (Geneva: Zoé, 1998), 57–61 (p. 57).
[4] On Le Bris and the movement, see Charles Forsdick, '*Fin de Siècle, Fin des Voyages*:
Michel Le Bris and Contemporary Travel Writing in French', in Michael Bishop and
Christopher Elson (eds.), *French Prose in 2000* (Amsterdam: Rodopi, 2002), 47–55. See
Ch. 6 for a fuller discussion of these issues.

narratives are at the same time salvaged and incorporated as a result of their supposed failure to reflect such orthodoxy.[5] The principal of these, Bouvier's *L'Usage du monde* (initially published in 1963, although not widely read until a new edition appeared in 1985), is contrasted in an article written shortly after the author's death with contemporary literary orthodoxies, dismissed by Le Bris as 'l'incroyable, l'essentielle *claustrophobie* de cette modernité-là' [the incredible, essential *claustrophobia* of that modernity].[6] This instrumentalization of Bouvier's text is striking for two reasons: on the one hand, the language used to distinguish it is essentially agoraphiliac, unquestioningly perpetuating an extroverted understanding of travel not necessarily suited to the rapidly changing circumstances of the late twentieth century; on the other, it denies the transformations that travel literature was undergoing in the often experimental work of a number of Bouvier's exact contemporaries.[7]

'L'Empire du signe' is itself clearly an unsubtle dismissal of the travel narrative customarily seen as representative of what Le Bris attacks, Barthes's *L'Empire des signes*, a text published in 1970 and accordingly a conveniently implicit foil in definitions of the nascent movement Le Bris himself represents. Barthes's text continues to attract sustained critical attention, often formulated in the light of a postcolonial critique of Orientalism. To cite only the principal examples of these recent readings, Roger Célestin, Marie-Paule Ha, Abdelkebir Khatibi, Diana Knight, and Lisa Lowe have all written substantial chapters, situating Barthes's Japanese text in relation to his earlier demystifications of exoticism and questioning the neo-Orientalist implications of the construction of a 'Japan' whose principal purpose is to further a Western critical project instigated in his earlier writing: i.e. what Goebel describes as a 'deconstructive critique of transcendental truth, determinate meaning, and epistemologically transparent language'.[8] For his most severe critics, Barthes's Orientalist Eurocentrism manifests itself

---

[5] Michel Le Bris, 'Manifeste (désabusé) pour une littérature (un peu plus) aventureuse', in *Le Grand Dehors* (Paris: Payot, 1992), 377–84 (p. 379).

[6] See Le Bris, 'La vie, si égarante et bonne', 58 (emphasis in original).

[7] For a discussion of the agoraphiliac impulse in travel literature, see Jean-Didier Urbain, *Ethnographe, mais pas trop* (Paris: Payot, 2003), 187–94.

[8] See Rolf J. Goebel, 'Japan as Western Text: Roland Barthes, Richard Gordon Smith, and Lafcadio Hearn', *Comparative Literature Studies*, 30/2 (1993), 188–205 (p. 189). For the principal recent studies of the text, see Célestin, *From Cannibals to Radicals*, 134–74, Ha, *Figuring the East*, 95–117, Abdelkebir Khatibi, *La Figure de l'étranger dans la littérature française* (Paris: Denoël, 1987), 57–85, Diana Knight, *Barthes and Utopia: Space, Travel, Writing* (Oxford: Clarendon, 1997), 141–65, and Lowe, *Critical Terrains*, 136–89.

in the neglect of the 'real'—by which is implied 'contemporary'—Japan; but such a critique on the one hand ignores the text's fascination not with the exotic but with the everyday, and on the other (and perhaps more importantly) fails to acknowledge that the shallow criterion of 'authenticity' on which less searching readings of travel literature tend to depend is helpfully replaced by a more fundamental questioning of what Barthes's projection of 'Japan'-as-text implies for representations of place.

In interviews, as Diana Knight makes clear, Barthes failed to distinguish the imagined 'Japan' of *L'Empire des signes* from the actual country in which he stayed.[9] The presence of an actual experience of travel accordingly persists. There is, as a result, a potentially convincing interpretation of the text as a travel narrative in its own right: indeed Barthes's reflections on the centrality of the intercultural experience of 'la rencontre' to travel itself haunt the text even though they appear to have the extra-textual status of handwritten jottings. To avoid such a reading becoming reductive, however, there is a need to foreground the text's metacritical status. In doing so, it is possible to suggest that Barthes's work casts light on a series of questions—about representation of the foreign, about representation in general, about language as a medium of representation, about reading other cultures and (more paradoxically) about reading one's own—that concern a number of post-war travel writers and are allied to radical transformations in the form in which they textualize their journeys. Travel emerges from *L'Empire des signes* as a hermeneutical experience or ethnographic activity as the traveller progresses, without the traditional textual support of maps and guides and street names, through the foreign city; as in a number of Italo Calvino's narratives of place, the culture travelled through becomes a text whose surface phenomena operate as signs to be deciphered.[10] Faced with the traveller's nightmare of heteroglossia, manifesting itself in 'un système symbolique inouï, entièrement dépris du nôtre' [an unheard-of symbolic system, one altogether detached from our own], Barthes does not resort to the refuge of monocultural, monolingual, received interpretations, to the control of 'notre inconnaisance de l'Asie grâce à des langages connus' [our incognizance of Asia by means of certain known languages], but instead transforms

---

[9] Knight, *Barthes and Utopia*, 146.
[10] For an associated reading of the traveller as semiologist, see David Scott, 'The Smile of the Sign: Semiotics and Travel Writing in Barthes, Baudrillard, Butor and Lévi-Strauss', *Studies in Travel Writing*, 7/2 (2003), 209–25.

incomprehension into possibility: 'descendre dans l'intraduisible, en éprouver la secousse sans jamais l'amortir, jusqu'à ce qu'en nous tout l'Occident s'ébranle' [to descend into the untranslatable, to experience its shock without ever muffling it, until everything Occidental in us totters].[11] At a time when, as Dean MacCannell suggests, tourists were becoming ever more sophisticated semiologists, Barthes describes a loss of semiotic mastery as his traveller is left with an accumulation of heterogeneous fragments—the word 'fragment' itself occurs six times in the sections on food alone—whose potential is ultimately not so much to reveal the travel narrative's desire to illuminate 'elsewhere' as to decentre and destabilize 'home'.[12] The verb 's'ébranler' used in the passage quoted above is clearly drawn from a post-1968 lexicon, and situates *L'Empire des signes* firmly in the ideological uncertainties of its time.

Barthes's travel narrative, decentred and discontinuous, challenges conventional understandings of the *récit de voyage* in ways similar to those he had already identified in his 1962 article in *Critique* on Michel Butor's *Mobile*. Barthes was one of the few contemporary critics to appreciate this text, to which the more common response was to dismiss its apparent structural chaos as 'absolument illisible' [absolutely unreadable] or as '[des] notations, qu'on dirait recopiées de catalogues par un enfant...' [observations that seem to have been recopied from catalogues by a child...].[13] There is a tendency, especially in *nouveau roman* criticism, to wheel out such reactionary voices—in this case, I have cited Robert Kanters and Pierre de Boisdeffre—for their retrospective comedy value, without identifying what Barthes called 'ce qui a été blessé' [what has been stung].[14] To identify the subject of Butor's textual experiment, attention should be paid to the text's opening paratextual marker, the map of the USA, which identifies this work as a travel narrative. The work seems, albeit temporarily, to adhere to a conventional understanding of order. In the case

---

[11] Roland Barthes, *L'Empire des signes* (Geneva: Skira, 1970), 7, 8, 11; *Empire of Signs*, trans. Richard Howard (London: Jonathan Cape, 1982), 3, 4, 6.

[12] See Dean MacCannell, *The Tourist: A New Theory of the Leisure Class* (London: Macmillan, 1976).

[13] Robert Kanters, 'L'Amérique en butorama', *Le Figaro littéraire*, 21 April 1962, 2; Pierre de Boisdeffre, '*Mobile* par Michel Butor', *La Revue de Paris*, May 1962, 169. Cited by F. C. St Aubyn, 'Michel Butor's America', *Kentucky Foreign Language Quarterly*, 11/1 (1964), 40–8 (pp. 40, 41).

[14] Roland Barthes, 'Littérature et discontinu', in *Essais critiques* (Paris: Seuil, 1964), 175–87 (p. 175).

of *Mobile*, the reading of the subsequent text seems to have represented for a number of critics an excessive challenge to conventional requirements regarding the travel narrative's continuity and clarity of meaning. As Barthes suggests, however, and as subsequent critics have illustrated at greater length, Butor's text is carefully, if not excessively ordered, and it is from the complex accumulation and juxtaposition of fragments and citations that meanings begin to emerge. The text is controlled by a series of patterns. Some of these are explicit (such as its alphabetical ordering of states, called by Barthes 'le plus insipide des ordres' [the most bland of orders],[15] or the use of distinctive typefaces to signal different voices, i.e. those of the traveller himself, of the source material he quotes, and of the dreamers of the American dream whose itineraries he crosses); others (such as the distinct use of four different time zones) remain more implicit. The search for strategies to hold together the text's fragments is reflected in the title. Although adjectivally *Mobile* seems to refer to the constant motion of cars crossing the continent, as a noun it alludes to heterogeneous fragments suspended individually yet joined on a unifying frame.

In pre-twentieth-century travel writing, textualization of 'travellees' and their culture had depended above all on strategies of containment and imposition of coherence; Butor, whose text should very much be read as the account of a French traveller released from European austerity into the consumerist abundance of 1950s America, foregrounds instead contingency, the chance inherent in anonymous encounters, the traveller's sense of powerlessness as initially inassimilable fragments of elsewhere seem to proliferate wildly. In short, he textualizes the great difficulty of negotiating one's way through and understanding other cultures. Butor's 'America'—and I use inverted comments here as with Barthes's 'Japan'—is characterized by a polyphony of voices, which causes a radical reassessment of the traveller/narrator's situation in the text; and this multiplication of voices is complemented by a proliferation of trajectories, both past and present, as the narrator's own journey narrative is challenged by those of his contemporaries whom he passes on the freeway, by those of earlier European emigrants, and by those of Native Americans progressively displaced. Butor's traveller is no longer the persistently sovereign individual of nineteenth-century travel accounts, but a character relativized by those whom he meets and by

---

[15] Roland Barthes, 'Littérature et discontinu', in *Essais critiques* (Paris: Seuil, 1964), 175.

whose traces his own itinerary is marked. As such, Butor's text is neither the failed experiment that many of his contemporary critics dismissed, nor the example of 'un modernisme qui déjà date un peu' [a modernism that is already a little out of date] that the *Mercure de France* critic identified.[16] Instead, it is a striking attempt to recast travel literature in the light both of the heteroglossia that contemporary travellers, responding to the perceived homogenization of the field of travel, increasingly acknowledged, and of the reframing of understandings of 'travel' whereby the term's restrictive meanings were radically overhauled in order to include a series of alternative journeys.

Yet in *Mobile*, we do not ultimately have the concluding statement of the *insaisissible*—the 'il n'y a rien à *saisir*' [there is nothing to grasp], with which *L'Empire des signes* concludes.[17] Butor's text, like Barthes's, re-enacts the experience of the traveller as fragments of elsewhere are encountered, processed, and steadily accumulated; but instead of maintaining a sense of radical alterity or of the unattainability of elsewhere—and clearly the tropological zones selected by the two authors, Japan and the USA, are significant in any understanding of the different approaches here—*Mobile* suggests that a potential unity underpins its apparent diversity. The structuring devices already mentioned, as well as the possible understanding of the title as substantive rather than adjective reflect this; but to suggest such unity Butor cites in particular the figure of the quilt. Describing the Shelburne Museum in Vermont, he writes: 'La partie la plus étonnante en est peut-être la collection de courtepointes, ou "quilts", en mosaïque d'étoffes. Ce "Mobile" est composé un peu comme un "quilt" ' [Perhaps their most remarkable feature is a collection of patchwork quilts. This 'Mobile' is composed somewhat like a quilt], and this is followed later in the text by long descriptions of the contents of three of these exhibits.[18] As Jean Duffy has noted, Butor himself refers to a series of very different analogies in his attempts to explain the construction of the text: cellular structures; the encyclopaedia, dictionary, or catalogue; the orchestral score; and the collage. Despite the range of contexts or media these imply, each suggests the text's capacity to suggest at the same time

---

[16] Philippe Sénart, 'Lettres-Actualités', *Mercure de France*, June 1962, 313. Cited by St Aubyn, 'Michel Butor's America', 48.

[17] Barthes, *L'Empire des signes*, 186; *Empire of Signs*, 109.

[18] Michel Butor, *Mobile: étude pour une représentation des États-Unis* (Paris: Gallimard, 1962), 45; *Mobile: Study for a Representation of the United States*, trans. Richard Howard (New York: Simon & Schuster, 1963), 28.

unrelatedness and correspondence, fragmentation and yet an underlying connectedness. In Duffy's terms, these analogies 'all draw attention to the prominence and interaction in *Mobile* of certain thematic and formal tensions, notably, similarity versus difference; connection versus disjunction; harmony versus discord; order versus disorder'.[19] It is the traveller's recognition of the tensions between the part and the whole, of the negotiation of such a passage between unity and diversity that similarly concerns Nicolas Bouvier, whose *L'Usage du monde* was published the year after *Mobile*. Before moving on to Bouvier's work, however, it is important to examine the reasons for bringing together the seemingly empirical *L'Usage du monde* with texts that epitomize what Le Bris, as we have seen, dismisses as a structuralist bracketing-off of the world.

By focusing initially on two very different texts by Barthes and Butor, what is suggested is that their travel narratives might be re-explored and reinterpreted in the light of the historical circumstances of their production—and especially in the light of the contemporary practices of mobility that were causing a rapid and radical reordering of elsewhere. Such a critical approach might proceed in the same way as Lynn Higgins countered criticism of the *nouveau roman* by situating and reassessing it in relation to a post-war crisis of narrative. It would be difficult to claim that there exists a *nouveau récit de voyage*, not least because the two authors' associations with the New Novel were either fleeting or tangential. No coherent corpus of travel texts answering to such a name exists, although the role of restlessness, mobility, and displacement in the *nouveau roman* itself is already a substantial one. Bringing together the texts by Barthes and Butor suggests that these authors respond, in very different ways, to the experience of place in a world emerging from colonialism and still affected by the results of the Second World War, and that their responses are concentrated in their reflections on issues relating to the textualization of the experience of place. On the one hand, their emphasis on the fragmentary and discontinuous reveals the accentuation of processes of change in the object of travel literature, change whose roots James Clifford identifies already in the 'poetics of displacement' developed by authors such as Segalen and Michaux; on the other, they take to an extreme the self-conscious, metatextual exploration of the representation of travel already initiated

[19] Jean Duffy, *Signs and Designs: Art and Architecture in the Work of Michel Butor* (Liverpool: Liverpool University Press, 2003), 194–5.

in texts such as *Equipée* and *Ecuador*. Travel literature has always inevitably depended on the processing of the fluid and fragmented, the recovery of elements of the journey from notes or from memory and their re-presentation in the would-be coherence of the text. Jonathan Raban points to the tension between the 'shapeless, endlessly shifting accumulation of experience' that is the journey, and the 'convention of guileless immediacy' and coherence to which many literary travel texts pretend; 'travelling', he writes, 'is inherently a plotless, disordered, chaotic affair, where writing insists on connection, order, plot, signification'.[20] What Barthes and Butor suggest most emphatically is that the task of travel writers is not necessarily to tidy up their experiences. Plotlessness, disorder, dislocation, even apparent chaos might have a creative potential of their own. It is a similar, but ultimately divergent interest in the aesthetics of fragmentation that underpins the travel project of the author whom Le Bris attempts to distance from their work, Nicolas Bouvier.[21]

NICOLAS BOUVIER: *LES MORCEAUX ÉPARS D'UNE MOSAÏQUE DÉTRUITE*

One of the more striking elements of Bouvier's literary style was the capacity to incorporate into his work self-sufficient, aphoristic fragments of a Montaignean simplicity, on which critics have a tendency to rely heavily in their explorations of his writing. From *L'Usage du monde*, for example: 'Un voyage se passe de motifs. [...] On croit qu'on va faire un voyage, mais bientôt c'est le voyage qui vous fait, ou vous défait' [Travel outgrows its motives. It soon proves sufficient in itself. You think you are making a trip, but soon it is making you—or unmaking you]; or, from the concluding sentence of 'Les Chemins du Halla San', in *Journal d'Aran et d'autres lieux*: 'Si on ne laisse pas au voyage le droit de nous détruire un peu, autant rester chez soi' [If we do not allow travel to destroy us a little, we might as well stay at home].[22]

---

[20] Jonathan Raban, *For Love and Money* (London: Picador, 1988), 246–7.

[21] Barthes's *L'Empire des signes* appeared five years before the original version of Bouvier's own *Chronique japonaise* (Paris: Payot, 1989 [1975]), and Bouvier also provided a number of illustrations for the former. Bouvier's text combines observations of contemporary Japan with a series of historical reflections.

[22] Nicolas Bouvier, *L'Usage du monde* (Paris: Payot, 1992 [1963]), 12; *The Way of the World*, trans. Robyn Marsack (Marlboro, Vt.: Marlboro Press, 1992), 16; and *Journal d'Aran et d'autres lieux* (Paris: Payot, 1990), 155.

It is on one such aphoristic fragment that I plan to focus in the remainder of this chapter, a sentence taken from a lesser-studied genre in which Bouvier also (and perhaps surprisingly, given the time-consuming refinement to which his texts were subjected) excelled, the interview. In the series of exchanges with Irène Lichtenstein-Fall, published in 1992 as *Routes et déroutes*, he claims in an answer to a question about the visual arts: 'je me bricole de petits morceaux de savoir comme on ramasserait les morceaux épars d'une mosaïque détruite, partout où je veux, sans esprit de système. [...] La seule chose qui me fasse accepter l'idée de vieillir, c'est de compléter cette mosaïque encore lacunaire' [I put together little pieces of knowledge in the same way as you might collect the scattered fragments of a destroyed mosaic, wherever the fancy takes me, without any sense of system. [...] The only thing that allows me to accept the idea of growing old is the thought that I might one day complete this still lacunary mosaic].[23] The intention in what remains of this chapter is to explore the detail of this comment, considering issues of fragmentation and restoration. The aim is to explore the usefulness of the mosaic as a model in more general considerations of Bouvier's work and of his aesthetics of travel, and in an albeit tentative conclusion about the role of the mosaic in Bouvier's work, it will be suggested that the form may permit negotiation of a passage through the world that avoids, on the one hand, either grand, unifying, relentlessly linear narratives, or, on the other, an understanding of space that is reliant on discontinuity and radical disconnectedness—i.e. a mode of travel that permits a route between the extremes (already apparent, as I have suggested, in the work of his contemporaries, with whom he is rarely associated, such as Butor) of unity and diversity.

As Lucien Dällenbach has suggested in his excellent study of the medium, *Mosaïques: un objet esthétique à rebondissements*, the complex history of the mosaic reveals a series of reinterpretations, of changes of fortune in reception, of rises and falls in status, of shifting re-emphases of its aesthetic or figurative qualities.[24] Although the work alludes to Bouvier only once in its discussion of what its author sees as a relentless return to the mosaic in the 1990s, the traveller and his work can nevertheless be read in the light of Dällenbach's understanding of

---

[23] Nicolas Bouvier, *Routes et déroutes: entretiens avec Irène Lichtenstein-Fall* (Geneva: Métropolis, 1992), 55.

[24] Lucien Dällenbach, *Mosaïques: un objet esthétique à rebondissements* (Paris: Seuil, 2001).

the medium and its contemporary uses.[25] For the critic, the initial twentieth-century resurgence of interest in the mosaic occurred in the 1950s, the moment of a post-war crisis in 'humanist' understandings of civilization: the fragmentary (as opposed to unifying) aspect of the mosaic had, for instance, a major influence on the *nouveaux romanciers* as these authors focused on discontinuity (and the works that could be produced from it).

According to Michel Le Bris, as has already been made clear, such attention to structure led in particular to the impoverishment of travel literature, with works such as Michel Butor's *Mobile* representing a then mainstream bracketing-off of the world, against which a text such as Bouvier's almost contemporary *L'Usage du monde* could not compete. While conflation of two very different texts is to be avoided, it has nevertheless been suggested that they both depend on the vision of a *monde-mosaïque*, according to which fragmentation and discontinuity are no longer seen as flaws but rather as potentially enabling devices in the traveller's translation of place. Both authors encompass a fragmented diversity within the unifying, classificatory framework of the travel text. However, whereas Butor's work depends either on patchwork (he claims, as is illustrated above, that the text is composed a little like a quilt) or on the alphabetical ordering that Roland Barthes, in 'Littérature et discontinu', describes as 'le degré zéro des classements' [degree zero of classification], Bouvier's adoption of the mosaic has a more clearly restorative function.[26] It does not respond to an overwhelming sense of discontinuity by celebrating the non-systematic; nor does it impose a patently arbitrary order where there is none. Instead, from fragments, it remodels a sense of order where this is perceived to have been lost.

It is this idea that brings the reader back to *Routes et déroutes*, in the light of whose comments on the mosaic *L'Usage du monde* may usefully be read. The latter text itself can be seen as part of a mosaic, for the textualization of his early journey from Geneva to Japan was transformed by Bouvier into a life-long project of which the final fragments—such as the brief account of the journey through India—continue to appear posthumously;[27] moreover, certain critics have

---

[25] Dällenbach mentions pupils at the Collège Nicolas-Bouvier in Geneva making a giant mosaic with 780 cardboard boxes which, seen from above, represented the face of their 'patron saint' (*Mosaïques*, 28).

[26] Butor, *Mobile*, 29; Barthes, 'Littérature et discontinu', 179.

[27] See e.g. Nicolas Bouvier, 'La descente de l'Inde', in *L'Œil du voyageur* (Paris: Hoëbeke, 2001), 101–15.

described the structure of the text itself in terms of the medium, with Jean-Xavier Ridon, for instance, calling it 'une mosaïque de pannes' [a mosaic of breakdowns].[28] However, in his account of the section of the journey from Geneva to the Afghan–Indian border, the term 'mosaïque' appears only once, describing the ceiling of a Tehran hotel room. The room is 'si exiguë et encombrée qu'il faut s'étendre sur les lits pour travailler' [so cramped and cluttered that you had to lie on the bed to work]; the ceiling is 'une mosaïque d'estagnons "BP" qui laissent filtrer le clair de lune' [a mosaic of BP petrol drums, which let in the moonlight].[29] What is striking here is the association of an aestheticized mosaic-effect (moonlight filtering through a petrol company's logos) with an accumulation of other assorted junk whose proliferation threatens to hinder the traveller's work of textualization of the journey.

More than any other text by Bouvier, *L'Usage du monde* is dominated by the catalogue, by lists of objects whose apparently haphazard, unprocessed accumulation reflects the experience of the traveller overwhelmed by places and people hitherto unencountered. The text opens with such a list, Bouvier's travelling companion Thierry Vernet's description in a letter of the market in Travnik, and this is followed by a series of lists of faces, smells, and objects that represent the raw material of Bouvier's account.[30] For the purposes of this chapter, two scenes of arrival, in Belgrade and Quetta, are perhaps the most illuminating:

Nous retrouvions la rue ensoleillée, l'odeur des pastèques, le grand marché où les chevaux portent des prénoms d'enfant, et *ce désordre de maisons éparses* entre deux fleuves, ce campement très ancien qui, aujourd'hui, s'appelle Belgrade.

We would find ourselves outside, in the sunny street again, with the scent of melons, the big market where horses bore children's names, and *houses scattered in a disorderly fashion* between two rivers—a very old encampment, which today is called Belgrade.

And in Quetta:

Autour de nous, la ville disposait largement le peu dont elle est faite: des pans d'ombre fraîche, des attelages de buffles gris, quelques portails de style victorien flanqués de guérites et de canons de bronze, et des ruelles sableuses où des

---

[28] Jean-Xavier Ridon, 'Pour une poétique du voyage comme disparition', in Christiane Albert, Nadine Laporte, and Jean-Yves Pouilloux (eds.), *Autour de Nicolas Bouvier; résonances* (Geneva: Zoé, 2002), 120–35 (p. 127).

[29] Bouvier, *L'Usage du monde*, 196; *The Way of the World*, 195.

[30] Bouvier, *L'Usage du monde*, 9.

vieillards enturbannés, de grande prestance, flottaient sur de beaux vélos graissés et silencieux. *Une ville éparse*, légère comme un songe, pleine de répit, d'impondérable pacotille et de fruits aqueux.

Around us, the town laid out at intervals the little it was made up of: patches of cool shade, teams of grey buffaloes, a few gateways in the Victorian style, flanked by warriors and bronze cannon, and little sandy streets where old, turbaned men with great presence floated along on handsome bicycles that were well-oiled and silent. *A sparse town*, as fragile as a dream, full of repose, shoddy goods as light as smoke, and watery fruit.[31]

In neither of these catalogues of disjointed fragments is the term mosaic used; it is the adjective 'épars' (in 'ce désordre de maisons éparses' and 'Une ville éparse'), however, that resonates with Bouvier's comments on the mosaic underpinning his work—'les morceaux épars d'une mosaï-que détruite'—with which this section of the chapter began.

What these extracts underline is Bouvier's focus on the creative potential of the traveller reconstructing patterns from scattered fragments whose previously existing configurations have been eroded and broken up. For this notion of reconstruction is not automatically associated with the mosaic, as there is customarily a distinction—increasingly lost, Dällenbach claims, in the conflations of the 1990s—between the mosaic and the jigsaw, between what Dällenbach calls a 'totalité inédite, donc à inventer' [brand new totality, which is therefore to be invented] and a 'totalité préexistante qu'il s'agit de reconstituer' [pre-existing totality, which it is a matter of reconstituting].[32] There is a risk, however, of misreading Bouvier's comments in the interview, and misunderstanding the nature of the 'reconstruction' they imply—for reconstruction does not necessarily imply restoration, the salvaging of fragments does not automatically lead to a nostalgic desire to recreate what is deemed original or authentic. Bouvier's work is certainly underpinned by a belief in the potential harmony of origins and the possibility of rediscovering traces of such harmony. Barthes and Bouvier are both motivated by an interest in Zen Buddhism, but whereas the former is drawn to the sense of void at its heart, the latter seems more attracted by a minimalism that permits reconstruction of a lost equilibrium from its remaining traces. In the title text of *Le Hibou et la baleine*, for instance, he describes a 'parenté avec le monde animal' [connection

---

[31] Ibid. 32; *The Way of the World*, 32 (my emphasis); and *L'Usage du monde*, 256; *The Way of the World*, 225 (my emphasis).

[32] Dällenbach, *Mosaïques*, 62.

with the animal world], linked to the foundational experience of 'cette Arche où nous vivions plutôt serrés mais tous ensemble et où, pendant mille interminables journées de pluie, de solides connivences se sont établies' [that Ark where we lived together in rather cramped conditions—but together all the same—and where, during a thousand days of interminable rain, a firm sense of complicity was established].[33] With the Ark stranded on Mount Ararat he continues, however, 'cette grande ménagerie s'est vidée; chacun est retourné à ses affaires [...] comme si cette cohabitation n'avait été qu'un songe' [this great menagerie was emptied, and everyone returned to their own business [...] as if this cohabitation had been a mere dream]. Commenting on this anecdote in his brief essay on Bouvier, Vahé Godel tampers with etymology to link this 'Arche' to the Greek 'arkhè', meaning 'beginning' or 'origin', and summarizes Bouvier's project in the following terms: ' "Trouver une langue" qui puisse restituer l'Unité perdue' ['Discovering a language' that would be able to restore the lost Unity].[34] Such lost unity is reflected in what Bouvier describes, in the section of the interviews devoted to the mosaic, as 'une sorte d'ensemble harmonique, polyphonique' [a sort of harmonious, polyphonic ensemble].[35]

In one of the first full critical studies of Bouvier, Adrien Pasquali similarly comments on the author's focus on origins and the possibilities of continuity they imply, identifying his adherence (on the one hand) to the spatial notion of a Eurasian 'continuité continentale' [continental continuity] that links China to Switzerland, challenging traditional Orientalist binaries, and (on the other) to the chronological axes of 'filiations écrites' [written filiations] that link Asia, Europe, and North America.[36] Bouvier's work does not reflect, however, a nostalgic yearning for these lost origins. In constructing through his work a 'monde-mosaïque', he explores instead the tensions that can be contained in this particular art form between such imagined unity and the experience of everyday discontinuity with which it coexists, between such purported uniformity and the diversity to which it is closely related. Bouvier's world-as-mosaic protects heterogeneity whilst allowing discontinuous elements to coexist in a homogenizing frame. It is no longer what

---

[33] Nicolas Bouvier, *Le Hibou et la baleine* (Geneva: Zoé, 1993), 7.

[34] Vahé Godel, *Nicolas Bouvier: 'faire un peu de musique avec cette vie unique'* (Geneva: Métropolis, 1998), 20.

[35] Bouvier, *Routes et Déroutes*, 55.

[36] Adrien Pasquali, *Nicolas Bouvier: un galet dans le torrent du monde* (Geneva: Zoé, 1996), 27, Bouvier, *Journal d'Aran*, 113, and *Le Hibou et la Baleine*, 55-7.

Dällenbach calls a ' "signifié flottant", [...] un terme "attrape-tout" [...] démuni de tout pouvoir différenciateur' ['floating signified', [...] a 'catch-all' term [...] lacking all power of differentiation].[37] Instead, in Bouvier's work, the mosaic seems to offer travel literature a middle course between representations of place and culture that are (on the one hand) fixed, essentialized, hierarchical, and (on the other) chaotic, entropic.[38] Instead of emphasizing one of the polarized understandings of the medium—unity (privileged in literal understandings) or discontinuity (privileged in metaphorical uses)—Bouvier maintains and exploits this tension between them and uses this as the foundation for his textualization of travel.

To understand further the writerly implications of Bouvier's use of the mosaic, there is a need to explore his attitude to those fragments to which he is drawn in particular and to which I allude in the chapter's title—i.e. rubbish—and to situate his attitude to this in relation to a more general use of debris and waste in travel writing. As Barthes and Butor show, rubbish is far from being the only form of fragmentation that the traveller encounters: Barthes's text describes none, and for Butor, apart from on two occasions when he describes 'papiers sales, / mégots, / assiettes de carton, / sandales dépareillées, / bouchons de tubes' [dirty papers, / cigarette butts, / paper plates, / odd sandals, / bottletops] bobbing in the sea, or 'les ordures qui flottent sur l'eau' [the garbage floating in the water], debris is more the absent yet implied end-product of the consumerism on which the text focuses.[39] Rubbish is, nevertheless, one of the most recurrent forms of fragmentation described in travel writing, and comes to epitomize the fragmentation with which these two authors experiment.

In relation to rubbish and travel, the most immediately apparent reference is undoubtedly Claude Lévi-Strauss's often-anthologized threnody for travel and travel literature in the opening section of *Tristes Tropiques*, entitled 'La Fin des voyages' [An End to Journeying], cited at the start of this chapter. Elsewhere is no longer associated with refuge, but with refuse—for the creation of rubbish is an unequivocal sign or

[37] Dällenbach, *Mosaïques*, 39.

[38] In this way, Bouvier's use of the mosaic is similar to the description of Creoleness as a 'mosaïque constitutive' [constituent mosaic] in Jean Bernabé, Patrick Chamoiseau, and Raphaël Confiant's *Éloge de la créolité* (Paris: Gallimard, 1993), 27, 89. The authors also claim: 'La Créolité c'est "le monde diffracté mais recomposé", un maelström de signifiés dans un seul signifiant: une Totalité' [Creoleness is 'the world diffracted but recomposed', a maelstrom of signifieds in a single signifier: a Totality], ibid 27, 88.

[39] Butor, *Mobile*, 278, 322; trans. Howard, 168, 193.

trace of human presence, the proliferation of litter a clear indicator of widespread social mobility. Lévi-Strauss's images of contamination and of the transformation of travel into a salutary voyage of confirmation are, however, far from unique, and debris forms a central element in the entropic vision of an earlier traveller, Victor Segalen. Travelling in Polynesia in 1903, Segalen, as a naval doctor, is obliged to intervene in the disaster area of the cyclone-struck Tuomotu archipelago.[40] What he describes both in the *Journal des îles* and in 'Vers les sinistrés', the official account of the tour of duty written for *Armée et Marine*, is the stripped and rubbish-strewn coral he discovers there: 'c'est un sol bousculé [...] recouvert d'un humus sinistre, d'une boue désséchée au soleil de choses informes, délavées, broyées, disloquées, pilées: [...] des chambranles de fenêtres, des cadres de bicyclettes [...] et toujours des pneus, des guidons' [it is disturbed ground [...] covered with [...] mud dried out in the sun, scattered with shapeless, faded, crushed, broken, shattered objects: [...] window frames, bicycle frames [...] and endless tyres and handlebars].[41] It is in the official article that he adds, in a phrase that Lévi-Strauss seems subsequently to echo: 'tous ces relents tristes d'une vie hybride en voie de perversion civilisée' [all these sad traces of a hybrid way of life in the process of being perverted by civilization].[42] For Segalen and Lévi-Strauss, rubbish is the by-product of Western imperialism, cultural and otherwise, and is emblematic of an exoticist view of the world whereby contact leads to pollution and progressively negative hybridization, and to which the only response is salvage of those traces of indigeneity that remain.[43] In terms of rubbish theory, the trash the traveller encounters is not simply and neutrally valueless but has instead a regrettably 'negative value'.[44]

The study of rubbish draws us, however, into considerations of shifting systems of value and of perceptions of status. Whereas, customarily, value and status are linked to possessions, rubbish theory suggests they are reflected in what we can afford to discard. Bouvier's traveller—no

---

[40] On this subject, see the Postface below.

[41] Victor Segalen, *Journal des îles*, in *Œuvres complètes*, i. 395–479 (p. 414).

[42] Victor Segalen, 'Vers les sinistrés', in *Œuvres complètes*, i. 513–19 (p. 516).

[43] Segalen and Lévi-Strauss's focus on debris foreshadows its recurrent role in contemporary travel texts, such as Gianni Celati's *Adventures in Africa*, trans. Adria Bernardi (Chicago, Ill.: University of Chicago Press, 2000). For Celati, West Africa is strewn with 'dust and garbage' (p. 6), 'mounds of trash' (p. 90) that characterize the perceived decay of the cultures through which he travels.

[44] See Michael Thompson, *Rubbish Theory: The Creation and Destruction of Value* (Oxford: Oxford University Press, 1979).

longer a confident, sovereign individual, but pared down to a minimal identity, vulnerable, and at times self-effacing to the point of a threatened disappearance that, unlike Barthes's nothingness, is never quite fully achieved—develops a mode of perception whereby value is granted to what others would dismiss as valueless or negatively valued. Travel narratives often describe a neutral experience, with elsewhere projected as monotonous and valueless. Segalen, on Easter Sunday 1903, writes in his *Journal des îles*: 'Huit jours de mer. Navigation dite "heureuse". Plate, tiède, sans vent, sans mer, sans rien' [Eight days at sea. So-called 'pleasant' sailing. Flat, tepid—no wind, no sea, no anything]; Michaux, crossing the Atlantic just over two decades later, repeats these impressions: 'On aura parcouru quatre mille milles et on n'aura rien vu [...]; en un mot: rien! rien!' [We are going to have travelled 4,000 miles, and we will have seen nothing [...]; in a word: nothing! nothing!].[45] In contrast with Barthes's concluding 'there is nothing to grasp', Bouvier himself refuses to find 'nothing'. The word is excluded from his lexicon—in the catalogue already quoted that marks the arrival at Quetta, he claims, for instance: 'la ville disposait largement *le peu* dont elle est faite' [the town laid out at intervals *the little* it was made up of], and it is the idea of a minimalist 'peu' that repeatedly replaces the dismissively annihilating 'rien'.[46]

In the later *Journal d'Aran*, Bouvier makes this point clear by claiming that 'Rien est un mot spécieux qui ne veut rien dire. *Rien* m'a toujours mis la puce à l'oreille' [Nothing is a specious word that has no meaning. *Nothing* has always set me thinking].[47] Bouvier's texts are strewn with what others would dismiss as nothing: waste, organic or manufactured, excrement or rubbish. His attitude to this debris diverges radically from that of Segalen and Lévi-Strauss, and echoes instead an idea of the world-as-constant-change whose earliest articulation is perhaps to be found in Heraclitus's *Fragments* (79 or 124 according to the edition): in Marcel Conche's translation, 'De choses répandues au hasard, le plus bel ordre, l'ordre-du-monde', or in T. M. Robinson's, 'The most beautiful order [in the universe?] is a heap of sweepings, piled up at random'.[48] The text of the fragment is doubtful,

[45] Segalen, *Journal des îles*, 419; Michaux, *Ecuador*, 17.
[46] Bouvier, *L'Usage du Monde*, 256; *Way of the World*, 225, my emphasis.
[47] Bouvier, *Journal d'Aran*, 31.
[48] See Heraclitus, *Fragments*, trans. and ed. Marcel Conche (Paris: PUF, 1986), 276, and *Fragments*, trans. and ed. T. M. Robinson (Toronto: University of Toronto Press, 1987), 71. For a discussion of Heraclitus' similar influence on the thought of Edouard Glissant, see Ridon, *Le Voyage en son miroir*, 128.

and Robinson makes the point that 'attempts at interpretation should therefore be treated with more than the usual dose of scepticism', but the reader's attention is held by Conche's claim, that the text 'affirme le droit, dans le monde, du désordre et du hasard' [asserts the right for disorder and chance to exist in the world].[49] Disordered, scattered debris is not necessarily a hindrance to Bouvier's experience of travel; it is rather the raw material on which that experience is inevitably to be built and with which the traveller engages both pragmatically and inquisitively. Taking an image from dance and music, Bouvier aestheticizes the rubbish that bobs around the coast of Aran and transforms it into a 'grande sarabande d'ordures et de détritus vagabonds qui tournent autour de l'île au gré de la bourrasque et des courants marins' [great swirling mass of rubbish and floating detritus that is tossed around the island as the gusts of wind and ocean current dictate].[50] In Korea, the sacred route to a Buddhist monastery—worn by pilgrims' footsteps, engraved with Chinese and Korean characters—becomes '*the old shittrack again*', 'étincel[ant] de bouteilles brisées; [...] ponctué d'étrons secs' [sparkling with broken bottles; [...] punctuated with dried turds].[51] What is *imagined* clashes with what is *experienced*, and Bouvier debunks exoticist anticipation (and the denial of coevalness with which this is customarily associated). A moment of *panne*—breakdown, here, of expectation—is transformed to underline the everyday juxtapositions that the contemporary traveller must face.

Bouvier assembles fragmentary, often discarded traces of elsewhere—anecdotes, experiences, photographs, material objects, recorded snatches of music, fleeting contact with 'travellees'—and presents these as the text of the journey, which progresses with seeming discontinuity yet is controlled by the frames of the narrative. This aspect of the text is perhaps most clearly illustrated in an episode at Quetta, in *L'Usage du monde*, during which the narrator's initial manuscript is

---

[49] Robinson, *Fragments*, 162; Conche, *Fragments*, 277.

[50] Bouvier, *Journal d'Aran*, 4.

[51] *Journal d'Aran*, 125. Excrement—human or animal—is a recurrent aspect of Bouvier's travel accounts, but it is not the negative currency in a denigratory textual or social economy described by Dominique Laporte in *Histoire de la merde (Prologue)* (Paris: Christian Bourgois, 1978). Instead, as part of the revalorization of the somatic and scatological that characterizes much of Bouvier's work, it represents an inevitable everyday element of the cultures through which he travels, neither avoided nor suppressed. As such, Bouvier's travel writing differs radically from that of authors such as V. S. Naipaul, for whom faecal matter becomes, in S. Shankar's terms, a 'marker of the ontological status of India'. See *Textual Traffic: Colonialism, Modernity, and the Economy of the Text* (New York: State University of New York Press, 2001), 153.

accidentally disposed of on a rubbish tip, 'dans la poussière avec les immondices et les troncs de choux' [in the dust along with unmentionable muck and cabbage stalks].[52] The substantial 'travail de l'hiver' [winter's work] is eventually unearthed, after a journey of excavation through the rubbish, as 'un agrégat noir et misérable' [a black, poverty-stricken medley], a literally homogenized account of the journey which the narrator is forced to abandon.[53] The search for this initial, ultimately unsatisfactory version, however, had entailed sifting through a carefully catalogued mass of disparate debris, and it is such seemingly banal, unexotic fragments that not only dominate this particular episode but also, once collected, eventually constitute the mosaic of the final account: an accumulation of individual elements, not a seamless text.[54] The world is accordingly perceived and experienced as discarded fragments of a potential mosaic, and such perception and experience have a structural and even epistemological impact on Bouvier's subsequent representation and understanding of his journey.

Bouvier claims to Patricia Plattner in the film version of *Le Hibou et la baleine*: 'Je n'ai rien d'un conquérant' [There is nothing in me of a conqueror],[55] and in his work there is indeed no search for pristine spaces, no discourse of disappointment at the discovery that others have not only travelled there before, but also left material traces. Instead, there is an acceptance of place *as he finds it* and a willingness to work with the raw materials with which travel presents him. The mosaic may seem to operate, in certain contexts, as a device of postmodern levelling, dissolving differences and permitting travellers to ignore the exclusions on which their own self-definition depends. For Bouvier, the mosaic becomes instead a means of reflecting complexity and not of flattening it out: the fragments he brings together range from traces of other journeys that relativize his own to evidence of historical awareness that gives texture to the surfaces of the present. Elements of the journey are therefore treated individually, but also in relation to those that precede or follow them. There is a risk, of course, that such a practice contributes to the perpetuation of certain ideological assumptions relating to travel, for 'mosaïque' and 'musée' share the same etymological

---

[52] Bouvier, *L'Usage du Monde*, 283; *Way of the World*, 249.

[53] Bouvier, *L'Usage du Monde*, 285; *Way of the World*, 252.

[54] See also Bouvier, *Chronique japonaise*, 274–5, in which the author describes the construction of the text from scrawled, disparate, and often discarded notes.

[55] Cited by Ridon, 'Pour une poétique du voyage comme disparition', 122.

roots, and the same potential for fixity and control.[56] Bouvier as traveller certainly is a collector, but in the amateur or artisanal sense of a 'colporteur' or peddler as opposed to any systematically appropriative understanding. Collection in this sense, as Italo Calvino suggests, is closely allied to the processes of textual accumulation that characterize the travel writer's activity, triggered by 'cette obscure folle envie qui pousse tout autant à rassembler une collection qu'à tenir un journal, c'est-à-dire du besoin de transformer le cours de sa propre existence en une série d'objets sauvés de la dispersion, ou en une série de lignes écrites, cristallisées en dehors du flux continu des pensers' [that obscure and foolish desire that motivates people to put together a collection or keep a diary, i.e. the need to transform the course of one's own existence into a series of objects salvaged from dispersal, or into a series of written lines, crystallized outside the continuous flow of thought].[57]

In conclusion, I return to the distinction between the jigsaw and the mosaic, between what Dällenbach calls the 'Opus magnum' of a divinely inspired pattern and the 'opus incertum' (or *œuvre incertaine*) constructed from broken, recycled materials or disparate fragments brought together from a variety of sources.[58] Whereas the aim of the early mosaic, often elevated from view, was to disguise discontinuity and emphasize unity, current metaphorical uses of the term seem to underline a celebratory sense of residual diversity, in contrast to the threat of all-encroaching globalization. Bouvier eschews such polarized, systematic understandings: he goes beyond the exotic to discover the specific, but works then to reinsert what is apparently fragmented into a framework of interconnections in which continuity and discontinuity, unity and diversity, harmony and variation are allowed to coexist. The challenges inherent in travel explored by Barthes and Butor similarly concern Bouvier, but he seems to transform the dislocated fragments he finds into a very different world picture. As a final image to illustrate this unexpected coexistence, I cite Bouvier's 1953 poem, 'Le point de non-retour' [The point of no return], a text subsequently redrafted as prose in *L'Usage du monde*, in which the fractal, fragmentary detail of a series of scattered fragments—'des racines blanchies rejetées par la mer', 'de menus éclats de bambou', and 'un tout petit poisson' [blanched roots rejected by the sea; slivers of

---

[56] Dällenbach, *Mosaïques*, 38.
[57] Italo Calvino, *Collection de sable*, trans. Jean-Paul Manganaro (Paris: Seuil, 1986), 13.
[58] Dällenbach, *Mosaïques*, 63.

bamboo; a small fish]—are contrasted with the 'fabuleux champignon d'orage' [enormous mushroom cloud], overarching as it rises above the Crimea and stretches as far as China.[59] Here is an image of continuity and discontinuity, of the microscopic and macroscopic, of unity and diversity in which can be seen a clear trace of Bouvier's 'mosaïque encore lacunaire'.

---

[59] Nicolas Bouvier, *Le Dehors et le Dedans* (Geneva: Zoé, 1997), 15. See also *L'Usage du Monde*, 87–90.

6

Journeying Now:
New Directions in Contemporary
Travel Literature in French

> The future of travellers' tales [...] lies in their reading, in culti-
> vating new arts of reading them. My prescription is to stay at home
> and do just that.[1]

> La banalité n'est pas dans le monde. Elle est toujours dans le
> regard. Et l'important n'est pas dans le fait que le monde soit (ou
> non) 'rincé de son exotisme', mais dans le fait qu'un jour il puisse
> être perçu ainsi. Alors, dans tous les cas, qu'il soit ou non 'rincé',
> l'essentiel n'est-il pas de se débarrasser de cette désagréable im-
> pression et de réinventer l'exotisme de ce monde?[2]

> Banality is never in the world. It is always in the gaze. What is
> important is not whether (or not) the world is 'rinsed of its exoti-
> cism', but whether one day it will be perceived as such. Whether it
> is washed out or not, is not the main thing to get rid of this
> unpleasant impression and to reinvent the world's exoticism?

FOR those concerned with the study of French-language literatures and
cultures, one of the principal changes in recent decades has involved the
progressive 'decolonization' of their object of study. The rapid proliferation, if not so rapid critical recognition, of a body of postcolonial
Francophone texts has led to the elaboration of an understanding of
francophone space that extends far beyond its traditional restriction to

---

[1] Adrian Rifkin, 'Travel for Men: from Claude Lévi-Strauss to the Sailor Hans', in
George Robertson et al. (eds.), *Travellers' Tales: Narratives of Home and Displacement*
(London: Routledge, 1994), 216–24 (p. 223).

[2] Urbain, *Secrets de voyages*, 438–9.

the boundaries of the Hexagon.[3] One of the aims of this volume has been to suggest that such a development has been accompanied and complemented by the parallel emergence of an interest in a body of texts, for the sake of convenience dubbed 'travel literature in French', that similarly challenges the reduction of understandings of Frenchness to a national model. Both postcolonial literature and travel literature in French suggest that cultures cannot be perceived as self-sufficient, but are more usefully understood in transcultural terms as mutually inter-dependent according to shifting patterns of power, representation, knowledge, and influence.

Although identifying and acquiring texts written in French produced outside France, especially from regions such as Polynesia, may remain challenging, the study of postcolonial literatures in French has been rapidly facilitated over the past decade or so by the wider dissemination and increased availability of books produced by publishing houses across the Francophone world. Reading travel narratives could until very recently be seen as an equally difficult as well as often more troubling process of unearthing what, in a different context in relation to the nineteenth-century novel, Margaret Cohen has called the 'great unread'.[4] This observation is as true of the shelf-loads of travel narra-tives and reportage from the period of New Imperialism that were rapidly relegated to the library stacks in the aftermath of decolonization as it is of contemporary works belonging to a genre whose journalistic associations continue to render it particularly perishable or ephemeral. The practices of reading and publishers' priorities in the later twentieth century led, however, to a selective reversal of this situation. The republication and anthologization of earlier material was supplemented by the commercially expedient packaging of new travel narratives. Such a practice is clearly associated with what Graham Huggan dubs the 'marketing of the margins', a process already discussed in the introduc-tion to this volume. A popular appetite for such material was matched by renewed scholarly interest, especially in North America, where postcolonialism's rapid emergence created a discipline in search of a canon. In the introduction to their *Companion to Travel Writing*, Peter Hulme and Tim Youngs describe their subject as a 'vast, little explored

---

[3] On these processes, see Forsdick and Murphy (eds.), *Francophone Postcolonial Stud-ies: A Critical Introduction*, and Stovall and van den Abbeele (eds.), *French Civilization and Its Discontents*.

[4] Margaret Cohen, *The Sentimental Education of the Novel* (Princeton, NJ: Princeton University Press, 1999).

area'.[5] The rapid proliferation over the past decade of centres, journals, collections, and other academic texts devoted to travel writing reflects the equally rapid expansion in scholarly activity, as well as the need to provide intellectual apparatus and epistemological underpinnings to permit its further development.

For the purposes of this study, attention is restricted to the renewal of interest in travel narratives in French, although any such restriction of travel literature along national lines is challenged by the mobility of such texts that, like their authors, tend to shift between cultures.[6] These processes of re-evaluation may be linked to a more general shift in the anglophone academy, affecting fields of inquiry such as French studies, whereby popular cultural forms have steadily replaced canonical literary texts as objects of study. There is a need to recognize, however, that reading the *récit de voyage* seems to involve more complex critical practices than those implied by the study of, for instance, the *bande dessinée* or *polar*. For the rise of travel literature not only crystallizes a series of concerns central to contemporary literary and cultural studies, relating to colonial and postcolonial issues: interculturality, translation, the desire to describe grounds of comparison according to which the metropolitan and non-metropolitan may coexist in a non-hierarchical relationship; it also poses a series of questions about the nature and future of the field in which scholars operate. For those working on French-language material, studying travel suggests either that French studies is firmly and literally interdisciplinary, situated in the space between a series of other disciplines; or that francophone material (with the epithet understood in its most inclusive senses) should in fact be situated in those other disciplines—such as postcolonial or translation studies. It also raises questions about the sustainability of definitions of Modern Foreign Languages in relation to national boundaries. The opening section of this chapter is concerned with the practical ways in which these current critical considerations coincide with and yet diverge from both the French publishing phenomenon known as 'le travel writing' and the movement that underpins this, *Pour une littérature voyageuse*.

---

[5] Hulme and Youngs, *Cambridge Companion to Travel Writing*, 1.
[6] See Siobhán Shilton, '*Une littérature qui dise le monde*? Contemporary French Travel Writing and the Challenge of Postcoloniality', in Peter Davies, Catriona Cunningham, and Cristina Johnson (eds.), *Contemporary Francophone Identities* (Glasgow: University of Glasgow French and German Publications, 2002), 135–49.

CONTRE *UNE LITTÉRATURE VOYAGEUSE*

French interest in travel literature, as has been explored above, became apparent in the 1980s when a series of publishers launched new series dedicated to the publication—or republication—of travel narratives. Michel Le Bris, former editor of *La Cause du Peuple*, journalist, and Robert Louis Stevenson scholar, created the now substantial Voyageurs series for Payot in 1988. He then built on this activity to launch the journal *Gulliver* and the Étonnants Voyageurs festival in Saint-Malo.[7] Although *Gulliver*'s development has been sporadic,[8] the festival has grown steadily to become one of France's major and most heavily attended annual literary events outside Paris. No longer devoted solely to travel writing, it now welcomes a series of other authors—especially of detective fiction and postcolonial literature—who share the festival's interest in what the organizers dub 'une littérature qui dise le monde'. The meaning of the phrase remains hazy, although its apparently neo-realist grounding in empirical contact with the world marks a clear departure from what Le Bris dismisses as the 'mise entre parenthèses du monde' by which, as was explained in the previous chapter, he characterizes French literature from the 1950s to the 1970s.

Early attempts to define the objectives of the *Pour une littérature voyageuse* movement were largely dependent on such negation, on its members' progressive distancing from a series of literary straw men that included the self-sufficiency and self-satisfaction of French literature, the pernicious and persistent legacies of Structuralism and the *nouveau roman*, and the emergence of new genres such as autofiction.[9] In 1992, however, a multi-authored manifesto appeared, taking as its title what would be understood as the movement's name. An unsigned preface appears to be the work of Le Bris himself, but the tone of the contributions is otherwise eclectic, extending from Nicolas Bouvier's subtle

[7] For a discussion of Le Bris's work, see Forsdick, '*Fin de Siècle, Fin des Voyages*'.
[8] Thirteen issues in three years, followed by a relaunch of three issues by Librio in 1998–9.
[9] Michel Le Bris has been the principal activist in attempts to forge a coherent identity that unites the largely fragmented collaborators in the movement. He has written a series of anti-theoretical 'theoretical' texts, such as 'Introduction—ce simple mystère: raconter des histoires', in *Une amitié littéraire: Henry James–Robert-Louis Stevenson* (Paris: Verdier, 1987), 7–73, and several essays included in *Le Grand Dehors*; the Étonnants voyageurs festival also invariably features authors whose critical interventions echo with his own position, such as Pierre Jourde whose *La Littérature sans estomac* (Paris: Esprit des péninsules, 2002) targets what it sees as the asphyxiation of contemporary French literature.

reflection on travel as an 'exercice de disparition' [disappearance exercise] to Jean-Luc Coatalem's statement on travel and nostalgia.[10] The collection encompasses, therefore, a variety of contemporary attitudes, ranging from progressive erosion of the travelling self in face of the Other to the self's active reassertion as a dominant, sovereign individual. What is striking, however, is the attempt—seen largely through paratextual features such as title, preface, and concluding bibliography—to impose coherence, to write a justificatory narrative of the movement's emergence, and to elaborate a credible genealogy. The editor's opening comments are defensive, dismissing suspicion of Anglo-Saxon dominance of 'le travel writing' and claiming a French pedigree by asking: 'pas Français vraiment, un Segalen, un Cendrars, un Michaux, un Kessel?' [not really French, a Segalen, a Cendrars, a Michaux, a Kessel?].[11] This conflation of identities—Breton, Swiss, Belgian, and French—and the exclusion of difference it implies are also reflected in the 'repères historiques' with which the volume concludes. Claiming a post-Marxist impetus, the movement's 'années charnières' are said to be 1976–7, during which a series of undeniably important travel texts appeared: Michel Chaillou's *Le Sentiment géographique*, Jacques Lacarrière's *Chemin faisant*, Michel Le Bris's *L'Homme aux semelles de vent*, Jacques Meunier's *Les Gamins de Bogota*, and Kenneth White's *Les Limbes incandescents*.[12]

It is the account of works published over the subsequent fifteen years that becomes confusing: details of texts by contemporary authors are mingled with those of earlier authors being simultaneously republished—Victor Segalen and Robert Louis Stevenson are, for instance presented alongside Jean Rolin; Peter Fleming and Ella Maillart alongside Nicolas Bouvier; and translations (largely from English) into French are similarly absorbed into what becomes a decontextualized, ahistorical glory-hole. What is troubling is the lack of texture, the failure to acknowledge that for readers of travel writing, more perhaps than for those of any other genre, three issues remain paramount: the processes of translation and the domestication of difference, an

---

[10] See Nicolas Bouvier, 'La clé des champs', in *Pour une littérature voyageuse*, 41–4 (p. 44).

[11] 'Notes de l'éditeur', in *Pour une littérature voyageuse*, 7–15 (p. 8).

[12] See Michel Chaillou, *Le Sentiment géographique* (Paris: Gallimard, 1976), Jacques Lacarrière, *Chemin faisant* (Paris: Payot, 1992 [1977]), Michel Le Bris, *L'Homme aux semelles de vent* (Paris: Grasset, 1977), Jacques Meunier, *Les Gamins de Bogota* (Paris: Lattès, 1977), and Kenneth White, *Les Limbes incandescents* (Paris: Denoël, 1976).

understanding of historical context, and a nostalgia for earlier forms. There emerges from this synthesis of texts written by a variety of almost exclusively European travellers a concept of travel that does little to reflect any late twentieth-century context: travel remains a Western practice, agoraphilic, implicitly masculine and explicitly solitary.[13] The clear risks of nostalgia—and more explicitly of 'imperialist nostalgia'—implicit in such an exclusive definition surface in a number of texts by authors associated with the movement. Jean-Luc Coatalem speaks, for instance, of his quest, through travel, for 'ces colonies d'antan, vestiges d'un passé qui me manque, d'une aventure qui m'a échappé, m'échappe encore, me pousse à toutes les hypothèses' [these colonies of yesteryear, traces of a past that I miss, of an adventure that eluded me, that still eludes me, that drives me to speculate wildly];[14] and this search for traces of the past is linked to an entropic view of travel's decline characterized most clearly by Alain Borer's intervention in the manifesto. The recognition that 'le plus loin où nous puissions aller est ici-même' [the furthest we can go is back here] does not imply the same reordering of the field of travel that it does for some travellers (such as Maspero, discussed below), but alludes instead to the risk of the end of travel.[15]

There are certain indications of a recasting of the movement's parameters in a more inclusive manner. Since 1993, when the event's theme was 'Écritures métissées', the participation of postcolonial Francophone authors (as well as of authors of immigrant origin working in France) at the annual Saint-Malo festival has increased. By bringing together the literature and culture of southern France and North Africa, for instance, the focus of the 1998 festival on the Mediterranean, described as a 'zone de tous les brassages et de toutes les fractures, sans cesse déchirée, meurtrie, et toujours renaissante' [area of all mixtures and fractures, incessantly split, bruised, and yet always in a

---

[13] There are notable exceptions, both in contributions to the collection of essay and in the bibliography (in which V. S. Naipaul and Ella Maillart stand out as respectively the only non-European and women writers), but there is an overwhelming sense that the manifesto reinforces a traditional, aristocratic discourse of anti-tourism and solitary travel characterized, in Jean-Didier Urbain's terms, by an overt 'agoraphilia' and an associated refusal to address the implications of Empire. On the apparent exclusion of women authors from the *Pour une littérature voyageuse* movement, see Forsdick, 'Hidden Journeys'.

[14] Jean-Luc Coatalem, 'Un mauvais départ', in *Pour une littérature voyageuse*, 83–6 (p. 85).

[15] See Alain Borer, 'L'Ère de Colomb et l'ère d'Armstrong', in *Pour une littérature voyageuse*, 17–40 (p. 35).

state of renewal], highlighted once again the potential contribution of travel to any ongoing reflection on the complexities of contemporary world culture.[16] In its rhetoric at least, what is emerging alongside these overtly nostalgic tendencies from the *Pour une littérature voyageuse* movement is a vision of diversity, based more on interchange than autonomy. This vision appears to counter metanarratives of entropy and loss in order to privilege the emergence of new cultural matrices. Any such commitment to the identification and representation of diversity in the contemporary world is problematized, however, by the continued adherence to previous models of intercultural contact. The position on 'travel' set out in the manifesto would seem, however, to persist; a second edition of the text, published to coincide with the tenth anniversary of the festival in 1999, remained entirely unchanged. Alain Borer's statement about the decline of travelling—'Les peuples voyagent peu. Ce sont quelques individus, guère plus nombreux en proportion, qui voyagent pour les autres' [People do not travel much. It is only a few individuals, hardly more numerous in proportion, who travel on behalf of others]—not only reflects this process of prescriptive definition, reliant on assumptions relating to the decline of diversity on which 'real' travel depends; but it also contradicts a more general effort throughout the 1990s to expand, decolonize, and democratize the concept of 'travel'.[17]

As the widespread practice of anti-tourism reveals, 'travel' is often defined in terms of such exclusion: would-be 'travellers' identify themselves not with positive attributes, but by distancing themselves from other characters, many of whom are similarly in (some form of) transit: tourists themselves, indigenous carriers, vagrants, migrants, and so on. This attempt to cling on to an earlier understanding of the practices encompassed by the verb 'voyager' can be seen most clearly in Jacques Lacarrière's brief contribution to the manifesto, 'Le bernard-l'hermite ou le treizième voyage'. This text is an attempt to describe 'le seul voyage qui vaille' [the only valid type of travel] by rejecting a catalogue of a dozen definitions in order to reach his own chosen understanding. For Lacarrière, the underlying principle of travel is a belief in its possible purity or authenticity, and the elevation of a particular type of Western traveller as its privileged practitioner. Lacarrière's ideal

---

[16] See Michel Le Bris, 'Avant-propos', in Michel Le Bris and Jean-Claude Izzo (eds.), *Méditérrannées* (Paris: Librio, 1998), 7. Edouard Glissant nevertheless usefully contrasts the Mediterranean with Caribbean in *Introduction à une poétique du Divers*, 14.

[17] See Borer, 'L'Ère de Colomb et l'ère d'Armstrong', 19.

transforms travel writing into a transparent vessel, the travel writer into 'un crustacé parlant dont l'esprit, dépourvu de carapace identitaire, se sent spontanément chez lui dans la culture des autres' [a talking crustacean whose mind, stripped of any shell of identity, spontaneously feels at home in others' cultures].[18] If the travel narrative is seen as a form of translation of elsewhere, then Lacarrière's traveller-translator belongs to an earlier understanding of these processes, whereby the text produced could be judged in terms of innocence and faithfulness. There is a clear divergence between this position and the contribution of recent developments in Translation Studies to the criticism of travel literature, i.e. in particular the knowledge that 'travel writers constantly position themselves in relation to their point of origin in a culture and the context they are describing'.[19] Moreover, what is of most interest in Lacarrière's list of excluded categories of mobility is its fiction of unrelatedness, its implicit decontextualization, and its denial of the connection Simenon highlighted in the 1930s: a connection between journeys that are often not only simultaneous, but also may share the same spatial parameters and even means of transport. For the would-be traveller's desire for self-distinction is eroded and broken down in what Mary Louise Pratt has described as the 'contact zone', a space criss-crossed by very different journeys, but where various itineraries temporarily converge and are forced to interact. Whereas Lacarrière excludes from his definition 'le voyage civil forcé (l'exilé, le déplacé, le déporté)' [the forced civilian journey (exiled, displaced, or deported people)], this is precisely the type of journey that James Clifford has absorbed, not without criticism, into the concept of travel in his essay 'Traveling Cultures'.

bell hooks responded to Clifford with the claim that '[h]olding on to the concept of "travel" as we know it is also a way to hold on to imperialism', and Patrick Holland and Graham Huggan point to the failure of the 'traveling culture' paradigm to accept that 'traversals are always already gendered'.[20] With these attenuating caveats relating to gender and ethnicity in mind, however, we may use Clifford's claim that

---

[18] Jacques Lacarrière, 'Le bernard-l'hermite ou le treizième voyage', in *Pour une littérature voyageuse*, 105–7 (p. 107).

[19] Susan Bassnett, *Comparative Literature: A Critical Introduction* (Oxford: Blackwell, 1993), 99.

[20] See bell hooks, 'Representations of Whiteness in the Black Imagination', in *Black Looks: Race and Representation* (Boston, Mass.: South End, 1992), 165–78 (p. 173), and Holland and Huggan, *Tourists with Typewriters*, 111.

'we need to listen to a wide range of "travel stories" (not "travel literature" in the bourgeois sense)' to cast light on the theory and practice of the *Pour une littérature voyageuse* movement.[21] Such 'travel stories' are not ignored; they are admitted, however, only under the banner of 'World Fiction' so that traditional understandings of 'travel literature' remain intact. In the same year as the second edition of the movement's manifesto was published, an issue of *Gulliver* devoted to 'World Fiction' appeared. Le Bris's introduction, drawing on undifferentiated notions of 'créolisation' and 'créolité', describes 'le monde basculant sous nos yeux' [the world toppling over before our very eyes] and recognizes the resultant emergence of 'de nouvelles lignes de partage, nettes, qui interrogent chacun, obligent à se déterminer' [new, distinct dividing lines that text each of us, force us to make up our minds].[22] It is encouraging that he refuses to pigeonhole the literature from France and Britain's former colonies as 'un genre, une catégorie exotique' [a genre, an exotic category]; but in failing to acknowledge the postcolonial—or even neocolonial—status of this literary production, in decontextualizing it as the product of a postmodern, post-historical world that is '[m]étissé, coloré, polyglotte' [hybrid, colourful, polyglot], he ends up risking precisely that.[23]

The choice as opening text of a translation into French of Pico Iyer's much commented 1993 article in *Time* magazine, 'The Empire Writes Back', compounds this risk.[24] As Graham Huggan has suggested in *The Postcolonial Exotic*, Iyer's piece, like the Booker prize whose recent laureates it celebrates, deploys the term 'postcolonial' as a 'strategically malleable' codeword for various conflated transnational operations.[25] The result, in Huggan's terms, is a 'naively celebratory global cosmopolitan sensibility in which conspicuous inequalities of technological resources and international divisions of labour are elided, and where the continuing anti-imperialist concerns of contemporary postcolonial writing are emptied out'.[26] Allusions in the translation of Iyer's article

---

[21] Clifford, 'Traveling Cultures', 38.

[22] Michel Le Bris, 'Editorial', *Gulliver*, 3 (1999), 7–13 (p. 8). On the distinction between 'créolisation' and 'créolité' (and Glissant's preference for the former), see Diva Damato, 'Edouard Glissant et le manifeste *Éloge de la Créolité*', in Yves-Alain Favre and Antonio Ferreira de Brito (eds.), *Horizons d'Edouard Glissant* ([n.pl.]: JSD Editions, 1992), 245–53.

[23] Le Bris, 'Editorial', 9.

[24] Pico Iyer, 'The Empire Writes Back', *Time*, 8 February 1993, 46–51.

[25] Huggan, *The Postcolonial Exotic*, 110.

[26] Ibid. 121.

to 'la nouvelle vague transculturelle' [the new transcultural wave] and 'la nouvelle fiction transcontinentale' [the new transcontinental fiction] suggest this sense of a carnivalesque celebration of late modern culture whose ambiguous yet productive grounding in postcoloniality is at best obscured and at worst denied.[27]

To understand this manœuvre, an awareness of French hostility to postcolonial criticism, regularly dismissed as Anglo-Saxon didacticism, is useful. Michel Le Bris has been one of the most vociferous critics of postcolonial approaches to travel literature, hostile in particular to the work of Edward Said. In a series of interviews, *Fragments du royaume*, he describes Said's *Orientalism* as 'l'hystérisation de toute pensée, le refus de toute complexité, de toute nuance' [the hystericization of all reflection, the refusal of all complexity or attenuation], parodying the work's thesis as a monolithic response to the homogeneous reality of intercultural contact.[28] What Le Bris dismisses above all in Said, however, is his insistence on contextualization, which jars with an understanding of travel perceived as an accumulation of epiphanic moments, travel writing as a strategy of radical decontextualization. Le Bris claims, in the 1990 issue of *Gulliver* devoted to travel, that the travel writer's privilege is to 'échapp[er], quoi qu'en disent les doctes, aux déterminations du "social-historique" ' [escape, no matter what the erudite might say, from the strictures of the 'socio-historical'], adding that 'un texte c'est précisément ce qui ne peut être réduit à ses contextes' [a text is precisely what cannot be reduced to its contexts].[29] In this restatement of the literary value of travel literature—as opposed to the documentary or journalistic status of travel writing—Le Bris seems to suggest that the successful travel account is characterized by what is gained in the individual's textual translation of an experience of elsewhere. Such a gain, however, often emerges precisely as a result of the author's uneasy awareness of his or her situation, of the unstable or changing relationship between traveller and travellee. By insisting on the traveller's hermeticism in relation to context, by claiming privileged elevation above issues of history, ethnicity, gender, and access to velocity, Le Bris still clings to a concept of travel that belongs to an earlier period.

---

[27] Pico Iyer, 'L'Empire contre-attaque, plume en main', *Gulliver*, 3 (1999), 15–29 (pp. 18, 20).

[28] Michel Le Bris, *Fragments du royaume* (Vénissieux: Paroles d'Aube, 1995), 197.

[29] Michel Le Bris, 'Écrire le poème du monde', *Gulliver*, 2–3 (1990), 4–11 (p. 5).

The Étonnants Voyageurs festival itself has diversified, setting up a number of 'micro-festivals' in locations such as Bamako, Dublin, and Montana. However, the conflation of traditions and discourses which such a process risks remains, as I have suggested, highly problematic. At the same time, the continued privileging of an exclusive definition of travel perpetuates certain distinctions and prevents potentially troubling contrapuntal readings of metropolitan and non-metropolitan accounts of displacement. The movement purports to advocate a full exploration and representation of global diversity, and by involving authors and thinkers such as Édouard Glissant and Patrick Chamoiseau may have the potential to do so. However, its combative self-definition in relation to the strands of contemporary French literature of which its principal spokesmen disapprove prevents any sustained self-critique; it perpetuates certain understandings of travel that served not only to police access to and appreciation of diversity, but also to fix that diversity in an imaginary geography bound by exoticist hierarchies and assumptions relating to certain forms of space. As a result, it prevents full engagement with and illumination of the differentiated networks of cultural interactions that journeys within and between cultures have revealed and continue to reveal. Consequently the cover-all category of 'une littérature qui dise le monde' risks becoming meaningless as the world it purportedly describes defies articulation when viewed according to grids that are increasingly unsuitable for interpreting its globalized and transnational structures. The *Pour une littérature voyageuse* movement requires a fresh focus and increased rigour of self-definition in order to avoid losing its way in the twenty-first century. In the two sections that follow, the chapter outlines some alternative itineraries, neither wholly unproblematic nor wholly divorced from the practices (as opposed to manifesto claims) of the movement itself.

ALTERNATIVE ITINERARIES I: DECELERATION

The preceding critique of the *Pour une littérature voyageuse* movement, inasmuch as the loose body of material that title encompasses can be described as a coherent movement, should not be seen as a denial of alternative modes of thinking about (and practising) travel and its textualization. According to Jean-Didier Urbain, whose semiological re-evaluation of both travel and its principal motivations and practitioners constitutes the most pioneering French contribution to considerations of these issues in recent years, what is most striking is the attempt to, in the terms of this chapter's epigraph, 'réinventer l'exotisme de ce monde' [reinvent the world's exoticism].[30] It is this emphasis on perception and the relational value of travel literature that is central to a number of recent developments concerning both forms of travel and the field in which this travel occurs.

It was suggested in the introduction to this book that dromomania, or a pathological propensity to walk away from home, may be seen as the site of a number of anxieties relating to late nineteenth-century travel (and the culture in which that travel took place). Although in the late twentieth century, this particular disorder had been replaced by what Hacking dubs other 'transient mental illnesses', walking continued to play a central role in considerations of travel's future. The threat to walking—as well as various robust responses to such a threat—has become a central element of recent travel literature in French. There is indeed a series of contemporary *dromomanes* who eschew mechanized transport and revert to pedestrian journeys that allow not only a renegotiation of the relationship between the traveller and the space of travel, but also a sustained reflection on what it means to travel today. Bernard Ollivier, a self-confessed 'autophobe', is one such walker whose *Longue marche* describes the initial stages of a projected journey from the Mediterranean to China along the Silk Route.[31] The return to walking of which his work is a part is far from straightforward. For reasons that will be explored later in this section, Ollivier's text illustrates (without necessarily falling into) a number of the pitfalls that occasionally threaten to undermine modern journeys on foot: a nostalgia for premodern forms of transport, an aristocratic (and even self-righteous) sense of choosing the only 'authentic' means of travel, and an increasingly exaggerated sense of physical exploit or challenge.

---

[30] For a discussion of Urbain's work, see Charles Forsdick, 'Viator in Fabula: Jean-Didier Urbain and Contemporary French Approaches to Travel', *Studies in Travel Writing*, 4 (2000), 126–40. The failure of many of the growing number of English-language scholars working in the field of travel to acknowledge Urbain's work reflects both the importance of translation but also the marked bifurcation of intellectual trends in this area along language-specific lines; this situation is likely to be remedied in part at least, however, with the translation of *Sur la plage* (Paris: Payot, 1994) into English: *At the Beach*, trans. Catherine Porter (Minneapolis: University of Minnesota Press, 2003).

[31] Ollivier's project was undertaken over three stages between 1999 and 2002, and published in three subsequent volumes: *Longue marche* (Paris: Phébus, 2000), *Vers Samarcande* (Paris: Phébus, 2001), and *Le Vent des Steppes* (Paris: Phébus, 2003).

Although along his route he is harassed and impeded by dogs, robbers, suspicious locals, and officious army officers, Ollivier's main obstacle is the succession of car and bus drivers who stop their vehicles, offer him a lift, assure him there will be no charge, and then leave convinced that this traveller who has refused their offer must be mad. This re-emergent diagnosis of a contemporary variation on dromomania is encapsulated in a question central to Ollivier's account, a direct echo of des Esseintes: 'A quoi bon marcher quand on peut se déplacer en voiture?' [What is the point of walking when we can travel by car?].[32] This implies a threatened sense of redundancy, as if the bipedalism that distinguishes *homo sapiens* from other mammals is becoming so increasingly archaic that walking is even seen as a pathological aberration. The journey recounted in *Longue marche*, as well as a recent series of numerous other walking journeys, provides a sustained response to Ollivier's question. It offers at the same time a retort to reservations about the expansion and renewal of travel literature articulated in the first section of this chapter. Postmodern thought foregrounds travel and the body as two of its principal themes; it is consequently not surprising that walking—the reinscription of corporeality into mobility—has also attracted increasing attention in a variety of fields. The return of walking can, accordingly, be linked to a series of returns that characterize late twentieth-century literature and culture: of experience, of the body, of the subject, of travel, and—since walking is often allied so closely to notions of narrative continuity—of the *récit*. In fact, instead of being an element in a series, it is possible to present walking as a nexus, as the activity in which these other returns are distilled in order to coexist as a working system. However, it is not simply the uses of walking that are at stake, but also the use—and feasibility—of travel itself. Ollivier's rhetorical 'À quoi bon marcher?' is accordingly linked closely to the fin-de-siècle refrain of 'À quoi bon bouger?'

Inspired largely by a reading of Lévi-Strauss, for example, Adrian Rifkin prophesies, in the epigraph to this chapter, such a demise: 'the future of travellers' tales [...] lies in their reading, in cultivating new arts of reading them. My prescription is to stay at home and do just that.' The antithesis of travel is not, however, simply 'staying at home'. In 'Les Catanautes des cryptocombes—des iconoclastes de l'ailleurs', a recent study of Michel Le Bris and Kenneth White (another author whose work is central to the 1992 anthology *Pour une littérature*

---

[32] Ollivier, *Longue marche*, 94.

voyageuse), Jean-Didier Urbain has criticized, along similar lines to the first section of this chapter, certain contemporary discourses of travel that are often dependent on rhetorical strategies of aristocratic self-distinction. Countering what he describes as a 'tyrannie agoraphile', Urbain offers a supplement to La Fontaine's fables with his own account of the flea and the albatross. In this, he focuses on more modest travellers, 'les voyageurs de l'immédiat', for whom the journey is not necessarily a matter of dimension, distance, or a superficially geographical exoticism, and cites as an illustration François Maspero on the RER or Julio Cortazar and Carole Dunlop on the motorway from Paris to Marseilles. He concludes: 'par l'atomisation du trajet, la *lenteur* provoquée remplace la durée des longs parcours' [by fragmenting travel, *slowness* replaces the duration of long journeys].[33]

Urbain's own emphasis on deceleration—as well as the punctuation and reconfiguration of space it allows—underlines walking's potential status as an innovative mode of both contemporary travel and artistic engagement with the outside world. Yet studying walking remains problematic, not only as a result of the profusion of literary and artistic uses to which such an everyday activity has lent itself, but also of the overdetermined range of cultural associations and memories triggered by what Rebecca Solnit calls in *Wanderlust* 'the most obvious and the most obscure thing in the world'.[34] The verticality of walking, allowing free use of the hands, development of the brain, and gradual elevation of sight as the principal sense, was the first marker of a species becoming human.[35] In terms of evolution, therefore, walking remains double-edged, a reminder of the physiological changes that placed humanity in a dominant position, but, at the same time, since walking as a means of locomotion has changed little, a persistent link to the pre-technological past. The history of human transportation represents a struggle to transcend the biological limitations of bipedalism, but this struggle occurs against a backcloth of the steady fragmentation of the meanings of walking into, for instance, revolutionary walking (or the march) as a means of political protest; spiritual walking (or the pilgrimage) as a renegotiation of individual faith, exploratory and scientific walking (or the small step of an astronaut) as a sign of the realignment of the

---

[33] Jean-Didier Urbain, 'Les catanautes des cryptocombes—des iconoclastes de l'Ailleurs', *Nottingham French Studies*, 39/1 (2000), 7–16 (p. 12; emphasis in the original).

[34] Rebecca Solnit, *Wanderlust: A History of Walking* (New York: Viking, 2000), 3.

[35] On this subject, see Yves Coppens and Brigitte Senut (eds.), *Origine(s) de la bipédie chez les hominidés* (Paris: Éditions du CNRS; Cahiers de Paléoanthropologie, 1991).

individual's relationship to (outer) space, and competitive walking (such as the Paris–Strasburg road race, founded in 1926) as a sporting activity that can have powerful implications for national identity.[36]

Walking as movement is a mechanical, anatomical, and natural activity; the choice of walking as a philosophical, political, spiritual, or aesthetic experience shifts according to cultural and historical context, and its meaning is invariably informed by that context. At a time when the pedestrian has become an increasingly endangered species, often seen as an obstacle to the free movement of traffic, there is a renewed creative interest in walking to be found in a variety of media in the late twentieth century and an emphasis on its potential as performance.[37] In this sense, walking is asserted as one of those activities which both Virilio and de Certeau describe as a means of refiguring the compression of time and space, of opening up spaces of resistance in which time, memory, and the body can be reintroduced. A similar sense of reinscription of the walker can be seen in a specific use of the peripatetic in Emmanuel Poirier's 1997 film *Western*. This is a road movie in which the car is rapidly written off, so that the protagonists are reduced to travelling on foot. The sudden deceleration of the action imposes a new rhythm on the film, because of which focus alters—in the act of walking—from space to time. There is an emphasis on individual episodes rather than on the speed of continuous duration. This in turn allows a shift from the fleeting or panoramic to a more detailed, microscopic reflection on contemporary French identity as the protagonists Paco and Nino try (never quite successfully) to fit in to a variety of situations—a reflection rendered all the more complex as a result of the Russian and Catalan origins of the two main characters and of the situation of the action on the far Western tip of Brittany. Walking becomes a means of exploring two elements central to contemporary identity formation: hybridity and periphery.

[36] On the social meanings of walking, see André Rauch (ed.), *La Marche, la vie: solitaire ou solidaire, ce geste fondateur* (Paris: Autrement, 1997).

[37] In his 1992 series of *Promenades pour Robert Walser* (some of which are included in his *Œuvre incomplète* (Paris: Éditions du Centre Pompidou, 1997)), e.g. the artist Jean-Jacques Rullier focuses on the implications of speed (or its lack) in walking for the experience and perception of time and space. What Rullier develops is a new cartography, dependent on an understanding of walking as an erratic progress whose form is largely dependent on the retrospective, selective ordering of memory and the senses, moving beyond rational and technological processes of mapping which flatten and delineate space. Several British artists are also inspired by the creative and performative potentials of walking. Of these, the most prominent are perhaps Richard Long and Hamish Fulton.

It is the account of a more ambitious journey on foot across France that may be seen to inaugurate the focus on walking found in contemporary travel literature in French. Jacques Lacarrière's *Chemin faisant* describes a 1,000-km walk through France in the early 1970s. The journey has an emphasis on peripheries, beginning in Alsace—'ces marches de la Germanie'—and concluding in the Basque country—'les marches de l'Espagne'. These two poles marking the diversity of Frenchness, whilst also revealing (like *Western*) the potentially privileged status of walking in explorations of identity and of the sense of place. The sense of travel on foot allowing access to what is often unseen or occluded is recurrent in contemporary literature, whether Philippe Delerm describes the 'plaisir minuscule' of walking in damp espadrilles or Patrick Modiano maps out more urban journeys on foot in his search for traces of Dora Bruder.[38] Again, in such dispersed examples, interpretations of walking risk over-determination; but the emphasis on walking in contemporary travel accounts is particularly significant for it forces the reader to consider definitional issues relating to travel literature itself. No longer understood solely in terms of a superficial geographical exoticism, this still hazily defined genre is linked accordingly to issues of the intercultural representation of otherness, of the freighting of experience by memory, of the relationship between narrating/travelling subject and the world narrated/travelled. Read in the context of such generic issues, walking as travel acquires a privileged status—in Jacques Lacarrière's terms, it is neither utilitarian 'marche routinière' ['routine walking'] nor exhausting 'marche routière' ['long-distance walking'], but a subversively constructive and clandestine 'marche buissonière'.[39] In this third mode of the peripatetic, an intricate exchange between perception, reflection, and memory begins to emerge. Because of the bodily nature of walking and the bombardment of the senses it entails, the walker actively engages with the world and relies on perception to negotiate a passage through it. He or she benefits from a kinaesthetic, tactile, active, and participatory presence, increasingly prevented elsewhere by what Michel de Certeau, in *L'Invention du quotidien*, dubs the 'enfermement du voyageur' [enclosure of the traveller] associated with most mechanical means of

---

[38] See Philippe Delerm, *La Première gorgée de bière et autres plaisirs minuscules* (Paris: Gallimard, 1997), 64, and Patrick Modiano, *Dora Bruder* (Paris: Gallimard, 1997). Delerm has also published an illustrated account of walks in Normandy, *Les Chemins nous inventent* (Paris: Stock, 1997).

[39] Lacarrière, *Chemin faisant*, 16.

transport.[40] In walking, all the senses are activated, permitting the world to be experienced as a complex system (of which we are an integral part) rather than as a disjointed series of objects and individuals. In this way, awareness of and attention to both detail and what is traditionally remote allow access to a degree of diversity often ignored as a result of its microscopic or marginal status.

In his eulogy of deceleration, *Du Bon Usage de la lenteur*, Pierre Sansot focuses on walking as one of the everyday practices whose reassessment would encourage more critical reflection on urbanism and an anthropology of the senses.[41] The idea of 'usage de la lenteur' that emerges from this text—as well as a series of other contemporary works on slowness[42]—is paradoxical and reliant on the untranslatable ambiguity of the word 'usage'. (Nicolas Bouvier similarly exploits this polysemy in the title of his major text, *L'Usage du monde*.) For 'usage' not only implies a specific practice—of slowness, of walking, of the external world—but also encapsulates the steady erosion of that practice. The perceived eccentricity (or even threateningly pathological status) of the walker and the anachronistic nature of walking itself have already been illustrated by reference to the constant interruptions of Bernard Ollivier's journey which cause the walker to struggle for 'le droit de marcher' [the right to walk].[43] Sensing himself 'regardé comme une bête curieuse' [watched like a strange animal], the journalist Emmanuel de Roux, on a walking journey along the Paris meridian, experienced a similar feeling of alienation: 'Je m'aperçois que le piéton est devenu aussi incongru en rase campagne qu'un cheval de labour. Marcher en dehors d'une zone urbaine relève d'un comportement archaïque, sinon suspect' [I have noticed that the pedestrian stands out in the open countryside as much as a cart-horse. Walking outside urban areas has become an archaic—even suspect—form of behaviour].[44]

[40] Michel de Certeau, *L'Invention du quotidien*, i. *Arts de faire* (Paris: Gallimard, 1990), 165.

[41] Pierre Sansot, *Du Bon Usage de la lenteur* (Paris: Payot, 1998). Sansot develops these ideas in his subsequent *Chemins aux vents* (Paris: Payot, 2000).

[42] See also Jacques Réda, 'Éloge modéré de la lenteur', in *Recommandations aux promeneurs* (Paris: Gallimard, 1988), 85–94, Rémi Villedecaze, *Traité de la promenade* ([n.pl.]: Éditions du Bon Albert, 1997), David Le Breton, *Éloge de la marche*, and the dossier on 'Éloge de la lenteur', *Télérama*, 6–12 May 2000, 12–18.

[43] Ollivier, *Longue marche*, 106.

[44] Emmanuel de Roux, *On a marché sur la Méridienne: de la Mer du Nord aux Pyrénées* (Paris: Fayard, 2001), 15.

The elaboration of such a sense of solitude can of course be part of a traveller's rhetorical strategy of self-justification, and this is clearly a procedure from which certain accounts of walking journeys are not exempt. Moreover, there is a risk that in responding to the denigration of walking by denigrating mechanized transport in turn, travellers compete for 'authenticity' and lose sight of the coexisting range of strategies that permit the traveller to approach self and other. The moral condemnation of speed and nostalgia for deceleration ignore the fact that motorized transport—and, in particular, collective transport—can be a valuable contact zone in its own right. The late twentieth-century focus on walking remains, however, more complex, for in the tachocratic context of what Paul Virilio has dubbed 'dromology' (i.e. the increasing acceleration not only of weaponry and transport, but also of everyday life), walking as an alternative means of transport acquires a disruptive and even transgressive status. Travelling on foot is transformed into a potentially clandestine, subversive activity. Rémi Villedecaze asks in *De la promenade*: 'tout promeneur ne prend-il pas le maquis?' [Doesn't every walker go underground?], and encapsulates a recurrent sense that the walker is not only an outsider but also an outlaw.[45] A seemingly extravagant Lacarrière goes further: 'Marcher ainsi de nos jours—et surtout de nos jours—ce n'est pas revenir aux temps néolithiques, mais bien plutôt être prophète' [Being a walker nowadays—nowadays especially—is not returning to Neolithic times; instead, it is acting as a prophet].[46]

The normalization of speed has made the body seem weak, fragile, and anachronistic. As David Le Breton has made clear in his writings on the anthropology of the (Western) body, the progressive erasure of the corporeal is a generalized post-industrial phenomenon linked to rapid changes in work, leisure, sanitation, hygiene, and medicine.[47] This suppressed consciousness of physicality is a marker not only of the healthy body, however, but also of the travelling body; with the mechanization of transport, the traveller's body has become increasingly inactive and superfluous, seated in 'movement' from one place to another. In a text already cited, Saint-Pol-Roux describes this steady erosion of corporeality: 'On va de plus en plus vite comme afin de se débarrasser grain à grain de son poids corporel' [We travel ever more quickly, as if we are trying to shake off the weight of our bodies—bit

---

[45] Villedecaze, *De la promenade*, 16.   [46] Lacarrière, *Chemin faisant*, 190.
[47] See esp. *Anthropologie du corps et modernité* (Paris: PUF, 2000).

by bit].[48] The poet's reflections on speed seem to relate more to a nineteenth-century wariness than to the enthusiasm of his Modernist contemporaries, but what characterizes his thought—and what Paul Virilio has identified in it—is not a retrospective longing, but instead an alarmingly precursory awareness of the role of ever-increasing acceleration in social organization and transformation. In *Vitesse*, Saint-Pol-Roux describes the reduction of the active body of the traveller into a passive state of motorized immobility, sensing a reframing of space, as if the car seat can be equated with a cinema seat.[49]

Saint-Pol-Roux's originality was not, however, centred in this identification of a renewed aesthetics of travel—underlining the separation and exclusion of the traveller—since this was also referred to by a number of his contemporaries;[50] instead, what remains striking in *Vitesse* and *La Randonnée* is not only the awareness of relative speed (distinguishing walking from the car, or the car from the aeroplane) that merely transforms travel, but also the insight into absolute speed, 'la vitesse infinie,' which—through the connection of departure and arrival—threatens to erase the space of travel itself.[51] This coincidence of departure and arrival—'être arrivé avant qu'être parti' [arriving without having left]—prefigures Virilio's interest in the tyranny of speed and the ultimate time–space compression that is its logical conclusion.[52] In Virilio's work, the search in modern arms technology for a strategic weapon that will simulate the speed of light is placed in the vanguard of developments in everyday culture. Achievement of the speed of light obliterates the difference between 'here' and 'there,' and, by reducing the traveller to stasis and the world to nothing, renders physical travel unnecessary: 'l'annihilation de temps et de l'espace par les hautes vitesses substitue la vastitude du vide à celle de l'exotisme et du voyage' [the annihilation of time and space by high speeds substitutes the vastness of emptiness for that of exoticism and travel].[53] Although the achievement of absolute speed remains perhaps a distant possibility, its currency as a valid concept continues to increase, and the distinct idea of relative speed accordingly requires attenuation: ever-increasing acceleration distances travellers from the slowness of walking and edges them closer to the possibility of absolute speed. The interim result is a sense of anchoritic speed that occludes the outside world, encloses the

---

[48] Saint-Pol-Roux, *La Randonnée*, 20.   [49] Saint-Pol-Roux, *Vitesse*, 25, 30.
[50] See, e.g. Morand, *Flèche d'Orient*, 41.   [51] Saint-Pol-Roux, *Vitesse*, 53.
[52] Saint-Pol-Roux, *La Randonnée*, 21.
[53] Paul Virilio, *Esthétique de la disparition* (Paris: Galilée, 1980), 119.

traveller, and (as jet travel illustrates most clearly) identifies the journey with a delocalized vector. Travel is thereby reduced to displacement, and direct perception accordingly eroded.

In the light of these shifts, it is the element of deceleration that becomes central to walking's potential as an alternative means of travel and of often-microscopic perception of diversity.[54] There is a risk, however, that praise of walking becomes part of a generalized anti-speed discourse. Speed alters the individual's perception of the world, and much anti-tourist literature, in particular, inevitably focuses on what is judged as the excessive rapidity of mass travel. The contemporary return to the peripatetic is certainly not motivated, however, by purely anti-modernist nostalgia for the exoticism associated with poor, slow travelling conditions. Contemporary eulogies of slowness—such as Pierre Sansot's *Du Bon Usage de la lenteur*—accept that, on purely utilitarian grounds, the 'lenteur–vitesse' debate was resoundingly lost long ago. Walking is no longer presented as a competing means of locomotion. There is, moreover, an acceptance that travel on foot cannot be presented as a more 'authentic' means of displacement. In *L'Idiot du voyage*, Jean-Didier Urbain has explored the delusory romanticization of what he calls the 'incontournable lenteur de la marche' [unavoidable slowness of walking] of an era before mechanization: 'Le pèlerin de jadis n'appréciait pas la lenteur de la marche: il la subissait. Le randonneur contemporain l'apprécie au contraire dans sa différence' [Long ago, pilgrims did not have a liking for the slowness of walking; they put up with it. Today's walkers, on the other hand, appreciate slowness because of its difference].[55] The contemporary walk—and the imposed slowness that accompanies it—is seen instead as the positive (and often even eccentric) choice of an alternative means of perception, or what Sansot calls another way of existing.[56]

Therefore, what underlies and differentiates contemporary commentary on the dominance of speed—such as Jacques Lacarrière's sanguine reflection on the garage owner too busy to go out walking: 'Il n'y a pas de dimanche pour les autos' [There is no Sunday for cars]—is an awareness of the radical and irreversible effects of such acceleration

---

[54] The emphasis on slowness as a source of resistance is of course not restricted to travel. In reaction to fast food, the gastronomic equivalent of mass tourism, for instance, a 'slow food' movement has emerged. See Carlo Petrini, *Slow Food: The Case for Taste*, trans. William McCuaig (New York: Columbia University Press, 2003).

[55] Urbain, *L'Idiot du voyage*, 121, 133.

[56] Sansot, *Du bon usage de la lenteur*, 37.

on all aspects of existence.[57] As Jacques Réda suggests in his 'Recommandations aux promeneurs,' the achievement of absolute speed will
inevitably lead to an instinctive nostalgia for rapidity, just as the
achievement of relative speed triggered a longing for slowness.[58] This
is why Jean-Claude Bourlès's focus in *Une Bretagne intérieure* on the
implications of the humble act of walking for the recovery of time is so
striking. When he claims about his journey through Brittany: 'Celui-ci
se fera à pied, vieille manie d'approcher un pays en égrenant le temps
des routes, seul moyen de comprendre et retenir, sinon l'essentiel, du
moins ce qui lui ressemble' [this one will take place on foot, going back
to the old habit of approaching a country by marking out the time of its
routes, the only way to understand and retain if not the essential, at
least an approximate version of it], he draws attention to the detail that
the walk can offer.[59] He also implies an understanding of travel that
foregrounds time as opposed to space, and suggests in the word 'égr-
ener' (repeated elsewhere in the text where it serves as a verbal leit-
motif) that the decelerated rhythms of walking nevertheless allow a
'telling' of space that reveals concealed or erased memories and patterns. Lacarrière claims similarly, in a remark that could equally be
applied to his wider travels around the Mediterranean: 'je me rends
compte combien se déplacer ainsi tout au long des chemins, musarder à
travers la France est affaire de temps beaucoup plus que d'espace'
[I realized how much travelling like this along these paths, dawdling
across France, is about time as much as it is about space].[60]

The recovery of time inherent in deceleration counters the aesthetics
of (increasing) separation that characterizes mechanized transport by
replacing it with an aesthetics of proximity. This shift of focus, perspective, and dimension was already present in Saint-Pol-Roux, whose
work laid the foundations for the return of walking in the later twentieth century. He writes: 'On ne voyage vraiment qu'à pied, sinon
l'homme n'est qu'un bagage animé' [We only really travel on foot—if
not, people are only propelled like luggage],[61] a judgement echoed by
his contemporary, the Swiss poet Gustave Roud, who describes in his
Petit traité de la marche en plaine the unexpected physical and sensual

---

[57] Lacarrière, *Chemin faisant*, 47.
[58] Réda, 'Recommandations aux promeneurs', 88.
[59] Jean-Claude Bourlès, *Une Bretagne intérieure* (Paris: Gallimard, 1998), 15.
[60] Lacarrière, *Chemin faisant*, 277.
[61] Saint-Pol-Roux, *Vitesse*, 38.

pleasures triggered by walking.[62] In such a phenomenological under-standing of travel privileging the physical over the geographical by concentrating on journeys close to home, Roud describes a sensual rediscovery of the outside world and a re-engagement with the often-unforeseen experiences afforded by walking. The emphasis is on direct contact, not only with the outside world but also with other people, with the result that walking becomes an activity with an anthropo-logical as well as an ethical dimension. An exposed and mud-caked Bourlès describes the ever-present threat of *la panne*: 'Dans cet univers de giboulées, il n'y a que la boue qui ne change pas d'idée, retenir le pied, ralentir la marche, ajouter de la fatigue à la fatigue, menacer le corps dans son bel équilibre' [In this land of sudden downpours, only the mud is constant, restricting movement of the feet, slowing down walking, exacerbating tiredness, threatening the body's fine balance].[63] The vulnerability of walkers leaves them open to the possibilities of otherness, whilst such a reduction of the world to the dimensions of the self forces the individual to understand his or her place in relation to the Other.

Walking emerges accordingly as a positive and practical response to prophesy of the end of travel and the entropic exhaustion of elsewhere. It provides an alternative to the recycling of older modes of travel described above. An aesthetics of proximity underlines the walker's status as a clandestine or interstitial figure who gains access to what is often ignored or inaccessible. Proximity reveals a degree of detail and underlines the potentially inexhaustible diversity of the space in which travel takes place. It is, as a result, a negentropic—or anti-entropic—strategy, reminiscent of Benoît Mandelbrot's theory of the 'fractal geometry of nature'. Like the traveller transported in a state of anchor-itic speed, standard geometry cannot perceive the complexity, irregu-larity, and fragmentation of nature. In a chapter entitled 'How Long is the Coast of Britain', Mandelbrot shows how the length of coastline increases in proportion to its scale on a map: 'with greater detail, subbays and sub-subpeninsulars appear, and so forth. Each adds to the measured length'.[64] Suggesting that cartographic measurement leads only to the conclusion that 'the typical coastline's length is very

---

[62] See *Essai pour un paradis, suivi du Petit traité de la marche en plaine* (Lausanne: Bibliothèque des Arts, 1984 [1932]).

[63] Bourlès, *Une Bretagne intérieure*, 20.

[64] Benoît Mandelbrot, *The Fractal Geometry of Nature* (New York: W. H. Freeman, 1983 [1977]), 26.

large and so ill determined that it is best considered infinite', he proposes a more direct method in the field:

Imagine a man walking along the coastline, taking the shortest path that stays
no farther from the water than the prescribed distance E. Then he resumes his
walk after reducing his yardstick, then again, after another reduction; and so on,
until E reaches, say, 50 cm. Man is too big and clumsy to follow any finer detail.
[...] In principle, Man could follow such a curve down to finer details by
harnessing a mouse, then an ant, and so forth. Again, as our walker stays
increasingly closer to the coastline, the distance to be covered continues to
increase with no limit.[65]

The emphasis on walking and re-walking not only undermines the
concept of fixed, objective geographic length, but also suggests the
potential inexhaustibility of the field of travel when the walker is
reinscribed physically in time and space.[66]

Developing this idea of ever-increasing proximity, Rémi Villedecaze
claims that walking is a type of 'enracinement' [taking root], and such
reinscription of the figure in the landscape underlines the corporeal
nature of travel.[67] With the atrophic effects of mechanization on the
body and the transformation of means of transport into prostheses, the
physicality of walking can lend itself to the culture of exploit or challenge, to the contemporary toying with contingency that David Le
Breton explores in *Passions du risque*. As Rebecca Solnit comments in
Wanderlust, however, 'the necessary combination of silver tongue and
iron thighs seems to be a rare one', and very few walking journeys that
succeed as travel accounts are equally successful as record-breaking acts
of defiance.[68] Emmanuel de Roux's walk along the Paris meridian ends
with renunciation, as deep snow forces the traveller to give up his
already visible goal in the Pyrenees; Bernard Ollivier's experience is
even more striking, for what begins as an apparently foolhardy exploit—a transcontinental hike from Istanbul to Xi'an—turns into an
exploration of the boundaries of the travelling body.

In a mock eulogy at the outset of *Chemin faisant*, Jacques Lacarrière
stresses these physiological underpinnings of the walking journey:

    [65] Mandelbrot, *The Fractal Geometry of Nature*, 26.
    [66] Although Mandelbrot focuses on the fractal dimension of natural phenomena, the
application of this notion to travel may also illuminate journeys through the built environment. Georges Perec's *Tentative d'épuisement d'un lieu parisien* (Paris: Bourgois, 2000
[1975]), for example, may be read as a vertical journey into the fleeting and often ignored
diversity of a small area of Paris.
    [67] Villedecaze, *De la promenade*, 47.
    [68] Solnit, *Wanderlust*, 129.

'Avant tout, je chanterai les pieds. Que la Muse m'inspire, car le sujet prête à sourire. Les pieds, nos pieds. Qui nous portent et que nous portons' [Above all else, I shall sing the feet's praises. I shall need inspiration from the Muses as the subject is likely to raise a smile. Feet, our feet. Which carry us and which we carry].[69] Rhythmic, repeated contact with the ground wears away the body and the walk becomes a process whereby the walker discovers the limits of his or her own physicality. David Le Breton describes the paradoxical contemporary situation of the body: spirited away from consciousness until pain or physical failure remind us of its presence, it is no longer the centre of the being, but has become in many ways an obstacle, or a cumbersome and painful support.[70] Walking is a challenge to the implications of this analysis, a reassertion of the body's pivotal role. Bernard Ollivier follows closely the effects of what he calls 'le rôdage d'une longue marche' [the breaking in which is part of a long walk], constantly examining in the opening stages of *Longue marche* his 'peau martyrisée' [martyred skin].[71] The practical implication of this apprenticeship is an emphasis on physicality, often to the detriment of perception: 'Je marche replié sur ma douleur, aveugle à l'environnement' [I walk bent double in pain, blind to my surroundings], and the first volume of Ollivier's journey actually ends in total breakdown as his body is transformed into a 'loque' [wreck] when he is only a few kilometres from the Iranian border. The narrator states baldly: 'Je ne peux plus marcher' [I can no longer walk].[72] Avoiding a sense of risk for risk's sake, Ollivier's text allows a re-exploration of one of the fundamentals of travel, the sense of physical investment. In relation to this, the roots of the word 'travel' are often cited: i.e. the Vulgar Latin 'tripalium', meaning three-pronged instrument of torture. This resort to etymology is particularly apt for walking. For the walker, travel is undergone actively, not experienced passively; it is the definition of the self as well as that of travel that are at stake, for—to borrow an idea from Nicolas Bouvier, already cited in Ch. 5—'Si on ne laisse pas au voyage le droit de nous détruire un peu, autant rester chez soi' [If we do not let the journey destroy us a little, we might as well stay at home].[73]

Except in unexpected moments of its failure, mechanized transport cushions and distances the body from its surroundings, whilst at the

---

[69] Lacarrière, *Chemin faisant*, 15.
[70] Le Breton, *Anthropologie du corps et modernité*, 128–9.
[71] Ollivier, *Longue marche*, 66, 61.   [72] Ibid. 65, 300.
[73] Bouvier, *Journal d'Aran*, 155.

same time privileging the gaze. In reinserting the body in the outside
world, walking does not elevate one sense above the others, but allows
reactivation of the senses in travel; at the same time, it triggers processes
of memory and allows access to layers of space that are eroded and
often lost in accelerated journeys. It is in these fields of sensation and
memory that walking perhaps offers the most fruitful contribution to
contemporary considerations of travel literature. Journeys on foot
undermine the sovereignty of the gaze, the hypertrophy of the eye
associated with mechanized travel. The reintegration of the body into
space allows, for example, much-neglected olfactory or auditory journeys,[74] and smell and sound are central to Lacarrière's *Chemin faisant*.
His is a primarily rural journey, but the routes he follows sporadically
cross major roads where the traveller rediscovers 'tout un monde
d'odeurs et de bruits que j'avais oublié' [a whole world of smells and
sounds I had forgotten].[75] The rhythms of walking are linked to processes of remembering and forgetting, of loss and recovery, and there is
at times a risk that the resulting account of the journey becomes
nostalgic in an anti-modernist sense. In presenting contemporary
France as a palimpsest, elements of which are obscured by urbanization
and by the acceleration of everyday life, Lacarrière attempts to disclose
the diversity of what he describes in the title of a later text as the
'country under the bark'.[76] The choice of rural as opposed to urban
space is significant, however, for travel may be seen to become a means
of hallucinating a 'lost' France whose links to the contemporary country are increasingly tenuous and even suspect.

For Lacarrière, such uncovering is at the same time recovery, for the
walking journeys of contemporary travel literature are characterized by
a fear of memory loss. Whereas intertextuality and the spectres of
previous travellers are often presented as elements of the exhaustion
of travel, walking journeys are not necessarily about immediacy or
pristine experience. They focus instead on regrounding and reconnec-
tion. Contemporary walkers stress how the physical act of walking
depends largely on immediate memory for its creative reconstitution:
Bourlès relies on 'la mémoire qui, l'heure venue, fera le tri, imposera ses
choix' [memory, which—when the time comes—will sift and make its
choices], and *Chemin faisant* is dependent on 'un travail construit,

---

[74] On olfactory journeys, see Pierre Sansot, *La France sensible* (Paris: Payot, 1995
[1985]), 53.
[75] Lacarrière, *Chemin faisant*, 127.
[76] Jacques Lacarrière, *Le Pays sous l'écorce* (Paris: Gallimard, 1980).

ordonné, réfléchi qui a trié, éliminé, conservé ou rejeté, en fonction des processus de la mémoire' [a job of construction, ordering and reflection which has sifted, eliminated, kept, or rejected according to the processes of memory].[77] There is a greater emphasis, however, on remembering as an activity that accompanies walking and is modulated by the rhythms of the peripatetic. Accordingly, walking seems to become a conscious means of reactivating or recovering the past. Bourlès and Lacarrière are drawn by the patterns of the landscape revealed by the processes of walking. They see travelling on foot as a means of discovering obscured traces of the past—Lacarrière calls crossing the landscape: 'feuilleter un livre ancien aux pages très jaunies' [flicking through an old book with very yellowing pages], and his proximity to place results in a sensitivity to 'les vieilles voies de transhumance' [the old paths of transhumance] running alongside modern roads.[78] Bourlès's walking journey, motivated by a series of childhood memories (and especially that of a map of Brittany), similarly relates the path of the walker to that of 'un chemin de mémoire, autrement plus ardu' [another, more arduous path—that of memory].[79] He too experiences the reordering of geography described by Lacarrière according to which administrative or constructed borders yield to more subtle geographic, ecological, or pre-modern boundaries.

Although not necessarily inspired by any narrow regionalism, the reflections of these travellers may nevertheless be associated with a nostalgic longing for a hazy 'France profonde'. Eschewing the geographical field of an earlier exoticism, however, these contemporary 'voyageurs de l'immédiat' [travellers of the everyday] seem drawn more to journeys at home—but the 'home' they project is a restricted one, far removed from the contemporary France explored by a traveller such as François Maspero discussed below. In his 1985 study *La France sensible*, Sansot described a country which was more of an imagined construct, 'un fait d'imagination' reliant on a sum of individual memories, than a quantifiable geographical entity. Walking through France seems to have become a means of recovering elements of this catalogue of smells, images, memories, and associations that constitutes a version of a country, to have become a means of repositioning aspects of the present in relation to the past. This implicit dislocation of past and present suggests, however, that such journeying may not ultimately be

---

[77] Bourlès, *Une Bretagne intérieure*, 171; Lacarrière, *Chemin faisant*, 205.
[78] Lacarrière, *Chemin faisant*, 107, 86.   [79] Bourlès, *Une Bretagne intérieure*, 31.

the most successful means of connecting with the contemporary field of
travel. Bourlès describes his own forgetting of the Brittany of his childhood as a form of disorientation: 'Le vrai déracinement ne commence-
t-il pas par l'oubli d'une terre? De son odeur et de son nom?' [Doesn't
true uprooting begin when people forget a region? Its smell and its
name?].[80] In the light of this comment, it is striking that Lacarrière, in
his preface to *Flâner en France*, considers walking as a type of reorien-
tation that allows reinvestment of memories.[81] Journeys on foot can be
read as an integral element of the contemporary response to those who
prophesy the demise of travel. With the undermining of the exclusive
notions on which Romantic understandings of travel depended (such as
restricted access, aristocratic solitude, expansive dimensions, and perilous exploits), travel is brought home and related increasingly to the
exploration of the everyday.

   Despite the necessary reservations articulated above about the nostalgic overtones of certain pedestrian journeys in rural spaces, the
return of walking is part of France's ongoing renegotiation, through
travel, of its relationship to itself and to the Other. As a mode of travel,
however, the peripatetic is not to be reduced to a series of variations on
bipedalism. A number of the features of walking explored in this
chapter—deceleration, proximity, reinvestment of the body in travel,
a return of memory and the senses—are inherent in recent accounts of
motorized journeys as well, as if speed and separation from the external
spaces of travel are no longer inevitable aspects of travelling by car or
rail. Adoption of the rhythms and practices of walking can put a
spanner in the works of the motorized journey. In *La France fugitive*,
for example, Michel Chaillou describes a journey through France in a
diminutive Renault Twingo, the account of which recalls in several
respects the 2CV journeys of the 1950s and 1960s described above.
With the experience of place supplemented by the texts of old guidebooks, he aims to 'voyager nez dans les livres, un œil sur la route, un
autre recto verso' [travel with his nose buried in books, one eye on
the road, another scanning the pages].[82] There is no fixed itinerary, only
a resolve to avoid major routes and to approach the peripheral. Chaillou's text is a reaction against what he calls 'cet escamotage perpétuel
du TGV' [the TGV's permanent whisking away], and describes an

   [80] Bourlès, *Une Bretagne intérieure*, 144.
   [81] Jacques Lacarrière (ed.), *Flâner en France: sur les pas de dix-huit écrivains
d'aujourd'hui* (Paris: Pirot, 1987), 11–19.
   [82] Chaillou, *La France fugitive*, 299.

impossible goal to which the fractal, peripatetic mode of his journey only manages an approximate approach: 'cette France de toutes les Frances se dérobant sans cesse de nos instants' [that France which is the sum of all the different versions of France, constantly slipping away from the present moment].[83] In *Paysage fer*, François Bon in turn provides a response to Chaillou's denigration of the high-speed train. The narrator explores the repetition of a single railway journey from Paris to Nancy and charts the shift from the initial separation of traveller and space of travel to a more complex sense of interaction. There is a privileging of the visual as the experience of travel is seen as 'retinal flow', but the hazy saturation of initial journeys gives way to a progressive accumulation and ordering of detail.[84]

Whereas Bourlès, Ollivier, and Lacarrière emphasize the potentially resistant status of the body walking through contemporary travel literature, Chaillou and Bon—as well as the works of Maspero and Cortazar mentioned above—suggest that the contribution of the peripatetic to modes of travel is not restricted to journeys on foot alone—nor uniquely to rural journeys.[85] In Rousseau, there was a culmination of the Romantic belief that philosophical reflection had found its ideal occasion in the walk. In the late twentieth-century texts on which this article has focused, there seems to be a suggestion that it is in the differing rhythms and practices of walking that a number of issues relating to contemporary travel can be most powerfully addressed and explored.

ALTERNATIVE ITINERARIES 2: DOMESTIC JOURNEYS

Many of Jacques Lacarrière's principal journeys have been in Greece, and his travels within this country are recounted in a number of texts. Despite the reservations expressed above regarding both the exclusive definition of the traveller provided in his contribution to the manifesto and the restricted, rural France to which *Chemin faisant* refers, it might be argued that one of Lacarrière's principal contributions to

[83] Ibid. 17, 178.
[84] François Bon, *Paysage fer* (Paris: Verdier, 2000), 17, 35.
[85] Maspero describes his journey in pedestrian terms as 'une ballade le nez en l'air' [a nonchalant sort of stroll, not an enquiry] (*Les Passagers du Roissy-Express* (Paris: Seuil, 1990), 20; *Roissy Express: A Journey through the Paris Suburbs*, trans. Paul Jones (London: Verso, 1994), 13).

contemporary travel literature involves the elaboration of a Mediterranean space that encompasses, without the customary imbalance towards its northern shore and to the detriment of the Maghreb, the
diversity of all cultures centred on the sea. By stressing its status as a
journey through France from the Germanic north-east to the Hispanic
south-west, *Chemin faisant* may be seen, in part at least, to encompass a
space, the domestic space of France itself, whose persistent diversity
defies the homogeneity that its progressive modernization seems to
imply. Deceleration is accompanied by an equally radical reassessment
of the field of travel, a recognition that if elsewhere may appear transformed, then any reconfiguration of travel should perhaps begin at
home. It is in relation to such a domestic—and not domesticating—
response that Urbain offers his supplement to La Fontaine's fables. In
his own account of the flea and the albatross, he privileges over those
who require vast distances and open spaces the more modest travellers,
'les voyageurs de l'immédiat', interested in places closer to home and
prepared to explore hidden dimensions of the everyday. Urbain's fable
directly targets Michel Le Bris and Kenneth White, describing their
'tyranny of scale and immensity' [tyrannie de l'étendue et de l'immen-
sité];[86] with them he contrasts the 'cryptonautes' or explorers of the
Parisian catacombs, whose clandestine journeys beneath the surface of
the capital reformulate an understanding of travel according to restriction, slowness, and the rediscovery of elsewhere in the here-and-now.

Looking for textual accounts of such atomization of the journey's
space and such fragmentation of its time, Urbain cites two texts mentioned above in relation to a peripatetic mode of travel available to
motorized as well as to pedestrian journeys: François Maspero's account of RER travel, and Julio Cortazar and Carole Dunlop's narrative
of a motorway journey from Paris to Marseilles. Of these, for reasons
that will become apparent, it is on François Maspero's *Les Passagers du
Roissy-Express* that I intend to focus.[87] Maspero's journey through the
Parisian *banlieues* with the photographer Anaïk Frantz is in many ways
a redefinitional text, engaging with received ideas about French identity, for although published in 1990, the itinerary described in *Les
Passagers du Roissy-Express* was undertaken the previous year, against

---

[86] Urbain, *Ethnologue, mais pas trop*, 19.
[87] The two texts are closely associated: Maspero writes in his 1993 postface to the
English translation of *Les Passagers du Roissy-Express*: 'if I hadn't read that book, perhaps
I would never even have dared to write mine' (*Roissy Express*, 262).

the backcloth of the bicentenary of the French Revolution.[88] At the same time, the text is a sustained reflection on the field of travel, the practices of travel, and the ways in which travel is textualized.

In line with a number of contributors to the *Pour une littérature voyageuse* movement manifesto discussed above, Maspero's text adopts a resigned tone regarding the impossibility of travel: 'Tous les voyages ont été faits. Ils sont à la portée de quiconque peut se payer le charter. Tous les récits de voyage ont été écrits' [All the journeys have been done. They are within reach of anyone who can afford a charter ticket. All the accounts of journeys have been written].[89] Countering such defeatism and employing ludically a series of recognizable generic markers, Maspero's narrator initially adopts the inflated discourse of exploration and danger customarily associated with earlier travel accounts; but he then appears to deflate his hyperbolic claims and confirm this entropic view of travel by revealing the parodic modesty of the journey chosen: a month-long descent of the RER-B line, without contact with Paris itself for the duration of the journey, alighting at each suburban station and stopping overnight in its environs. When he dubs this project 'un vrai voyage' [a real journey] or 'un *grand* voyage' [a *really big* journey], and proceeds to discuss it in terms of the cartographic uncertainties that had challenged earlier travellers, his friends' reaction—like that of the reader—is incredulity.[90] Yet there is seriousness to this journey belied by the often-ludic tone of its account. Despite the ironic 'Express' of his title, Maspero presents the decelerated, domestic journey as a response to the perceived end of travel. One of his principal aims is rediscovery of the obscured complexities not of the exotic (travel's customary domain), but of the everyday. He does not so much leave home as rediscover it, renegotiating in the process his relationship to 'home' itself. The purported collapse of both the field and practice of travel is countered by a sense of their potentially constant reinvention.

---

[88] Although the Bicentenary context remains implicit in the text, Maspero subsequently underlines its importance: in the postface to the English translation, for instance, he describes the journey (in peripatetic terms) as: 'a pleasant stroll among my own people, in this country of mine, in the spring of the French Revolution bicentenary year' (p. 268). References in the text itself to the Bicentenary remain deliberately ambivalent: a gardener tending some Bastille-shaped topiary is Algerian (*Les Passagers*, 101).

[89] Maspero, *Les Passagers*, 13; *Roissy Express*, 8. Although Maspero has never been directly involved in the movement, excerpts from *Les Passagers* appeared as 'Drancy' in *Gulliver*, 4 (1990), 124–41.

[90] Maspero, *Les Passagers*, 15, 19 (emphasis in the original); *Roissy Express*, 9, 12.

As Max Silverman states in his discussion of postmodern urban space
in France: 'The local is now more global: that is, a hybrid space composed of a mosaic of diverse pieces from diverse places.'[91] Underpinning
Maspero's account is a similar awareness of the contradictions and
unevenness inherent in the representation of urban space. His itinerary
slices through the vast suburban periphery of Paris, offering a cross-
section and exploring the tensions between the capital and the surrounding shapeless mass or 'magma informe' from which it endeavours
to distinguish itself.[92] The monolithic term *la banlieue* reflects the
refusal to differentiate implied by such a reductive description. As
Maspero remarks, this buffer zone between Paris and *la Province* is
for many Parisian 'un désert de dix millions d'habitants, une suite de
constructions grises indifférenciées' [a desert containing ten million
inhabitants, a series of indistinct grey buildings].[93] It is a monotonous
landscape in which anonymous figures coalesce or are demonized as an
undifferentiated mass reminiscent of the nineteenth-century 'classes
dangereuses' described by Louis Chevalier.[94] The term *la banlieue*
suggests a homogenizing approach to the vast and well-populated

---

[91] Max Silverman, *Facing Postmodernity: Contemporary French Thought on Culture
and Society* (London: Routledge, 1999), 74.

[92] One conclusion of Maspero's journey, while underlining the ways in which official
structures such as the public transport network entrench spatial divisions, points to the
arbitrary and imaginary nature of any boundary dividing Paris from its *banlieues*. In
Balkans-Transit (Paris: Seuil, 1997), a text outlining the author's 1990s journeys in the
former Yugoslavia, Maspero describes himself, as a child, building a jigsaw of Europe in
which each piece represented an individual country (p. 9). The memory encompasses not
only the division and fragmentation ensured by the borders of each individual piece, but
also the possibility of assembling these fragments into the continuity of a continental land
mass. Fragmentation and reconstruction, discontinuity and continuity, issues underpinning Maspero's Balkan journey as he witnesses the rapid marginalization of elements of a
culture and population that were previously both multi-ethnic and plurilingual, are also
central to Maspero's earlier domestic journey described in *Les Passagers du Roissy-
Express*.

[93] Maspero, *Les Passagers*, 24; *Roissy Express*, 16.

[94] See Louis Chevalier, *Classes laborieuses, classes dangereuses à Paris pendant le
première moitié du XIXe siècle* (Paris: Plon, 1958). In an excellent chapter on Maspero,
Jean-Xavier Ridon describes *la banlieue* as 'un espace qui ne trouve pas facilement les
moyens de sa propre représentation et où ses habitants oscillent entre une visibilité extrême
et une forme généralisée d'oubli' [a space which does not easily achieve the means to
represent itself and whose inhabitants swing between an extreme visibility or a generalized
form of amnesia]. See *Le Voyageur en son miroir*, 75. Silverman adds that the term *la
banlieue* has become 'the major euphemism for the racialization (and fragmentation) of
city space, symbolically representing the anxieties and sense of crisis of our age, from the
fear of drugs, violence, AIDS and religious fundamentalism to the more general "malaise"
of Western democratic societies' (*Facing Postmodernity*, 75).

area that surrounds the twenty Parisian *arondissements*, historically home to a diverse population further supplemented in recent years by postcolonial migration.[95] At the same time, however, what Maspero sees as the contradictory fragmentation of this space ('espace morcelé, espace en miettes' [space broken into bits and pieces]) is seen as a challenge; in both guidebooks and the Parisian imagination, dependent respectively on alphabetical ordering or centre–periphery models of geography, interconnections between areas of *la banlieue* have been eclipsed.[96] Maspero's aim is to reflect through travel the striking diversity of a plurality of *banlieues* while nevertheless seeking continuities between its fragments. Maspero's traveller repeatedly underlines his natural rootedness within the city itself, and constructs his persona as an 'insider' figure, a Parisian intellectual far removed from the lives of the people through whose space he travels; yet Maspero himself, known (as the text reminds us) as a radical publisher in the 1950s and 1960s instrumental in the dissemination of anti-colonial texts, may also be seen as a counter-cultural figure and intellectual outsider.[97] The texts plays on these contradictions and underlines the instabilities of identity they imply. The *dépaysement* inherent in travel, despite the apparent modesty in geographical terms of the particular journey undertaken, triggers an experience of dislocation and marginalization. As the journey is textualized, it becomes clear that Maspero aims to challenge a series of conventions, narrative and otherwise, that characterize the 'dominant' culture to which he belongs. As such, as I shall explain further below, Maspero's voice might be allied to other representations of *la banlieue* as a potential site of travel found in the work of a series of recent authors of immigrant origin.

The historical context of this descent of the RER-B line situates its author in relation to a series of issues regarding memory and identity. The theme of commemoration, and the risks of the consensus to which a practice has a tendency to lead, is central to the text, whether the narrator is concerned with Drancy or with the Bicentenary of the Revolution itself. In choosing to travel through an area of France rarely

---

[95] See Tyler Stovall, 'From Red Belt to Black Belt: Race, Class, and Urban Marginality in Twentieth-Century Paris', *L'Esprit Créateur*, 41/3 (2001), 9–23.

[96] See Maspero, *Les Passagers*, 21–2; *Roissy Express*, 13.

[97] On this subject, see Maspero's autobiographical reflections, *Les Abeilles et la guêpe* (Paris: Seuil, 2002).

subject to the tourist gaze,[98] Maspero challenges both the (predominantly rural) tradition of the domestic journey and the associated version
of home on which many accounts of journeys to other cultures depend.
The projected stability of the domestic space often serves in the travel
narrative as a fixed point of reference against which the baroque and
often threatening diversity of elsewhere is judged; that this space is often
associated with a regional, pre-urban idyll underlines its imagined,
often nostalgic status. It was such a reimagining of the French nation
that the 1989 Bicentenary allowed. A country beset with those *fin-
de-siècle* crises already discussed in the introduction to this volume
was able to project, through the processes of republican commemoration, the image of a unified France in which elements perceived as
exterior or exotic were incorporated without undermining the integrity
of a unified 'Frenchness'. Perhaps one of the most marked illustrations
of this manœuvre was Jean-Paul Goude's 1989 *Opéra Marseillaise*, a
controversially multiculturalist celebration of the Republican tradition
that stage-managed French tolerance and openness whilst ignoring the
material conditions faced by those of immigrant origin in contemporary
France.[99] Maspero's journey is a constant challenge to such republican
ideology, moving beyond an objective recognition of multi-ethnicity to
underline France's transformation into a multicultural, polyvocal space.
In selecting the space between the capital and the regions, the author
deliberately focuses on the construction of margins, with the marginal
understood in terms of existing material conditions as well as of
the processes that structure, consolidate, and perpetuate actual lived
experience.

Studies of travel literature have a tendency to take means of transport for granted, but in Maspero's text the choice of the train is central
to the narrative's impact. The RER line is a site of transit, linking the
urban centre with its suburban periphery; like the airport at its

[98] Since the publication of Maspero's text, there has been a shift of emphasis. See e.g.
Banlieues de Paris (Paris: Guide du Routard, 2001), and *La France des écrivains* (Paris:
Gallimard, 1997), the second of which includes an entry on Maspero's text. See Cyril
Jarton, 'Le passager du Roissy-Express: François Maspero', 114–16.

[99] For a discussion of the *Opéra Marseillaise*, see Laurent Dubois, '*La République
métisée*: Citizenship, Colonialism, and the Borders of French History', *Cultural Studies*,
14/1 (2000), 15–34 (pp. 18–20), and Steven Laurence Kaplan, *Farewell, Revolution:
Disputed Legacies, France 1789/1989* (Ithaca, NY: Cornell University Press, 1995), 270–
330. For an excellent reflection on hybridity in contemporary France, see Jennifer Yee,
'*Métissage* in France: a Post-Modern Fantasy and its Forgotten Precedents', *Modern and
Contemporary France*, 11/4 (2003), 411–26.

north-eastern extremity,[100] it is a striking example of what Marc Augé dubs a 'non-lieu' [non-place], an anaesthetized location disjointed from any wider context by its transformation into a space in which dwelling or travel (as opposed to more neutral displacement) seems impossible.[101] Closely policed, the train line provides a particularly striking example of the 'enfermement du voyageur'.[102] For travellers originating from the city's centre, the centripetal line of the railway turns *la banlieue* into a space passed through and never granted the status of destination in its own right. By travelling for only a few minutes a day, alighting and exploring the area around the station on foot or by other public transport, Maspero and Frantz submit the journey to a different logic, disrupting its North–South vector with other tangential trajectories. The conventional itinerary is atomized. As the travellers slow down, they discover a different texture of place, they replace the panoramic or panoptic with the microscopic or partial, and they gain access to what might be classed as a fractal dimension of urban space.[103] In Jean-Xavier Ridon's terms, through the practices of travel, the 'non-place' is transformed into a place in its own right.[104] When the travellers reach Drancy, for example, their journey takes on an archaeological guise as they cut through the historical strata of place: the conventional, horizontal vectors of travel are transformed into a vertical equivalent.[105] The supposed 'suite de constructions grises indifférenciées' achieves marked differentiation: Maspero and Frantz shift between the bucolic and the pluri-ethnic contexts of their chosen field of travel, discovering its marked diversity.[106]

The project or idea on which the journey depends is not a simple conceit whereby the proximate is ingeniously and benignly exoticized.

---

[100] Maspero describes the airport as 'cet espace hors de tout temps et de tout espace réels' [that space outside of real time and space] (*Les Passagers*, 13; *Roissy Express*, 7).

[101] See Marc Augé, *Non-lieux* (Paris: Seuil, 1992).

[102] On the symbolic meanings of the policing of the RER, see Dubois, 'La République métisée', 16–17.

[103] There is a conscious refusal of panoramic views and what Mary Louise Pratt describes as the 'monarch-of-all-I-survey' trope: on the Arceuil viaduct, for instance, Frantz is prevented by the poor weather conditions from taking the picture that such a high vantage point would seem to permit (*Les Passagers*, 292–5). See Pratt, *Imperial Eyes*, 205–6.

[104] See Ridon, *Le Voyage en son Miroir*, 79.

[105] On the concept of the 'vertical' journey, see Cronin, *Across the Lines*, 19.

[106] For a discussion of the role of travel in the discovery of diversity in *Les Passagers*, see Alexandre Dauge-Roth, 'Quelles *espèces d'espaces* pour *Les Passagers du Roissy-Express*? Lectures de la banlieue comme lectures du quotidien', *French Literature Series*, 24 (1997), 153–70 (pp. 160–2).

Underpinning the text is a real sense of risk that becomes apparent on those occasions when the journey itself appears to be on the point of grinding to a halt, when the identity of the would-be tourists becomes subject to suspicion; but these moments of near breakdown in the journey are transformed into opportunities for creative reflection. The detached, third-person narration of *Les Passagers* is supplemented by a series of photographs by Maspero's co-traveller Frantz.[107] It is customarily the photographer who shows a marked sensitivity to the element of exchange inherent in the travellers' encounters. She uses photography as a means of negotiating contact and dialogue rather than seizing images; the photograph operates not as an illustration of the journey or as proof of its account's authenticity, but as a heuristic means of incorporating the lives of those encountered and teasing out their voices. Her apparently inexplicable failure to negotiate the right to take a picture on one occasion is therefore surprising, especially as it leads the journey to a moment of crisis or 'dérapage' (meaning both a 'faux pas' and a 'skidding out of control').[108] Having omitted to request permission to photograph a group of Malians, Frantz is challenged for what is perceived as a lack of respect and good manners. Her error is twofold: not only, in the eyes of the Malians, has she as an outsider assumed the right to photograph; but also, against the rationale of the journey, she has taken the picture voyeuristically, 'de très loin', neglecting the attention to detail on which other encounters depend.[109] In a particularly rich description of the exchange that follows, Maspero alludes to a number of features central to the rest of the account. Already, in an encounter with Madame Zineb, hospitality had been refused, and the narrator makes no attempt to disguise the un-

---

[107] For a discussion of the text–image interrelationship, see Peter D. Osborne, *Travelling Light: Photography, Travel and Visual Culture* (Manchester: Manchester University Press, 2000), 185, and Ridon, *Le Voyage en son miroir*, 89–92.

[108] The passage must additionally be read in the context of French judicial attitudes to the photographic image and debates regarding the ethics of photography. Frantz's customary procedure of negotiating the right to an image may be contrasted, for instance, with Luc Delahaye's photographing of passengers on the Paris metro with a hidden camera. See *L'Autre* (London: Phaidon, 1999). For a further commentary on this passage, see Ridon, *Le Voyage en son miroir*, 94.

[109] Maspero, *Les Passagers*, 127. After the episode, Frantz repeats this aspect: 'C'est idiot: cette photo, prise de si loin, n'avait de toute façon aucun intérêt' [It's stupid—the photo was of no interest anyway, taken from so far away] (*Les Passagers*, 128; *Roissy Express*, 100).

comfortable situation to which this refusal led.[110] The meeting with the Malians provides a similar reflection on the clash of systems of hospitality and exchange, and on the need to negotiate intercultural—or perhaps here, more accurately, intracultural—contact. The scene reveals a clash of attitudes regarding both the sharing of space and the ways in which dialogue and exchange are to be conceptualized. The passage begins by focusing on a scene apparently 'exotic' within this French setting (the adjective itself is used, and the lexical choices reveal the otherness of the artefacts described): 'sous des arbres, un étal de fruits exotiques, de mangues, de tubercules; des Africains en boubous, assis, désœuvrés; un joueur de tamtam' [under some trees is a stall of exotic fruit, mangos, tubers; Africans in boubous sit idly around, and someone is playing the tomtoms]; but as the text proceeds, these exoticist markers of a hackneyed African travel narrative (fruit, clothing, music, men deep in discussion squatting on their haunches) are progressively normalized and absorbed into their French context.[111]

Maspero and Frantz are initially presented as travellers confident in their roles and at home in their context; yet there is a marked shift of emphasis away from the appearance of the 'travellees' towards a reflection on the identity of the travellers themselves. The latters' effortless and unthinking superiority is transformed into malaise and even guilt, as their tourism becomes a suspicious practice. One source of the Malians' disapproval is a clear anxiety regarding their status in France: Maspero provides assurance that he and Frantz are neither police nor journalists. By inadvertently triggering this moment of crisis, the travellers are forced to reflect on their own vulnerability as well as on that of other travellers sharing the same space. Underpinning the text is an awareness of the status of many Malians in France in the 1980s whose status as 'clandestins' had not yet, through progressive politicization, been transformed into 'sans-papiers'.[112] In such a context, taking what

[110] See Mireille Rosello, *Postcolonial Hospitality: The Immigrant as Guest* (Stanford, Calif.: Stanford University Press, 2001), 68–77. Frantz returns to visit Madame Zineb once the journey is over (*Les Passagers*, 48–9), and a similar possibility underpins the exchange with the Malians.

[111] Maspero, *Les Passagers*, 127; *Roissy Express*, 99. The interdependency of France and its (former) colonies is underlined when one interlocutor alludes to the role of the *tirailleurs sénégalais*: 'mon père s'est battu pour la France' [my father fought for France].

[112] Maspero's awareness of the ways in which legal status affects the relationship to place is made clear in the text: 'refuge, ghetto, oasis, citadelle, tout dépend du passeport, du permis de séjour et de la carte de travail de celui qui en franchit le seuil' [refuge, ghetto, oasis or citadel—it all depends on the passport, green card or work permit of the person who walks through the door] (*Les Passagers*, 242; *Roissy Express*, 192). A group of

at first appears to be an exotico-touristic snapshot becomes a potential act of policing. Temporarily at least, the text permits no firm sense of home for either of the parties involved in the encounter, no straightforward binary of traveller and travellee: as Mireille Rosello comments, 'when strangers meet strangers, each becomes not only a potential host and also a potential guest, but also, at least for Maspero, a potential enemy'.[113] This episode concludes, however, with the possibility of return ('un jour, c'est promis, s'ils se retrouvent, à Paris, peut-être' [one day, he promises, perhaps if they meet in Paris]), as if the crisis has enabled the situation to evolve, communication to improve, and the possibility of dialogue and even connection to emerge.[114] What Maspero foregrounds is an understanding that representation of diversity may be seen as a process of dialogue and negotiation, challenging the Orientalist assumption (whose grasp reaches far beyond the hazy geographical area implied by that epithet) that: 'they cannot represent themselves; they must be represented'.[115] In Max Silverman's terms, 'Maspero's narrator [. . .] seeks to make connections in a space which has become fragmented, diversified and uprooted from its anchorage in a spatio-temporal and social context.'[116] Such creation of connections does not lead, however, to an understanding of space that rejects any differentialist or separatist model of diversity for a celebratory and integrative one in which all barriers are suddenly erased. The narrator's aim is to challenge spatial binaries disseminated by the media according to which diversity becomes dichotomy, and to tease out—by walking, talking, and writing—the more complex, shifting patterns undergirding the field of travel.

Malian men recruited by Jean-Paul Goude to play *tirailleurs sénégalais* in his Bicentenary parade were reluctant to rehearse as they feared attempts to lure them onto the infamous charter flights to Mali. See Corine Lesnes, 'Ultimes répétitions aux Champs-Elysées: les tambours de maître Goude', *Le Monde*, 13 July 1989, 15, and Laurence Kaplan, *Farewell, Revolution: Disputed Legacies*, 294. On the subject of these flights, see Didier Daeninckx, *Lumière noire* (Paris: Gallimard, 1993), and Med Hondo's film version of the novel. The Malians employed to act out Republican ideals actually illustrated the limitations of those ideals and the instability of those dwelling in the margins of the French Republic.

[113] Rosello, *Postcolonial Hospitality*, 75. On Maspero's 'pulsions sécuritaires', see e.g. *Les Passagers*, 316.

[114] Maspero, *Les Passagers*, 128; *Roissy Express*, 100.

[115] I cite here Said's much quoted epigraph to *Orientalism*, borrowed from Karl Marx's *Eighteenth Brumaire of Louis Bonaparte*.

[116] Silverman, *Facing Postmodernity*, 92. Here Silverman contrasts François with the nineteenth-century tradition of the flâneur as well as the practices of voyeurism.

Maspero and Frantz's uncharacteristic assumptions regarding their right to photograph those they meet trigger active refusal, but the resistance underpinning this reflects an essential element of the travelogue in question: far from being accorded the walk-on parts customarily written for 'travellees' in much conventional travel literature, inhabitants of the *banlieues* are granted central, even equal roles in their journey account. *Les Passagers* accordingly encourages a rethinking of the rules of cross-cultural contact. Indeed, the *banlieues* it represents may be seen as a domestic illustration of the 'contact zone', in which preconceived ideas relating to identities and the connections between them are challenged and even undermined. The travellers' identities are themselves destabilized and rendered vulnerable as, subjected to a series of questions, they forfeit any assumed right to enquire: who are they? how do others see them? how tenable is their project? what does it feel like to dwell in another's margins, to become an outsider onto whom another's fear of the Other is projected? It is significant that to the question of identity, Maspero replies by foregrounding his work as translator, and what may initially appear to be an obfuscatory response allowing him to disguise his other roles in fact casts light on the whole journey narrative.[117] *Les Passagers* presents travel as an intersemiotic, interlingual, intralingual, and intercultural experience. The encounter analysed above underlines the ways in which the text explores the clash of sign systems whilst at the same time exposing the traveller's responsibility as translator. Recent translation studies have problematized the common failure by the various users of translations to acknowledge the work that goes into transforming an original text into its alternative version; this myth of effortless, seamless transfer ignores the obstacles, dilemmas, and material processes that underpin the production of a translation. A similar situation pertains to travel accounts, where obstacles to the textual translation of elsewhere tend to be transformed into sources of bathetic humour or more commonly factored out. Maspero's account describes travellers wrestling with the space of travel, with the objects that fill this space, and with the people who inhabit it; as such, it self-consciously acknowledges obstacles to translation, but in acknowledging such obstacles reveals the diversity of the space through which its producers travel and the

---

[117] Katherine Gantz's claim that translation is a 'fact of [Maspero's] work with no real bearing on this encounter in the suburbs' would appear too hasty. See 'Dangerous Intersections: The Near-Collision of French and Cultural Studies in Maspero's *Les Passagers du Roissy-Express*', *The French Review*, 73/1 (1999), 82–93 (p. 89).

complexity of their relationship to that space and its inhabitants.[118] In
Maspero, re-exploration of the domestic space becomes its redefinition.
Home and away are no longer differentiated, dependent on a mosaic
approach to diversity in which the familiar may be coterminous with
the unfamiliar but remains distinct from it; instead, there is an unpredictable and occasionally uneasy integration whereby the once unfamiliar is embedded in the once familiar, creating new matrices of cultural
interaction.

Central to this complexity is an awareness that the apparent linearity
of the Roissy-Express is intersected by a multitude of competing itineraries: not simply the recorded tangents and arabesques permitted by
Maspero and Frantz's disruption of the journey's logic, but also a series
of other routes, both historical and contemporary, that increasingly
crowd out the single journey announced at the text's opening in such
hyperbolic terms. Not only therefore is the space of travel revealed to be
a palimpsest;[119] but also the status of the traveller within that space is
relativized, seen as part of a network of competing journeys that undermines any claims to primacy the traveller may initially seem to enter-
tain. These competing journeys, whether witnessed or recounted, are
often merely sketched, and those undertaking them accordingly retain
an element of mystery: crossing the parc du Sausset in Aulnay-sous-
Bois, for instance, the travellers encounter one such figure:

Carrefours compliqués. Ils coupent droit. Devant eux marche un homme, un
Africain, qui porte sa valise sur la tête. Il quitte la route et s'éloigne par les
jachères. Plus loin une femme et ses enfants sortent de la brousse. Il existe

---

[118] I diverge here from Gantz's observation that: 'Self-reflexivity is also in short supply;
his largely uninspected position of privilege detracts from the credibility of his social
commentary.' See 'Dangerous Intersections', 91–2. Max Silverman seems more accurate
in noting Maspero's clear awareness both of his lack of necessary cultural competence and
of the links between social status and access to mobility (*Facing Postmodernity*, 167 n. 5).
As Mireille Rosello adds, as a result of the 'interesting textual hybridity' of this third- and
not first-person travel narrative, the reader is constantly if obliquely aware of Anaïk's
silent presence and her likely divergence from François's own reactions (*Postcolonial
Hospitality*, 71–2).

[119] In alluding to 'affiches lacérées à faire crever d'envie Raymond Hains' (p. 64),
Maspero associates his text with the torn posters of the Nouveau réalisme movement.
Hains, the principal 'affichiste', cut down layered and ripped posters from advertising
hoardings and presented these huge pieces as works of art. Parallels with *Les Passagers* are
suggestive: these 'affiches lacérées' questioned artistic agency and creative intervention
since anonymous passers-by and municipal officials were as important or perhaps more
important in their production than the artist himself; moreover, Hains's 1961 exhibition,
'La France déchirée', including FLN and OAS posters, was a clear engagement with
essential if then suppressed issues relating to French identity.

comme cela aux confins du monde des contrées apparemment inhabitées où l'on voit parfois surgir sur les routes des gens qui cheminent vers d'improbables destinations.[120]

They come to complicated crossroads, and tack right. Walking in front of them is an African with a suitcase on his head. He leaves the road and heads off over the rough ground. Further along, a woman and her children come out of the scrub. There are places like that at the end of the world, where you sometimes see people spring out on to the road and head off towards improbable destinations.

This complex crossroads reflects not only the physical uncertainties of the journey, but also the interconnecting itineraries by which the routes of the journey are constituted.

It is to be stressed, however, that *Les Passagers* reveals more than an awareness of competing itineraries, which can be found elsewhere, both in the exclusive definitions of Lacarrière discussed above or in the fleeting references to others' journeys in an author such as Coatalem;[121] instead, the relativizing implications of other journeys have a more profound impact on the text, on the travellers' identities it freights, and on the understanding of the field through which they journey. When, towards the end of the text, the travellers' identities appear to fragment, this is not only as a result of fatigue or greater familiarity with the southern section of the RER-B line; it is also a direct result of this relativization, and the subsequent deflation and even trivialization to which this seems to lead. Maspero's account both invites a contrapuntal awareness of competing journeys and underlines the implications of such an awareness for conventional understandings of travel literature. His aim is to operate in a space in which he and Frantz are outsiders—or even marginal figures—whilst allowing to emerge, through both the practice and (textual and photographic) account of their journey, the voices and experiences of those 'marginal' figures they meet.[122] The traveller's autocratic and aristocratic discourse of self-sufficiency is replaced with a more precarious conception of travel literature that invites the reader to prise open conventional definitions of travel. The popularity of Maspero's text, rapidly become central to any canon of

---

[120] Maspero, *Les Passagers*, 44; *Roissy Express*, 31.

[121] See Jean-Luc Coatalem, *Suite indochinoise: récit du voyage au Vietnam* (Paris: Le Dilettante, 1999), 139–40.

[122] A reflection on the mechanisms and structures of marginality underpins Frantz's photographic work. See Anaïk Frantz and François Maspero, *Paris bout du monde* (Levallois Perret: Manya, 1992), 8.

French cultural studies, is perhaps rooted in its implicit dialogues with a whole series of other texts and cultural products that have been seen to explore the complexities of contemporary France (and of a more general francophone space of which France is merely a part).[123] In relation to *Les Passagers* should be read a series of other narratives, by those born or raised in the *banlieues*, that recount similar journeys through contemporary France: texts by authors such as Azouz Begag, Mehdi Charef, Soraya Nini, and Mounsi; moreover, Maspero and Frantz's itinerary might be considered in relation to journeys adopting a reverse itinerary, from the suburbs into Paris, such as that included by Mathieu Kassovitz in *La Haine* in which the three protagonists, Said, Hubert, and Vinz, venture into 'les beaux quartiers'. With Maspero's travelogue, the understanding of travel is opened to explore its relationship to other modes of displacement such as migrancy and marginalization. The notion of a fixed centre or a domestic space on which travel often depends is itself undermined. The Île de France—and, by implication, France itself—is revealed, by the traveller's interaction with it, to be a shifting, dynamic, heterogeneous, and subtly subdivided space.

---

[123] Considering the popularity of the text, Katherine Gantz claims that it belongs to 'a hybridized genre by forging a literary work out of a cultural studies project—namely, the examination of everyday society in the Parisian suburban periphery'. See 'Dangerous Intersections', 82.

Postface
From the Cultures of Travel to
Travelling Cultures

> Many different kinds of people travel, acquiring complex know-
> ledges, stories, political and intercultural understandings, without
> producing 'travel writing'. [...] Travel, in this view, denotes a
> range of material, spatial practices that produce knowledges, stor-
> ies, traditions, comportments, musics, books, diaries, and other
> cultural expressions.[1]

WHILST Maspero's self-conscious travel text certainly belongs to the
peripatetic tradition discussed in parallel to it in the previous chapter, it
serves at the same time as a critique of many pedestrians' cultural self-
sufficiency and even self-satisfaction. The contemporary tradition of
walking narratives in French offers an invaluable reflection on the
practices of travel; at the same time, it illuminates travel's potential to
uncover, in spaces seemingly threatened by progressive homogenization, evidence of the potential 'réseau d'un filigrane très ténu' described
by Segalen and discussed in the introduction to this volume. What these
texts often omit, however, is any sustained engagement, along the lines
apparent in *Les Passagers du Roissy-Express*, either with those new
patterns of diversity and hybridity revealed by the journey or with the
implications of these new configurations for wider understandings of
travel itself. What Maspero makes clear is that any potentially roman-
ticized focus on walking must be cautiously contextualized: for many
travellers, for basic material reasons, walking is a necessity not a choice,
since it remains one of the principal modes of transport for migrants
and the homeless.[2] As Susan George's concept of 'fast castes' underlines, a traveller's relationship to a mode of transport depends very

---

[1] Clifford, 'Traveling Cultures', 34–5.
[2] A similar point is made by Christopher Prendergast, who criticizes de Certeau's
commentary on the subversive potential of urban roaming: 'for [the homeless] "walking"
the streets reflects less a challenge to the power of those who own the city than one of the
miserable effects of that power'. See *Paris and the Nineteenth Century* (Oxford: Blackwell,
1992), 211. Cited by Max Silverman, *Facing Postmodernity*, 79–80.

much on individual circumstances: slowness is a luxury for those with access to the means of acceleration, a curse to those without.[3]

As the discussion of the *Pour une littérature voyageuse* movement has demonstrated, one not uncommon response to any such recognition of tachocracy (and the differentiated access to means of mobility this implies) is the continuation of exclusive definitional processes. 'Travel' is grasped according to earlier understandings of the concept, the 'traveller' projected in terms of a specific matrix of gender, class, and ethnicity. While certain strands of travel literature continue to contribute to the perpetuation of these previous versions, James Clifford and others have pointed to the failings of any such yearning for a status quo ante. While certain travel narratives may choose to erase the material transformations of those chosen fields, it is nevertheless true that many earlier understandings of travel have been challenged, and for the most part undermined, by contemporary practices of mobility. One of the aims of this study, however, has been to suggest that the conventional purposes of travel literature have been progressively called into question not only as a result of mechanization or tourism, but also because those traditionally objectified and pacified by the travel narrative have increasingly gained access themselves to means of (self-)representation.

The travel narrative's educational or documentary alibi of cultural transfer risks becoming redundant when the erstwhile 'travellee', traditionally mute in Western journey narratives, begins not only to travel back but also to write back. Thus, the postcolonial recognition of the Empire travelling back to the former colonial centre is accompanied by an urgent need to rethink both travel and the ways in which we construct and read the diverse practices that this term encompasses. As recent works by authors as diverse as Nicole-Lise Bernheim, Nicolas Bouvier, and François Maspero have suggested, the traveller's unquestioning representation of the cultures through which he or she travels has given way to a more anxious and self-aware engagement with cultural diversity.[4] The notion of a specific 'culture of travel' may as a result be seen increasingly to suggest a troubling self-sufficiency, implying that Western travellers still interact with, react to, and represent traces of diversity perceived elsewhere according to sets of values

---

[3] See Ch. 4 above.
[4] For a discussion of Nicole-Lise Bernheim and the reassessment of travelling, dwelling, and intercultural contact that her narratives imply, see Charles Forsdick, 'Reading Twentieth-Century Women's Travel Literature in French', in Arzu Etensel Ildem (ed.), *Seuils et Traverses 4* (Ankara: University of Ankara Press, 2004), 361–73.

provided by their own cultures of origin and formulated with no reference to their destinations; such a domestication of other cultures and failure to reflect their inherent complexity or even opacity encapsulates the processes of exemplification to which the term 'exoticism' itself is often reduced. The binaries in which such assumptions are grounded—Western/non-Western, active/passive, viewing/viewed, mobile/static, modern/traditional—yield increasingly, however, to more complex models: the postcolonial migration of people to and from the former colonial centres leads to an acceleration of the hybridization of cultures that has always existed (if it has not always been acknowledged as such);[5] those whose movement in a colonial economy of travel was closely policed by centre–periphery vectors achieve the right to travel and to articulate the experience of their own journeys. The result is a prising open of understandings of travel, a concept whose definition according to the Victorian model of self-distinction and unquestioning self-assertion, still perpetuated in particular in certain forms of advertising, becomes increasingly difficult to sustain. Instead of obscuring the uneven mechanics of intercultural connection, studying travel becomes a means of revealing the ambiguities and imbalances of contact between cultures. Michael Cronin has written: '[T]he general decline in foreign-language learning in the English-speaking world in recent years can be attributed in part to the ready identification of English as the sole language of globalization but also to the desire to maintain the benefits of connectedness without the pain of connection.'[6] The proliferation of certain understandings of travel, in which the differences between and within cultures are eclipsed by an acceptance of monoculture, has had a parallel and associated effect. It is, however, an inclusive, contrapuntal grasp of travel, open to a range of travellers and journeys wider than that to which the term has traditionally been restricted, that transforms this concept into a privileged site for consideration of the 'pain of connection' in the contemporary world.

---

[5] For an illustration, in a French context, of the ways in which a myth of self-sufficiency is challenged by historical recognition of France's long-standing reliance on foreign contributions to national identity, see Stovall and van des Abbeele (eds.), *French Civilization and its Discontents*, and Peter Sahlins, *Unnaturally French: Foreign Citizens in the Old Régime and After* (Ithaca, NY: Cornell University Press, 2004). Stovall and van des Abbeele's collection suggest that France itself has been shaped by global processes of creolization; Sahlins considers the absorption of foreigners into notions of French nationality in the three centuries leading to the Revolution, underlining the fact that France has always been multicultural and multiethnic in the private sphere.

[6] Michael Cronin, *Translation and Globalization* (London: Routledge, 2003), 49.

FROM DISCOVERY TO OPENNESS: POSTCOLONIAL JOURNEYS

One of the most obvious textual manifestations of these shifts is to be found in postcolonial literature in French, a heterogeneous body of texts that often relies on travel thematically but also offers a major contribution to more clearly epistemological considerations of the uses of mobility. In a study pioneering in this field, *Journeys through the French African Novel in French*, Mildred Mortimer addresses the various uses of the journey motif—a staple element of many African oral narratives—in a number of works of Maghrebian and sub-Saharan Francophone fiction. What her book makes clear is that, in addition, travel within or between colonial and postcolonial spaces becomes a constitutive element of post-war Francophone writing. This very general observation further illustrates the exclusive practices according to which contemporary French definitions of travel literature operate, for the texts in question are invariably seen as 'Francophone' fiction and accordingly remain doubly distanced from a French tradition of literary travel. Many early novels, such as Camara Laye's *L'Enfant noir* and Cheikh Hamidou Kane's *L'Aventure ambiguë*, fictionalize the dilemmas of the colonially centripetal journey of acculturation undertaken by many young colonial subjects from their country of origin to France itself, with the latter associating these later twentieth-century displacements with the earlier twentieth-century journeys to Europe of the *tirailleurs sénégalais*.[7] The uneasiness regarding intersections of travel and identity articulated by Kane prepares for subsequent journey narratives by authors such as Rachid Boudjedra, Mengouchi and Ramdane, and Pius Ngandu Nkashama, all of whom investigate the ambiguous and vulnerable status of the postcolonial francophone traveller in contemporary France.[8] Travel indeed becomes a principal motif in texts by French authors of immigrant origin, such as Azouz Begag and Mounsi, as they attempt to articulate their marginalization within accepted notions of Frenchness and to describe the journeys between cultures on which their everyday existence depends. It is also in these

---

[7] The experiences of a *tirailleur sénégalais* (including his journey from Senegal to Morocco and then France) are described in the text customarily presented as the first sub-Saharan African novel in French, Bakary Diallo's assimilationist *Force-Bonté* (Dakar: Nouvelles Éditions Africaines, 1985 [1927]).

[8] See Rachid Boujedra, *Topographie idéale pour une agression caractérisée* (Paris: Denoël, 1975), Mengouchi and Ramdane, *L'Homme qui enjamba la mer* (Paris: Veyrier, 1978), and Pius Ngandu Nkashama, *Vie et mœurs d'un primitif en Essone Quatre-vingt-onze* (Paris: L'Harmattan, 1987).

accounts of postcolonial journeys that women's voices are heard directly, with authors such as Assia Djebar and Leila Sebbar providing a challenge to spatial norms created along gender lines.

Sebbar, the Algerian-born novelist now resident in France, describes a series of young female protagonists for whom travel through France and North Africa becomes a means of exploring self-identity. They attempt to understand their interstitial or marginal location by collecting fragments of their personal histories. For many of them, a return home is impossible, for such a location does not exist, and so they dwell in travel, transforming mobility into the foundations of identity. These journey accounts, however, transform the quest for individual identity into an exploration of wider cultural identities. The eponymous heroine of *Les Carnets de Shérazade*, for instance, hitching a lift through the regions of France, undertakes a postcolonial alternative to the journey of that other national epic from a century before, *Le Tour de la France par deux enfants*.[9] The role of the protagonists of the Third Republic textbook, written in the aftermath of the Franco-Prussian War, was to consolidate the national space from which Alsace-Lorraine had recently been amputated and to perform, through travel, a strengthening of national borders by galvanizing Republican unity.[10] Sebbar's text may rely on the same peripatetic structure, but she uses travel and the impressions it triggers as a means of superimposing traces of the historical North African and Turkish presence in France over the contemporary realities of migration. From a late twentieth-century perspective, solid national boundaries become decidedly fuzzy and permeable, especially when Shérazade reminds the driver of the lorry in which she is travelling that the Arabs occupied the south of France for almost three centuries, from the late 700s—i.e. for twice as long as the French occupation of Algeria.[11] The history of annexation, colonization, and cultural assimilation around the Mediterranean basin, Sebbar implies, is longer than and rather different from the versions often peddled in France itself. Careful exploration of that history suggests that assumptions of superiority as

---

[9] See Leila Sebbar, *Les Carnets de Shérazade* (Paris: Stock, 1985), and G. Bruno, *Le Tour de la France par deux enfants* (Paris: Belin, 1977).

[10] On this subject, see Jacques and Mona Ozouf, '*Le Tour de la France par Deux Enfants*: le petit livre rouge de la République', in Nora (ed.), *Les Lieux de mémoire*, i. 277–301.

[11] See Sebbar, *Les Carnets de Shérazade*, 264–5. For a discussion of this aspect of the text, see Anne Donadey, *Recasting Postcolonialism: Women Writing Between Worlds* (Portsmouth, NH: Heinemann, 2001), 123.

well as myths of national identity based on ethnic or cultural purity are both unfounded and unsustainable. The implications for travel are clear: conventional understandings of the practice built around the nation state are increasingly difficult to sustain, for a growing awareness of globalized or transnational formations triggers what may be seen as the journey's definitive crisis.[12]

For reasons discussed above, the historical emergence of travel writing and the traditional policing of its boundaries have often excluded non-white authors from this genre.[13] Non-fictional (if not non-fictionalized) accounts of journeys by, for example, black Francophone travellers nevertheless exist, and there are notable examples—such as Bernard Dadié's trilogy, describing journeys to Paris, Rome, and New York—of travel narratives that provocatively toy with the overlap between the autobiographical and the novelistic. Michel-Tété Kpomassie's account of a journey from the Ivory Coast, via France, to Greenland, adds a new dimension to the notion of travelling in a francophone Black Atlantic space, but it is one of Édouard Glissant's early texts, the rarely studied *Soleil de la Conscience*, that merits close attention for its transformation of the journey theme into a tool for more sustained understanding of culture and identity.[14] As Romuald Fonkoua has suggested convincingly, travel is one of the devices central to an understanding of Glissant's work, in which the author repeatedly rereads, redefines, and reinterprets the meanings of the journey.[15] *Soleil de la Conscience* is indeed one of the first coherent articulations in the French-language tradition of a concept of postcolonial travel. Instead of using the conceit of ethnographic reversal, whereby the one-time exoticizer France is itself in turn exoticized, Glissant identifies a more troubling and self-reflexive version of the journey in which traditional *dépaysement* is no longer an option. For the Caribbean traveller emerging from a French education, France becomes an inevitable mix of the exotic and the instantly recognizable, with the travellees who inhabit

---

[12] For a fuller discussion of the role of travel in Sebbar's work, see Donadey, *Recasting Postcolonialism*, 119–39, and Mortimer, *Journeys through the French African Novel*, 177–94.

[13] Discussion of the relationship between travel writing and ethnicity, unlike of that between the genre and gender, remains relatively sparse. A useful resource is, however, *The Journal of African Travel Writing*, founded in 1996.

[14] See Michel-Tété Kpomassie, *Un Africain au Groenland* (Paris: Flammarion, 1981), and Edouard Glissant, *Soleil de la Conscience* (Paris: Gallimard, 1998 [1955]).

[15] See Romuald Fonkoua, *Essai sur une mesure du monde au XXe siècle: Édouard Glissant* (Paris: Honoré Champion, 2002), esp. 33–62.

the distant country associated with a peculiar familiarity.[16] The first experience of snow is contrasted on several occasions with the climate of home, the 'espace ensoleillé de la mémoire' [sunny space of memory],[17] but the journey does not depend on any shallow exoticism but is instead a sustained questioning, with both ontological and epistemological implications, of postcolonial travel.

It is a commonplace to note that the travel narrative implicitly and yet invariably reveals more about the traveller's home culture than that of the culture travelled through: in the regularly cited terms of John Szarkowski's observations on (late twentieth-century American) photography, it is more a 'mirror, reflecting the portrait of the artist who made it' than a 'window, through which one might better know the world'.[18] In the Western travel narrative this often results from the travellers' transformation of elsewhere into a screen onto which their own individual or collective dilemmas are projected. In Glissant, however, such self-reflection becomes the primary purpose of the text, not so much erasing the specificity of the France through which he travels as using it to prepare for an ongoing reflection on the role of travel (and subsequently other associated practices of mobility such as *errance*) in the elaboration of what he would subsequently dub a 'Caribbean discourse'. Glissant's journey is accordingly a variation on what Edward Said dubbed the 'voyage in', a trajectory allowing those undertaking it to 'enrichir [leur] silence sur la nouvelle grève' [enrich their silence on a new shore].[19] However, the travel narrative avoids the customary polarities of 'home' and 'elsewhere' in order to project a more integrated field of travel—'Car nous sommes, tous, réunis sur un seul rivage' [For we are all assembled on a single shore]— and to describe the more complex, uneven yet interdependent exchanges that characterize Glissant's subsequent concept of postcolonial 'Relation': 'il n'y aura plus de culture sans toutes les cultures, plus de civilisation qui puisse être métropole pour les autres' [there will no longer be any culture without all cultures, no civilization that might be seen as the centre of the others].[20]

---

[16] Fonkoua describes this slippage between the familiar and unfamiliar in terms of a quasi-schizophrenic response, as the traveller is forced to negotiate the gap between the history of France studied at school and the geography of the Caribbean experienced whilst growing up. See *Essai sur une mesure du monde*, 36.

[17] Glissant, *Soleil de la Conscience*, 52.

[18] John Szarkowski, *Mirrors and Windows: American Photography Since 1960* (New York: Museum of Modern Art, 1978), 25.

[19] Glissant, *Soleil de la Conscience*, 33.

[20] Ibid. 72, 13–14.

Whereas some critics reject the notion of travel or 'le voyage' as a result of its colonial connotations and what they see as the trivialization of forced journeys such as the transatlantic traffic in slaves, Glissant seems to share with James Clifford a desire to cling on to the term precisely because of what the latter dubs its 'historical taintedness'.[21] Despite its adoption of alternative terms such as *errance* that seem to underline the traveller's ambiguous status, Glissant's work persistently engages with the assumptions of Western travel, with the writings of Western travellers (such as Segalen) and with the contribution of travel to the Enlightenment project. His aim is to wrest back travel from a reductively colonialist understanding and to redeploy the concept as a means of understanding the new patterns of intercultural relating that have emerged in the period perceived as the wake of Empire. In the exhortation: 'Ne partez pas de votre rive pour un voyage de découverte ou de conquête. / Laissez faire au voyage' [Don't leave your shore for a journey of discovery or conquest. / Let the journey run its own course], his conception of travel converges with that of other late twentieth-century travellers such as Nicolas Bouvier.[22] His approach to the concept's origins, however, diverges from such understandings, for Glissant stresses that one of the foundational elements of Caribbean culture and history was the trauma and rupture inherent in the enforced journeys of the Middle Passage. Moreover, Caribbean identity is presented as fundamentally relational, dependent on a series of axes—transatlantic, trans-American, trans-Caribbean—represented by imperceptible connections as well as actual journeys. The challenge for Glissant is to rethink and restructure travel, a practice customarily reliant on fixed cultures and binary relationships, when fixity or rootedness is no longer a constituent element of identity.

---

[21] Clifford writes: 'I hang on to "travel" as a term of cultural comparison precisely because of its historical taintedness, its associations with gendered, racial bodies, class privilege, specific means of conveyance, beaten paths, agents, frontiers, documents, and the like. I prefer it to more apparently neutral, and "theoretical", terms, such as "displacement", which can make the drawing of equivalences between historical experiences too easy' ('Traveling Cultures', 39). Commenting on this exploration by Clifford of the limits of 'travel', bell hooks concedes, in the terms of this chapter's epigraph, that 'to answer the questions he poses is to propose a deconstruction of the conventional sense of travel, and put alongside it, or in its place, a theory of the journey that would expose the extent to which holding on to the concept of "travel" as we know it is also a way to hold on to imperialism' ('Representations of Whiteness in the Black Imagination', 173). Drawing on Césaire's *Cahier d'un retour au pays natal*, Fonkoua coins the term 'voyage sérieux' to differentiate the experience of black travellers in Europe. See 'Le "voyage à l'envers" ', 133.

[22] Glissant, *Traité du Tout-Monde*, 59.

As Jean-Xavier Ridon has explained, it is in particular in the essays constituting the four volumes of Glissant's *Poétique* that this re-elaboration or reconceptualization of travel is performed.[23] In these key texts, by adopting the figure of the rhizome and associating with this the practices of *errance*, Glissant moves away from an understanding of travel as an autonomous or even dialectical means of identity construction in order to present the journey as a more open process of mutual exchange. In Ridon's terms:

Glissant offre un nouveau concept qui essaye d'intégrer à l'idée du voyage le principe d'un déracinement préliminaire—et qui, à la place de l'idée de découverte de l'autre, mettrait celle d'une ouverture à l'autre. La différence étant que la découverte finit toujours par reproduire un principe d'appropriation alors que l'ouverture est avant tout un système de mise en relation.[24]

Glissant proposes a new concept that endeavours to integrate into the notion of travel the principle of a preliminary uprooting—and that replaces the notion of discovery of the other with an openness to the other. The difference being that discovery always ends up reproducing a principle of appropriation whereas openness is primarily a system of putting cultures in contact with each other.

Travel then becomes a figure central to the Glissantian concept of 'la Relation' [Relating], an understanding of persistent cultural diversity that avoids the inequalities of globalization or assimilative exoticism, challenges the foreseeable equilibrium of hybridity, and at the same time reflects the unpredictability inherent in creolization.[25] Dominant Western understandings of travel as an exclusive practice that creates immobile and mute travellees depend on a sense of fixed, unitary identity; this is to be contrasted with a more inclusive understanding of the term according to which the traveller-travellee binary becomes a

---

[23] See Ridon, *Le Voyage en son miroir*, 125. It should be noted that, despite its partial translation into English, Glissant's work has not yet made the impact on postcolonial criticism that one might have expected. English-language versions exist of: *Caribbean Discourse: Selected Essays*, trans. J. Michael Dash (Charlottesville: University Press of Virginia, 1989), and *Poetics of Relation*, trans. Betsy Wing (Ann Arbor: University of Michigan Press, 1997).

[24] Ridon, *Le Voyage en son miroir*, 132.

[25] It should be remembered that Glissant prefers the dynamic term 'créolisation' as opposed to the static or essentialist 'créolité' to describe the unpredictable and unfinished processes of intercultural contact. On Glissant's attitude to the Créolité movement, see Damato, 'Edouard Glissant et le manifeste *Éloge de la Créolité*'. This opposition is central to his essay 'Le Chaos-monde', in which he formulates it in terms of a contrast between the fixity of the infinitive 'être' and the process implied by the present participle 'étant'. See 'Le Chaos-monde, l'oral et l'écrit'.

redundant one.[26] In 'Traveling Cultures', James Clifford refers to Glissant in passing, in relation to Vivek Dhareshwar's notion of a dynamic 'postcolonial habitus'.[27] There are, however, very clear connections between on the one hand the postcolonial understanding of diversity underpinning the Martiniquan's concept of an interlocking 'Tout-Monde' and the US ethnographer's notion of 'traveling cultures'. Glissant's 'Tout-Monde' emerges from this concept of Relating, and articulates a rhizomatic worldview in which different cultures interrelate and overlap without losing their distinctiveness; Clifford's 'traveling cultures' similarly challenges notions of rootedness in order to present individual cultures as sites characterized simultaneously by dwelling and travelling, by a geographical locatedness and yet at the same time a dependency on connections with elsewhere.

From the notion of a distinctive culture of travel—or even coexisting cultures of travel—associated with a specific national space and elaborated by travellers departing from and returning to that space, we shift therefore to more complex models. The understandings of travel presented by both Glissant and Clifford acknowledge more openly those transnational and transcultural practices and formations that undermine excessively neat and increasingly unsustainable understandings of home and elsewhere; they privilege the unpredictability of contact between cultures, and accordingly challenge the reductive teleologies that entropic versions of this often imply; without erasing the differences between cultures and the individuals who represent them, they present nevertheless an alternative version of travel, belied to be sure by certain colonial and neocolonial performances of the practice, but nevertheless illuminating the coexistence and interdependence present, latently or otherwise, in intercultural contact.

TRAVELLING FRENCH POLYNESIA

Clifford's reflections in *Routes* emerge from his earlier recognition in *The Predicament of Culture*, cited above, that '[a]longside this

---

[26] Although Glissant does not refer directly to Pratt's traveller-travellee binary, it is implicit in his analysis of travel as a Western colonizing practice: 'Je peux penser que ma force est dans le Voyage (je fais l'Histoire) et que ta différence est immobile et muette' [I can think that my strength is in Travel (I make history) and that your difference is static and mute]. See *Introduction à une poétique du Divers*, 30.

[27] Clifford, 'Traveling Cultures', 30.

narrative of progressive monoculture a more ambiguous "Caribbean" experience may be glimpsed'.[28] Glissant's own work straddles the local and global, identifying in the Caribbean microcosm a paradigm with potentially wider applications.[29] The concluding section of this study will focus, however, on another group of islands whose potential role in postcolonial considerations of travel and culture has so far been eclipsed by a privileging of the Caribbean: French Polynesia.[30] This final regional case study, following the more theoretical and abstract reflections on postcolonial travel above, underlines the constant need in this field of inquiry to contextualize or to negotiate the gap between the general observation and its particular application. Focusing on Tahiti and the archipelago surrounding it permits in a sense a return to this volume's point of origin, not only in that it was Tahiti that triggered Segalen's own early twentieth-century reassessment of exoticism, but also in that colonial activity in the South Pacific is in many ways essential to understanding representations of cultural diversity, and the myths, figures, and assumptions on which these depend, in a French and Francophone context.

When Cyclone Zoe struck the Solomon Islands in late December 2002, giving that area of Melanesia the coverage in the world media it only rarely seems to merit, it was possible to suggest parallels with a similar disaster, almost exactly a century previously, that had devastated part of Polynesia. For although, perhaps especially in the French imagination, 2003 marked the centenary of Gauguin's death on

---

[28] See Clifford, *The Predicament of Culture*, 15.

[29] On this subject see Ralph Ludwig, 'Écrire la parole de nuit', in *Écrire la 'parole de nuit'*, 13–25 (p. 20).

[30] A similar case could be made for the island cultures of the Indian Ocean. See Françoise Lionnet, 'Créolité in the Indian Ocean: Two Models of Cultural Diversity', *Yale French Studies*, 82 (1993), 101–12, and Françoise Vergès, 'The island of wandering souls: processes of creolisation, politics of emancipation and the problematic of absence of Reunion Island', in Rod Edmond and Vanessa Smith (eds.), *Islands in History and Representation* (London: Routledge, 2003), 162–76. Edmond and Smith make a more general point that postcolonial criticism has tended to maintain a continental focus, marginalizing islands as 'negligible, purely strategic sites'. See 'Editors' introduction', in *Islands in History and Representation*, 1–18 (p. 5). In *The Word, the Pen and the Pistol: Literature and Power in Tahiti* (Albany: State University of New York Press, 2001), Robert Nicole provides one of the first comprehensive postcolonial engagements with Western representations of Tahiti as well as Tahitian self-representations. His text attempts in particular to attenuate Edward Said's Orientalism with reference to the Polynesian context (see esp. pp. 6–10), and articulates a clear sensitivity to the pitfalls inherent in attempts by an external observer 'to speak for Maohi' (p. 167). For a further attempt to interpret the work of Said in a South Pacific context, see also Patrick D. Morrow, *Post-Colonial Essays on South Pacific Literature* (Lewiston, NY: Edwin Mellen, 1998), 7–18, 169–75.

Hiva-Oa, it was a cyclone in the Tuamotu archipelago that had a more marked effect on the everyday life of the French Pacific in 1903. Both of these events were recorded by Victor Segalen, at that time recently arrived in Tahiti on a tour of duty as a naval doctor. Although the impact on the author's work of his 'significant missed rendez-vous' with the French painter has, as is suggested in Ch. 2 above, been well documented, less attention has been paid to his analysis of the cyclone, bringing relief to whose victims was one of his first official duties. The parallels between the Melanesian disaster in 2002 and the Polynesian cyclone a century earlier are striking: in both cases, despite advances in technology over the intervening period, the survival of the inhabitants was only confirmed once relief parties had actually arrived; in both cases, major damage was caused to buildings, crops, and the water system; and in both cases, images of devastation seemed to unsettle received Western images of Pacific society and culture as, in Segalen's terms, 'l'Europe casanière apprendra que les îles [...] existent, puis-qu'elles viennent d'être dévastées' [stay-at-home Europe will learn that the islands exist because they have just been devastated].[31] A recurrent detail of this devastation involves the cyclone's unearthing of bones— bones whose sacrilegious strewing across the islands' beaches was seen by Segalen as an indication of the disruption of links between past and present, of what he describes elsewhere, in *Pensers païens*, as 'le naufrage de tout notre passé tahitien' [the shipwreck of our whole Tahitian past].[32]

It is this image of disruptive, chaotic fragmentation, not in contem-porary Melanesia but in early twentieth-century Polynesia, that allows us to understand not only Segalen's imagination of this region but also, by extension, the more complex tradition of French-language represen-tations in which late nineteenth- and early twentieth-century figures such as Gauguin, Segalen, and Loti play a central role. In the processes of interpretation that Segalen's thought has undergone in the work of certain postcolonial and postmodern critics, apparent divergences from his contemporaries have been accentuated and convergences eclipsed. As is demonstrated in Ch. 2, it was certainly in Polynesia, especially in the formally experimental novel *Les Immémoriaux*, that the author's complex and critical understanding of exoticism emerged; rarely

---

[31] Segalen, 'Vers les sinistrés', 513.
[32] Segalen, *Pensers païens*, in *Œuvres complètes*, i. 383–93 (p. 386). In Segalen's account of Fakarava, 'le cimetière seul a pâti, violé par la tempête' [the cemetery alone suffered, violated by the storm] ('Vers les sinistrés', 518)

explored, however, are the links between his analysis of entropic cultural decline in the Polynesian writings and a similar analysis found in the work of Segalen's near contemporaries, such as Gauguin and Loti. Edward Hughes has recently identified 'familiar shared perspectives in the work of all three', including 'the infantilization of the Polynesian Other, the lament for a moribund culture'.[33] The account of the cyclone in the Tuamotu Archipelago exemplifies such a tendency. On the one hand, it ensures portrayal of the Polynesians as dependent victims; on the other, and perhaps more importantly, the natural disaster illustrates what Segalen sees as the decidedly unnatural cultural processes triggered by Western contact. The description of debris strewn chaotically across the beach on Hikuera, the account of which in the *Journal des îles* has already been discussed in a different context in Ch. 5, clearly illustrates this point: 'une boue déséchée de choses informes, délavées, disloquées, broyées, pilées; de ce débris mesquins et piteux qui, mieux que des ruines, atteignent à une plus absolue navrance' [dried mud containing shapeless, faded, broken, crushed things; some of that worthless and sorry debris that, more so than ruins, reaches an appearance of extreme distress].[34] Segalen sees the intermingled fragments of indigenous and Western artefacts as evidence of the inexorable, systematic, teleological decline of Polynesian culture that resulted from initial contact with European travellers. It is in the following that this entropic version of cultural process becomes clear, for hybridity—'une vie hybride'—is associated with an exclusively negative outcome, i.e. 'perversion civilisée', or the adulteration of indigenous culture as a result of contact with the West.

As Rod Edmond and Vanessa Smith outline in their introduction to *Islands in History and Representation*, the insular space has long had an ambiguous status in Western thought: 'Were islands the detritus of crumbling continents or the seeds of new ones? Did they constitute points of ending or of origin?'.[35] This ambiguity, they claim, has progressively been replaced in a globalized geography by a tendency to view islands as 'sites of cultural stagnation', with their isolation 'thought of as disabling, damagingly cut off from modernity rather than a utopian alternative to it'.[36] Self-sufficient insular space lends itself, however, to the spatialization of concepts such as entropy or globalization: it may be seen as a site of resistance to the former and

---

[33] Hughes, *Writing Marginality*, 40.   [34] Segalen, 'Vers les sinistrés', 516.
[35] Edmond and Smith, 'Editors' introduction', 1.   [36] Ibid. 8.

as an anachronistic stumbling block to the transcontinental flows of the latter; or it may be cast as a restricted space in which takes place the sustained and rapid erosion of an indigenous culture subject to the fatal impact of external influences. In the light of this, it is not unusual that Segalen's concept of 'le Divers' depends on a belief in the perpetuation of self-sufficient, discrete, insular cultures, on resistance to what he casts variously in his work as 'déchéance' or 'globulicide', resistance to the processes of hybridization crystallized in *Le Maître-du-Jouir* in the character of mixed ethnicity, Sara, whom 'Gauguin' dismisses in violent terms as lacking the ethnic and cultural purity in which his vision of Polynesian culture is grounded.[37] This rejection of a character situated between cultures reflects the more general reliance of Western expectations of Polynesia on the maintenance of polarized differences: the protagonist in *Le Mariage de Loti*, for instance, so fearful of disappointment on arrival in colonial Tahiti, refuses to go ashore for three days.[38] His account of Polynesia, like Segalen's, is characterized by a *fin-de-siècle* focus on the decline of an aristocratic lineage, a condemnation of influences (specifically French and Chinese) seen as external, and an aestheticization of extinction, of 'le charme de ceux qui vont mourir' [the charm of those about to die].[39] The text concludes in terms with which Segalen's cyclone account echoes: 'tout était fini dans la fange' [everything had finished in the mud], claims Loti, as his narrator suffers a nightmare vision in which palm trees are uprooted and a corpse seemingly unearthed.[40]

These gradations of exoticization—ranging from what is customarily seen as Loti's superficial, exploitative engagement, to Gauguin and Segalen's more subtle investigations of indigenous culture—disguised a more uniform instrumentalization of Polynesia in the French culture of travel relating to the region.[41] The pattern of islands serves not only as an arena in which the tensions and contradictions of a colonial identity are played out; it is also the often abstract backcloth against which an entropic understanding of exoticism develops, and as a result of which a retrogressive 'salvage exoticism', denigrating the contemporary and exalting a disappeared past, begins to emerge. Such retrospection is a

---

[37] See Segalen, 'Essai sur l'exotisme', 775, and *Journal des îles*, 440.
[38] See Pierre Loti, *Le Mariage de Loti*, in *Romans* (Paris: Presses de la Cité, 1989), 133–254 (p. 137).
[39] Ibid. 205.
[40] Ibid. 252.
[41] On this subject, see Hughes, *Writing Marginality*, 9–40.

clear response to a situation identified by Pierre-Yves Toullelan in *Tahiti colonial*: it was in the late nineteenth and early twentieth century that Polynesia underwent a process of transformation more rapid than that seen after initial contact a century before.[42] As has been demonstrated in Ch. 1, it is a clear salvage impulse that is inherent in the sense of imperialist nostalgia. This impulse underpins the work of Gauguin, Segalen, and Loti, and remains the dominant mode in subsequent twentieth-century representations of Polynesia, from Simenon's account of the mediocre settler community and the stage-managed indigenous culture in *Touriste de banane* to Jean Reverzy's description of agonizing, pathological decline in *Le Passage*.[43] A common strand concerns the contemporary islands' status as a positive danger to the modern French traveller, as if again hybridization is to be understood only in terms of dislocation, contamination, and deterioration.

While the fantasy of a Polynesian paradise maintains a stubborn hold on the popular imagination (as the 2001–2 exhibition at the Musée des arts africains et océaniens on *Kannibals et Vahinés* proved),[44] contemporary Polynesia, whose postcolonial rather than strictly post-colonial status remains a troubled and complex one, is more accurately associated with riots and nuclear tests.[45] Jean-Luc Coatalem's recent travel account of a journey in Gauguin's footsteps, *Je suis dans les mers du Sud*, is one of the most recent contributions to the French literature of Polynesia, clearly drawing on and contributing to the culture of travel to which that region has given rise. The text acknowledges and yet simultaneously dismisses this socio-political

---

[42] Pierre-Yves Toullelan, *Tahiti colonial* (Paris: Publications de la Sorbonne, 1994).

[43] Jean Reverzy, *Le Passage* (Paris: Julliard, 1954), and Georges Simenon, *Touriste de bananes* (Paris: Gallimard, 1936).

[44] See *Kannibals et Vahinés* (Paris: Réunion des musées nationaux, 2001).

[45] Commenting on French Polynesia's relationship to metropolitan France, Kareva Mateata-Allain describes the region as 'symbolically *post*(-)colonial'. See 'Ma'ohi Women Writers of Colonial French Polynesia: Passive Resistance toward a *Post*(-)colonial Literature', *Jouvert*, 7/2 (2003), <http://social.chass.ncsu.edu/jouvert/v7i2/mateat.htm>, para 2, accessed 1 Nov. 2004. Robert Nicole comments perceptively on the strategies used by French law to infantilize and criminalize those advocating 'alternate versions of Maohi cultural history' (*The Word, the Pen, and the Pistol*, 162). He concludes, however, that France's growing commitment to Europe, the end of the strategic alibi permitted by the Cold War, and the politically disastrous nuclear policies in the 1990s may signal the advent of growing autonomy and even independence (p. 201). Jean Chesneaux and Nic Maclellan claim nevertheless that a persistent presence of French, even after independence and in an increasingly multilingual context, will perpetuate a 'saine et féconde diversité' [healthy and fruitful diversity] in the predominantly anglophone Pacific. See *La France dans le Pacifique: de Bougainville à Mururoa* (Paris: La Découverte, 1992), 233.

reality.[46] The Papeete he describes is 'pollué par les enseignes' [polluted by signs], 'saturé de circulation et de feux rouges' [saturated with traffic and traffic lights], characterized, in a phrase reminiscent of Segalenian rhetoric, by a 'sentiment de bric-à-brac' [feeling of bric-à-brac].[47] Coatalem is a travel writer associated since its inception with the *Pour une littérature voyageuse* movement. His work is characterized by a retrospective longing for the sepia tones of the colonial period. His reliance on journeys in others' footsteps—to which the polysemic 'suis' of his title, first person singular form of both 'être' and 'suivre', 'to be' and 'to follow', bears witness—is a clear response to prophecy of 'la fin des voyages', a nostalgic re-rooting of contemporary travel in its earlier forms. The implications of such a manœuvre for the geographical and cultural context of travel are, however, clear, for Coatalem tends to travel more through books (i.e. the 'six kilos de bouquins' [6 kg of books] he carries with him) than through space itself.[48] He explores (in what he calls an 'essai personnel') an autobiographical mode of travel writing, in order, through oblique dialogue with Gauguin and Segalen, to recover his own past (and in particular the early years of his life spent in Tahiti) and to articulate, often through strategic quotation of Gauguin, his longing for that past.[49]

The present is seen as tarnished: 'En ce début de siècle, le nôtre, Papeete n'a rien d'idyllique' [At the beginning of this century, our own, there is nothing idyllic left in Papeete], and with this qualification, 'le nôtre', Coatalem seems to refer back to the previous century's opening, suggesting accordingly a continuity and signalling the parallels between two Tahitis, colonial and post-/neocolonial.[50] Despite frustration with Polynesian indifference towards Gauguin, he aims to gain access—through reading correspondence, visiting the sites of his paintings, and discovering artefacts (such as Gauguin's sewing machine)—to the artist's presence, as if a process of 'floculation' had left 'des particules, des éclairs, les effluves d'une présence' [particles, glints, the lingering aroma of a presence].[51] The search is an unpredictable, uneven, and ultimately frustrating one. It culminates in the description of an arch-

---

[46] Jean-Luc Coatalem, *Je suis dans les mers du Sud: sur les traces de Paul Gauguin* (Paris: Grasset, 2001).

[47] Ibid. 146.

[48] Ibid. 134.

[49] Ibid. 271. e.g. 'C'est la Tahiti d'autrefois que j'aimais' [It was old Tahiti I loved], 128.

[50] Ibid. 146.

[51] For a discussion of Polynesian indifference towards Gauguin, see ibid. 120. See also 130, 133.

aeological exploration of the site of Gauguin's *fare* in which the narrator shares its excavators' ambivalent response—'ce plaisir qui ressemble pour moitié à du désarroi' [this pleasure that is half like distress]—to the banal objects this uncovers: lumps of paint, nails, bottles, fragments of *faïence*, teeth, a glass syringe.[52] As relics of the artist, these are 'objets miraculeux'; as contemporary artefacts, they are a chaotic collection of rusted and broken junk, Segalen's post-cyclone debris. Coatalem's text ends, therefore, with a contemporary version of the discourse of disappointment to be found in earlier twentieth-century works: a literal illustration of salvage exoticism forces the narrator, drawing on his imagination alone, to return to the photograph of one of Gauguin's subjects, with which the text—and the journeys it recounts—began.

Coatalem's Tahiti is one in which it is only traces of past diversity that are dredged up; it is an island space in which a fragmented, tarnished present contains few if any residual traces of a historical moment that is itself increasingly considered to have been both fragmented and tarnished. Unsurprisingly for a tradition whose principal mode is a nostalgic one, denigration of the contemporary and its reduction to passivity, inactivity, debasement, and worthlessness are staple elements of French representations of Tahiti. Reynaldo Hahn's opera, *L'Île du rêve*, inspired by Loti, was staged in Tahiti shortly before the narrator's stay, and Coatalem is surprised by such an endeavour in which the contemporary population were 'non plus figurants mais acteurs' [no longer extras, but actors].[53] The Polynesians in his own text, however, have for the most part the status of 'travellees' with walk-on parts, passive observers of Western mobility, subject of and to the traveller's reflections and gaze. What Coatalem ignores, however, are the marginalized and yet increasingly articulate and insistent voices of contemporary Polynesian literature, voices that challenge Western representations and on which, by way of conclusion, the final section of the postface will focus.

CONCLUSION: REWRITING POLYNESIAN SPACE

The writings of French travellers in Polynesia—like much material that falls into the hazy category of 'travel literature'—tend to say more about the culture from which their authors originate than the one that

---

[52] Ibid. 301–4.   [53] Ibid. 136.

they purport to describe; they treat the region either as a blank space on which Western texts are to be written, or as a laboratory in which Western ideas are to be tested and elaborated. In an intertextual process described by Robert Nicole as 'sedimentation', travellers tend to rely on, echo, and supplement the accounts of those in whose footsteps they follow. One way of rereading, recontextualizing the Western traveller's subjectivity is to situate it, contrapuntally, in relation to accounts of the host culture produced by its own inhabitants. For a long time such an approach was impractical in a Polynesian context, for indigenous accounts either mimicked a Western tradition or were non-existent. With the possible exception of Segalen's *Les Immémoriaux*, the project of whose Tahitian translation was never completed, the works available to Polynesian authors seeking to textualize their culture and identity represented heavy baggage, belonging to a Western archive from which indigenous voices were excluded: 'L'océan de livres se brise sur le récif du silence polynésien' [Waves of books break on the reef of Polynesian silence].[54] Henri Hiro alluded to the problem in an interview published in *I Mua*: 'Si tu étais venu chez nous, nous t'aurions accueilli à bras ouverts. Mais tu es venu ici chez toi, et on ne sait pas comment t'accueillir chez toi' [If you had come to our island, we would have welcomed you with open arms. But you came to your island, and we cannot welcome you in your own space].[55] However, a contrapuntal approach to texts such as Coatalem's—and the implicit attenuation this allows—has been made possible by the late twentieth-century publication of texts by authors such as Flora Devatine, Louise Peltzer, Chantal Spitz, and Taaria Walker who seek precisely to recover this sense of a 'chez nous' and to project this place as a dynamic, 'travelling' culture in its own right, capable of self-assertion and self-expression. Their aim is, in the terms of Robert Nicole's analysis of the Tongan anthropologist Epeli Hau'ofa, 'to redefine their identities in ways that avoid and reject the accepted theories that they are hopeless and helpless victims lost in the powerful currents of an aggressive age of globalization'.[56]

All four women contributed to a recent issue of the *Bulletin de la Société des Études Océaniennes*, devoted to an exploration of the legacy

---

[54] Louise Groznykh-Pelzner, cited in Jean Chesneaux (ed.), *Tahiti après la bombe: quel avenir pour la Polynésie?* (Paris: L'Harmattan, 1995), 23.

[55] Cited by Odile Gannier, 'Tahiti: de l'exotisme à l'exil', *Mots Pluriels*, 17 (2001), <http://www.arts.uwa.edu.au/MotsPluriels/MP1701og.html>.

[56] Nicole, *The Word, the Pen, and the Pistol*, 12.

of Loti and entitled *Supplément au Mariage de Loti.*[57] Spitz provided
one of the few discordant Francophone voices during the centenary
celebrations of Gauguin's death, claiming that the painter contributed
to: 'ces mythes réducteurs qui de la Nouvelle-Cythère à la maison du
jouir nous établissent dans une identité immuable immobile nous rédui-
sent au silence à l'absence nous laissent sans voix sans consistance.
Peuple insonore' [these reductive myths, from New Cythera to the
house of pleasure, that fix us in an unchanging, static identity, reduce
us to silence and absence, leave us without voice or reality. A soundless
people].[58] The dominant mode in this timely revisionist retort is one of
challenging refusal of such an ever-present intertext, with Devatine
herself rejecting, in almost Glissantian terms, '[c]e choc des cultures
où tout est connu, fixé, d'avance' [that clash of cultures in which the
outcome is known and fixed in advance].[59] The alternative model of
intercultural contact to which she implicitly refers counters the pessimistic predictability of entropic drift towards monoculture that dominates French representations of Polynesia. Instead, emphasizing the
dynamic, unpredictable configurations triggered when cultures are
brought into contact, she seems to seek an alternative cultural history,
encapsulated in Michel Panoff's notion (for some overly optimistic) of
'Tahiti métisse', a concept which presents Polynesian culture as 'un
organisme vivant, toujours prêt à se régénérer et à s'adapter aux conditions imprévues' [a living organism, always ready to be regenerated
and adapted to unforeseen circumstances].[60] Panoff's analysis is to be
welcomed as it counters dominant French representations of Polynesia
by rejecting systematic or reductive models of intercultural contact. At
the same time, it underlines the importance of indigenous agency. There
are clear risks here, however, of a revisionist reading of French Polynesian history. This apology for Tahitian hybridity might be seen to
downplay the demographic and cultural upheaval caused by colonization. Such an interpretation may, in a contemporary context, allow a
celebratory sense of cross-cultural contact to eclipse not only increasing

[57] Through Gauguin's references to the author, Loti remains an intertext in Coatalem
(*Je suis dans les mers du Sud*, 100).

[58] See Chantal Spitz, 'Héritage et confrontation'. This text read during the Gauguin
centenary conference at the University of French Polynesia at Punaauia (6–8 March 2003)
is available on the invaluable 'île en île' website: <http://www.lehman.cuny.edu/ile.en.ile/
paroles/spitz_gauguin.html> (accessed 1 Nov. 2004).

[59] Flora Devatine, *Tergiversations et rêveries de l'ecriture orale: Te Pahu a Hono'ura*
(Papeete: Au Vent des Îles, 1998), 198.

[60] Michel Panoff, *Tahiti métisse* (Paris: Denoël, 1989), 21.

evidence of a harmful globalized economy, but also what commentators have dubbed 'le syndrome de la Franconésie', i.e. the maintenance of Franco-Polynesian axes as a reaction to Anglophone hegemony in the Pacific.[61] Moreover, the syncretic, acculturated local culture, heavily influenced by Christianity and dubbed by Alain Babadzan a 'nouvelle tradition', that emerged post-contact is now itself threatened with further change as a result of rapid shifts caused by the presence and activity over three decades, until the mid-1990s, of the Centre d'Expérimentation du Pacifique.[62] Many of the population are now, in Jean-Jo Scemla's terms: 'câblés, connectés, salariés, fonctionnarisés, embourgeoisés' [with cable TV, internet connections, regular salaries, jobs for life, middle-class comforts].[63] Such rapid shifts challenge Panoff's optimistic vision, articulated in contrast to his condemnation of the assimilationist policies imposed on the Anglophone Pacific, of a progressive process of Franco-Tahitian mutual influence, or what might subsequently be cast as transculturation.[64] Moreover, the human damage caused by nuclear testing, tourism, and industrial activity has been supplemented by ecological disasters such as the 1985 cyclones from which the coconut industry has never really recovered.

What is striking in Panoff's text, however, is the recognition of indigenous agency, for his model of a Tahitian hybridity counters assumptions regarding the 'impuissance des peuples de couleurs face à "l'impact fatal" de l'expansion européenne' [powerlessness of indigenous people when faced with the 'fatal impact' of European expansion].[65] A nationalist, independentist response to this progressive assimilation has involved the search for a pre-contact culture, but even radical activists have avoided the excesses of chronic introversion,

[61] For a discussion of 'Franconesia', see Chesneaux and Maclellan, *La France dans le Pacifique*, 112.

[62] See Alain Babadzan, *La Nouvelle Tradition* (Paris: Orstom, 1983). On threats to this 'nouvelle tradition', see Jean-Jo Scemla, 'Polynésie française et identité maohie', in Jean Chesneaux (ed.), *Tahiti après la bombe: quel avenir pour la Polynésie?* (Paris: L'Harmattan, 1995), 19–51 (p. 30).

[63] Scemla, 'La littérature dans le Pacifique: le cas tahitien', *Notre Librairie*, 143 (2001), 112–23 (p. 118). Chantal Spitz sees these developments in terms of a similar drift towards immobility. The Tahitians are seen as a 'troupeau en transhumance vers les lumières le bruit la pollution la consommation' [herd migrating towards lights, noise, pollution, consumption], dreaming of 'une carrière costumée cravatée climatisée dans une administration moquettée lambrisée capitonnée' [a dressed-up, tie-wearing, air-conditioned career in a carpeted, lined, padded administration] ('Héritage et confrontation').

[64] See Panoff, *Tahiti métisse*, 230.

[65] Ibid. 77.

with key figures such as Henri Hiro rejecting 'indépendance en tant que coupure' [independence understood as a clean break]. It is such a desire to negotiate a location between the local and the global, between the past and the future that has inspired much recent Polynesian writing, with authors responding, as does Coatalem with the image of the artefacts drawn from the well, to an apparent fragmentation or disloca-tion of indigenous culture, to chaos. The chaotic, however, is increas-ingly understood in a positive Glissantian sense. What has emerged from the work of Devatine, Peltzer, and Walker is a constructive response to the *métissage* that underpins this cultural situation, a re-sponse that may be read in relation to a similar process in the Franco-phone Caribbean. Indeed, the authors of the *Éloge de la créolité* suggest a connection that might usefully be explored for the Polynesian case, along the same lines as Françoise Lionnet's contrastive reading of Indian Ocean creoleness:

Nous, Antillais créoles, sommes donc porteurs d'une double solidarité:
– *d'une solidarité antillaise (géopolitique) avec tous les peuples de notre Archipel, quelles que soient nos différences culturelles: notre Antillanité;*
– *d'une solidarité créole avec tous les peuples africains, mascarins, asiatiques et polynésiens qui relèvent des mêmes affinités anthropologiques que nous: notre créolité.*

We, the Caribbean Creoles, enjoy, therefore, a double solidarity:
– *a Caribbean solidarity (geopolitical) with all the peoples of our Archipelago regardless of our cultural differences—our Caribbeanness; and*
– *a Creole solidarity with all African, Mascarin, Asian, and Polynesian peoples who share the same anthropological affinities as we do—our Creoleness.*[66]

There are distinct differences, of course, ethnic, linguistic, and histor-ical, but the parallels are clear: both cultures were exoticized by alien-ating French written representations; both were tempted by the possibility of return to a 'pays natal'; yet both now, accepting what the *créolistes* call an 'irruption dans la modernité', seek a solution that responds to the '*agrégat interactionnel ou transactionnel* des éléments culturels [...] que le joug de l'Histoire a réuni sur le même sol' [*inter-actional or transactionnal* [*sic*] *aggregate* of [...] cultural elements, united on the same soil by the yoke of history].[67]

---

[66] Bernabé, Chamoiseau, and Confiant, *Éloge de la Créolité*, 33, 94.
[67] Ibid. 26, 87 (emphasis in original).

In *Lettre à Poutaveri*, Louise Peltzer replies to Victor Segalen, describing the initial stages of missionary contact and filling in the period during which the latter's protagonist in *Les Immémoriaux* was forced to wander away from home; perhaps more sympathetic towards the French travellers than Segalen's account, Peltzer explores issues of translation and bilingualism, and ends with an apology for a Tahitian concept of language, clearly addressed to contemporary readers, that stresses its performative, organic nature. The novel is written in French, however, and it is through point of view rather than language that the author explores her aims. Flora Devatine, on the other hand, in *Tergiversations et rêveries de l'écriture orale*, has produced a long text in which she 'tahitianizes' French, gallicizes Tahitian, and searches for a language of contemporary Polynesia, moving beyond an *oralité–écriture* distinction, that is suitable to articulate a hybrid, 'creolized' identity. Her aim is dual: 'reconquête de la parole' [reconquest of spoken language] and 'apprivoisement de l'écriture' [taming of writing], and the dogged refrain of 'Et j'écris' reflects the author's persistence in the search for a written form in which 'polynésianité' [Polynesianness] may be articulated.[68] Images of fragmentation characterize the context to which she responds: Polynesian culture is 'rapiécée maladroitement par l'histoire' [patched together clumsily by history]; the Polynesians themselves constitute a 'peuple-patchwork, cosmopolite, à des degrés divers' [patchwork-people, cosmopolitan to varying degrees].[69] And this is the imagery that underpins Taaria Walker's *Rurutu: mémoires d'avenir d'une île australe*, the chronological contradictions of whose title recall Glissant's own 'vision prophétique du passé' [prophetic vision of the past].[70] Her image of the Pacific involves progressive creolization, as Polynesia is seen as a travelling culture, dependent on the convergence of different peoples, a process now reversed in the creation of a substantial diaspora. The text is provocative, equating Francocentric politicians with 'extra-terrestres'; at the same time, however, in a section entitled 'Les Polynésiens de l'an 2000', she counters Gauguin's and Loti's anti-Chinese racism by underlining the positive results of the

[68] Devatine, *Tergiversations et rêveries de l'écriture orale*, 37, 145.
[69] Ibid. 9, 184.
[70] See Taaria Walker's *Rurutu: mémoires d'avenir d'une île australe* (Papeete: Haere Po, 1999). Walker is also known as Pare. For Glissant's use of this phrase, see *Monsieur Toussaint* (Paris: Seuil, 1986), 7. For a discussion of the phrase, see Juris Silenieks, 'Glissant's Prophetic Vision of the Past', *African Literature Today*, 11 (1980), 161–8.

assimilation of the first Chinese family into Rurutu.[71] She celebrates, in a quotation that inverts any traditional understanding of purity, the multi-ethnicity of her island, inhabited by 'des Rurutu blonds aux yeux verts ou bleus, des Rurutu noirs et crépus, des Rurutu aux yeux bridés et aux cheveux raides, portant des noms européens et chinois, anglais et français, tous fiers d'être de purs Rurutu' [blond Rurutus with green and blue eyes, black and frizzy-haired Rurutus, Rurutus with slanting eyes and straight hair, with European and Chinese names, French and English names, all proud to be pure Rurutus].[72]

Walker's *Rurutu* offers a convincing reading of Polynesia as a travelling culture, both in terms of its past, present, and future. As such, she is part of the current questioning and reconfiguring of travel as a practice: who travels? what constitutes travel? what are the links between travel and culture? In the narrator's version of familiar genealogies, the inhabitants of the island are presented according to an image of individuals floating at sea, at the mercy of the currents, reaching the uninhabited island, and slowly developing a creolized culture. The narrator presents herself as a traveller through French Polynesia, and her contemporary island is itself characterized by departure and arrival: the triennial Me celebrations, for instance, marking the arrival of the Gospel on Rurutu, bring back to the island those members of its diaspora spread throughout the Pacific as well as in France and the USA.[73] Walker presents Rurutu as a multiethnic space whose inhabitants' identity depends on constant connections with elsewhere, either through their origins or regular travel: 'Rurutu', she concludes, 'adopte toutes les cultures et les religions sans abandonner la sienne' [adopts all cultures and religions without abandoning its own].[74] French readings of Polynesia, including those of Bougainville and Diderot, endeavoured to concentrate Western issues in a distant, insular space. Tahiti continues—as Coatalem's text suggests—to appear in French travel writing as a post-lapsarian space with prelapsarian appeal, haunted by the spectres of previous Western representations. Yet Polynesian authors such as Walker have begun to elaborate alternative, projective versions of their own culture whose challenge to such neo-exoticist practices still

---

[71] See Loti, *Le Mariage de Loti*, 154, and Bengt Danielsson and Patrick O'Reilly, 'Gauguin journaliste à Tahiti et ses articles des *Guêpes*', *Journal de la Société des Océanistes*, 21 (1965), 1–53.

[72] Walker, *Rurutu*, 111

[73] See ibid. 56, 27.

[74] Ibid. 129.

embedded in certain strands of French travel literature has repercussions—in the same way as does the work of the Caribbean *créolistes*—far beyond the archipelago from which they originate. The disparate islands of Polynesia have never been fixed or immobile. Even before Western contact, their society was both inwardly and outwardly dynamic, dependent for survival on a highly mobile network of journeys and interrelationships. Western intervention and the anthropological analysis that accompanied it often reduced such dynamism to the movement of past migrations, erecting new boundaries (including those persistent ones dividing Polynesia, Melanesia, and Micronesia) that restricted any exchange of peoples and cultural artefacts. Connections were eroded in part at least so that patterns of indigenous resistance could be seen as isolated, fragmented, and lacking co-ordination, and the island space was progressively transformed into one characterized by claustrophobia.[75] In such a context, the notion that travelling was a European preserve became commonplace, and French travel literature became a privileged forum for the perpetuation of such assumptions regarding mobility and sessility, dynamism and stagnation. Fabian's temporal notion of a denial of coevalness has a clear spatial correlate in this colonialist reduction of culture to narrowly defined geographical boundaries. In a postcolonial world, as Walker makes clear, such restriction has broken down and the Pacific has become diasporic, dependent on interconnecting vectors of migration and return.

It is in these processes that the island space plays a key role. Syncretism, Relation, hybridity, creolization, transculturation: all of these processes imply a travelling within and between cultures, a multiplication of identities that may ultimately be seen to undermine the notion of unitary identity itself. It is the geographical as opposed to cultural boundedness of the Polynesian island that potentially offers a solution, proposing a new understanding of that stable identity on which concepts of travel have traditionally depended. Countering the entropic erosion of diversity that underpins much French travel literature in the twentieth century, whilst at the same time challenging the congratulatory response to such apocalypticism found in postmodern celebrations of hybridity and instability, the island metaphor, in Edmond and Smith's terms, invites 'not the equilibrium of métissage, but an incessant

---

[75] On this subject, see Daniel Margueron, *Tahiti dans toute sa littérature*, 39.

oscillation between notions of fixed and relational identities'.[76] As such, the balance of singularity and diversity on which travel depended throughout the twentieth century may be seen to persist; but this postcolonial version of persistence obliges us to challenge residually hierarchical notions of cultural diversity, whilst at the same time exploring self-reflexive understandings of travel in which exclusion and monologue are replaced with reciprocity and dialogue.

[76] Edmond and Smith, 'Editors' introduction', 14. Here they draw on Chris Bongie, *Islands and Exiles: the Creole Identities of Post/Colonial Literature* (Stanford, Calif.: Stanford University Press, 1998), 3–24.

Bibliography

ANON, *Excursions daguerriennes: vues et monuments les plus remarquables du globe*, 2 vols. (Paris: Lerebours, 1841).

—— *Autour du Monde par les Boursiers de Voyage de l'Université de Paris* (Paris: Alcan, 1904).

—— *Pour une littérature voyageuse* (Brussels: Complexe, 1992).

—— *La France des écrivains* (Paris: Gallimard, 1997).

—— 'L'étonnant paradoxe de la littérature de voyage', *Livres de France*, 208 (1998), 36–8.

—— 'L'Exotisme au féminin', *Les Carnets de l'exotisme*, 1 (2000).

—— 'Éloge de la lenteur', *Télérama*, 6–12 May 2000, 12–18.

—— 'Tirailleurs en images', *Africultures*, 25 (2000).

—— *Banlieues de Paris* (Paris: Guide du Routard, 2001).

—— *Kannibals et Vahinés* (Paris: Réunion des Musées Nationaux, 2001).

ABLEY, MARK, *Spoken Here: Travels Among Threatened Languages* (London: Heinemann, 2004).

AFFERGAN, FRANCIS, *Exotisme et altérité* (Paris: PUF, 1987).

AGERON, CHARLES-ROBERT, 'L'Exposition coloniale de 1931: mythe républicain ou mythe impérial?', in Pierre Nora (ed.), *Les Lieux de mémoire*, 3 vols. (Paris: Gallimard/Quarto, 1997), i. 493–515.

AHMAD, AIJAZ, *In Theory: Classes, Nations, Literatures* (London: Verso, 1992).

—— 'The Politics of Literary Postcoloniality', *Race and Class*, 36/3 (1995), 1–20.

ALEXANDRE, DIDIER, 'Henri Michaux, le barbare', *Revue d'Histoire Littéraire de la France*, 95/2 (1995), 199–217.

APTER, EMILY, *Continental Drift: From National Characters to Virtual Subjects* (Chicago, Ill.: University of Chicago Press, 1999).

ARCHER-STRAW, PETRINE, *Negrophilia: Avant-Garde Paris and Black Culture in the 1920s* (London: Thames & Hudson, 2000).

ARNOLD, A. JAMES, 'Perilous Symmetry: Exoticism and the Geography of Colonial and Postcolonial Culture', in Freeman G. Henry (ed.), *Geo/graphies: Mapping the Imagination in French and Francophone Literature and Film* (Amsterdam: Rodopi, 2003), 1–28.

ASHCROFT, BILL, 'On the Hyphen in Post-Colonial', *New Literatures Review*, 32 (1996), 23–32.

—— GRIFFITHS, GARETH, and TIFFIN, HELEN, *Key Concepts in Post-Colonial Studies* (London: Routledge, 1998).

AUGÉ, MARC, *Non-lieux* (Paris: Seuil, 1992).

BABADZAN, ALAIN, *La Nouvelle Tradition* (Paris: Orstom, 1983).

BALDENSPERGER, DENIS, 'Il y a 50 ans: Citroën lance "la Croisière jaune" ', *Historia*, 413 (1981), 93–101.

BANCEL, NICOLAS, BLANCHARD, PASCAL, and LEMAIRE, SANDRINE, '1931! Tous à l'Expo…', *Polémique sur l'histoire coloniale, Manière de voir*, 58 (2001), 46–9.

—— 'De la mémoire coloniale à l'histoire', *Francophone Postcolonial Studies*, 1/1 (2003), 8–24.

—— —— BOETSCH, GILLES, DEROO, ERIC, and LEMAIRE, SANDRINE, (eds.), *Zoos humains: de la vénus hottentote aux reality shows* (Paris: La Découverte, 2002).

BARTHES, ROLAND, 'La nouvelle Citroën', in *Mythologies* (Paris: Seuil, 1957), 150–2.

—— 'Mythologie de l'automobile', in *Œuvres completes*, ed. Eric Marty, 3 vols. (Paris: Seuil, 1993), i. 1136–42. (First published, as 'La voiture, projection de l'ego', in *Réalités*, October 1963.)

—— 'Littérature et discontinu', in *Essais critiques* (Paris: Seuil, 1964), 175–87.

—— *L'Empire des signes* (Geneva: Skira, 1970); *Empire of Signs*, trans. Richard Howard (London: Jonathan Cape, 1982).

BARTKOWSKI, FRANCES, *Travelers, Immigrants, Inmates: Essays in Estrangement* (Minneapolis: University of Minnesota Press, 1995).

BASSNETT, SUSAN, *Comparative Literature: A Critical Introduction* (Oxford: Blackwell, 1993).

—— 'Travel and Gender', in Peter Hulme and Tim Youngs (eds.), *The Cambridge Companion to Travel Writing* (Cambridge: Cambridge University Press, 2002), 225–41.

BAUDOT, JEAN-CLAUDE, and SÉGUÉLA, JACQUES, *La Terre en rond* (Paris: Flammarion, 1960).

BAUDRILLARD, JEAN, *La Transparence du mal: essai sur les phénomènes extrêmes* (Paris: Galilée, 1990).

BEAUSOLEIL, JEANNE (ed.), *Jean Brunhes autour du monde: regards d'un géographe / regards de la géographie* (Boulogne: Musée Albert Kahn, 1993).

—— and DELAMARRE, MARIEL J.-BRUNHES (eds.), *Les Archives de la Planète*, 2 vols. ([n.pl.]: Cuénot, 1978–9).

—— and ORY, PASCAL (eds.), *Albert Kahn 1860–1940: réalités d'une utopie* (Boulogne: Musée Albert Kahn, 1995).

BENGUIGUI, YAMINA, *Mémoires d'immigrés* (Paris: Pocket, 2000 [1997]).

BENIAMINO, MICHEL, *La Francophonie littéraire: essai pour une théorie* (Paris: L'Harmattan, 1999).

BERCHET, JEAN-CLAUDE, 'La préface des récits de voyage au XIXe siècle', in György Tverdota (ed.), *Écrire le récit de voyage* (Paris: Presses de la Sorbonne Nouvelle, 1994), 3–15.

BERLINER, BRETT A., *Ambivalent Desire: The Exotic Black Other in Jazz-Age France* (Amherst: University of Massachusetts Press, 2002).

BERNABÉ, JEAN, CHAMOISEAU, PATRICK, and RAPHAËL, CONFIANT, *Éloge de la créolité* (Paris: Gallimard, 1993).

BERNHEIM, NICOLE-LISE, *Chambres d'ailleurs* (Paris: Payot, 1999 [1986]).

—— *Saisons japonaises* (Paris: Payot, 2002 [1999]).

—— *Couleur cannelle: une plantation biologique à Ceylan* (Paris: Arléa, 2002).

BESSIÈRE, JEAN, 'Retiring President's Address', *ICLA Bulletin*, 21/1 (2002), 4–17.

—— and MOURA, JEAN-MARC (eds.), *Littératures postcoloniales et représentations de l'ailleurs: Afrique, Caraïbe, Canada* (Paris: Champion, 1999).

BHABHA, HOMI, *The Location of Culture* (London: Routledge, 1994).

DE BLIGNIÈRES, PASCAL, *Albert Kahn, les jardins d'une idée* (Paris: Éditions la Bibliothèque, 1995).

BLANCHARD, PASCAL, 'L'union nationale: la "rencontre" des droites et des gauches à travers la presse et autour de l'exposition de Vincennes', in Pascal Blanchard and Sandrine Lemaire (eds.), *Culture coloniale: la France conquise par son empire, 1871–1931* (Paris : Autrement, 2003), 213–31.

BODIN, L., and TOUCHARD, J., *Front Populaire, 1936* (Paris: Armand Colin, 1976).

BON, FRANÇOIS, *Paysage fer* (Paris: Verdier, 2000).

BONGIE, CHRIS, *Exotic Memories: Literature, Colonialism, and the Fin de Siècle* (Stanford, Calif.: Stanford University Press, 1991).

—— *Islands and Exiles: the Creole Identities of Post/Colonial Literature* (Stanford, Calif.: Stanford University Press, 1998).

BONHOMME, MARIE, 'Les jardins d'Albert Kahn: une hétérotopie?', in Jeanne Beausoleil and Pascal Ory (eds.), *Albert Kahn 1860–1940: Réalités d'une utopie* (Boulogne: Musée Albert Kahn, 1995), 97–105.

—— and DELAMARRE, MARIEL JEAN-BRUNHES, 'La méthode des missions des *Archives de la Planète*', in Jeanne Beausoteil (ed.), *Jean Brunhes autour du monde: regards d'un géographe / regards de la géographie* (Boulogne: Musée Albert Kahn, 1993), 194–219.

BORER, ALAIN, *Rimbaud en Abyssinie* (Paris: Seuil, 1984).

—— 'L'Ère de Colomb et l'ère d'Armstrong', in *Pour une littérature voyageuse* (Brussels: Complexe, 1992), 17–40.

BORM, JAN, and LE DISEZ, JEAN-YVES (eds.), *Seuils et Traverses*, 2 vols. (Brest: CRBC; Versailles: Suds d'Amériques, 2002).

BOUJEDRA, RACHID, *Topographie idéale pour une agression caractérisée* (Paris: Denoël, 1975).

BOURLÈS, JEAN-CLAUDE, *Une Bretagne intérieure* (Paris: Gallimard, 1998).

BOUVIER, NICOLAS, *L'Usage du monde* (Paris: Payot, 1992 [1963]); *The Way of the World*, trans. Robyn Marsack (Marlboro, Vt.: The Marlboro Press, 1992).

BOUVIER, NICOLAS, *Chronique japonaise* (Paris: Payot, 1989 [1975]).

—— *Journal d'Aran et d'autres lieux* (Paris: Payot, 1990).

—— 'La clé des champs', in *Pour une littérature voyageuse* (Brussels: Complexe, 1992), 41–4.

—— *Routes et déroutes: entretiens avec Irène Lichtenstein-Fall* (Geneva: Métropolis, 1992).

—— *Le Hibou et la baleine* (Geneva: Zoé, 1993).

—— *Le Dehors et le Dedans* (Geneva: Zoé, 1997).

—— *L'Œil du voyageur* (Paris: Hoëbeke, 2001).

BRAHIMI, DENISE, 'Enjeux et risques du roman exotique', in Alain Buisine and Norbert Dodille (eds.), *L'Exotisme: actes du colloque de Saint-Denis de la Réunion, 1988*, Cahiers CRLH-CIRAOI, 5 (Paris: Didier-Érudition, 1988), 11–18.

BRÉCHON, ROBERT, *Michaux* (Paris: Gallimard, 1959).

BRIGGS, ASA, and SNOWMAN, DANIEL (eds.), *Fins de Siècle: How Centuries End 1400–2000* (New Haven, Mass.: Yale University Press, 1996).

BROOME, PETER, 'Henri Michaux and Travel: From Outer Space to Inner Space', *French Studies*, 39 (1985), 285–97.

BROUTELLE, MARTHE, *Paris–Cap Nord en 2CV* ([n.pl.]: Scorpion, 1965).

BRUNO, G., *Le Tour de la France par deux enfants* (Paris: Belin, 1977).

BRUSH, STEPHEN G., 'Thermodynamics and History', *Graduate Journal*, 7 (1967), 477–566.

—— *The Temperature of History: Phases of Science and Culture in the Nineteenth Century* (New York: Burt Franklin, 1978).

BUISINE, ALAIN, *L'Orient voilé* (Cadeilhan: Zulma, 1993).

—— and DODILLE, NORBERT (eds.), *L'Exotisme: actes du colloque de Saint-Denis de la Réunion, 1988*, Cahiers CRLH-CIRAOI, 5 (Paris: Didier-Érudition, 1988).

BUTOR, MICHEL, *Mobile: étude pour une représentation des États-Unis* (Paris: Gallimard, 1962); *Mobile: Study for a Representation of the United States*, trans. Richard Howard (New York: Simon & Schuster, 1963).

BUZARD, JAMES, *The Beaten Track: European Tourism, Literature and the Ways to Culture* (Oxford: Clarendon, 1993).

CADILHAC, P.-É., 'Promenade à travers les cinq continents', *L'Illustration*, 23 May 1931, 73–6.

CALVINO, ITALO, *Collection de sable*, trans. Jean-Paul Manganaro (Paris: Seuil, 1986).

CARIO, LOUIS, and RÉGISMANSET, CHARLES, *L'Exotisme: la littérature coloniale* (Paris: Mercure de France, 1911).

CARRITHERS, MICHAEL, *Why Humans Have Cultures: Explaining Anthropology and Social Diversity* (Oxford: Oxford University Press, 1992).

CAUMERY, and PINCHON, J. P., *Bécassine voyage* (Paris: Gautier-Languereau, 1921).

CELATI, GIANNI, *Adventures in Africa*, trans. Adria Bernardi (Chicago, Ill.: University of Chicago Press, 2000).

CÉLESTIN, ROGER, *From Cannibals to Radicals: Figures and Limits of Exoticism* (Minneapolis: University of Minnesota Press, 1996).

—— DALMOLIN, ELAINE, and ABBEELE, GEORGES VAN DEN (eds.), 'Travel and Travelers', *Sites*, 5/1 (2001).

DE CERTEAU, MICHEL, 'La beauté de la mort', in *La Culture au pluriel* (Paris: Seuil, 1993 [1974]), 45–72; 'The Beauty of the Dead', in *Heterologies: Discourse on the Other*, trans. Brian Massumi (Manchester: Manchester University Press, 1986), 119–36.

—— *L'Écriture de l'histoire* (Paris: Gallimard, 1975).

—— *L'Invention du quotidien*, i. *Arts de faire* (Paris: Gallimard, 1990).

CÉSAIRE, AIMÉ, *Discours sur le colonialisme* (Paris: Présence Africaine, 1955).

CHAILLOU, MICHEL, *Le Sentiment géographique* (Paris: Gallimard, 1976).

CHEVALIER, LOUIS, *Classes laborieuses, classes dangereuses à Paris pendant la première moitié du XIXe siècle* (Paris: Plon, 1958).

CHATEAUBRIAND, *Mémoires d'Outre-Tombe*, ed. J.-C. Berchet, 4 vols. (Paris: Garnier, 1998 [1849–50]).

CHESNEAUX, JEAN (ed.), *Tahiti après la bombe: quel avenir pour la Polynésie?* (Paris: L'Harmattan, 1995).

—— and MACLELLAN, NIC, *La France dans le Pacifique: de Bougainville à Mururoa* (Paris: La Découverte, 1992).

CHÉVRIER, JACQUES, 'L'esprit "fin de siècle" dans quelques romans coloniaux des années 1890–1910. Le cas de l'Afrique noire', in Gwenhaël Ponnau (ed.), *Fins de siècle* (Toulouse: Presses universitaires du Mirail, 1989), 495–508.

CHOPPIN DE JANVRY, OLIVIER, 'Exotisme et jardins historiques ouverts au public (L'Isle-Adam, Jardins A. Kahn, Désert de Retz): vers la destruction ou la restauration d'un mythe', *Carnets de l'Exotisme*, 13 (1994), 85–92.

CLARK, STEVE (ed.), *Travel Writing and Empire: Postcolonial Theory in Transit* (London: Zed Books, 1999).

CLARKE, R. M. (ed.), *Citroën 2CV Gold Portfolio: 1949–1989* (Cobham: Brookland Books, [n.d.]).

CLET-BONNET, NATHALIE, 'Les bourses Autour du Monde: la fondation française, 1898–1930', in Jeanne Beausoleil and Pascal Ory (eds.), *Albert Kahn 1860–1940: réalités d'une utopie* (Boulogne: Musée Albert Kahn, 1995), 137–52.

CLIFFORD, JAMES, 'On Ethnographic Allegory', in James Clifford and George Marcus (ed.), *Writing Culture* (Berkeley: University of California Press, 1986), 98–121.

—— *The Predicament of Culture: Twentieth-Century Ethnography, Literature, and Art* (Cambridge, Mass.: Harvard University Press, 1988); *Malaise dans la culture: l'ethnographie, la littérature et l'art au XXe siècle* (Paris: École nationale des Beaux-Arts, 1996).

CLIFFORD, JAMES, 'Notes on Travel and Theory', *Inscriptions*, 5 (1989), 177–88.

—— 'Traveling Cultures', in *Routes: Travel and Translation in the Late Twentieth Century* (Cambridge, Mass.: Harvard University Press, 1997), 17–39.

COATALEM, JEAN-LUC, 'Un mauvais départ', in *Pour une littérature voyageuse* (Brussels: Complexe, 1992), 83–6.

—— *Je suis dans les mers du Sud: sur les traces de Paul Gauguin* (Paris: Grasset, 2001).

COHEN, MARGARET, *The Sentimental Education of the Novel* (Princeton, NJ: Princeton University Press, 1999).

COMPAGNON, ANTOINE, 'L'Exception française', *Textuel*, 37 (2000), 41–52.

CONDAT, ROBERT, 'Quelques points de repère dans les rapports entre Segalen et Saint-John Perse', *Littératures*, 9–10 (1984), 299–308.

CONDOMINAS, GEORGES, *L'Exotique est quotidien* (Paris: Plon, 1965).

CONSTANTIN-WEYER, MAURICE, *Le Flâneur sous la tente* (Paris: Stock, 1941).

COOMBES, ANNIE E., 'The Recalcitrant Object: Cultural Contact and the Question of Hybridity', in Francis Barker, Peter Hulme, and Margaret Iversen (eds.), *Colonial Discourse/Postcolonial Theory* (Manchester: Manchester University Press, 1994), 89–114.

COOPER, NICOLA, *France in Indochina: Colonial Encounters* (Oxford: Berg, 2001).

COPIN, HENRI, *L'Indochine dans la littérature française des années vingt à 1954: exotisme et altérité* (Paris: L'Harmattan, 2000).

COPPENS, YVES, and SENUT, BRIGITTE (eds.), *Origine(s) de la bipédie chez les hominidés* (Paris: Éditions du CNRS; Cahiers de Paléoanthropologie, 1991).

COQUIO, CATHERINE, 'Le Soir et l'aube: décadence et anarchisme', *Revue d'Histoire Littéraire de la France*, 99/3 (1999), 453–66.

CORNELOUP, MARIE MATTERA, 'Albert Kahn autour du monde, 1908–1909', in Jeanne Beausoleil and Pascal Ory (eds.), *Albert Kahn 1860–1940: réalités d'une utopie* (Boulogne: Musée Albert Kahn, 1995), 59–72.

CORNET, JACQUES, *Deux hommes, 2CV, en Asie* (Lyons: Jacques Cornet, 1957).

—— and LOCHON, HENRI, *Deux hommes, 2CV, deux continents* (Paris: Pierre Horay, 1954).

COUSTURIER, LUCIE, *Des inconnus chez moi*, ed. Roger Little, Autrement mêmes (Paris: L'Harmattan, 2001 [1920]).

CRONIN, MICHAEL, *Across the Lines: Travel, Language, and Translation* (Cork: University of Cork Press, 2000).

—— *Translation and Globalization* (London: Routledge, 2003).

DADIÉ, BERNARD, *Un nègre à Paris* (Paris: Présence Africaine, 1959).

—— *La Ville où nul ne meurt* (Paris: Présence Africaine, 1968).

—— *Patron de New York* (Paris: Présence Africaine, 1969).

DAENINCKX, DIDIER, *Meurtres pour mémoire* (Paris: Gallimard, 1984).

—— *Lumière noire* (Paris: Gallimard, 1993).

—— *Cannibale* (Paris: Verdier, 1998).

—— *Le Retour d'Ataï* (Paris: Verdier, 2002).

DÄLLENBACH, LUCIEN, *Mosaïques: un objet esthétique à rebondissements* (Paris: Seuil, 2001).

DAMATO, DIVA, 'Edouard Glissant et le manifeste *Éloge de la Créolité*', in Yves-Alain Favre and Antonio Ferreira de Brito (eds.), *Horizons d'Édouard Glissant* ([n.pl.]: JSD Éditions, 1992), 245–53.

DANIELSSON, BENGT, and O'REILLY, PATRICK, 'Gauguin journaliste à Tahiti et ses articles des *Guêpes*', *Journal de la Société des Océanistes*, 21 (1965), 1–53.

DASH, J. MICHAEL, '*Caraïbe Fantôme*: The Play of Difference in the Francophone Caribbean', *Yale French Studies*, 103 (2003), 93–105.

DAUGE-ROTH, ALEXANDRE, 'Quelles *espèces d'espaces* pour *Les Passagers du Roissy-Express*? Lectures de la banlieue comme lectures du quotidien', *French Literature Series*, 24 (1997), 153–70.

DAULIAC, J.-P., *La Croisière jaune 1931–32* ([Mougins]: Éditions de l'automobiliste, 1986).

DAUPHINÉ, JOËL, *Canaques de la Nouvelle Calédonie à Paris en 1931: de la case au zoo* (Paris: L'Harmattan, 1998).

DAVIDSON, ROBYN, 'Introduction', in *The Picador Book of Journeys* (London: Picador, 2001), 1–7.

DEKKERS, MIDAS, *The Way of All Flesh: A Celebration of Decay*, trans. Sherry Marx-Macdonald (London: Harvill, 2000).

DELAHAYE, LUC, *L'Autre* (London: Phaidon, 1999).

DELAMARRE, JEAN-BRUNHES, MARIEL, and BEAUSOLEIL, JEANNE, 'Deux témoins de leur temps: Albert Kahn et Jean Brunhes', in Jeanne Beausoleil (ed.), *Jean Brunhes autour du monde: regards d'un géographe / regards de la géographie* (Boulogne: Musée Albert Kahn, 1993), 91–107.

DELERM, PHILIPPE, *Les Chemins nous inventent* (Paris: Stock, 1997).

—— *La Première gorgée de bière et autres plaisirs minuscules* (Paris: Gallimard, 1997).

DERDERIAN, RICHARD L., 'Algeria as a Lieu de mémoire: Ethnic Minority Memory and National Identity in Contemporary France', *Radical History Review*, 83 (2002), 28–43.

DÉRIVE, JEAN, '*Un nègre à Paris*: intertexte et contexte', *Komparatistische Hefte*, 15–16 (1987), 177–95.

DERRIDA, JACQUES, *Archive Fever: A Freudian Impression* (Chicago, Ill.: University of Chicago Press, 1996).

DEVATINE, FLORA, *Tergiversations et rêveries de l'ecriture orale: Te Pahu a Hono'ura* (Papeete: Au Vent des Îles, 1998).

DIALLO, BAKARY, *Force-Bonté* (Dakar: Nouvelles Éditions Africaines, 1985 [1927]).

DONADEY, ANNE, ' "Une certaine idée de la France": The Algeria Syndrome and Struggles over "French" Identity', in Steven Ungar and Tom Conley (eds.), *Identity Papers: Contested Nationhood in Twentieth-Century France* (Minneapolis: University of Minnesota Press, 1996), 215–32.

—— *Recasting Postcolonialism: Women Writing Between Worlds* (Portsmouth, NH: Heinemann, 2001).

DUBOIS, LAURENT, '*La République métisée*: Citizenship, Colonialism, and the Borders of French History', *Cultural Studies*, 14/1 (2000), 15–34.

DUFFY, JEAN, *Signs and Designs: Art and Architecture in the Work of Michel Butor* (Liverpool: Liverpool University Press, 2003).

DUHAMEL, ALAIN, *Le Complexe d'Astérix: essai sur le caractère politique des Français* (Paris: Gallimard, 1985).

DUNCAN, JAMES, and GREGORY, DEREK (eds.), *Writes of Passage: Reading Travel Writing* (London: Routledge, 1999).

DURAND, JEAN-FRANÇOIS, 'Regards sur la culture arabo-musulmane dans le récit de l'ère coloniale (1890–1912)', in David Murphy (ed.), *Remembering Empire* ([n.pl.]: Society for Francophone Postcolonial Studies, 2002), 13–36.

DURING, SIMON, 'Postcolonialism and Globalization', *Meanjin*, 51/2 (1992), 339–53.

EARWAKER, NICOLA, *Travels with a 2CV: An Epic Journey by Citroën 2CV from London to Karachi* (London: Javelin Books, 1988).

EAGLETON, TERRY, 'In the Gaudy Supermarket', *London Review of Books*, 21/10 (1999), 3–6.

—— 'A Spot of Firm Government', *London Review of Books*, 23/16 (2001), 19–20.

ECHENBERG, MYRON, *Colonial Conscripts: the 'Tirailleurs Sénégalais' in French West Africa, 1857–1960* (Portsmouth, NH: Heinemann; London: James Currey, 1991).

EDMOND, ROD, 'The Pacific/Tahiti: Queen of the South Sea Isles', in Peter Hulme and Tim Youngs (eds.), *The Cambridge Companion to Travel Writing* (Cambridge: Cambridge University Press, 2002), 139–55.

—— and SMITH, VANESSA (eds.), *Islands in History and Representation* (London: Routledge, 2003).

EDWARDS, ELIZABETH (ed.), *Anthropology and Photography, 1860–1920* (New Haven, Conn.: Yale University Press, 1992).

—— 'Performing Science: Still Photography and the Torres Straits Expedition', in Anita Herle and Sandra Rouse (eds.), *Cambridge and the Torres Straits. Centenary Essays on the 1898 Anthropological Expedition* (Cambridge: Cambridge University Press, 1998), 106–35.

EHRENBURG, ILYA, *The Life of the Automobile*, trans. Joachim Neugroschel (London: Pluto, 1985 [1929]).

ELSNER, JAS, and RUBIÉS, JOAN-PAU (eds.), *Voyages and Visions: Towards a Cultural History of Travel* (London: Reaktion, 1999).

ETCHERELLI, CLAIRE, *Élise ou la vraie vie* (Paris: Denoël, 1967).

EZRA, ELIZABETH, *The Colonial Unconscious: Race and Culture in Interwar France* (Ithaca, NY: Cornell University Press, 2000).

FABIAN, JOHANNES, *Time and the Other: How Anthropology Makes its Object* (New York: Columbia University Press, 1983).

FAESSEL, SONIA, 'Simenon, Gary: deux lectures du mythe de Tahiti. *Touriste de bananes* et *La Tête coupable*', *Travaux de littérature*, 10 (1997), 379–95.

FANON, FRANTZ, *Pour la révolution africaine* (Paris: Maspero, 1964).

FARGE, ARLETTE, *Le Goût de l'archive* (Paris: Seuil, 1989).

FONKOUA, ROMUALD, 'Le "voyage à l'envers": essai sur le discours des voyageurs nègres en France', in Romuald Fonkoua (ed.), *Les Discours de voyages: Afrique–Antilles* (Paris: Karthala, 1998), 117–45.

—— (ed.), *Les Discours de voyages: Afrique–Antilles* (Paris: Karthala, 1998).

—— *Essai sur une mesure du monde au XXe siècle: Edouard Glissant* (Paris: Honoré Champion, 2002).

FORSDICK, CHARLES, 'Victor Segalen and Museology: Stage-Management of the Exotic in an Age of Entropy', *French Cultural Studies*, 6 (1995), 385–412.

—— 'L'Exote mangé par les hommes', in Charles Forsdick and Susan Marson (eds.), *Reading Diversity* (Glasgow: Glasgow French and German Publications, 2000), 1–20.

—— 'Viator in Fabula: Jean-Didier Urbain and Contemporary French Approaches to Travel', *Studies in Travel Writing*, 4 (2000), 126–40.

—— *Victor Segalen and the Aesthetics of Diversity: Journeys between Cultures* (Oxford: Oxford University Press, 2000).

—— 'Sight, Sound, and Synesthesia: Reading the Senses in Victor Segalen', in Michael Syrotinski and Ian Maclachlan (eds.), *Sensual Reading: New Approaches to Reading and Its Relation to the Senses* (Lewisburg, Pa.: Bucknell University Press; London: Associated University Presses, 2001), 229–47.

—— '*Fin de Siècle, Fin des Voyages*: Michel Le Bris and Contemporary Travel Writing in French', in Michael Bishop and Christopher Elson (eds.), *French Prose in 2000* (Amsterdam: Rodopi, 2002), 47–55.

—— 'Hidden Journeys: Gender, Genre and Twentieth-Century Travel Literature in French', in Jane Conroy (ed.), *Cross-Cultural Travel: Papers from the Royal Irish Academy International Symposium on Literature and Travel* (New York: Peter Lang, 2003), 315–23.

—— 'Reading Twentieth-Century Women's Travel Literature in French', in Arzu Etensel Ildem (ed.), *Seuils et Traverses 4* (Ankara: University of Ankara Press, 2004), 361–73.

FORSDICK, CHARLES, and MURPHY, DAVID (eds.), *Francophone Postco-lonial Studies: A Critical Introduction* (London: Arnold, 2003).

FOSTER, SHIRLEY, *Across New Worlds: Nineteenth-Century Women Travel-lers and their Writings* (Hemel Hempstead: Harvester, 1990).

FOURASTIÉ, JEAN, *Les Trente Glorieuses: ou, La Révolution invisible de 1946 à 1975* (Paris: Fayard, 1979).

FRANTZ, ANAÏK, and MASPERO, FRANÇOIS, *Paris bout du monde* (Leval-lois Perret: Manya, 1992).

FRÉMIOT, ANNE (ed.), *Fin de siècle?* ([Nottingham]: Department of French, University of Nottingham, 1998).

FULLAGER, SIMONE, 'Narratives of Travel: Desire and Movement in Femi-nine Subjectivity', *Leisure Studies*, 21 (2002), 57–74.

FUSSELL, PAUL, *Abroad: British Literary Travelling Between the Wars* (New York: Oxford University Press, 1980).

GALLAGHER, MARY, *La Créolité de Saint-Jean Perse* (Paris: Gallimard, 1998).

GANNIER, ODILE, *La Littérature de voyage* (Paris: Ellipses, 2001).

—— 'Tahiti: de l'exotisme à l'exil', *Mots Pluriels*, 17 (2001), <http://www.arts. uwa.edu.au/MotsPluriels/MP17010g.html>, accessed 1 Nov. 2004.

GANTZ, KATHERINE, 'Dangerous Intersections: The Near-Collision of French and Cultural Studies in Maspero's *Les Passagers du Roissy-Express*', *The French Review*, 73/1 (1999), 82–93.

GAZAÏ, CAROLINE, and GAILLET, GENEVIÈVE, *Vacances en Iran* (Paris: Berger-Levrault, 1961).

GEERTZ, CLIFFORD, 'The Uses of Diversity', *Michigan Quarterly*, 5/1 (1987), 105–23.

GELLNER, ERNEST, 'The Mightier Pen?', *Times Literary Supplement*, 19 February 1993, 3–4.

GENETTE, GÉRARD, *Palimpsestes: la littérature au second degré* (Paris: Seuil, 1982).

GEORGE, SUSAN, 'Fast Castes', in Jeremy Millar and Michiel Schwartz (eds.), *Speed: Visions of an Accelerated Age* (London: The Photographers' Gallery; Whitechapel Art Gallery, 1998), 115–18.

GIDE, ANDRÉ, *Journal, 1889–1939* (Paris: Gallimard, Pléiade, 1951).

GIRARDET, RAOUL, *L'Idée coloniale en France de 1871 à 1962* (Paris: La Table Ronde, 1972).

GLISSANT, ÉDOUARD, *Soleil de la Conscience* (Paris: Gallimard, 1998 [1955]).

—— *Monsieur Toussaint* (Paris: Seuil, 1986).

—— *Caribbean Discourse: Selected Essays*, trans. J. Michael Dash (Charlottes-ville: University Press of Virginia, 1989).

—— *Poétique de la Relation* (Paris: Gallimard, 1990); *Poetics of Relation*, trans. Betsy Wing (Ann Arbor: University of Michigan Press, 1997).

—— 'Le chaos-monde, l'oral et l'écrit', in Ralph Ludwig (ed.), *Écrire la 'parole de nuit': la nouvelle littérature antillaise* (Paris: Gallimard, 1994), 111–29.

—— *Introduction à une poétique du divers* (Paris: Gallimard, 1996).

—— *Traité du Tout-Monde* (Paris: Gallimard, 1997).

GODEL, VAHÉ, *Nicolas Bouvier: 'faire un peu de musique avec cette vie unique'* (Geneva: Métropolis, 1998).

GODET, ROBERT, *En 2 CV vers les hauts lieux de l'Asie* (Paris: Amiot-Dumont, 1954).

GOEBEL, ROLF J., 'Japan as Western Text: Roland Barthes, Richard Gordon Smith, and Lafcadio Hearn', *Comparative Literature Studies*, 30/2 (1993), 188–205.

GOULEMOT, J.-M., LECURU, J., and MASSEAU, D., 'Les siècles ont-ils une fin?', in Pierre Citti (ed.), *Fins de siècle: colloque de Tours 4–6 juin 1985* (Bordeaux: Presses universitaires de Bordeaux, 1990), 17–33.

GREWAL, INDERPAL, *Home and Harem: Nation, Gender, Empire, and the Cultures of Travel* (London: Leicester University Press, 1996).

GRUBER, JACOB W., 'Ethnographic Salvage and the Shaping of Anthropology', *American Anthropologist*, 72 (1970), 1289–99.

HA, MARIE-PAULE, *Figuring the East: Segalen, Malraux, Duras, and Barthes* (New York: State University of New York Press, 2001).

HAARDT, GEORGES-MARIE, and AUDOUIN-DUBREUIL, LOUIS, *La Croisière noire: expédition Citroën Centre-Afrique* (Paris: Plon, 1927).

HACKING, IAN, *Mad Travellers: Reflections on the Reality of Transient Mental Illness* (London: Free Association Books, 1999).

HADDON, ALFRED CORT, 'The Saving of Vanishing Knowledge', *Nature*, 55 (1897), 305–6.

HALL, STUART, 'When was "the Post-Colonial"? Thinking at the Limit', in Iain Chambers and Lidia Curti (eds.), *The Post-Colonial Question: Common Skies, Divided Horizons* (London: Routledge, 1996), 242–60.

HAMBURSIN, OLIVIER (ed.), *Voyage et littérature: sens et plaisirs de l'écriture pérégrine* (Amay: Maison de la poésie d'Amay, 2001).

HARGREAVES, ALEC G., 'The Challenges of Multiculturalism: Regional and Religious Differences in France Today', in William Kidd and Siân Reynolds (eds.), *Contemporary French Cultural Studies* (London: Arnold, 2000), 95–110.

—— and McKINNEY, MARK (eds.), *Post-Colonial Cultures in France* (London: Routledge, 1997).

HAWTHORNE, SUSAN, 'The Politics of the Exotic: The Paradox of Cultural Voyeurism', *Meanjin*, 48 (1989), 259–68.

HERACLITUS, *Fragments*, trans. and ed. Marcel Conche (Paris: PUF, 1986).

—— *Fragments*, trans. and ed. T. M. Robinson (Toronto: University of Toronto Press, 1987).

HILL, TRACEY (ed.), *Decadence and Danger: Writing, History and the Fin de Siècle* (Bath: Sulis, 1997).

HO CHI MINH, *Textes 1914–1969*, ed. Alain Ruscio (Paris: L'Harmattan, 1990).

HODEIR, CATHERINE, and PIERRE, MICHEL, *L'Exposition coloniale* (Brussels: Complexe, 1991).

HOLDEN, LEN, 'More than a Marque. The Car as Symbol: Aspects of Culture and Ideology', in David Thoms, Len Holden, and Tim Claydon (eds.), *The Motor Car and Popular Culture in the 20th Century* (Aldershot: Ashgate, 1998), 28–40.

HOLLAND, PATRICK, and HUGGAN, GRAHAM, *Tourists with Typewriters: Critical Reflections on Contemporary Travel Writing* (Ann Arbor: University of Michigan Press, 1998).

HOOKS, BELL, 'Representations of Whiteness in the Black Imagination', in *Black Looks: Race and Representation* (Boston, Mass.: South End, 1992), 165–78.

HUGGAN, GRAHAM, 'The Postcolonial Exotic', *Transition*, 64 (1994), 22–9.

—— *The Postcolonial Exotic: Marketing the Margins* (London: Routledge, 2001).

HUGHES, EDWARD J., *Writing Marginality in Modern French Literature: From Loti to Genet* (Cambridge: Cambridge University Press, 2001).

HULME, PETER, and YOUNGS, TIM (eds.), *Cambridge Companion to Travel Writing* (Cambridge: Cambridge University Press, 2002).

HUYSMANS, J.-K., *À Rebours* (Paris: Garnier-Flammarion, 1978 [1884]).

IYER, PICO, 'The Empire Writes Back', *Time*, 8 February 1993, 46–51; 'L'Empire contre-attaque, plume en main', *Gulliver*, 3 (1999), 15–29.

JACK, BELINDA, ' "Mirages de Paris": Paris in Francophone Writing', in Michael Sheringham (ed.), *Parisian Fields* (London: Reaktion 1996), 150–61.

JACKSON, JULIAN, *The Popular Front in France: Defending Democracy, 1934–38* (Cambridge: Cambridge University Press, 1988).

—— ' "Le temps des loisirs": Popular Tourism and Mass Leisure in the Vision of the Front Populaire', in M. S. Alexander and H. Graham (eds.), *The French and Spanish Popular Fronts: Comparative Perspectives* (Cambridge: Cambridge University Press, 1989), 226–39.

JAMIN, JEAN, 'Objets trouvés des paradis perdus: à propos de la Mission Dakar-Djibouti', in Jacques Hainard and Roland Kaehr (eds.), *Collections passion* (Neuchâtel: Musée d'ethnographie, 1982), 69–100.

—— 'De l'humaine condition de Minotaure', in *Regards sur Minotaure: La Revue à tête de bête* (Geneva: Musée d'art et d'histoire, 1987), 79–87.

JOHNSON, RANDAL, 'Tupy or not Tupy: Cannibalism and Nationalism in Contemporary Brazilian Literature and Culture', in John King (ed.), *Modern Latin American Fiction: A Survey* (London: Faber & Faber, 1987), 41–59.

JOPPA, F., 'Situation de *Mirages de Paris* d'Ousmane Socé dans le roman néo-africain', *Présence Francophone*, 1 (1970), 219–32.

JOUBERT, JEAN-LOUIS, 'Poétique de l'exotisme: Saint-John Perse, Victor Segalen et Édouard Glissant', in Alain Buisine and Norbert Dodille (eds.), *L'Exotisme: Actes du colloque de Saint-Denis de la Réunion, 1988*, Cahiers CRLH-CIRAOI, 5 (Paris: Didier-Érudition, 1988), 281–91.

JOURDE, PIERRE, *La Littérature sans estomac* (Paris: Esprit des péninsules, 2002).

KAPLAN, CAREN, *Questions of Travel: Postmodern Discourses of Displacement* (Durham, NC: Duke University Press, 1996).

KAPLAN, STEVEN LAURENCE, *Farewell, Revolution: Disputed Legacies, France 1789/1989* (Ithaca, NY: Cornell University Press, 1995)

KEILLER, PATRICK, 'Sexual Ambiguity and Automotive Engineering', in Peter Wollen and Joe Kerr (eds.), *Autopia: Cars and Culture* (London: Reaktion, 2002), 342–53.

KHATIBI, ABDELKEBIR, *La Figure de l'étranger dans la littérature française* (Paris: Denoël, 1987).

KNIGHT, DIANA, *Barthes and Utopia: Space, Travel, Writing* (Oxford: Clarendon, 1997).

KOSHAR, RUDY, *German Travel Cultures* (Oxford: Berg, 2000).

KPOMASSIE, MICHEL-TÉTÉ, *Un Africain au Groenland* (Paris: Flammarion, 1981).

KRITZMAN, LAWRENCE D., 'A Certain Idea of French: Cultural Studies, Literature and Theory', *Yale French Studies*, 103 (2003), 146–60.

KUISEL, RICHARD, *Seducing the French: The Dilemma of Americanization* (Berkeley and Los Angeles: University of California Press, 1996).

LACARRIÈRE, JACQUES, *Chemin faisant* (Paris: Payot, 1992 [1977]).

—— *Le Pays sous l'écorce* (Paris: Gallimard, 1980).

—— (ed.), *Flâner en France: sur les pas de dix-huit écrivains d'aujourd'hui* (Paris: Pirot, 1987).

—— 'Le bernard-l'hermite ou le treizième voyage', in *Pour une littérature voyageuse* (Brussels: Complexe, 1992), 105–7.

—— 'Nous ne sommes plus des paramécies', *Gulliver*, 11 (1993), 31–3.

LAPORTE, DOMINIQUE, *Histoire de la merde (Prologue)* (Paris: Christian Bourgois, 1978).

LAROUSSI, FARID, and MILLER, CHRISTOPHER L. (eds.), 'French and Francophone: The Challenge of Expanding Horizons', *Yale French Studies*, 103 (2003).

LARSON, R., 'Ethnography, Thievery and Cultural Identity: A Rereading of Michel Leiris's *L'Afrique fantôme*', *PMLA* 112 (1997), 229–42.

LAUDE, PATRICK, *Exotisme indochinois et poésie: étude sur l'œuvre poétique d'Alfred Droin, Jeanne Leuba et Albert de Pouvourville* (Paris: Sudestasie, 2000).

LAVENIR, C. B., *La Roue et le stylo: comment nous sommes devenus touristes* (Paris: Odile Jacob, 1999).

LAWRENCE, KAREN R., *Penelope Voyages: Women and Travel in the British Literary Tradition* (Ithaca, NY: Cornell University Press, 1994).

LAYEC, CLAUDE, *Au Long Cours en 2CV* (Paris: Presses de la Cité, 1968).

LÉAUTAUD, PAUL, *Journal littéraire*, 19 vols. (Paris: Mercure de France, 1954–6).

LEBEL, ROLAND, *Histoire de la littérature coloniale en France* (Paris: Larose, 1931).

LEBOVICS, HERMAN, *True France: The Wars over Cultural Identity, 1900–1945* (Ithaca, NY: Cornell University Press, 1992).

LE BRETON, DAVID, *Passions du risque* (Paris: Métailié, 1991).

—— *Anthropologie du corps et modernité* (Paris: Quadrige/PUF, 2000).

—— *Éloge de la marche* (Paris: Métailié, 2000).

LE BRIS, MICHEL, *L'Homme aux semelles de vent* (Paris: Grasset, 1977).

—— (ed.), *Une amitié littéraire: Henry James–Robert-Louis Stevenson* (Paris: Verdier, 1987).

—— 'Écrire le poème du monde', *Gulliver*, 2–3 (1990), 4–11.

—— 'Le Grand Retour de l'aventure', *Carnets de l'exotisme*, 5 (1991), 51.

—— *Le Grand Dehors* (Paris: Payot, 1992).

—— *Fragments du royaume* (Vénissieux: Paroles d'Aube, 1995).

—— 'La vie, si égarante et bonne', in *Le Vent des routes: hommages à Nicolas Bouvier* (Geneva: Zoé, 1998), 57–61.

—— (ed.), *Étonnants Voyageurs: anthologie des écrivains de Gulliver* (Paris: Flammarion, 1999).

—— and IZZO, JEAN-CLAUDE (eds.), *Méditérrannées* (Paris: Librio, 1998).

LEED, ERIC, *The Mind of the Traveler: From Gilgamesh to Global Tourism* (New York: Basic Books, 1991).

LEFÈVRE, GEORGES, *La Croisière jaune: expédition Citroën centre-Asie* (Paris: L'Asiathèque, 1990 [1933]).

LEIRIS, MICHEL, *L'Afrique fantôme* (Paris: Gallimard, 1934).

—— *Cinq études d'ethnographie* (Paris: Denoël; Gonthier, 1969).

—— *Zébrages* (Paris: Gallimard, 1992).

LESNES, CORINE, 'Ultimes répétitions aux Champs-Elysées: les tambours de maître Goude', *Le Monde*, 13 July 1989, 15.

LESOURD, MICHEL, 'L'appropriation du monde', in Jeanne Beausoleil (ed.), *Jean Brunhes autour du monde: regards d'un géographe / regards de la géographie* (Boulogne: Musée Albert Kahn, 1993), 15–47.

LÉVI-STRAUSS, CLAUDE, *Tristes Tropiques* (Paris: Plon, 1955); *Tristes Tropiques*, trans. John and Doreen Weightman (London: Cape, 1973).

LINHART, ROBERT, *L'Établi* (Paris: Minuit, 1978).

LINHART, VIRGINIE, *Volontaires pour l'usine: vie d'établies 1967–1977* (Paris: Seuil, 1994).

LINON-CHIPON, SOPHIE, MAGRI-MOURGUES, VÉRONIQUE, and MOUSSA, SARGA (eds.), *Miroirs de textes: récits de voyage et intertextualité* (Nice: Publications de la Faculté des Lettres, Arts et Sciences Humaines de Nice; Paris: Centre de Recherches sur la Littérature des Voyages, 1998).

LIONNET, FRANÇOISE, 'Créolité in the Indian Ocean: Two Models of Cultural Diversity', *Yale French Studies*, 82 (1993), 101–12.

LITTLE, ROGER, 'Death by Water: Socé's Fara and Lacrosil's Cajou', *ASCALF Bulletin*, 23 (2001), 6–22.

—— 'World Literature in French; or Is Francophonie Frankly Phoney?', *European Review*, 9/4 (2001), 421–36.

LOCHON, HENRI, *En 2CV chez les primitifs de la Sierra mexicaine* (Lyons: Vinay, 1956).

LOSELLE, ANDREA, *History's Double: Cultural Tourism in Twentieth-Century French Writing* (New York: St Martin's Press, 1997).

LOTI, PIERRE, *Romans* (Paris: Presses de la Cité, 1989).

LOUBET, JEAN-LOUIS, *Histoire de l'automobile française* (Paris: Seuil, 2001).

LOWE, LISA, *Critical Terrains: French and British Orientalisms* (Ithaca, NY: Cornell University Press, 1991).

LUDWIG, RALPH (ed.), *Écrire la 'parole de nuit': la nouvelle littérature antillaise* (Paris: Gallimard, 1994).

MACCANNELL, DEAN, *The Tourist: A New Theory of the Leisure Class* (London: Macmillan, 1976).

MACCLANCY, JEREMY (ed.), *Exotic No More* (Chicago, Ill.: University of Chicago Press, 2002).

MACQUEEN, BOB, and MCNAMARA, JULIAN, *The Life and Times of the 2CV* (Cambridge: Great Ouse, 1982).

MAFFI, LUISA, 'Introduction: On the Interdependence of Biological and Cultural Diversity', in *On Biocultural Diversity: Linking Language, Knowledge and the Environment* (Washington DC: Smithsonian Institution, 2001), 1–50.

MAIGNE, VINCENETTE, 'Exotisme: évolution en diachronie du mot et de son champ sémantique', in R. Antonioli (ed.), *Exotisme et création: actes du colloque international de Lyon, 1983* (Lyons: Hermès, 1985), 9–16.

MANCERON, GILLES, *Segalen* (Paris: Lattès, 1992).

—— 'Koké et Tépéva: Victor Segalen dans les pas de Gauguin', in *Gauguin—Tahiti: l'atelier des tropiques* (Paris: Éditions des Musées nationaux, 2003), 322–33.

MANCERON, HENRY, and SEGALEN, VICTOR, *Trahison fidèle*, ed. Gilles Manceron (Paris: Seuil, 1985).

MANDELBROT, BENOÎT, *The Fractal Geometry of Nature* (New York: W. H. Freeman, 1983 [1977]).

MANN, MICHAEL, *The Sources of Social Power* (Cambridge: Cambridge University Press, 1986).

MARGUERON, DANIEL, *Tahiti dans toute sa littérature: essai sur Tahiti et ses îles dans la littérature française de la découverte à nos jours* (Paris: L'Harmattan, 1989).

MARTIN, JEAN-PIERRE, *Henri Michaux* (Paris: Gallimard, 2003).

MASON, PETER, *Infelicities: Representations of the Exotic* (Baltimore, Md.: Johns Hopkins University Press, 1998).

MASPERO, FRANÇOIS, 'Drancy', *Gulliver*, 4 (1990), 124–41.

—— *Les Passagers du Roissy-Express* (Paris: Seuil, 1990); *Roissy Express: A Journey through the Paris Suburbs*, trans. Paul Jones (London: Verso, 1994).

—— *Balkans-Transit* (Paris: Seuil, 1997).

—— *Les Abeilles et la guêpe* (Paris: Seuil, 2002).

MATEATA-ALLAIN, KAREVA, 'Ma'ohi Women Writers of Colonial French Polynesia: Passive Resistance toward a Post(-)colonial Literature', *Jouvert*, 7/2 (2003), <http://social.chass.ncsu.edu/jouvert/v7i2/mateat.htm>, accessed 1 Nov. 2004.

MATHY, JEAN-PHILIPPE, 'The Resistance to French Theory in the United States: A Cross-Cultural Inquiry', *French Historical Studies*, 19 (1995), 331–47.

MAUROIS, ANDRÉ, *L'Amérique inattendue* (Paris: Mornay, 1931).

MAYAUX, CATHERINE, 'Victor Segalen et Saint-John Perse: deux poètes en Chine', *Europe*, 696 (1987), 117–25.

MENDELSON, DAVID, 'Le "Voyage en Orient" et le renouvellement de l'écriture fin-de-siècle', in Gwenhaël Ponnau (ed.), *Fins de siècle: Terme–Évolution–Révolution* (Toulouse: Presses universitaires du Mirail, 1989), 295–301.

MENGOUCHI and RAMDANE, *L'Homme qui enjamba la mer* (Paris: Veyrier, 1978).

MÉNIL, RENÉ, *Antilles déjà jadis* (Paris: Jean-Michel Place, 1999).

MESNARD, JEAN, and NIDERST, ALAIN (eds.), *Les Récits de voyage* (Paris: Nizet, 1986).

MEUNIER, JACQUES, *Les Gamins de Bogota* (Paris: Lattès, 1977).

—— *Le Monocle de Joseph Conrad* (Paris: La Découverte, 1987).

MICHAUX, HENRI, *Ecuador* (Paris: Gallimard, 1929).

—— *Un barbare en Asie* (Paris: Gallimard, 1933).

MILLAR, JEREMY, and SCHWARTZ, MICHIEL (eds.), *Speed: Visions of an Accelerated Age* (London: The Photographers' Gallery; Whitechapel Art Gallery, 1998).

MILLE, PIERRE, 'A l'Exposition coloniale: vue d'ensemble', *Revue des deux mondes*, 51/3 (1931), 265–87.

—— *Barnavaux aux colonies, suivi d'Écrits sur la littérature coloniale*, ed. Jennifer Yee, Autrement mêmes (Paris: L'Harmattan, 2002).

MILLER, CHRISTOPHER, *Nationalists and Nomads: Essays on Francophone African Literature and Culture* (Chicago, Ill.: University of Chicago Press, 1998).

MILLER, DANIEL, 'Driven Societies', in Daniel Miller (ed.), *Car Cultures* (Oxford: Berg, 2001), 1–33.

MILLS, SARA, *Discourses of Difference: An Analysis of Women's Travel Writing and Colonialism* (London: Routledge, 1991).

MITCHELL, TIMOTHY, 'Orientalism and the Exhibitionary Order', in Nicholas B. Dirks (ed.), *Colonialism and Culture* (Ann Arbor: University of Michigan Press, 1992).

MODIANO, PATRICK, *Dora Bruder* (Paris: Gallimard, 1997).

MONICAT, BÉNÉDICTE, *Itinéraires de l'écriture au féminin: voyageuses du 19e siècle* (Amsterdam: Rodopi, 1996).

MONTALBETTI, CHRISTINE, *Le Voyage, le monde et la bibliothèque* (Paris: PUF, 1997).

MORAND, PAUL, 'Exotisme et cosmopolitisme', *Carnets de l'exotisme*, 10 (1992), 79–80. (First published 1924.)

—— *Le Voyage* (Monaco: Éditions du Rocher, 1994 [1927]).

—— *Flèche d'Orient* (Paris: Gallimard, 1932).

—— *Éloge du repos* (Paris: Arléa, 1996). (First published as *Apprendre à se reposer* (Paris: Flammarion, 1937).)

MORIN, EDGAR, *Commune en France: la métamorphose de Plozevet* (Paris: Fayard, 1967).

MORROW, PATRICK D., *Post-Colonial Essays on South Pacific Literature* (Lewiston, NY: Edwin Mellen, 1998).

MORTIMER, MILDRED, *Journeys through the French African Novel* (Portsmouth, NH: Heinemann; London: James Currey, 1990).

MORTON, PATRICIA A., *Hybrid Modernities: Architecture and Representation at the 1931 Colonial Exposition, Paris* (Cambridge, Mass.: MIT Press, 2000).

MOSES, CLAIRE GOLDBERG, 'Made in America: "French Feminism" in Academia', in Roger Célestin, Eliane DalMolin, and Isabelle de Courtivron (eds.), *Beyond French Feminisms: Debates on Women, Politics and Culture in France, 1981–2001* (New York: Palgrave Macmillan, 2003), 261–84.

MOURA, JEAN-MARC, 'Francophonie et critique postcoloniale', *Revue de littérature comparée*, 1 (1997), 59–87.

—— *L'Europe littéraire et l'ailleurs* (Paris: PUF, 1998).

—— *La Littérature des lointains: histoire de l'exotisme européen au XXe siècle* (Paris: Champion, 1998).

—— 'Littérature coloniale et exotisme: examen d'une opposition de la théorie littéraire coloniale', in Jean-François Durand (ed.), *Regards sur les littératures coloniales*, 2 vols. (Paris: L'Harmattan, 1999), ii. 21–39.

—— *Littératures francophones et théorie postcoloniale* (Paris: PUF, 1999).

MOURALIS, BERNARD, *Les Contre-littératures* (Paris: PUF, 1975).

MOUREAU, FRANÇOIS (ed.), *Métamorphoses du récit de voyage* (Paris: Champion; Geneva: Slatkine, 1986).

MUDIMBE-BOYI, ELISABETH, 'Travel, Representation, and Difference, or How Can One Be a Parisian?', *Research in African Literatures*, 23/3 (1992), 25–39.

MURPHY, DAVID, 'De-centring French Studies: Towards a Postcolonial Theory of Francophone Culture', *French Cultural Studies*, 13/2 (2002), 165–85.

MYERS, GREG, 'Nineteenth-Century Popularizations of Thermodynamics and the Rhetoric of Social Prophecy', in Patrick Brantlinger (ed.), *Energy and Entropy: Science and Culture in Victorian Britain* (Bloomington: Indiana University Press, 1989), 307–38.

NICOLE, ROBERT, *The Word, the Pen and the Pistol: Literature and Power in Tahiti* (Albany: State University of New York Press, 2001).

NÍ LOINGSIGH, AEDÍN, 'Éxil et perception du temps chez Tilli et Socé', *ASCALF Bulletin*, 16–17 (1998), 3–21.

NKASHAMA, PIUS NGANDU, *Vie et mœurs d'un primitif en Essone Quatre-vingt-onze* (Paris: L'Harmattan, 1987).

NORINDR, PANIVONG, *Phantasmatic Indochina: French Colonial Ideology in Architecture, Film and Literature* (Durham, NC: Duke University Press, 1996).

O'CONNOR, ALAN, *Raymond Williams: Writing, Culture, Politics* (Oxford: Blackwell, 1989).

O'HANLON, REDMOND, *Into the Heart of Borneo* (Edinburgh: Salamander, 1984).

—— *In Trouble Again: A Journey between the Orinoco and the Amazon* (London: Hamilton, 1988).

OLLIVIER, BERNARD, *Longue marche* (Paris: Phébus, 2000).

—— *Vers Samarcande* (Paris: Phébus, 2001).

—— *Le Vent des Steppes* (Paris: Phébus, 2003).

ORTIZ, FERNANDO, *Cuban Counterpoint: Tobacco and Sugar*, trans. Harriet de Onís (Durham, NC: Duke University Press, 1995 [1947]).

OSBORNE, PETER D., *Travelling Light: Photography, Travel and Visual Culture* (Manchester: Manchester University Press, 2000).

OVERY, RICHARD, 'Heralds of Modernity: Cars and Planes from Invention to Necessity', in Mikulás Teich and Roy Porter (eds.), *Fin de siècle and its Legacy* (Cambridge: Cambridge University Press, 1990), 54–79.

OZOUF, JACQUES and MONA, '*Le Tour de la France par Deux Enfants*: le petit livre rouge de la République', in Pierre Nora (ed.), *Les Lieux de mémoire*, 3 vols. (Paris: Gallimard/Quarto, 1997), i. 277–301.

PANOFF, MICHEL, 'Une valeur sûre: l'exotisme', *L'Homme*, 26/1–2 (1986), 287–96.

—— *Tahiti métisse* (Paris: Denoël, 1989).

PASQUALI, ADRIEN, *Le Tour des horizons: critique et récits de voyages* (Paris: Klincksieck, 1994).

—— *Nicolas Bouvier: un galet dans le torrent du monde* (Geneva: Zoé, 1996).

PEREC, GEORGES, *Tentative d'épuisement d'un lieu parisien* (Paris: Bourgois, 2000 [1975]).

PETREY, SANDIE, 'Language Charged with Meaning', *Yale French Studies*, 103 (2003), 133–45.

PETRINI, CARLO, *Slow Food: The Case for Taste*, trans. William McCuaig (New York: Columbia University Press, 2003).

PIERRE, JOSÉ (ed.), *Tracts surréalistes et déclarations collectives 1922–1939: tome 1 1922–1939* (Paris: Le Terrain vague, 1980).

PIERROT, J., '*L'Afrique fantôme* de Michel Leiris ou le voyage du poète de l'ethnographe', in Jean Mesnard and Alain Niderst (eds.), *Les Récits de voyage* (Paris: Nizet, 1986), 189–241.

PIETERSE, JAN NEDERVEEN, 'Globalization as hybridization', in Mike Featherstone, Scott Lash, and Roland Robertson (eds.), *Global Modernities* (London: Sage, 1995), 45–68.

VAN DER POEL, IEME, and BERTHO, SOPHIE (eds.), *Traveling Theory: France and the United States* (Madison, NJ: Fairleigh Dickinson University Press; London: Associated University Presses, 1999).

POINDRON, ERIC, *Belles étoiles: avec Stevenson dans les Cévennes* (Paris: Flammarion, 2001).

POLEZZI, LOREDANA, *Translating Travel: Contemporary Italian Travel Writing in Translation* (Aldershot: Ashgate, 2001).

—— 'Did someone just travel all over me? Travel writing and the travellee...', in Jan Borm and Jean-Yves Le Disez (eds.), *Seuils et Traverses: enjeux et écriture du voyage*, 2 vols. (Brest: CRBC; Versailles: Suds d'Amériques, 2002), ii. 303–12.

POLIAKOV, L., *Le Mythe aryen: essai sur les sources du racisme et du nationalisme* (Paris: Calmann-Lévy, 1971).

PORTER, DENNIS, '*Orientalism* and Its Problems', in Patrick Williams and Laura Chrisman (eds.), *Colonial Discourse and Post-Colonial Theory: A Reader* (New York: Columbia University Press, 1994), 150–61.

POSTEL, PHILIPPE, *Victor Segalen et la statuaire chinoise: archéologie et poétique*, Bibliothèque de Littérature générale et comparée, 31 (Paris: Honoré Champion, 2001).

PRATT, MARY LOUISE, *Imperial Eyes: Travel Writing and Transculturation* (London: Routledge, 1992).

PRENDERGAST, CHRISTOPHER, *Paris and the Nineteenth Century* (Oxford: Blackwell, 1992).

PRZYBOS, J., 'Voyage du pessimisme et pessimisme du voyage', *Romantisme*, 61 (1988), 67–74.

PUTNAM, WALTER, 'Myth, metaphor, and music in "Le Voyage" ', in William J. Thompson (ed.), *Understanding 'Les Fleurs du mal': Critical Readings* (Nashville, Tenn.: Vanderbilt University Press, 1997), 192–213.

RABAN, JONATHAN, *Coasting* (London: Collins Harvill, 1986).

RABAN, JONATHAN, *For Love and Money* (London: Picador, 1988).

RAIMOND, MICHEL, *La Crise du roman: des lendemains du naturalisme aux années vingt* (Paris: J. Corti, 1966).

RAMAL-CALS, JEANNE, 'Souvenir de l'Exposition coloniale', *Les Œuvres libres*, 126 (1931), 7–22.

RATHJE, WILLIAM L., and MURPHY, CULLEN, *Rubbish! The Archaeology of Garbage* (New York: HarperCollins, 1992).

RAUCH, ANDRÉ (ed.), *La Marche, la vie: solitaire ou solidaire, ce geste fondateur* (Paris: Autrement, 1997).

RAZAC, OLIVIER, *L'Écran et le Zoo: spectacle et domestication, des expositions coloniales à Loft Story* (Paris: Denoël, 2002).

RÉDA, JACQUES, 'Éloge modéré de la lenteur', in *Recommandations aux promeneurs* (Paris: Gallimard, 1988), 85–94.

REICHLER, CLAUDE, 'Le deuil du monde', *Traverses*, 41–2 (1987), 134–45.

RENARD, JULES, *Journal*, ed. Léon Guichard and Gilbert Sigaux (Paris: Gallimard, 1960).

REVERZY, JEAN, *Le Passage* (Paris: Julliard, 1954).

REYNOLDS, JOHN, *André Citroën: The Man and the Motor Cars* (Stroud: Sutton, 1996).

RICHARDS, THOMAS, *The Imperial Archive: Knowledge and the Fantasy of Empire* (London: Verso, 1993).

RIDON, JEAN-XAVIER (ed.), 'Errances urbaines', *Nottingham French Studies*, 39/1 (2000).

—— 'Pour une poétique du voyage comme disparition', in Christiane Albert, Nadine Laporte, and Jean-Yves Pouilloux (eds.), *Autour de Nicolas Bouvier; résonances* (Geneva: Zoé, 2002), 120–35.

—— *Le Voyage en son miroir: essai sur quelques tentatives de réinvention du voyage au 20e siècle* (Paris: Kimé, 2002).

RIFKIN, ADRIAN, 'Travel for Men: from Claude Lévi-Strauss to the Sailor Hans', in George Robertson et al. (eds.), *Travellers' Tales: Narratives of Home and Displacement* (London: Routledge, 1994), 216–24.

ROBERTSON, ROLAND, 'Glocalization: Time–Space and Monogeneity–Heterogeneity', in Mike Featherstone, Scott Lash, and Roland Robertson (eds.), *Global Modernities* (London: Sage, 1995), 25–44.

RONY, FATIMA TOBING, *The Third Eye: Race, Cinema and Ethnographic Spectacle* (Durham, NC: Duke University Press, 1996).

ROOT, DEBORAH, *Cannibal Culture: Art, Appropriation and the Commodification of Difference* (Boulder, Col.: Westview, 1996).

ROSALDO, RENATO, *Culture and Truth: The Remaking of Social Analysis* (London: Routledge, 1993).

ROSELLO, MIREILLE, *Postcolonial Hospitality: The Immigrant as Guest* (Stanford, Calif.: Stanford University Press, 2001).

—— 'Unhoming Francophone Studies: A House in the Middle of the Current', *Yale French Studies*, 103 (2003), 123–32.

ROSS, KRISTIN, *Fast Cars, Clean Bodies: Decolonization and the Reordering of French Culture* (Cambridge, Mass.: MIT Press, 1995).

ROUAUD, JEAN, *Les Champs d'Honneur* (Paris: Minuit, 1990).

ROUD, GUSTAVE, *Essai pour un paradis, suivi du Petit traité de la marche en plaine* (Lausanne: Bibliothèque des Arts, 1984 [1932]).

DE ROUX, EMMANUEL, *On a marché sur la Méridienne: de la Mer du Nord aux Pyrénées* (Paris: Fayard, 2001).

—— 'Comment s'est bâtie Alger la Blanche', *Le Monde*, 19 August 2003, 20.

RULLIER, JEAN-JACQUES, *Œuvre incomplète* (Paris: Éditions du Centre Pompidou, 1997).

SABATÈS, FABIEN, *La Croisière Noire Citroën* ([n. pl.]: Eric Baschet, 1980).

SACHS, WOLFGANG, *The Love of the Automobile: Looking Back in the History of our Desires*, trans. Don Reneau (Berkeley: University of California Press, 1992).

SAHLINS, PETER, *Boundaries: The Making of France and Spain in the Pyrenees* (Berkeley: University of California Press, 1989).

—— *Unnaturally French: Foreign Citizens in the Old Régime and After* (Ithaca, NY: Cornell University Press, 2004).

SAID, EDWARD W., *Orientalism* (Harmondsworth: Penguin, 1991 [1978]); *L'Orientalisme: l'Orient créé par l'Occident* (Paris: Seuil, 1980).

—— 'Traveling Theory', in *The World, the Text and the Critic* (London: Vintage, 1991), 226–47. (First published 1983.)

—— *Culture and Imperialism* (London: Chatto & Windus, 1993); *Culture et impérialisme* (Paris: Fayard; Le Monde diplomatique, 2000).

—— 'Traveling Theory Reconsidered', in Robert M. Polhemus and Roger B. Henkle (eds.), *Critical Reconstructions* (Stanford, Calif.: Stanford University Press, 1994), 251–65.

—— 'Afterword to the 1995 Printing', in *Orientalism*, rev. edn. (Harmondsworth: Penguin, 1995), 329–54.

SAINT-POL-ROUX, *Vitesse* (Mortemart: Rougerie, 1973).

—— *La Randonnée* (Mortemart: Rougerie, 1978).

SANSOT, PIERRE, *La France sensible* (Paris: Payot, 1995 [1985]).

—— *Du Bon Usage de la lenteur* (Paris: Payot, 1998).

—— *Chemins aux vents* (Paris: Payot, 2000).

SANTAOLALLA, ISABEL (ed.), *'New' Exoticisms: Changing Patterns in the Construction of Otherness* (Amsterdam: Rodopi, 2000).

SARTRE, JEAN-PAUL, 'D'une Chine à l'Autre', in *Situations V* (Paris: Gallimard, 1964), 7–24.

SCEMLA, JEAN-JO, 'Polynésie française et identité maohie', in Jean Chesneaux (ed.), *Tahiti après la bombe: quel avenir pour la Polynésie?* (Paris: L'Harmattan, 1995), 19–51.

SCEMLA, JEAN-JO, 'La littérature dans le Pacifique: le cas tahitien', *Notre Librairie*, 143 (2001), 112–23.

SCHLICK, YAËL, 'Re-Writing the Exotic: Mille, Segalen, and the Emergence of *Littérature coloniale*', *Dalhousie French Studies*, 35 (1996), 123–34.

—— 'The "French Kipling": Pierre Mille's Popular Colonial Fiction', *Comparative Literature Studies*, 34/3 (1997), 226–41.

SCHWARTZ, HILLEL, *Century's End: An Orientation Manual Toward the Year 2000* (New York: Currency Doubleday, 1996).

SCHWARTZ, VANESSA R., *Spectacular Realities: Early Mass Culture in Fin-de-Siècle Paris* (Berkeley: University of California Press, 1998).

SCOTT, DAVID, 'The Smile of the Sign: Semiotics and Travel Writing in Barthes, Baudrillard, Butor and Lévi-Strauss', *Studies in Travel Writing*, 7/2 (2003), 209–225.

SEBBAR, LEILA, *Les Carnets de Shérazade* (Paris: Stock, 1985).

SEGALEN, VICTOR, *Lettres de Chine* (Paris: Plon, 1967).

—— *Œuvres complètes*, 2 vols., ed. Henry Bouiller (Paris: Laffont, 1995).

—— *Essay on Exoticism: An Aesthetics of Diversity*, trans. and ed. Yaël Rachel Schlick (Durham, NC: Duke University Press, 2002).

—— *Correspondance*, 2 vols. (Paris: Fayard, 2004).

SHANKAR, S., *Textual Traffic: Colonialism, Modernity, and the Economy of the Text* (New York: State University of New York Press, 2001).

SHAPIRO, RON, 'In Defence of Exoticism: Rescuing the Literary Imagination', in Isabel Santaolalla (ed.), *'New' Exoticisms: Changing Patterns in the Construction of Otherness* (Amsterdam: Rodopi, 2000), 41–9.

SHELTON, M.-D., 'Primitive Self. Colonial Impulses in Michel Leiris's *L'Afrique fantôme*', in E. Barkan and R. Bush (eds.), *Prehistories of the Future: The Primitivist Project and the Culture of Modernism* (Stanford, Calif.: Stanford University Press, 1995), 326–38.

SHILTON, SIOBHÁN, '*Une littérature qui dise le monde?* Contemporary French Travel Writing and the Challenge of Postcoloniality', in Peter Davies, Catriona Cunningham, and Cristina Johnson (eds.), *Contemporary Francophone Identities* (Glasgow: University of Glasgow French and German Publications, 2002), 135–49.

SILENIEKS, JURIS, 'Glissant's Prophetic Vision of the Past', *African Literature Today*, 11 (1980), 161–8.

SILVERMAN, MAX, *Facing Postmodernity: Contemporary French Thought on Culture and Society* (London: Routledge, 1999).

SIMENON, GEORGES, *Touriste de bananes* (Paris: Gallimard, 1936).

—— *A la recherche de l'homme nu*, ed. Francis Lacassin (Paris: 10/18, 1976).

DE LA SIZERANNE, ROBERT, 'Le bon et le mauvais exotisme', *Revue des deux mondes*, 51/5 (1931), 597–616.

SMITH, SIDONIE, *Moving Lives: Twentieth-Century Women's Travel Writing* (Minneapolis: University of Minnesota Press, 2001).

SMYTH, GERRY, 'The Politics of Hybridity: Some Problems with Crossing the Border', in Ashok Bery and Patricia Murray (eds.), *Comparing Postcolonial Literatures: Dislocations* (Basingstoke: Macmillan, 2000), 43–55.

SNOW, C. P., *The Two Cultures and a Second Look* (Cambridge: Cambridge University Press, 1964).

SOCÉ, OUSMANE, *Mirages de Paris* (Paris: Nouvelles Éditions Latines, 1964 [1937]).

SOKAL, ALAN, and BRICMONT, JEAN, *Impostures intellectuelles* (Paris: Jacob, 1997).

SOLNIT, REBECCA, *Wanderlust: A History of Walking* (New York: Viking, 2000).

SONTAG, SUSAN, *On Photography* (London: Allen Lane, 1977).

SPEAR, THOMAS (ed.), *La Culture française vue d'ici et d'ailleurs* (Paris: Karthala, 2002).

SPITZ, CHANTAL, 'Héritage et confrontation', <http://www.lehman.cuny. edu/ile.en.ile/paroles/spitz_gauguin.html>, accessed 1 Nov. 2004.

ST AUBYN, F. C., 'Michel Butor's America', *Kentucky Foreign Language Quarterly*, 11/1 (1964), 40–8.

STOVALL, TYLER, 'From Red Belt to Black Belt: Race, Class, and Urban Marginality in Twentieth-Century Paris', *L'Esprit Créateur*, 41/3 (2001), 9–23.

—— and ABBEELE, GEORGES VAN DEN (eds.), *French Civilization and Its Discontents* (Lanham, Md.: Lexington Books, 2003).

SUGNET, CHARLES, 'Vile Bodies, Vile Places: Travelling with *Granta*', *Transition*, 51 (1991), 70–85.

SUK, JEANNIE, *Postcolonial Paradoxes in French Caribbean Writing: Césaire, Glissant, Condé* (Oxford: Clarendon, 2001).

SURVÉLOR, ROLAND, 'Folklore, exotisme, connaissance', *Acoma*, 2 (1971), 21–40.

SYROTINSKI, MICHAEL, ' "When in Rome...": Irony and Subversion in Bernard Dadié's Travel-Writing', *The Journal of African Travel Writing*, 7 (1999), 66–79.

SZARKOWSKI, JOHN, *Mirrors and Windows: American Photography Since 1960* (New York: Museum of Modern Art, 1978).

TAFFIN, DOMINIQUE, 'Le Musée des Colonies et l'imaginaire colonial', in Nicolas Bancel, Pascal Blanchard, and Laurent Gervereau (eds.), *Images et Colonies: iconographie et propagande coloniale sur l'Afrique française de 1880 à 1962* (Nanterre: Bibliothèque de documentation internationale contemporaine; Paris: ACHAC, 1993), 140–3.

TAI, HUE-TAM HO, 'Remembered Realms: Pierre Nora and French National Memory', *History Cooperative*, 106/3 (2001), 38 paras. (<http://www. historycooperative.org/journals/ahr/106.3/aho00906.html>, accessed 1 Nov. 2004).

TEICH, MIKULÁS, and PORTER, ROY (eds.), *Fin de siècle and its Legacy* (Cambridge: Cambridge University Press, 1990).

TÉVANIAN, PIERRE, *Le Racisme républicain: réflexions sur le modèle français de discrimination* (Paris: L'Esprit frappeur, 2001).

THEROUX, PAUL, *The Kingdom by the Sea* (London: Hamilton, 1983).

THIBAULT, BRUNO, ' "Voyager contre": la question de l'exotisme dans les journaux de voyage d'Henri Michaux', *The French Review*, 63 (1990), 485–91.

—— *L'Allure de Morand: du Modernisme au Pétainisme* (Birmingham, Ala.: Summa Publications, 1992).

THOMAS, CHRIS D., et al., 'Extinction Risk from Climate Change', *Nature*, 427 (2004), 145–8.

THOMPSON, MICHAEL, *Rubbish Theory: The Creation and Destruction of Value* (Oxford: Oxford University Press, 1979).

THULLIER, PIERRE, 'Qui a peur de la thermodynamique?', in *Le Petit Savant illustré* (Paris: Seuil, 1989), 13–17.

TODOROV, TZVETAN, *Nous et les Autres: la réflexion française sur la diversité humaine* (Paris: Seuil, 1989).

TOUCHARD, PATRICE (ed.), *Le Siècle des excès, de 1880 à nos jours* (Paris: PUF, 1992).

TOULLELAN, PIERRE-YVES, *Tahiti colonial* (Paris: Publications de la Sorbonne, 1994).

TOWNSHEND, CHARLES, 'The Fin de Siècle', in Alex Danchev (ed.), *Fin de Siècle: The Meaning of the Twentieth Century* (London: Tauris Academic Studies, 1995), 198–216.

TVERDOTA, GYÖRGY (ed.), *Écrire le récit de voyage* (Paris: Presses de la Sorbonne Nouvelle, 1994).

UNGAR, STEVE, 'La France impériale en 1931: une apothéose', in Pascal Blanchard and Sandrine Lemaire (eds.), *Culture coloniale: la France conquise par son empire, 1871–1931* (Paris: Autrement, 2003), 201–11.

URBAIN, JEAN-DIDIER, *L'Idiot du voyage* (Paris: Payot, 1993).

—— *Sur la plage* (Paris: Payot, 1994); *At the Beach*, trans. Catherine Porter (Minneapolis: University of Minnesota Press, 2003).

—— *Secrets de voyage: menteurs, imposteurs et autres voyageurs invisibles* (Paris: Payot, 1998).

—— 'Les catanautes des cryptocombes—des iconoclastes de l'Ailleurs', *Nottingham French Studies*, 39/1 (2000), 7–16.

—— *Ethnographe, mais pas trop* (Paris: Payot, 2003).

VERGÈS, FRANÇOISE, 'The Island of Wandering Souls: Processes of Creolisation, Politics of Emancipation and the Problematic of Absence of Reunion Island', in Rod Edmond and Vanessa Smith (eds.), *Islands in History and Representation* (London: Routledge, 2003), 162–76.

VIART, DOMINIQUE, *Le Roman français au XXe siècle* (Paris: Hachette, 1999).

VIAU, GUY, *Le Tour d'Afrique en 2CV de quatre jeunes Français* (Paris: Amiot-Dumont, 1956).

VILLEDECAZE, RÉMI, *Traité de la promenade* ([n.pl.]: Éditions du Bon Albert, 1997).

VIRILIO, PAUL, *Vitesse et Politique* (Paris: Galilée, 1977).

—— *Esthétique de la disparition* (Paris: Galilée, 1980).

VOLODINE, ANTOINE, *Le Post-exotisme en dix leçons leçon onze* (Paris: Gallimard, 1998).

WALKER, TAARIA, *Rurutu: mémoires d'avenir d'une île australe* (Papeete: Haere Po, 1999).

WASSERMAN, RENATA, 'Re-inventing The New World: Cooper and Alencar', *Comparative Literature*, 36/2 (1984), 130–45.

—— *Exotic Nations: Literature and Cultural Identity in the United States and Brazil, 1830–1930* (Ithaca, NY: Cornell University Press, 1994).

WEBER, EUGEN, *France: Fin de Siècle* (Cambridge, Mass.: Belknap, 1986).

—— *The Hollow Years: France in the 1930s* (London: Sinclair-Stevenson, 1995).

WEINER, SUSAN (ed.), 'The French Fifties', *Yale French Studies*, 98 (2000).

WEST, SHEARER, *Fin de Siècle* (Woodstock, NY: Overlook, 1994).

WHITE, KENNETH, *Les Limbes incandescents* (Paris: Denoël, 1976).

WHITE, MATT, *Citroën 2CV: The Complete Story* (Ramsbury: Crowood, 1999).

WIK, HENRY, *Henry Ford and Grass-Roots America* (Ann Arbor: University of Michigan Press, 1972).

WILLIAMS, RAYMOND, *Politics and Letters* (London: New Left Books, 1979).

—— *The Country and the City* (London: Hogarth, 1985).

WOLF, JAMES B., 'Imperial Integration: The Car, the British and the Cape-to-Cairo Route', in Robert Giddings (ed.), *Literature and Imperialism* (Basingstoke: Macmillan, 1991), 112–27.

WOLGENSINGER, JACQUES, *L'Épopée de la Croisière jaune* (Paris: Laffont, 1970).

—— *La 2CV: Nous nous sommes tant aimés*, Découvertes 270 (Paris: Gallimard, 1995).

WOLLEN, PETER, and KERR, JOE (eds.), *Autopia: Cars and Culture* (London: Reaktion, 2002).

YEE, JENNIFER, *Clichés de la femme exotique* (Paris: L'Harmattan, 2000).

—— '*Métissage* in France: A Post-Modern Fantasy and its Forgotten Precedents', *Modern and Contemporary France*, 11/4 (2003), 411–26.

YOUNG, ROBERT J. C., *Colonial Desire: Hybridity in Theory, Culture and Race* (London: Routledge, 1995).

ZENCEY, ERIC, 'Some Brief Speculations on the Popularity of Entropy as Metaphor', *North American Review*, 271/3 (1986), 7–10.

—— 'Entropy as Root Metaphor', in Joseph W. Slade and Judith Yaross Lee (eds.), *Beyond the Two Cultures: Essays on Science, Technology and Literature* (Ames: Iowa State University Press, 1990), 185–200.

Index

Ingram Content Group UK Ltd.
Milton Keynes UK
UKHW010055050723
424579UK00001B/26